Practical Salesforce Development Without Code

Building Declarative Solutions on the Salesforce Platform

Second Edition

Philip Weinmeister

Apress®

Practical Salesforce Development Without Code: Building Declarative Solutions on the Salesforce Platform

Philip Weinmeister
Powder Springs, GA, USA

ISBN-13 (pbk): 978-1-4842-4870-6   ISBN-13 (electronic): 978-1-4842-4871-3
https://doi.org/10.1007/978-1-4842-4871-3

Managing Director, Apress Media LLC: Welmoed Spahr
Acquisitions Editor: Susan McDermott
Development Editor: Laura Berendson
Coordinating Editor: Rita Fernando

Cover designed by eStudioCalamar

Cover image designed by Freepik (www.freepik.com)

Distributed to the book trade worldwide by Springer Science+Business Media New York, 233 Spring Street, 6th Floor, New York, NY 10013. Phone 1-800-SPRINGER, fax (201) 348-4505, e-mail orders-ny@springer-sbm.com, or visit www.springeronline.com. Apress Media, LLC is a California LLC and the sole member (owner) is Springer Science + Business Media Finance Inc (SSBM Finance Inc). SSBM Finance Inc is a **Delaware** corporation.

For information on translations, please e-mail rights@apress.com, or visit http://www.apress.com/rights-permissions.

Apress titles may be purchased in bulk for academic, corporate, or promotional use. eBook versions and licenses are also available for most titles. For more information, reference our Print and eBook Bulk Sales web page at http://www.apress.com/bulk-sales.

Any source code or other supplementary material referenced by the author in this book is available to readers on GitHub via the book's product page, located at www.apress.com/9781484248706. For more detailed information, please visit http://www.apress.com/source-code.

Printed on acid-free paper

*To Gigi, who, while not necessarily understanding
any of the content within my books, has blessed me through
her consistent support and excitement.*

Table of Contents

About the Author

Philip Weinmeister, Salesforce MVP, is the VP of Product Management at 7Summits, where he is focused on building innovative components, apps, and bolts that enable impactful, transformative communities on the Salesforce platform. Phil is 20x Salesforce certified and has delivered numerous Sales Cloud, Service Cloud, and (primarily) Community Cloud solutions to a variety of organizations on Salesforce since 2010. He released the first edition of *Practical Salesforce.com Development Without Code* in 2015 (Apress); in 2018, he released *Practical Guide to Salesforce Communities* (Apress). He has been a Salesforce MVP since 2015. He was named the first-ever Community Cloud MVP in 2017, and, in 2018, he was named the Most Active Trailblazer by the Community Cloud team.

A graduate of Carnegie Mellon University with a double major in Business/IT and Spanish, Phil now resides in Powder Springs, GA. When he's not building solutions on Salesforce, he spends most of his "free" time with his amazing wife, Amy, and his children, Tariku, Sophie, Max, and Lyla. In addition to showing up at his kids' birthday parties as semi-superheroes, hoping for a winning season from the Arizona Cardinals, or rap battling his wife, he enjoys traveling, playing drums, and growing in his walk with Jesus.

Stay updated on Phil's most recent insights and blog posts by following him on Twitter (@PhilWeinmeister).

About the Technical Reviewer

David Litton is a Salesforce MVP and the Director of
Solutions Architecture at Ad Victoriam Solutions. He
has been working with Salesforce for more than 7 years
and began working with Salesforce as a customer before
transitioning to a partner. David has 18 Salesforce
certifications including Application Architect and System
Architect. He lives in Bigfork, Montana, with his wife
Missy and dog Ziggy. You can visit his Salesforce blog
at https://salesforcesidekick.com to see what he is
currently up to, and you can follow him on Twitter
(@DavidLittonSFDC).

About the Technical Reviewer

Acknowledgments

Amy Weinmeister: My wife has been unwaveringly supportive in so many ways to make this edition (and all of my past writings) a reality.

David Litton (Ad Victoriam): David has been a stellar technical reviewer, providing excellent and insightful feedback.

John Price (7Summits): John had my first book sitting on his desk long before we ever met. He has been a huge advocate of my thought leadership while at 7Summits and continues to keep my book at arm's reach.

Rita Fernando Kim and **Susan McDermott (Apress)**: Rita, Susan, and the entire Apress team provided top-notch support every step of the way.

Cindy Burns (EarthLink): Cindy believed in me early in my career and gave me numerous opportunities to grow and demonstrate my expertise.

Bill Loumpouridis (EDL Consulting): Bill saw potential in me and pushed me out of my comfort zone within the Salesforce ecosystem. I haven't looked back since!

And none of this would be possible without **Jesus**, who has redeemed me in his perfect grace. My career and abilities are gifts from him, and I desire to reflect him in all I do.

Foreword

In 2019, I celebrated my 12-year Salesforce anniversary. Then, as now, Salesforce operated on the founding principle: Make the Complex, Simple, and Make the Impossible, Possible. Since that time I have advanced from Business Analyst to Developer, to Architect, and finally to Salesforce Certified Technical Architect.

For those of you doing the math, that comes to about 40 seamless upgrades (releases) of the Salesforce platform. "Software" that I wrote on Salesforce in 2008 will work just as well in 2020 – although I'll admit my Unit Testing and Continuous Integration skills have come a long way since then.

Salesforce's own development tools have also come a long way, including the recent introduction of SalesforceDX for robust change management workflows. But their "development" capabilities – free developer environments, robust dev and test sandboxes, declarative-first development, and mandatory code quality and unit test coverage – have not changed much in all that time.

The Power of Metadata

In early 2007 I spent several months researching, learning, and writing a Business Requirements Document (BRD) for a Record Retrieval platform. The idea was simple: customers would come to my client asking to retrieve some kind of record (medical, legal, etc.), and the client would "retrieve" those records from wherever in the world they existed. The complexity lay in the massive amounts of approvals, paperwork, and process required to request, process, analyze, and deliver a combination of paper and (increasingly) digital documentation.

My solution was a metadata-driven platform designed to streamline the process from beginning to end. We had document generation, digital signatures, fax integration (sending and receiving), FTP drop boxes, image processing, sequence generation, workflow automation, email alerts, and more. The platform would run on a stack of 11 servers and be written in Microsoft's .Net Framework. The BRD and proposal weighed in at over 100 pages, 12 appendices, and several presentations.

It was a beautiful proposal. It would have worked. The record retrieval process would have been accelerated from weeks to days. It would have cost millions of dollars; the company would have had to hire a dozen new IT staff and as many developers. And it would have taken years to develop. The ROI just wasn't there.

The solution, which came from an outside consultant, was to build the system on Salesforce. In the end, the project took half the original estimated time and added no new IT staff. Document generation and signatures were handled by AppExchange apps, and the workflow and email automation were managed out of the box. Image processing and display were still handled by on-premise servers, but the amount of code required to integrate with Salesforce was a fraction of my original proposal.

And, although I'm no longer involved with that project, I am confident that the Salesforce configuration is still stable and functional. I doubt the other systems involved were so stable.

The Salesforce Dream

When I entered the Salesforce Ecosystem, there was no such thing as Trailhead. We were encouraged to spin up new developer environments, join the Developer Community, and test new functionality in sandboxes. And because there were very few trained "Salesforce Developers," we were required to learn how to meet business objectives using the declarative tools available to us.

And that is the Salesforce dream: that a Business Analyst can become an Administrator and can create a full-featured software application capable of running a department. Toss in a few AppExchange packages to provide specialized functionality and streamline processes, and you can run an entire company (all of the consulting companies I've worked for used Salesforce exclusively for their operations).

And, of course, not everything can be done using configuration. For those things that require complex logic and integrations, Salesforce provides industry standard, "opinionated" interfaces and tools with all the capabilities you need to create Enterprise-grade software.

All of Salesforce's documentation is available for free, as are Developer Edition accounts (I still have my first developer org). The guided and structured training environment of Trailhead has also added a new dimension of enjoyment and has sped up learning new Salesforce-related topics significantly.

Segue

This book is about creating practical, usable systems with a positive ROI by taking advantage of Salesforce's metadata-driven development. By focusing on declarative configuration, you can create value faster, your work will last longer, and you will get access to three releases a year of upgraded functionality.

I would also like to take this opportunity to invite you to the Salesforce Community. Later in this book you will learn how to create a developer environment, how to sign up for the Developer Community, and how to take your first Trailhead training. Salesforce is all about best practices, so whether you plan to configure Salesforce, become an on-platform developer, or want to learn how to integrate Salesforce with other technologies, you will learn skills and techniques that will benefit you and your career.

What are you waiting for?

Ernest W. Lessenger, MBA and Certified Technical Architect
Chief Platform Architect
Run Consultants

Introduction

Five years have passed since the introduction of the first edition of this book. In one sense, much has changed. This significantly updated version brings numerous valuable additions to the platform into focus, equipping readers with even more tools to use in their path to become declarative development rock stars. Terms like "Process Builder" and "Lightning Flow" weren't found in the first edition yet are now used in daily conversations among Salesforce solution builders.

In another sense, much has stayed the same. Salesforce's dedication to innovation has not wavered, resulting in a continual supply of releases with truly impactful functionality three times a year. Additionally, the platform has continued to manage a roadmap that enables meaningful solution development without the employment of code. While the declarative ecosystem has undoubtedly grown over the last few years, Salesforce's view of "clicks" has always been there. It just may be that the secret is finally out.

Second Edition

This edition is probably not a typical one. While new editions may usually see a couple areas getting augmented and a few mature topics being tightened up, an array of key additions have been added in this second edition of *Practical Salesforce Development Without Code*. In this edition, you will find brand new elements, including Lightning App Builder, Lightning Flow, Flow Builder, Process Builder, and more.

I have closely reviewed each and every other chapter, including relevant changes and updates to bring you to the current state of the platform and share new insights and guidance to help you on your declarative path. Some chapters from the first edition have been removed as new tools have moved into the forefront for building similar solutions.

Development Without Code

If you are scratching your head in response to the phrase "development with code" being used in the world of software and technology, let me assure you that this is not at all a paradox. While typical development requires the knowledge of a particular programming language, the creation of business applications on Salesforce does not. In this book, I will share tips, tricks, lessons learned, and the application of Salesforce features and functionality that do not require the utilization of code.

If you are a traditional, programmatic developer, keep reading! The content of this book will serve as the foundation to essentially unlimited customization of the platform. While I will not cover Apex, Visualforce, or any other languages, it's important to understand that a more traditional approach to development in Salesforce is almost always accompanied by "declarative" elements that are implemented via configuration, or "clicks." There are numerous occasions in which a particular configuration setting will be preferable over a solution built from scratch. Why reinvent the wheel when you can simply input your specifications and order one up? While the content directly applies to administrators, consultants, and analysts, there is also a significant value for any Salesforce developer looking to better understand the platform and produce reliable, extensible applications.

Why Develop Without Code?

Regardless of your role, you'll need to be able to make wise decisions when it comes to delivering functionality for your organization or client. Inevitably, you will encounter scenarios in which a solution can be delivered either with or without the use of code. There are unique pros and cons in every situation, but do consider a few key points that may support the decision to avoid using code:

- The need to consider Salesforce.com limits and parameters is significantly reduced or, at times, eliminated completely when building solutions using declarative means.

- Modifications are often more straightforward, as they may only require a change to a configuration setting, not to a line of code.

- No unit testing is required (Apex test classes, in contrast, must be written for custom Apex code).

- Knowledge transfer burdens are reduced, since an understanding of the particular feature or function is typically sufficient to quickly determine what a specific application is intended to do.

- Future maintenance is simplified. If, for example, an individual who built custom applications for you leaves abruptly, picking up the pieces is much simpler if the work was done declaratively.

Don't get me wrong – there are numerous scenarios that do warrant development *with* code and most of the best solutions I've seen including both declarative and programmatic aspects. Extending the platform to support functionality that simply does not exist "out of the box" or cannot be done via clicks is a perfect time to employ code-based solution.

Code Sightings

I would like to comment on the "no code" aspect of this book. First, you *will* find a few snippets of code sprinkled throughout the book. For example, with formula functions, a few occasions arise that require manual input. Here are two examples from Chapter 2:

```
BEGINS(City, "Ph")
```

```
AND(
    Escalated,
    Subject = "AS400 is no longer functioning"
)
```

In both examples, you can see text strings that have been manually typed (e.g., "Ph" and "AS400 …"). While the values were not set via configuration or "clicks," I do not consider this code in the traditional sense. It is expected that some scenarios will emerge that require you to manually input a value.

Second, you will encounter traditional code in Chapter 11. In that chapter, I cover development with the Web-to-Lead tool, for which some HTML-editing capability will come in handy. However, HTML-editing skills are not required to understand the chapter and apply the principles being taught.

In both cases, "code" takes a back seat to declarative development.

Glossary

Let's clarify a few terms that will assist you as you walk through the book. You will also likely encounter these terms often when living in the world of Salesforce.com.

- **Org**: An organization, or "org," represents a particular instance of Salesforce, whether in production or in a test environment. An org has a unique set of metadata and data that formulates the overall user experience.

- **Sandbox**: A *sandbox* is a nonproduction org that is associated with one production org and possibly other sandboxes. Salesforce allows deployments both from and to sandboxes from other sandboxes or even a production environment.

- **Declarative**: This term describes a method for configuration or development that does not require coding or programming but, rather, the utilization of UI-based components to set up an org.

- **Configuration**: In the Salesforce world, configuration refers to the management of settings via "clicks" to control a particular feature, tool, solution, or experience.

- **Customization**: In this book, *customization* is used to describe the utilization of the Salesforce platform to deliver solutions or functionality that is not available to users upon initial org activation (i.e., not available out of the box). Note that, in the world of Salesforce.com development, some individuals refer to traditional, code-based development as "customization."

- **Out of the box**: This term means different things to different people, so I want to be as clear as possible. For purposes of this book, *out of the box* signifies a feature, tool, or function that is ready for use without significant declarative development and definitely without any custom code. For example, workflow rules are supported out of the box, but a complex, custom-built solution that employs workflow rules would not be considered out of the box. Additionally, anything that requires customization via Apex or Visualforce is not considered out of the box.

Salesforce Editions

It is important to understand that a number of different editions of Salesforce exist. The edition that you are on depends on the licensing agreement that your organization shares with Salesforce.com. Certain features and tools are only available for particular editions, so make sure you are familiar with your edition and the corresponding functionality. You can find an overview of the different editions of Salesforce.com at `www.salesforce.com/editions-pricing/overview/`.

Developer Org/Environment

If you don't already have a Salesforce org in which you can follow my examples and build similar solutions, you'll want to obtain one. The good news is that Salesforce development environments are free and are provisioned very quickly. Navigate to `https://developer.salesforce.com/signup` and sign up for your own org today. I highly recommend that you follow along and try to create solutions based on what you are learning. Reading is a great thing, but obtaining hands-on experience is what will bring you the most long-term benefit.

A Final Word

Ultimately, my goal through this book is to help you succeed. There is nothing more gratifying to me, as an author, to hear how a book of mine has helped an individual grow his or her career.

If at first you don't succeed, try, try again. There was a starting point for all of us in the development ecosystem, so stay encouraged and motivated. If you are struggling to put a particular takeaway into practice, continue to study and apply what you have learned, and you'll find that things will eventually "click." Pun intended ... now go have some fun!

CHAPTER 1

The Salesforce Data Model: Objects, Fields, and Relationships

If you have any familiarity with Salesforce, you know that it has never failed to provide a continuous supply of rich features and functionality. One particular facet of its broad development platform clearly stands out as a prime starting point for developing without code on the Salesforce platform and will serve as the foundation for the rest of this book. That element is the Salesforce data model, which consists of objects, fields, and relationships. The data model serves as a framework for almost everything else you can do within the application. Once you understand objects, fields, and relationships within Salesforce, the other areas I will cover in this book will start to come into focus.

Because Salesforce has a wide variety of features and functionality, readers will vary greatly in terms of knowledge, development experience, business analysis/comprehension, and technical aptitude related to the platform. While some may see this chapter as a refresher before digging deeper, others will see it as more of a critical starting point.

Throughout this book, you will find step-by-step instructions to guide you through building out the platform yourself. I highly recommend taking a hands-on approach as you make your way through each chapter since it will allow you to recall the details more vividly and possibly answer some of your own questions along the way.

By the end of this chapter, you will

- Understand standard and custom fields, including the corresponding differences

- Be familiar with field types and when to use each of them

1

© Philip Weinmeister 2019
P. Weinmeister, *Practical Salesforce Development Without Code*,
https://doi.org/10.1007/978-1-4842-4871-3_1

- Know how to effectively create custom fields step by step

- Understand standard objects and their purpose

- Have learned about custom objects, including how to create your own custom object

- Know the importance of external objects and how to use them

- Understand how to effectively build relationships between different objects

Salesforce Fields

When you want to get familiar with a new system or application, it can help to have a frame of reference. To give you one, I might suggest that the fields in Salesforce are similar to the columns that you would find in a relational database table. Like database columns, Salesforce fields contain data of a specific type. But whereas in a database table, a column and row intersect to give you a field that contains the actual data, in Salesforce, a field is present on a record and can be populated with data.

However, it is important to point out where the comparison between database columns and Salesforce fields falls short. To be truly nontechnical, I might refer to a Salesforce field as a database column on steroids. A field in Salesforce has a number of related attributes and properties that make it much more robust than a simple database column.

Note   A **database column** is often referred to as a field. Regardless of how it is labeled, a column/field in a database has some significant differences from a Salesforce field.

To effectively meet your company's needs within Salesforce, having the right fields is an absolute must. As you will see in subsequent chapters, fields will be your most basic building block throughout the development process. You will not only need to identify what fields will be meaningful and valuable within your org, but also to build them with the appropriate attributes. In this chapter, I will review Salesforce fields in detail and provide you with a foundation for success when developing without code on the Salesforce platform.

Standard vs. Custom Fields

Once you begin developing solutions within Salesforce, you'll quickly become familiar with the terms *standard* and *custom*. Standard items, whether fields or objects, are elements that Salesforce produces for you. While you can control some of the attributes of standard items, you cannot directly control the creation of those elements. In a sense, standard elements are existing platform features. I say "in a sense" because some standard elements can be created as part of a separate process after your Salesforce instance is initially established. For example, when you create a custom object, standard fields are created automatically. The standard fields come along for the ride; you have no direct control over their presence.

The set of standard fields that is available to you depends on the object containing them. Standard objects each contain a unique, predefined set of fields. I will cover those later in this chapter when we dive into objects. For now, let's look at the minimal set of standard fields – those that are automatically created when an object is created:

- **Record Name (*Name*):** This can be a manually entered alphanumeric value (Text field) or an "auto-number" automatically generated by Salesforce.

- **Owner (*OwnerId*):** With some exceptions (see the "Master-Detail Relationship" section later in this chapter), the Owner field will be automatically created. Your Owner field will be populated with a User from your system.

- **Created By (*CreatedById*):** This is a special system-populated field that captures the User that created the record along with the date and time of the record creation.

- **Last Modified By (*LastModifiedById*):** Although this field is similar to Created By, it captures the User and Date/Time associated with the last record update instead of record creation.

Note   Last Modified By is actually a concatenation of two system fields: LastModifiedById and LastModifiedDate. However, users just see the concatenated Last Modified By field.

Attributes

Every field that you create in Salesforce has certain attributes that need to be defined. There are obvious examples, such as Name and, in some cases, Length. Other attributes provide depth for fields and allow them to be used properly in a variety of scenarios. You will want to get familiar with these attributes before creating your own fields; they include

- **Field Label**: The name of your field that is displayed to users.

- **Field Name**: The unique name of your field. Field Name is typically not shown to users, although it is possible to do so. Field Names can only contain alphanumeric characters and (nonconsecutive) underscores, must begin with a letter, and must end with a letter or number.

- **Description**: The Description field is purely for reference, used to explain the purpose and/or context of the field you are creating. It is highly recommended that you always populate Description even if the reason you are adding a field seems obvious.

- **Help Text**: The bubble text displayed to users upon hovering over a small question mark next to the field. Populating the Help Text field is not required and is most valuable when a user might have trouble understanding how to interact with or interpret a field.

- **Required**: This Checkbox must have a legitimately formatted value present before a record can be created or saved.

- **Unique**: By selecting the Unique Checkbox, you ensure that the field on a new or existing record cannot contain a value that matches that of the same field on another record. Unique can be configured to be case sensitive or case insensitive.

- **External ID**: This Checkbox serves as a record identifier for a field in a system or application outside of Salesforce. External IDs have special behavior when corresponding records are imported, either via the standard import wizards or the Apex Data Loader. Note that the External ID by itself does not guarantee that the field values are unique in Salesforce – the unique attribute is a separate function.

- **Default Value:** By setting the Default Value on a field, you can set an initial value on every record that is created. This value can be as straightforward as a string ("New") or a number ("5"). However, it can also be a formula that uses Salesforce's built-in formula functions and can even derive values from other fields/objects.

Note   The Field Name and Field API Name attributes are directly related. The API Name is referenced in code and formulas. You might have a custom field with a Field Name of "Book." In the API Name, "__c" (for custom) is automatically appended, making the API Name "Book__c". Standard fields do not have anything appended, so the Field Name is the same as the API Name.

All fields require a Field Label and Field Name. Description and Help Text are not required but are available on every field. The remaining attributes (Required, Unique, External ID, Default Value) are available for selection on a limited number of field types. See Table 1-1.

Table 1-1. *A Matrix of Field Attributes Available by Field Type*

Field Type	Required	Unique	External ID	Default Value
Auto Number			✓	
Formula				
Roll-Up Summary				
Lookup Relationship	✓			
Master-Detail Relationship				
External Lookup Relationship	✓			
Indirect Lookup Relationship				
Checkbox				
Currency	✓			✓
Date	✓			✓
Date/Time	✓			✓

(continued)

5

Table 1-1. (*continued*)

Field Type	Required	Unique	External ID	Default Value
Email	✓	✓	✓	✓
Geolocation	✓			
Number	✓	✓	✓	✓
Percent	✓			✓
Phone	✓			✓
Picklist				
Picklist (Multi-Select)				
Text	✓	✓	✓	✓
Text Area	✓			✓
Text Area (Long)				
Text Area (Rich)				
Text (Encrypted)	✓			
Time	✓			✓
URL	✓			✓

Custom Field Types

Every field within Salesforce has an associated type. When you create your own custom field in Salesforce, you will need to define a field type. A field's type (e.g., Number, Text, etc.) ensures that certain parameters and governing rules are enforced. It drives how users see and interact with the corresponding field. Salesforce provides a number of field types to choose from. The types available to you when you create a custom field are a subset of the full set of field types that exist in Salesforce; some types are only available via standard objects. Let's take a look at the custom field types and how they are used within the platform.

Note   The Lookup relationship, External Lookup relationship, Master-Detail relationship, and Roll-Up Summary field types will be covered in the "Salesforce Relationships" section later in this chapter.

Auto-Number

Auto-Number fields automatically generate a value for each new record based on a simple algorithm that incrementally inserts the numeric portion of the field's value for each new record. At the most basic level, you can create an Auto-Number field (e.g., "Auto-Generated Project Number") that starts with a value of 1 and increases by 1 for each subsequent record (see Table 1-2).

Table 1-2. Auto-Numbering Sequencing

	Record 1 Value	Record 2 Value	Record 3 Value
Auto-Generated Project Number	1	2	3

While you cannot control the size of the increment – Auto-Number fields always increase the numeric portion of the value by 1 – you can control the display format and the starting number of the field. The display format consists of two parts: (1) a numeric portion that is automatically increased and (2) optional static text that supplements the number. The numeric part is identified in the field setting with curly brackets ("{}"). The starting number setting identifies the first integer to be used.

Note   When you create an Auto-Number field, give careful consideration to how you format the static text component to provide as much meaning as possible. For example, "ANN-{0000}" would be a sensible format for an Announcement custom object and "PR-{0}" would work for a custom object called "Project." If possible, format the Auto-Number field so that a user might understand what it represents without needing to do additional research.

Table 1-3 shows some examples of Auto-Number display formats along with the corresponding field values that would actually display on a page, based on display format and starting number.

Table 1-3. *Example Values Based on Different Auto-Number Formats*

Display Format	Starting #	Record #	Field Value
{0}	1	1	**1**
{0000}	1	1	**0001**
ABC-{0}	1	1	**ABC-1**
ABC-{0}	1	155	**ABC-155**
ABC-{0}	1000	1	**ABC-1000**
ABC-{0}	1000	155	**ABC-1154**
ABC-{0000}	1	1	**ABC-0001**
ABC-{0000}	1	11315	**ABC-11315**
ABC-{0000}	1000	1	**ABC-1000**
ABC-{0000}	1000	11315	**ABC-12314**
Record_{0}	1	1	**Record_1**
Record_{0}	1	87	**Record_87**
Record_{0}	100	1	**Record_100**
Record_{0}	100	87	**Record_186**
{0000}-abc	1	1	**0001-abc**
{0000}-abc	1	52	**0052-abc**

Note   If you notice unexpected gaps in your Auto-Number sequences (e.g., "ABC-1" to "ABC-2" to "ABC-7"), you need to know two things: First, know that you have not lost your mind. It's unlikely that a rogue user is off deleting records; this is probably a result of records being created in Apex Test Classes. Second, you can adjust this. Go to **Setup ➤ Apex Test Execution ➤ Options**, select "Independent Auto-Number Sequence," and click "OK."

Additionally, date-related values can be used in Auto-Number fields. This is extremely handy if you want to have a built-in date/timestamp on a record. Table 1-4 shows some examples of Auto-Number fields with date-related sequences.

Table 1-4. *Example Values Based on Different Auto-Number Formats with Date/ Time Sequences*

Display Format	Starting #	Date	Record #	Field Value
{DD}{MM}{0}	1	July 9, 2021	1	**09071**
{0000}-{MM}{DD}	1	July 9, 2021	33	**0033-0709**
{MM}{DD}{YY}{0}	52	July 9, 2021	1	**070921-52**
{YYYY}-{000}	77	May 14, 2022	11	**2022-011**
{YY}-{MM}-{000}	77	May 14, 2022	22	**22-05-099**
{0000}-{DD}	1	April 1, 2023	1	0001-01
{MM}{DD}{0}	88	April 1, 2023	1	040188
{00000}{YYYY}	1	April 1, 2023	1000	010002023

Formula

The Formula field type allows you to construct a formula based on functions, statements, calculations, operations, user-defined values, and/or other field values that will be evaluated and return a corresponding value. Most commonly, Formula fields will involve derived values that are pulled in from other fields on the same object or from fields on related objects. For example, you may create a formula that evaluates one of the following values:

- A multiple of a currency value (e.g., amount)

- A date based on an existing date field plus a set number of days

- A true/false value derived from an IF statement that evaluates another field on the object

- Text inherited from a Parent object (as is)

Formulas will be valuable to you as you build solutions within Salesforce. I will dedicate multiple chapters in this book to understanding how formula fields work and how to effectively create them to address your business needs.

Note   Formulas will serve as one of the cornerstones for development without code and will be covered in detail in Chapters 2 and 3.

Checkbox

A Checkbox field is a Boolean expression, potentially containing one of two values: True or False. Within the standard Salesforce user interface, a Checkbox appears with a check for True and without a check for False. You have the option of setting the default value to either checked or unchecked when defining a Checkbox field.

Numeric Fields

Number, Currency, and Percent are three fields that are very similar in behavior, so I am grouping them together here. These field types store numeric values up to a total length of 18 digits. The digits include the total number of digits to the left of the decimal point (referred to as length) and to the right of it (referred to as decimal places). For example, you can create fields from these field types with a length of 16 + 2 decimal places, a length of 10 + 8 decimal places, and so forth. A field with a length of 18 would not be allowed to have any decimal places due to the total digit limit.

It is worth noting that each of these fields stores the corresponding number without any transformation of the value itself. For example, entering 50 in a Number field, a Currency field, and a Percent field would result in a value of 50 being stored in each field in the database (i.e., not "0.5" in the Percent field). Additionally, it's critical to understand that values with precision beyond the configured number of decimal places are rounded accordingly. For example, in a Number field with a length of 2 + 3 decimal places, a submitted value of "14.1448" would be modified to "14.145". The new value is the one actually stored in the field at that point; it is not simply a shortened representation of a longer field.

Note   The currency type (represented by an ISO currency code; e.g., USD, GBP, EUR, etc.) associated with a particular Currency field is not set at the field level; it is determined by a variety of contextual factors at the record, user, and org levels.

Date and Time Fields

Date, Date/Time, and Time fields contain date, date and time, and time values, respectively. There are a couple key points to understand about these fields: First, the format of the value will differ based on your context. In scenarios where a date or Date/Time field will be populated or edited by your users (e.g., within record detail pages, list views, reports, etc.), the format will be MM/DD/YYYY (e.g., "11/21/2020"). You may enter the year as "YY" and it will be converted to the full four-digit date, YYYY. In other scenarios (e.g., advanced developers using Apex or system administrators using the Data Loader), the format will be YYYY-MM-DD. See Table 1-5 and Figure 1-1 for how Date fields appear in different contexts.[1]

Table 1-5. *Display/Presentation of Date Values in Different Contexts*

Date	Salesforce Context	Displayed Value
November 21, 2020	Record detail page	**11/21/2020**
November 21, 2020	List view	**11/21/2020**
November 21, 2020	Report	**11/21/2020**
November 21, 2020	Apex trigger/class	**2020-11-21**
November 21, 2020	Data Loader	**2020-11-21**

Figure 1-1. *A Date field with the automatic date picker that appears in the UI*

---

[1]All Salesforce screenshots in this chapter © copyright Salesforce, Inc. Used with permission.

Date and Date/Time fields behave similarly. In the standard user scenarios previously described, Date/Time fields will need to be formatted in the UI as MM/DD/YYYY HH:MM AM/PM. For AM/PM, you would enter either "AM" or "PM." Hours should be entered in the 12-hour format. Like with the Date field, users may enter YY for a Date/Time field and allow Salesforce to automatically convert the value into a four-digit year. In the more datacentric scenarios previously described, the format will be YYYY-MM-DDTHH:MM:SSZ. The T and Z should be entered as is and do not need to be modified; the T stands for time and the Z stands for zone, as in time zone. By default, the value is entered in the user's local time zone. You can offset the time to a specific time zone, as shown in Table 1-6 and Figure 1-2. In that case, the Z is replaced with the time offset (e.g., "–05:00").

Table 1-6. *Date/Time Values (with Local Time and Time Zone Offset)*

Date/Time (UTC)	Time Zone	Data Loader/Apex Value	As Shown in UI in the Referenced Time Zone
November 21, 2020, 4:30 PM	UTC	**2020-11-21T16:30:00Z**	**11/21/2020 4:30 PM**
November 21, 2020, 4:30 PM	EST (UTC–5)	**2020-11-21T16:30:00Z-05:00**	**11/21/2020 11:30 AM**
November 21, 2020, 4:30 PM	PST (UTC–8)	**2020-11-21T16:30:00Z-08:00**	**11/21/2020 8:30 AM**

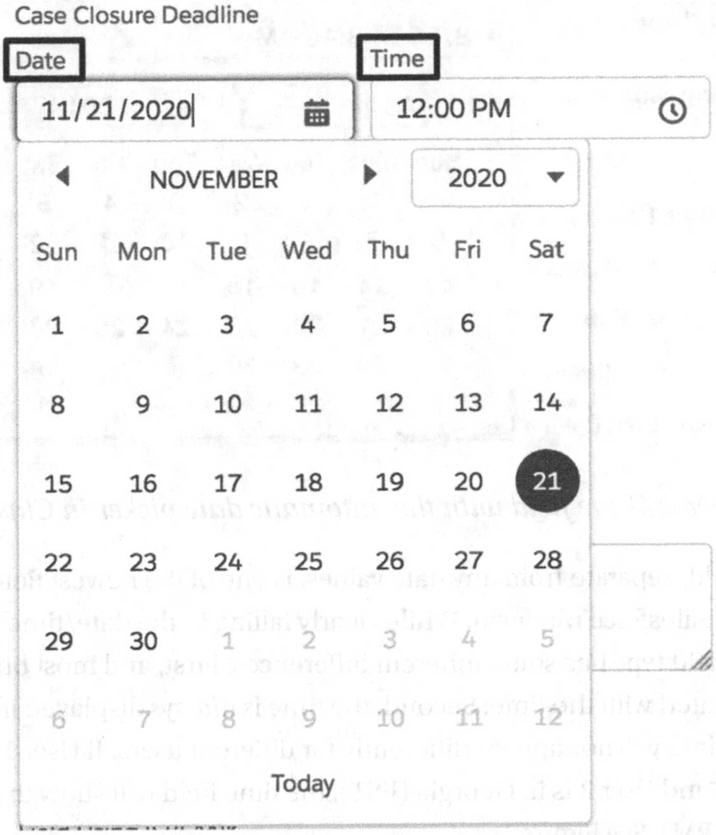

Case Closure Deadline

Figure 1-2. *A Date/Time field will provide both a date selector and a time selector in Lightning Experience*

Note   The time displayed to a user depends on the time zone set on his or her record. So, if a Date/Time field contains a time of 1:00 PM PST, it will display as 4:00 PM for users who have the time zone set to EST.

In Lightning Experience, corresponding date and time fields are both presented as part of a Date/Time field. This differs from the classic experience, where date and time were combined in one presented field. See Figure 1-3 for the classic view.

Figure 1-3. *A Date/Time field with the automatic date picker in Classic*

The Time field, separate from any date values, is one of the newest field types available on the Salesforce platform. While clearly falling in the date/time bucket of fields, the time field type has some inherent differences. First, and most obvious, there is no date associated with the time. Second, the time is *always* displayed in GMT. This means that the time will not appear differently for different users. If User 1 is in California (PST) and User 2 is in Georgia (EST), the time field will show the same value to both (e.g., 11:00 PM). See Figure 1-4.

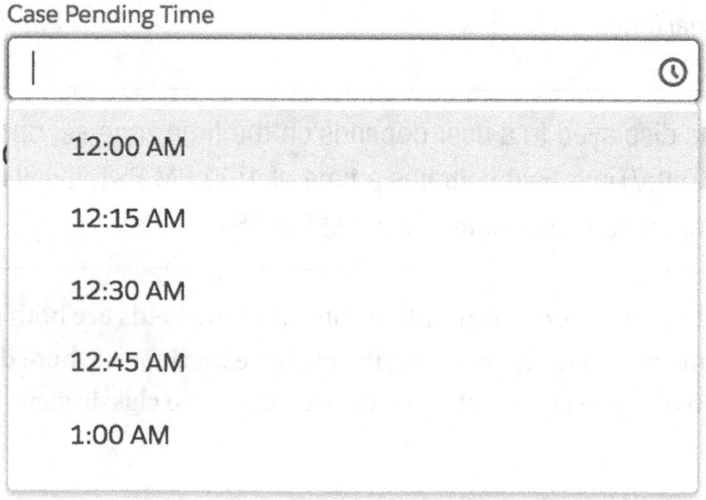

Figure 1-4. *Time fields have no date and are always in GMT*

Email

Email fields are essentially Text fields with specific, built-in formatting validations. Email fields must include

- An @ symbol

- Text before the @

- A period somewhere after the @

- Text immediately before and after the period

- No symbols other than underscores, hyphens, periods, characters, and @ symbols

Of course, Salesforce cannot fully validate an email based on these conditions. Try it yourself. You can enter "1-_@1.1" in the Email field and the value will be accepted. If you do want to expand the validations on this field, you can use the REGEX function within a validation rule. Both the REGEX function and validation rules will be covered in subsequent chapters.

Email fields have a built-in mailto: link that allows you to send an email to the specified address using your default email application upon clicking the address.

Geolocation

The Geolocation field type is relatively new to Salesforce. Geolocation actually contains two subfields: Longitude and Latitude. You can control how the value is displayed: in degrees, minutes, or seconds (DMS) or as a number with decimal places. Figure 1-5 contains four subfields related to the two Geolocation subfields. The first two fields represent the Longitude and Latitude for a DMS-formatted field; the second two fields represent a Decimal-formatted Geolocation field.

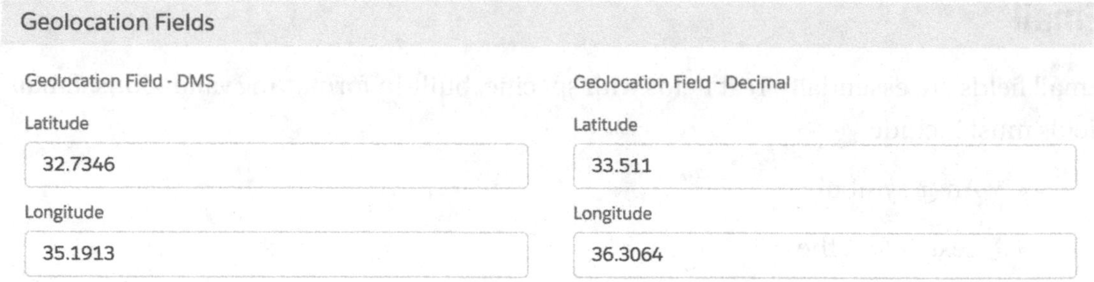

Geolocation Fields

Geolocation Field - DMS	Geolocation Field - Decimal
Latitude	Latitude
32.7346	33.511
Longitude	Longitude
35.1913	36.3064

Figure 1-5. *How the two Geodecimal fields (DMS and Decimal) appear when edited*

After saving your edit, Figure 1-6 shows what you will see in each field on the record detail page.

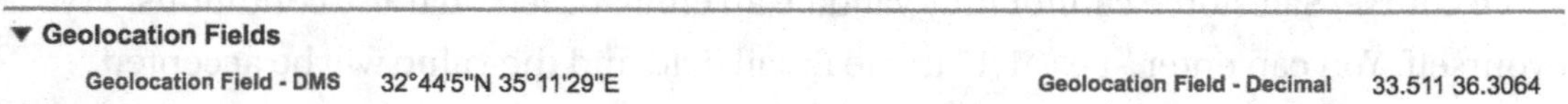

▼ **Geolocation Fields**

Geolocation Field - DMS	32°44'5"N 35°11'29"E	Geolocation Field - Decimal	33.511 36.3064

Figure 1-6. *The two Geodecimal fields after saving (view in Classic)*

You can set the number of decimals that are allowed in a Geolocation field. Like with other numeric fields, Salesforce will round a value that has more decimal places than it allows. For example, in a field with two allowed decimals places, a latitude of 35.505 would save as 35.51 and a latitude of 35.504 would save as 35.5 (note that the lagging zero is removed).

Phone

The Phone field is similar to the Email field in that it has a very specific context and use: in this case, the storage of a phone number. In terms of what data is allowed in the field, it is really a simple Text field. However, Phone fields can be used for manual or automatic dialing of phone numbers within certain applications. If the value in a Phone field does match a standard number of digits, it will be displayed as a standard phone number in the UX. For example, "2342342344" will display as "(234) 234-2344."

Note   The text allowed in a Phone field goes well beyond the scope of characters/ digits that would appear in real-world scenarios. I would recommend building out some validation rules to prohibit invalid entry of phone number values to maintain data integrity. Validation rules are covered in detail in Chapter 5.

Picklist

The Picklist fields, **Picklist** and **Picklist (Multi-Select)**, are used frequently within Salesforce and can be extremely valuable when building business processes into your application. Picklists behave most similarly to drop-down fields, although that term is completely abandoned on the Salesforce platform. With single Picklists, you can define a list of one or more values that can be selected, or picked, by users through the standard UI. Figure 1-7 shows a Picklist field called Stock Exchange. This field represents the exchange on which an Account's stock trades.

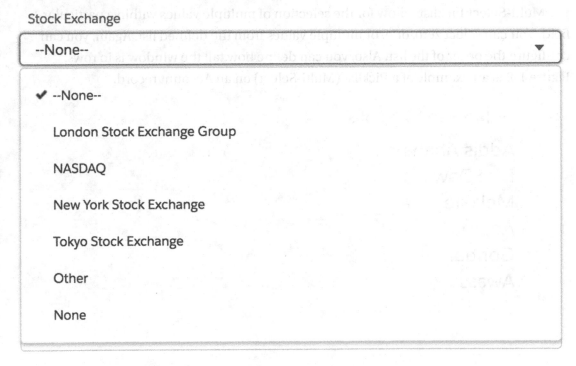

Figure 1-7. *Values from a Picklist field*

In addition to identifying the values that will be available, you will also define the sequence in which the values will appear and, optionally, the default (prepopulated) value for users.

Note   Including values such as "None" and "Other" has implications in your business process that need to be considered. Including "Other" may be necessary to prevent user frustration with a finite set of values, but it could have an adverse effect on reporting granularity. "None" is most useful when you want to ensure that users consider and select a value for a Picklist field even if no value applies. Alternatively, you can simply let them avoid making a selection, but there's the risk that the user may skip the field out of hastiness.

Multi-Select Picklists allow for the selection of multiple values within a particular field. You can select zero, one, or multiple values from the defined list. Again, you can configure the order of the list. Also, you can define how tall the window is in rows. Figure 1-8 is an example of a Picklist (Multi-Select) on an Account record.

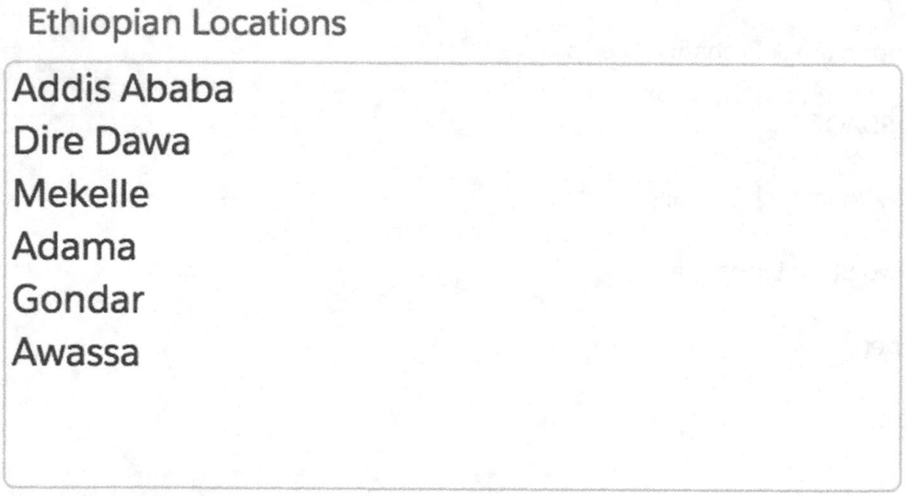

Ethiopian Locations

Addis Ababa
Dire Dawa
Mekelle
Adama
Gondar
Awassa

Figure 1-8. *A Multi-Select Picklist field during an edit*

Note   Perhaps the primary factor you will need to consider when creating a Multi-Select Picklist field is the implication for reporting. With a standard (single) Picklist field, you can easily obtain the count of records by Picklist value. That is not the case with a Multi-Select Picklist field.

Text Fields

You can create a variety of text fields in your data model. Table 1-7 is a summary of each.

Table 1-7. *A Matrix of Text Field Types and Their Related Attributes*

Text Field Type	Max Length	# Display Lines	Formatted Text	Images	Links
Text	255	1	No	No	No
Text (Encrypted)	175	1	No	No	No
Text Area	N/A	1–3*	No	No	No
Text Area (Long)	32,768	2–50	No	No	No
Text Area (Rich)	32,768	2–50	Yes	Yes	Yes

*You do not have control over the number of lines displayed for a Text Area field; this is driven by the context (page) and the length of the value in the field.

Encrypted fields allow characters to be masked and replaced with "x" or "*." The format of the masking can be configured as well. Standard users will not be able to see encrypted fields without the "View encrypted data" permission. A good example of how to use this field would be "Social Security Number."

URL

URL fields are text based and have a specific use and context. These fields store properly formatted hyperlinks and link to the specified URL upon the user clicking the hyperlink. Like Phone fields, URL fields have no restrictions on the amount of actual characters that can be entered. Previously, Salesforce considered the text input and identified whether a prefix (http://) was required. If the submitted value did *not* start with http:// or https://, Salesforce added the prefix "http://" to the text value in the field.

However, the URL field now simply links to the exact text in the field; there is nothing prepended to the saved string. For example, if "azcardinals" is entered as a value and then used, users would encounter a "This site can't be reached" message upon clicking the link. If `http://azcardinals.com` or simply "azcardinals.com" were entered, the IP address would be found and the Arizona Cardinals website would load. I recommend some basic validations of this field to ensure that no invalid characters are accidentally included in the URL value or, if required, to require that "http" is present.

Additional Field Types

Address and Name field types are not currently available when creating custom fields on custom objects, but are present on some standard objects. Name is a concatenation of multiple fields; address is actually a set of related fields and is referred to as a "compound" field. The Address and Name fields cannot be directly updated, but the individual field components of which they are comprised can. For example, you cannot update Billing Address on the Account object, but you can update Billing Street, Billing City, Billing State, and so on. The Address field type is comprised of the following fields: **Street**, **City**, **State/Province**, **Zip/Postal Code**, and **Country**. Lastly, if you enable State and Country/Territory picklists, you can use those in the corresponding state and country fields within addresses. The Name field type is a bit interesting, as its display doesn't always reflect its actual contents. For example, the Name field on a contact will show Salutation, First Name, and Last Name; however, Salutation is technically not part of the "Name" field in the database.

Creating a Custom Field

Each field type has a unique creation process. I previously described some of the elements that need to be considered when creating a corresponding field according to the field type. What follows is an overview of the creation process along with the key considerations. Keep in mind that the best way to get familiar with the process is to actually create a variety of fields with different field types.

Note   Relationship fields (Lookup, External, Master-Detail) have a more detailed creation process than the four-step process described in this section and will be addressed later in the chapter.

---

1. **Select a field type**: Carefully choose your field type from the provided list. Make sure to think about the exact use case and select the field type that makes sense for your business needs.

2. **Configure the field attributes**: Once you select your field type, you will have to set the attributes for the field. Each of these is covered in detail earlier in this chapter.

3. **Set up field-level security**: Establish the permissions to your new field that should be granted to existing profiles. Once you have set the field type and configured the related attributes for your field, you will need to set the visibility of and access to the field across the existing profiles. You have three options that can be applied. Table 1-8 is a matrix showing the Visible and Read-Only columns that you edit along with the CRUD (create, read, update, delete) equivalent of the corresponding combination.

Table 1-8. *Potential Field-Level Security Settings (Note: Create and Delete are managed at the record and object levels)*

Summary	Visible	Read-Only	CRUD Equivalent
No visibility/No ability to edit the field			N/A
Visibility/No ability to edit the field	Y	Y	R
Visibility/Ability to edit the field	Y		RU

Keep in mind that field-level security (FLS) may or may not have a direct impact on a user's experience. If a user does not have access to a particular record at all, full access via FLS does nothing to change that – the user still will not be able to see any of the fields on the record. Or she may be granted Read/Write access via FLS but a validation rule (these will be covered later in this book) may override that access and prevent her from editing the record. FLS, whether associated with a profile or a permission set, conveys the maximum access to a field that a user might have; the user might ultimately have less access based on other settings, but she will not have more access to the field than configured via FLS. Figure 1-9 is a look at the FLS settings page during custom field creation.

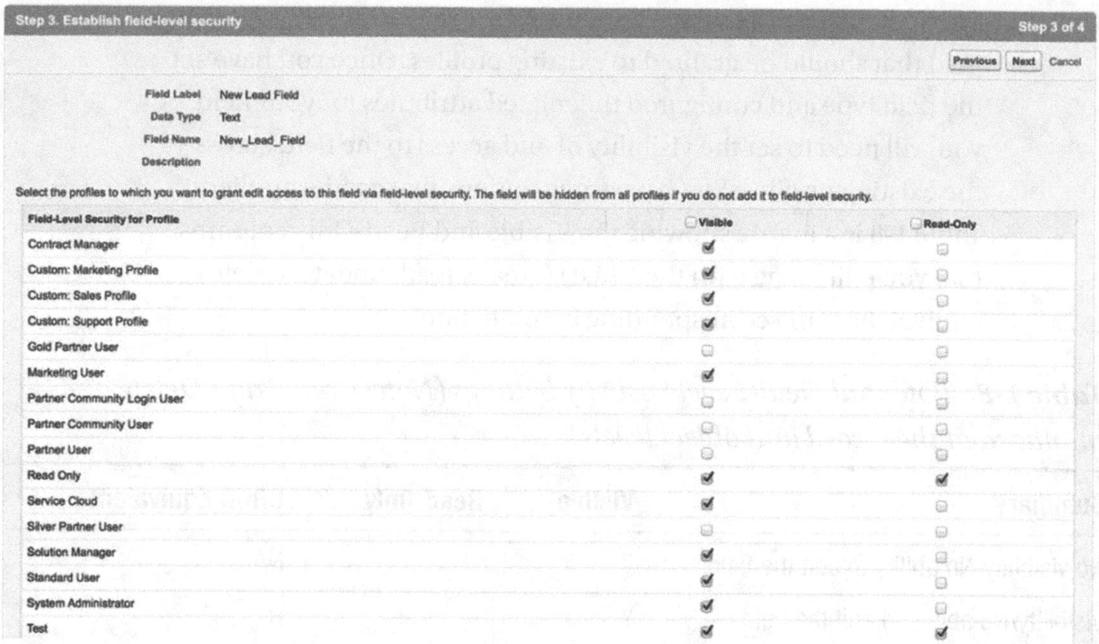

Figure 1-9. *Setting the field-level security for your field*

Note   Security considerations, including object and field permissions, are discussed in detail in Chapter 15.

---

4. **Add to page layouts:** The last step in the field creation process is only marginally helpful, and I'll explain why. You are given the option to automatically add the field you are creating to any of the page layouts for the corresponding object. If you are creating a Lead field and four page layouts exist for Leads, you can add the Lead field to any of those four layouts at your discretion, as shown in Figure 1-10.

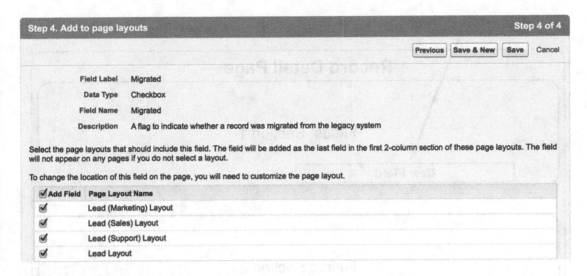

Figure 1-10. *Setting your page layout options*

This sounds like a nice time-saver, doesn't it? The problem is that you have no control over the field's location within the page layout, just whether it is present or not. Fields added to page layouts through this means are (almost) always added as the bottom, left-most field in the first section on the page layout, as shown in Figure 1-11. Long and rich text area fields are automatically added to a one-column section, if one exists.

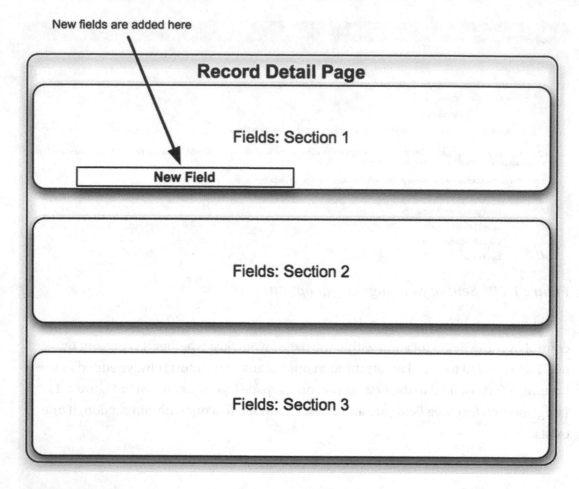

Figure 1-11. *Appearance of a new field when added during the creation process*

Except in the rare situation where you specifically want your field to appear in the bottom-left corner of the top-most field section on your page layout, you will need to go into your layout and edit it to move the field to the desired location. You may want to hold off on automatically adding a field to a page layout and just do it manually for two reasons:

- If you forget to update the corresponding page layout after creating it, your field will be in the wrong location.

- You have to update the page layout anyway and you will have additional control if you handle adding the field and moving it all at once.

That's it! You do want to spend some time thinking about your options before just breezing through the creation. You can always change your field settings later, but it's definitely easier to set up your field properly up front. Now, you're ready to move on to the world of objects.

Salesforce Objects

As you have seen in this chapter thus far, it is impossible to cover the breadth of Salesforce fields without at least touching on the objects in which those fields are contained. In this section, I will dive into the basics of objects and further prepare you to develop real-world business solutions on the Force.com platform.

Previously, I stated that fields in Salesforce are comparable to database columns. Along those same lines, we can compare Salesforce objects to database tables (again, on steroids). Each object contains a set number of standard fields along with any custom fields you create. At the intersection of those fields and the records will be your field values, similar to database fields. Table 1-9 includes a couple of basic charts that have a similar structure to each other.

Table 1-9. *Comparison Between a Salesforce Object and a Relational Database Table*

Salesforce Object			Relational Database Table		
	Field 1 (text)	Field 2 (number)		Column 1 (text)	Column 2 (number)
Record 1	My first record	100	Row 1	My first record	100
Record 2	My second record	200	Row 2	My second record	200
Record 3	My third record	300	Row 3	My third record	300

However, there is another layer entirely to objects. Like fields, objects have associated attributes and metadata that build their context and drive their use. I will now walk you through the object creation process, during which you will see the additional information that can be associated with a Salesforce object. To start, navigate to "Create ➤ Objects" in classic or "Object Manager" in Lightning Experience (from where you will click on "Create" as shown in Figure 1-12.

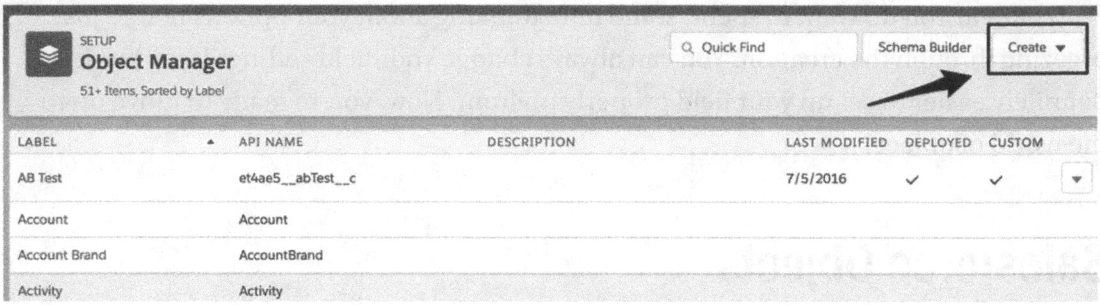

Figure 1-12. *Click the Create button on the Object Manager screen to initiate the creation of a new object*

Figure 1-13 is the initial screen you see when creating a custom object.

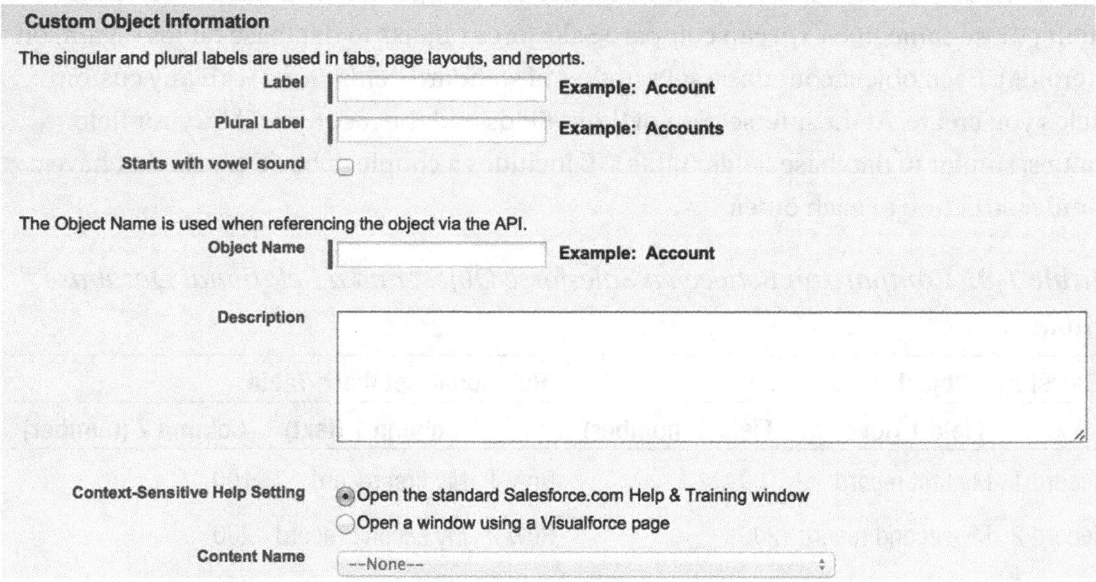

Figure 1-13. *Typical custom field attributes that can be set during field creation*

The first step in creating a custom object is to define its basic, key information. You'll set your label and plural label first. Salesforce doesn't want to assume what your grammatical application will be. What if you wanted to make an object called "Fish"? In that case, you might want the plural label to match label. The "Starts with vowel sound" is present for a similar reason: Salesforce does not inherently know that the starting letter in "hour" and "hot" sound different, but it does want to apply correct grammar rules. Setting that yourself helps to achieve that goal.

Like with Salesforce fields, you will need to provide an object name and, optionally, a description. I would again recommend using the object name that is automatically populated, unless it is critical to your business process that you set a specific name for a business purpose. And as tempting as it is to skip entering a description, the 10 seconds needed to enter one could pay off in spades. I can say from personal experience that a populated description has helped save a significant chunk of time more than once.

The next step is configuring the Record Name label and format for your object. Figure 1-14 shows the Record Name field, which will be the primary name field for your new records.

Figure 1-14. *Record Name as a text field*

As shown in Figure 1-15, you can either allow open text entry or you can automate it (without code) using the Auto-Number option. I recommend using the Auto-Number option when possible, as it provides you with a built-in ID that is automatically increased, in increments, with the creation of new records. In particular, it should be heavily considered when creating "child" objects that look up to other objects, as these typically don't require arbitrarily formatted names. It also serves as a nice reference when looking at a list of records.

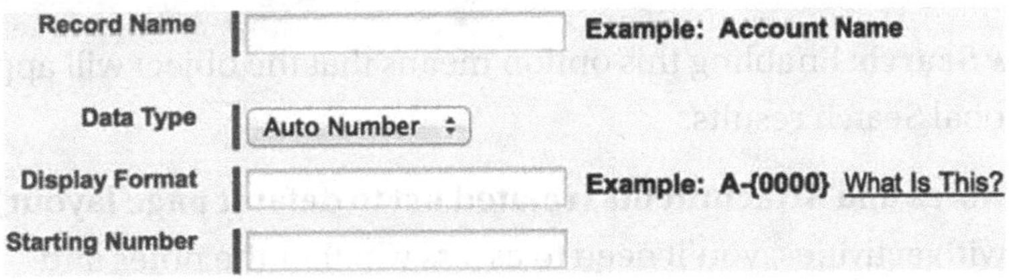

Figure 1-15. *Record Name as an Auto-Number field*

The last setting in this section determines the source for your content. You can either use the generic custom object page that Salesforce provides or your own custom page. If you don't have a specific help page ready for use, proceed with the Salesforce help page.

There are some additional attributes that you'll need to consider when creating your custom fields. Here's a summary of the remaining items:

- **Allow Reports**: Creates a custom report type for the object with which reports can be created for the new object.

- **Allow Activities**: Enables activities (tasks, events) to be associated with the record. Recommended only if activities make sense for the object. If the object does not require activities to be tracked against it, leave it unchecked. You can also enable it later.

- **Track Field History**: Allows changes made to the fields on the object to be tracked.

- **Allow in Chatter Groups**: Allows records of this object type to be associated with Chatter groups, either internally or in communities, via the Add Record button.

- **Allow Sharing**, **Allow Bulk API Access**, and **Allow Streaming API Access**: These three settings must either all be enabled or all be disabled. By default, they are enabled, making a custom object an "Enterprise Application" object. Disabling these features will convert the object to a "Light Application" object. The settings themselves allow for more advanced, robust interaction with the object.

- **Deployment Status**: Allows you to select "Deployed" if the object is ready for release to all users.

- **Allow Search**: Enabling this option means that the object will appear in Global Search results.

- **Add Notes and Attachments (related list to default page layout)**: Like with activities, you'll need to assess whether the notes and attachments are relevant. If so, select this option. Otherwise, leave off the clutter.

- **Launch New Custom Tab Wizard (after saving the custom object)**: Will users need to navigate to the records? Then definitely select this option. There's no need to select this option if it has more of a back-end or reporting function.

Note   The Object attributes that are configured at the time of object creation can easily be modified later by navigating back to the object in the Setup menu. For example, if your reporting needs change after object deployment, you can check the Allow Reports Checkbox when needed.

External Objects

External objects are similar to custom objects, but represent data in an external system (i.e., the data lives outside of Salesforce). Considering the age of the overall platform, external objects are relatively new. Once an external data source is established, an external object can be created from that data source. Table 1-10 breaks down the difference between the setup options available for custom objects and external objects.

Table 1-10. *Creation Options Available for Custom Objects and External Objects*

Setting	Custom Object	External Object
Label	✓	✓
Plural Label	✓	✓
Starts with Vowel Sound	✓	✓
Object Name	✓	✓
Description	✓	✓
Context-Sensitive Help Setting	✓ (2)	✓ (3)
Record Name	✓	
Data Type	✓	
Display Format	✓	
Starting Number	✓	
External Data Source		✓
Table Name		✓
Display URL Reference Field		✓

(continued)

Table 1-10. (*continued*)

Setting	Custom Object	External Object
Allow Reports	✓	✓
Allow Activities	✓	
Track Field History	✓	
Allow in Chatter Groups	✓	
Allow Sharing	✓	
Allow Bulk API Access	✓	
Allow Streaming API Access	✓	
Deployment Status	✓	✓
Allow Search	✓	
Add Notes & Attachments Related List	✓	
Launch New Custom Tab Wizard	✓	✓
Search Status		✓

Having an external object in place allows much simpler access to and interaction with data that is located outside Salesforce.

Salesforce Relationships

While relationships in Salesforce technically fall under the umbrella of field types, they warrant a closer look outside the scope of other more straightforward field types. Relationship fields are the last piece of the puzzle and allow you to connect everything in your data model together.

Relationship Field Types

To fully understand how relationships within Salesforce work, you must first have a firm grasp on the types of relationship fields that can be created.

Lookup Relationship

Along with the Master-Detail relationship field type, which will be discussed in the next section, the Lookup relationship is vastly different from all other field types and has significant implications for your Salesforce org. A Lookup relationship field actually modifies the interobject schema by creating Parent/Child links between objects. To clearly see the picture, first take a look at a two disparate, unrelated objects. As illustrated in Figure 1-16, the Contact and Idea objects have no native relationship with each other.

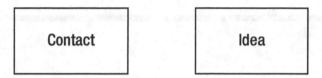

Figure 1-16. *Two disparate objects*

Unlike the Contact and Idea objects, the Contact and Account objects are, in fact, related. The Contact object has an "Account Name" Lookup relationship that creates a link between the two objects. In Figure 1-17, the Account object is shown above the Contact object since it is the Parent object and the Contact object is the Child.

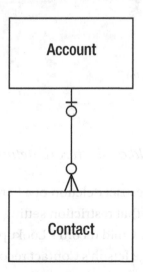

Figure 1-17. *Related Account and Contact objects, connected via a Lookup field*

Figure 1-17 shows the Crow's Foot entity-relationship notation for the relationship between the Account and Contact. A Contact can look up zero or one Account. An Account can go from zero-to-many Contacts and is not required to have any related

Contacts, but can be associated with however many you can add to it within the applicable limits of your org. When creating a Lookup relationship field, make sure to consider that it is a loose relationship; deletion of the parent record that is referenced in the Lookup field does not result in the child record's deletion. For example, take a look at Figure 1-18. In this image, you can see that the Contact record for George Jetson has a Lookup relationship to the Spacely Sprockets Account. If you delete the record of the parent, Spacely Sprockets, George Jetson's Contact record will not be deleted automatically; the Account field will simply no longer be populated.

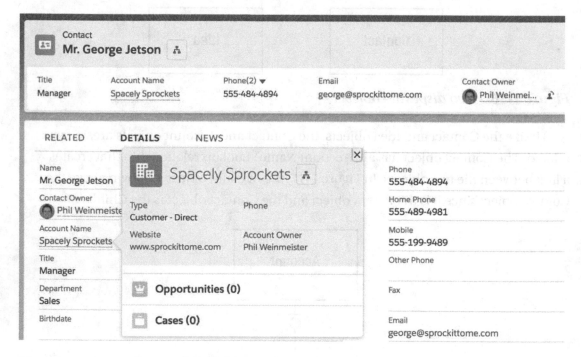

Figure 1-18. *A relationship field on the record detail page*

Salesforce does allow you to restrict deletion of a Parent record that is part of a Lookup relationship. By enabling that restriction setting, you require users to first remove or change the value in the Child record's Lookup field before deleting the Parent. In this case, you would edit George Jetson's Contact record, modify the Account Name Lookup, save the record, and then delete the Spacely Sprockets record. See Figure 1-19 for a view of this option.

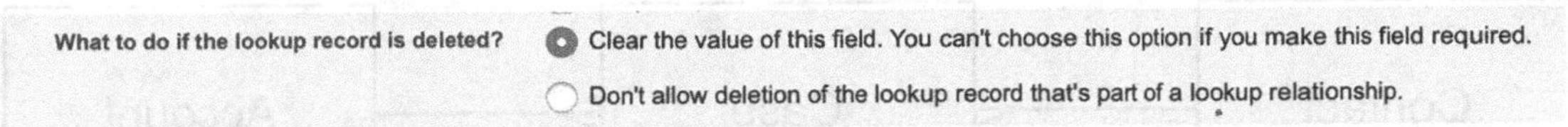

What to do if the lookup record is deleted?	⦿ Clear the value of this field. You can't choose this option if you make this field required.
	◯ Don't allow deletion of the lookup record that's part of a lookup relationship.

Figure 1-19. *Ability to control deletion of a lookup record*

Additionally, you can add a Lookup Filter to a Lookup relationship. A Lookup Filter will restrict the available records in a Lookup field based on defined criteria. Figure 1-20 shows the Filter Lookup setup screen for the Account lookup field on the Contact object.

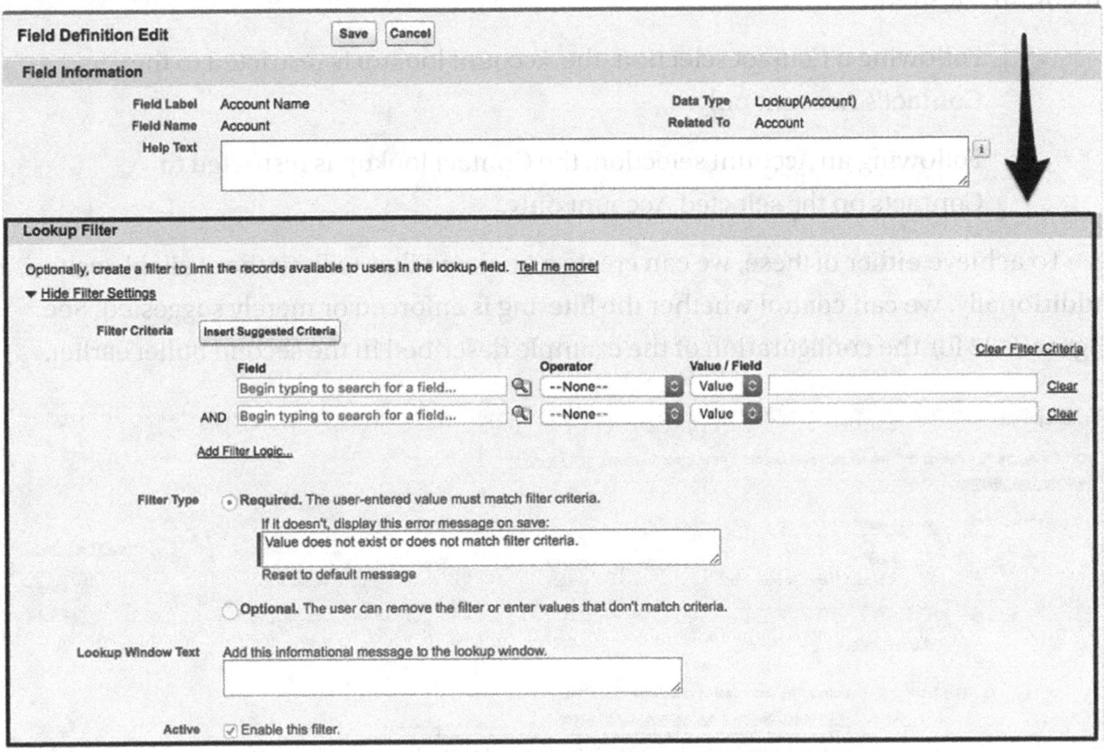

Figure 1-20. *A Lookup Filter helps to restrict the fields available to select in a Lookup field*

Let's take the Case object as an example. The Case object possesses lookup relationships to both Contact and Account; see Figure 1-21.

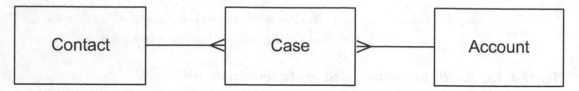

Figure 1-21. *The Case object possesses lookup relationships to both Contact and Account*

Although they don't apply to all organization's support scenarios, two scenarios are frequently desired:

- Following a Contact selection, the Account lookup is restricted to the Contact's Account only.

- Following an Account selection, the Contact lookup is restricted to Contacts on the selected Account only.

To achieve either of these, we can create a Lookup Filter to limit the available values. Additionally, we can control whether the filtering is enforced or merely suggested. See Figure 1-22 for the configuration of the example described in the second bullet earlier.

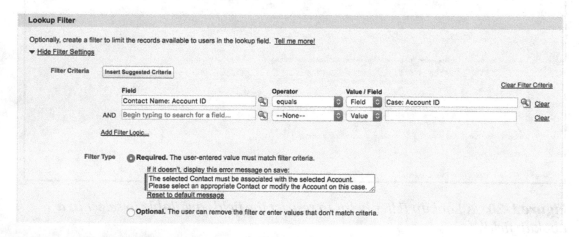

Figure 1-22. *A Lookup Filter to restrict the Contact values in the Contact Name lookup on a Case to Contacts associated with the selected Account*

External Lookup Relationship

If you have established an external data source and created an external object, you "unlock" a new field type: an external lookup relationship. This allows you to create a relationship between an object and a table in an external system, represented as an external object in Salesforce. The child object can be either an object in Salesforce (resulting in a Salesforce object looking up to an external object) or an external object (resulting in an external object looking up to an external object). Figure 1-23 shows this option on the "New Custom Field" screen.

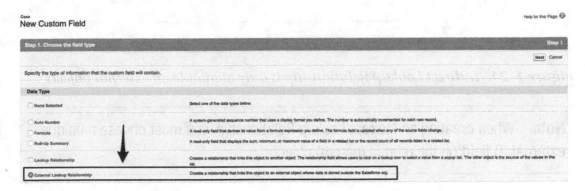

Figure 1-23. *An external lookup relationship*

Other than the fact that the selectable objects are external objects, no other differences exist in the setup process.

Note   A Lookup Relationship (instead of an External Lookup Relationship) can be created and associated to a parent that is an external object, but only if the external data includes a column that identifies related Salesforce records by their 18-character record IDs.

Indirect Lookup Relationship

The reverse of an external lookup relationship is an Indirect Lookup Relationship. This can only be created from an external object and is not visible on the new custom field screen for either custom or standard objects. Figure 1-24 shows the Indirect Lookup Relationship selection.

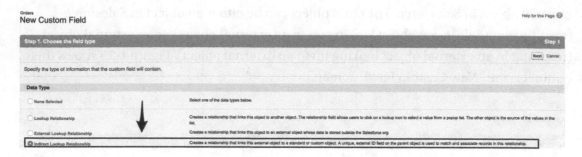

Figure 1-24. *Indirect Lookup Relationship is only available on external objects*

Note   When creating an Indirect Lookup Relationship, you must choose a unique external ID field on the related (parent) object.

Figure 1-25 shows a view of an internal object (Case) and an external object (Orders) and how lookup relationships between the objects would be labeled.

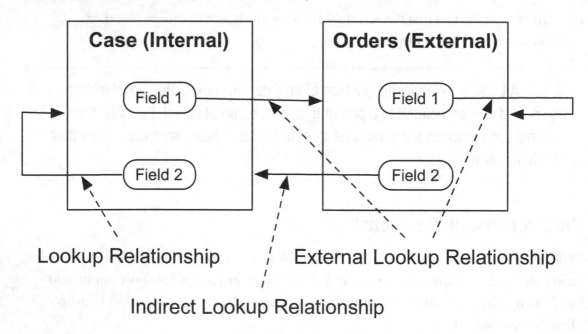

Figure 1-25. *Lookup relationships between and external and internal object*

Master-Detail Relationship

The Master-Detail relationship field type is very similar to a Lookup relationship. By creating a Master-Detail field, you build a relationship between a Child record and a Parent record. However, there are some critical differences between these two relationship field types:

- A Master-Detail relationship field must be populated. In other words, you cannot have an "orphaned" Child record that has a blank Master-Detail field. This is not the case with a Lookup field unless you specify that a Parent is required in the Lookup.

- A Child in a Master-Detail relationship does not have a standard Owner field; the owner of the Parent record, via inheritance, determines the owner for this relationship.

- Cascading deletion occurs when Parent/Master records are removed. In other words, all Child/Detail records will be deleted if the Parent record linked via a Master-Detail field is deleted.

- Master-Detail fields allow you to create Roll-Up Summary fields. They will be discussed in the next section.

Although a Master-Detail field must be populated, it can be "reparented" if configured accordingly. That means that you can change the associated Parent record after the Child record is created.

Roll-Up Summary

The Roll-Up Summary field type does not affect object relationships, but it builds directly upon the Master-Detail relationship. A Roll-Up Summary field is a great feature, which Salesforce makes available for creation any time you establish a Master-Detail field. The presence of an associated Master-Detail field is a requirement, since the Summary part of the field is directly related to the associated Child records. In Figure 1-26, you can see two different perspectives of how this works. On the left, you see that the Master-Detail field is created on the Detail, or Child, object. However, the Roll-Up Summary is set up on the Master, or Parent, object. On the right, you can see examples of actual records that might be present in this Master-Detail relationship. The presence of the Roll-Up Summary on the Master record makes sense since the summary will include a downward look across all of the children.

37

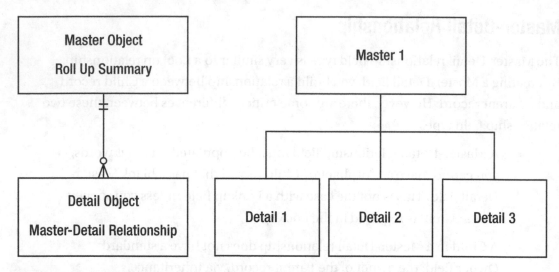

Figure 1-26. *A view of a Master-Detail relationship*

When you create a Roll-Up Summary, you are given the following options:

- **Object to summarize**: Note that the objects listed will be limited to those with Master-Detail relationships with the object you're working with.

- **Roll-Up type**: (COUNT, SUM, MIN, MAX) COUNT returns the number of all Child records on the selected object. SUM returns the sum of a specified Number or Currency field across Child records. MIN and MAX return the least/first or greatest/last value, respectively, from a specific Number, Currency, or Date field among Child records.

- **Filter criteria**: Allows you to specify criteria based on object fields to limit which Child records are included in the Roll-Up.

It might help to look at a few specific examples. Figure 1-27 represents the Master-Detail relationship between the Opportunity and Account objects, and Table 1-11 shows sample records at the detail level.

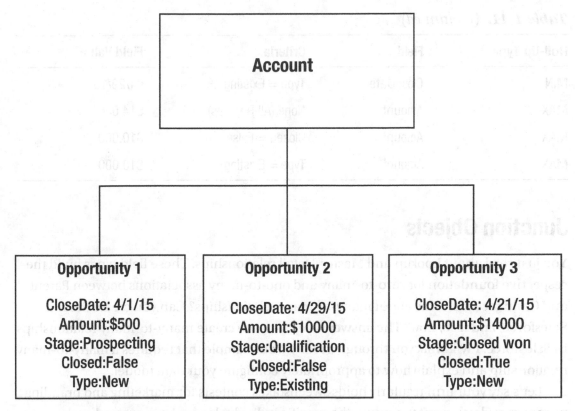

Figure 1-27. *Three Opportunities and their related Account*

Table 1-11. *Examples of Roll-Up Summary Fields and Their Values Based on the Records in Figure 1-27 Salesforce Data Model: Roll-Up Summary*

Roll-Up Type	Field	Criteria	Field Value
COUNT	N/A	None (All Records)	3
COUNT	N/A	Closed = False	2
COUNT	N/A	Type = Existing	1
SUM	Amount	None (All Records)	$24,500
SUM	Amount	Closed = False	$10,500
SUM	Amount	Type = Existing	$10,000
MIN	CloseDate	None (All Records)	04/01/15
MIN	CloseDate	Closed = False	04/01/15

(*continued*)

Table 1-11. (*continued*)

Roll-Up Type	Field	Criteria	Field Value
MIN	CloseDate	Type = Existing	04/29/15
MAX	Amount	None (All Records)	$14,000
MAX	Amount	Closed = False	$10,000
MAX	Amount	Type = Existing	$10,000

Junction Objects

You just read about Lookup and Master-Detail relationships. These field types build the respective foundation for zero-to-many and one-to-many associations between Parent and Child records. What about many-to-many relationships? Can you create those in Salesforce, and if so, how? The answer is yes; you *can* create many-to-many relationships in Salesforce. I will walk you through a real-world example that requires a many-to-many relationship and explain how to appropriately configure your data model.

Let's say your firm regularly holds sweepstakes contests for marketing and branding purposes and you want to capture the specific individuals who have entered each contest. Those individuals come from your pool of existing Contact records. In this case, the standard Campaign and Campaign Member objects would likely meet your needs, but we will use custom objects for the purposes of this discussion.

You could create a Sweepstakes object and relate Contacts to it via a Lookup relationship, as shown in Figure 1-28.

Figure 1-28. *Contact record related to a custom object "Sweepstakes"*

However, via a direct relationship to Sweepstakes, *a Contact can only be associated with one Sweepstakes.* That quickly becomes a problem as your Contacts start to apply for multiple Sweepstakes. This is where a "Junction object" comes into play. Instead of directly linking your Contact to a Sweepstakes, you can create a new custom object called a Sweepstakes Registrant and add two relationship fields to it, as shown in Figure 1-29.

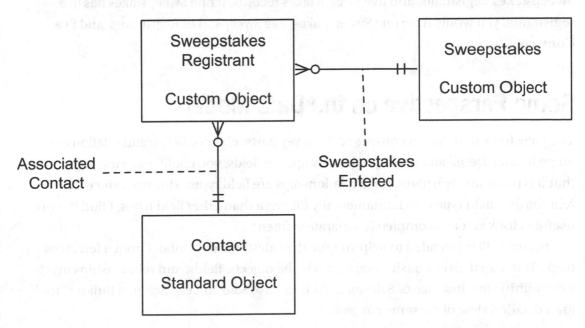

Figure 1-29. *Sweepstakes Registrant custom object serving as a Junction object*

41

Here is a breakdown of the various elements shown in Figure 1-29:

- **Sweepstakes Entered**: This Master-Detail field identifies a sweepstakes that the registrant is registered for. It is a Master-Detail field because a Sweepstakes Registrant cannot exist apart from a Sweepstakes.

- **Associated Contact**: This field identifies the person that registered for a particular Sweepstakes. Because you don't need a duplicate record of a person, you link to the "source" record, which is the Contact, and add any custom fields to the Sweepstakes Registrant record to provide additional context about his role as a registrant. This is a Master-Detail field because a Sweepstakes Registrant cannot exist apart from a Contact, at least in this case.

As a result, both Contacts and Sweepstakes can be associated with many Sweepstakes Registrants. That means that

- One Contact can be associated with many Sweepstakes.

- One Sweepstakes can be associated with many Contacts.

If one Contact is registered for five Sweepstakes, you would have one Contact, five Sweepstakes Registrants, and five Sweepstakes records. If one Sweepstakes has five registrants, you would have one Sweepstakes, five Sweepstakes Registrants, and five Contacts.

Some Perspective on the Data Model

The Salesforce data model consists of three key parts: objects, fields, and relationships. Since Master-Detail and Lookup relationships are fields, you could make the argument that it is really just two parts, since relationships are field types. However, since the relationship field type is so fundamentally different than other field types, I find it more useful to look at it as a completely separate element.

Figure 1-30 is intended to help you see the Salesforce data model from a few steps back. This visual gives a basic perspective of the objects, fields, and relationships that exist within your instance of Salesforce. You can use Salesforce's "Schema Builder" tool for a detailed view of the same content.

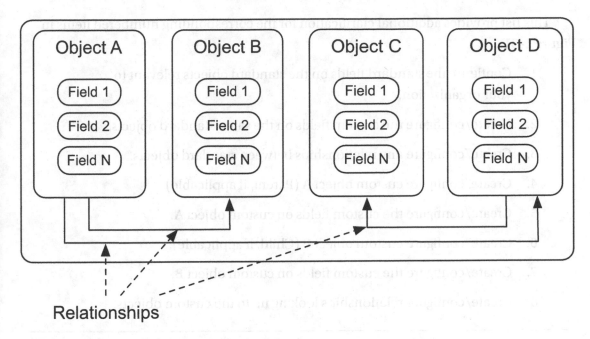

Figure 1-30. *A view of the data model*

More realistically, the creation of your data model will look like Figure 1-31.

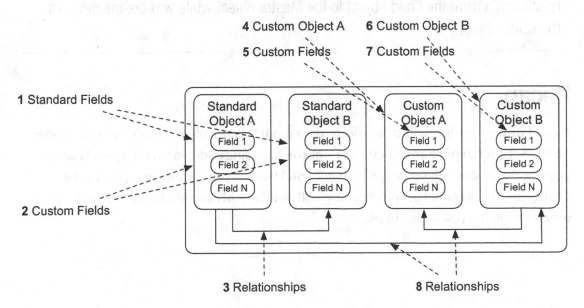

Figure 1-31. *A high-level suggested sequence for building out your data model*

This list provides additional clarification for the corresponding numbered items in Figure 1-31:

1. Configure the standard fields on the standard objects relevant to your organization.

2. Create/configure the custom fields on the same standard objects.

3. Create/configure any relationships between standard objects.

4. Create/configure custom object A (Parent, if applicable).

5. Create/configure the custom fields on custom object A.

6. Create/configure custom object B (Child, if applicable).

7. Create/configure the custom fields on custom object B.

8. Create/configure relationships looking up to the custom objects.

Note   Create Parent objects before Child objects to minimize the number of total steps required to build out your data model. This will allow you to add the relationship from the Child object to the Master object while you are building out the Child object.

Recap

A solid understanding of the Salesforce data model is critical for success as a developer on the Salesforce platform whether or not you are using code. In this chapter, I examined objects, fields, and relationships in detail and I walked you through the process for setting up a data model in your org. You will build on this foundation as you make your way through the rest of this book.

CHAPTER 2

Formula Functions: Your Building Block in Salesforce Formulas

Without hesitation, I would identify this chapter as one of the most important in this book. Along with the first chapter on the Salesforce data model, it will serve as the foundation for many of the upcoming chapters, as formula functions are used in a number of development areas within the Salesforce platform. If you understand how to properly build and apply functions within Salesforce, you will be able to develop successful custom solutions for yourself, your employer, and your clients.

Functions can be used in a number of different areas:

- Formula fields
- Workflow rules
- Field updates
- Validation rules
- Approval rules and rule steps
- Auto-response rules
- Escalation rules
- Assignment rules
- Custom buttons and links
- Process builder
- Flow (visual workflow)

© Philip Weinmeister 2019
P. Weinmeister, *Practical Salesforce Development Without Code*,
https://doi.org/10.1007/978-1-4842-4871-3_2

These areas comprise much of the focus of this book and a significant portion of your arsenal in developing custom solutions within Salesforce using clicks, not code. There are over 60 total functions available for use within Salesforce and that number continues to grow. In this chapter, I will dissect the most useful and applicable of them. Those functions that are not specifically covered in this chapter can be reviewed in more depth using Salesforce's online help documentation.

In this chapter, I will walk you through each function and review the following areas in relation to it:

- **Format**: The format and syntax of the function

- **Summary**: A summary of the function, including a concise description of how the function works

- **Application scenarios**: Examples of how you might apply the function in real-world situations

- **Usability**: The areas in Salesforce in which the function can be used

- **Other considerations**: Any additional tips or "gotchas" that might assist you when using the function

Although some of the scenarios described may not closely pertain to you or your business, they can offer a starting point for you to generate ideas. Once you grasp the basics of functions, you can start applying them in complex and powerful ways. In upcoming chapters, I will examine how to pull significant value out of formulas using an array of functions and related fields.

By the end of this chapter, you should

- Be familiar with the most useful Salesforce functions

- Understand Salesforce function syntax

- Understand how to apply functions at a basic level

Anatomy of a Salesforce Function

Understanding the anatomy of a function in Salesforce is the first step in properly utilizing it. Salesforce functions can be generally represented as follows:

```
FUNCTION_NAME(argument_1,...argument_n [, optional_argument])
```

Name

The name of the function being used is the FUNCTION_NAME. The name will always be followed by the opening parenthesis.

Arguments

The number of arguments in a function can vary. An argument is not required, as demonstrated through such functions as TODAY and NOW, which return the current date and the current date/time, respectively, without a single argument being provided. The type of arguments that can be used in functions can vary. For example, the argument required may be a

- Number (e.g., Amount)
- True or false value (e.g., Child_Account_Count__c > 0, IsClosed, etc.)
- Text string (e.g., "On Hold")
- Field of a specific type (e.g., a Multiselect Picklist field)

There are many more types of arguments that can be found within the array of Salesforce functions; these are just a few common examples.

Note   In functions, fields are represented by their full (API) name. For example, a field labeled "My New Field" might have an API name of My_New_Email__c. The label "My New Field" will not be referenced in the function examples; instead, you will see My_New_Field__c within the function.

Optional Arguments

An argument that can be provided but is not required is an optional_argument. Brackets, [], represent these optional arguments. For example, FUNCTION(text [, optional]) may be used as

```
FUNCTION(text) or
FUNCTION(text, optional)
```

Note   All functions with optional arguments have specified default behavior for when the optional arguments are omitted. Always know the default behavior before you decide that the optional arguments are unnecessary.

Salesforce Development Using Functions

Functions can be invoked in various areas within Salesforce. While it is important to understand function format and syntax, the actual use of functions requires no coding on behalf of the developing user. Salesforce provides a declarative method not only for producing a validly formatted function but also for inserting related fields.

The framework does, of course, allow for hard-coded input that falls outside of what Salesforce can deliver declaratively. For example, the SUBSTITUTE function calls for text strings as two of the arguments; unless you established each of those values in a custom setting or a custom metadata type (refer to Chapter 11 for more detail on how to build and use both options), you would need to manually type in your text values.

To develop using Salesforce formula functions, you can use the provided formula editors that exist in the majority of elements where functions can be developed. The formula editors allow you to use clicks to build your solution without memorizing syntax or format of the related functions you'll be using.

Let's take a look at the components of a formula editor.

The Function Selector

The function selector, when available, is located to the right-hand side of the development area as shown in Figure 2-1.

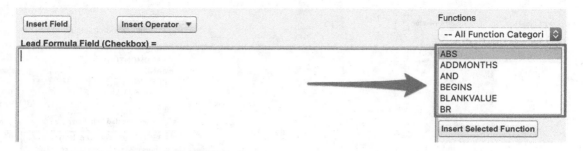

Figure 2-1. *The function selector allows you to declaratively insert functions into your formulas*[1]

To use the function selector

1. Select a function category from the list of displayed functions (optional).

2. Scroll down to and select the function to be used.

3. Click the "Insert Selected Function" button.

Note   You may double-click a function name to insert that function into your formula as an alternative to selecting the function name and clicking the "Insert Selected Function" button.

When you select a function, some information about it will be displayed below the function selector. Once you click the "Insert Selected Function" button, the function will be inserted into the development area as shown in Figure 2-2.

---

[1]All Salesforce screenshots in this chapter © copyright Salesforce, Inc. Used with permission·

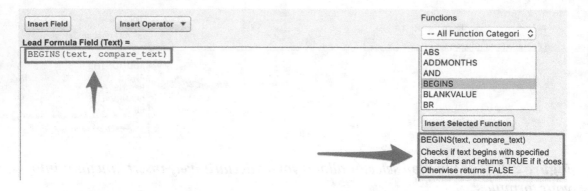

Figure 2-2. *The* BEGINS *function has been inserted into this formula using the function selector*

In this case, the BEGINS function was selected, and the following text was inserted into the development area:

BEGINS(text, compare_text)

Inserting a Field

Once you have the function in place, you can replace the default argument text with actual values. For example, you will want to replace text and compare_text in the BEGINS function shown in Figure 2-2. To insert a field

1. Double-click the text to be replaced.

2. Click the "Insert Field" button.

3. Select the lowest-level object or entity in which your field resides.

4. Select a Lookup field to traverse to a related object; repeat as needed (optional).

5. Select the field you want to insert into your function.

6. Click the "Insert" button.

Figure 2-3 shows the interface for selecting and inserting a field.

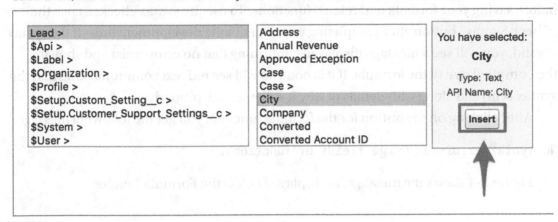

Insert Field

Select a field, then click Insert. Labels followed by a ">" indicate that there are more fields available.

Lead >	Address	You have selected:
$Api >	Annual Revenue	**City**
$Label >	Approved Exception	
$Organization >	Case	Type: Text
$Profile >	Case >	API Name: City
$Setup.Custom_Setting__c >	City	
$Setup.Customer_Support_Settings__c >	Company	Insert
$System >	Converted	
$User >	Converted Account ID	

Figure 2-3. *Inserting a field*

Once inserted, the formula function becomes

BEGINS(City, compare_text)

Inserting Text

In this example with the BEGINS function, you still have compare_text to replace. It's possible that you may want to replace this with another field, but it's more likely that you will manually replace it with the desired text. To do so, double-click the text and replace it with your desired text within quotes (e.g., "Ph") as follows:

BEGINS(City, "Ph")

Note   Function operators will frequently be used in your development without code. I will review details of operators in Chapter 3, "Formula Fields."

Checking Your Syntax

Although you are not required to use it, Salesforce provides a way to check your syntax before saving your formula and related functions. To use the syntax checker, click the "Check Syntax" button after completing your work in the development area. If the syntax is valid, you will see a message displayed confirming that no errors exist and showing the compiled size of the formula. If it is not, you will see red text communicating that the syntax is invalid along with details of why it will not work properly.

After clicking on the button for the formula function, you get the following message:

No syntax errors in merge fields or functions.

Figure 2-4 shows the message, as displayed below the Formula Builder.

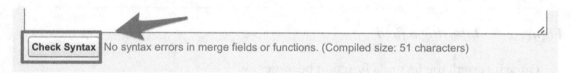

Figure 2-4. *The desired message after clicking "Check Syntax"*

Done! You've developed your first formula function within Salesforce.

Note   Manual validation of syntax is not required because validation is automatically performed upon saving your formula.

Using the Simple and Advanced Formula Editors

When building formula fields, Salesforce provides two types of formula editors to use: simple and advanced. The application of the simple formula editor is extremely limited in comparison to that of the advanced formula editor. Additionally, *you cannot develop with functions declaratively in a simple formula editor*. Figure 2-5 shows the main user interface for the simple formula editor.

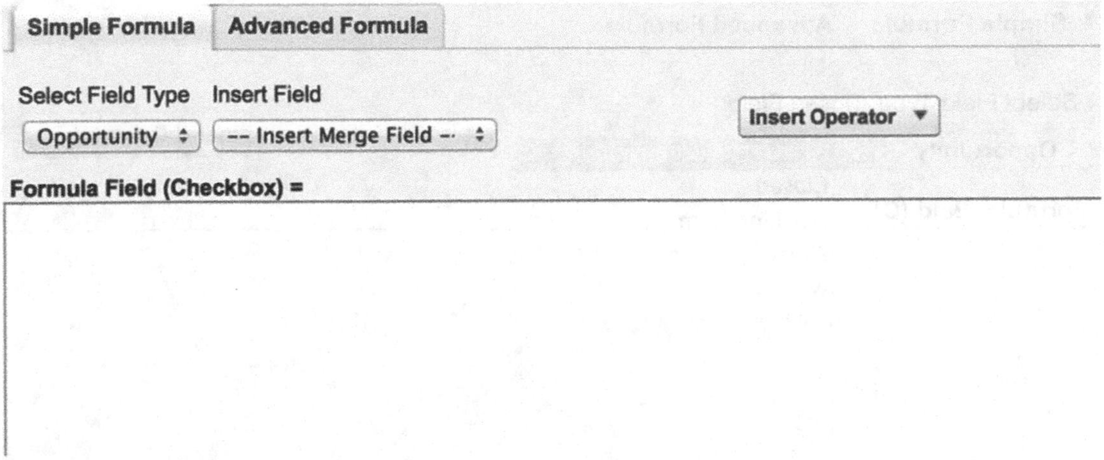

Figure 2-5. *The simple formula editor provides limited functionality when building formulas*

The idea here is that the simple formula editor is easy and quick to use. However, you'll notice a few drawbacks:

- Lookups cannot be performed declaratively to reference fields for use within functions.

- Only a limited number of fields are displayed in the field list.

- Operator choices are limited.

- A function "picker" is not available.

Figure 2-6 provides an example of the values displayed within the merge field dropdown when using the simple formula editor.

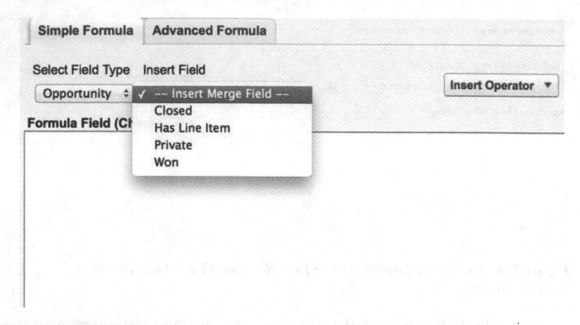

Figure 2-6. *Examples of available fields that can be used with functions in the simple formula editor*

The advanced formula editor provides access to more fields, operators, and most importantly, the function selector. The advanced formula editor is shown in Figure 2-7.

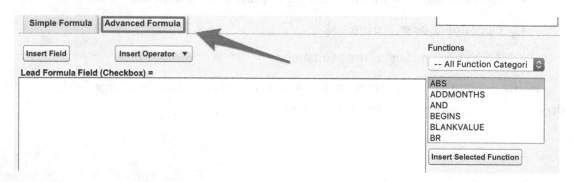

Figure 2-7. *Advanced formula editor*

Note Due to the limited scope and declarative capabilities of the simple formula editor, it is recommended that you use the advanced formula editor when building formula fields. Additionally, it is important to be aware that functions may significantly impact compile size and, as a result, approach or hit a formula field compile size limit. Make sure to review the current compile size limit, as posted by Salesforce, and understand your options.

Salesforce Formula Functions: A Deep Dive

Understanding basic function syntax and how to create functions using the provided editors lays the groundwork for the development of meaningful functions for real-life business situations. In this section, I will cover specific functions in detail and walk through hypothetical scenarios that show how these functions can be applied within your org. Clearly, there are many more possible scenarios for function usage than described in this chapter; you could write a separate book on example scenarios alone!

Note This section will cover certain key functions that are valuable to know. Some lesser-used or niche functions are not included here, but you can refer to Salesforce help documentation for a list of all Salesforce functions and their use.

ABS

The ABS function returns the absolute value of a number. The number can be specified, referenced via a field, or calculated.

Format

ABS(number)

Application Scenarios

Scenario 1: You want to calculate the difference between two numbers without the concept of sequence or rank among the data points.

55

Your organization uses Case management within the Salesforce Service Cloud. Internal business processes drive all new Cases to queues, from which customer service representatives within the corresponding queue pick them up. Internal service level agreements (SLAs) require that a representative post a Case comment within 5 minutes of ticket acceptance. The sequence is irrelevant; all that matters is that a customer service representative communicates with the customer right around the time that the Case is "picked up" by the representative (i.e., the representative assigns the Case to himself). You would use the following (custom) fields:

Time_to_Initial_Response__c (custom field on Case object);

Time_to_Initial_Acceptance__c (custom field on Case object)

The updated function:

```
ABS(Time_to_Initial_Response__c - Time to Initial Acceptance__c)
```

Note   Sequence is irrelevant when using the ABS function based on subtraction. ABS (field 1 - field 2) and ABS (field 2 - field 1) will have the same result.

Scenario 2: You want to know the difference between the actual amount and the initial expected revenue on a "Closed/Won" Opportunity. You only care how far off the initial expectation was (in dollars); you do not have interest in which of the two was actually larger. You would use the following fields:

Amount (standard field on Opportunity object)

Initial_Expected_Revenue__c (custom field on Opportunity object)

The updated function:

```
ABS(Amount - Initial_Expected_Revenue__c)
```

Usability

Table 2-1 shows the areas in which the ABS function can be utilized.

Table 2-1. *Allowed ABS Function Usage*

ABS			
Validation Rules	✓	Escalation Rules	✓
Workflow Rules	✓	Approval Rules	✓
Formula Fields	✓	Assignment Rules	✓
Auto-Response Rules	✓	Approval Step Rules	✓
Field Updates	✓	Custom Buttons & Links	✓
Process Builder	✓	Flow (Visual Workflow)	✓

Other Considerations

Although ABS will return a Number value, you can apply the ABS function to Percent and Currency fields in addition to Number fields. The ultimate output of your formula will always depend on your formula type, not the value returned by your Formula function. For example:

- **Formula (number)**: ABS (Currency_1 - Currency_2) – Difference between Currency_1 and Currency_2 in number format

- **Formula (currency)**: ABS (Number_2 - Number_1) – Difference between Number_2 and Number_1 in currency format

- **Formula (percent)**: ABS (Percent_2 - Percent_1) – Difference between Percent_2 and Percent_1 in percent format

ADDMONTHS

The ADDMONTHS function allows for a specified number of months to be added to a date. The function will automatically determine exactly how many days to add to the provided date.

Format

ADDMONTHS(Date,num)

Application Scenario

A news article will expire a certain number of months after creation. The number of months should be configurable for each record. Key fields:

> News__r.CreatedDate (standard field on custom "News" object);
>
> News__r.NumberOfMonths__c (custom field on custom "News" object)

The updated function:

ADDMONTHS(News__r.CreatedDate,News__r.NumberOfMonths__c)

Note   The function will automatically determine exactly how many days to add to the provided date. This is not a simple multiple of 30; it takes into consideration exactly which months come into play to provide an accurate result.

Usability

Table 2-2 shows the areas in which the ADDMONTHS function can be utilized.

Table 2-2. *Allowed ADDMONTHS Function Usage*

ADDMONTHS			
Validation Rules	✓	Escalation Rules	✓
Workflow Rules	✓	Approval Rules	✓
Formula Fields	✓	Assignment Rules	✓
Auto-Response Rules	✓	Approval Step Rules	✓
Field Updates	✓	Custom Buttons & Links	✓
Process Builder	✓	Flow (Visual Workflow)	✓

AND

The AND function checks whether all arguments are true and returns TRUE if all arguments are true or FALSE if one or more arguments are false.

Format

```
AND(logical1,logical2,...)
```

Application Scenarios

Scenario 1: You want to flag all opportunities that have an expected revenue greater than $5000 and a probability greater than 50 percent. You would use the following fields:

>Amount (standard field on Opportunity object)

>Probability (standard field on Opportunity object)

The updated function:

```
AND(
    Amount > 5000,
    Probability > 0.5
)
```

Scenario 2: You want to identify all cases that are Escalated and have a specific value in the Subject field. Let's assume that Subject line is "AS400 is no longer functioning". You would use the following fields:

>Escalated (standard field on Case object)

>Subject (standard field on Case object)

The updated function:

```
AND(
    Escalated,
    Subject = "AS400 is no longer functioning"
)
```

Usability

Table 2-3 shows the areas in which the AND function can be utilized.

Table 2-3. *Allowed AND Function Usage*

AND			
Validation Rules	✓	Escalation Rules	✓
Workflow Rules	✓	Approval Rules	✓
Formula Fields	✓	Assignment Rules	✓
Auto-Response Rules	✓	Approval Step Rules	✓
Field Updates	✓	Custom Buttons & Links	✓
Process Builder	✓	Flow (Visual Workflow)	✓

Other Considerations

You'll notice the term *Escalated* in the previous function (AND). This can be notated in longer form as *Escalated* = *true*. Since we're dealing with a Boolean field (Checkbox), the value returned is True or False. So, if you want to evaluate whether a Boolean field is true, the field name itself is sufficient.

Note   When evaluating a Checkbox field within a function, the field name itself is sufficient. There is no need for = *true* or = *false* in the statement.

Another approach for evaluating whether all arguments are AND() is by using the && operator. For example:

```
Amount > 5000 && Probability > 0.5
```

The decision to use the function AND or the operator && is purely based on personal preference. Both can be applied using clicks and there is no advantage to using one vs. the other in terms of how the formula is compiled.

Note   The AND function can be used interchangeably with a pair of ampersands. AND(`argument1, argument2`) is the equivalent of `argument1 &&` `argument2`.

BEGINS

The BEGINS function checks if specified text begins with specified characters and returns TRUE if it does. Otherwise, it returns FALSE.

Format

BEGINS(text, compare_text)

Application Scenarios

Scenario 1: You want to identify all Leads with a particular New York City area code and labeling them as high-priority Leads. In such an example, you would use the following field:

Phone (standard field on Lead object)

The updated function:

BEGINS(Phone, "202")

Scenario 2: You want to use the standard Product object within Salesforce and identify a certain type of product based on the name. You have a simple product-naming standard, with the first three letters conveying the product category. For example, "BRD-02293" is a Blu-ray disc and "DVD-15529" is a DVD. If you want to identify flag Blu-ray discs and emphasize them to users for special attention, you would use the following field:

Name (standard field on Product object)

The updated function:

BEGINS(Name, "BRD")

Usability

Table 2-4 shows the areas in which the BEGINS function can be utilized.

Table 2-4. *Allowed BEGINS Function Usage*

BEGINS			
Validation Rules	✓	Escalation Rules	✓
Workflow Rules	✓	Approval Rules	✓
Formula Fields	✓	Assignment Rules	✓
Auto-Response Rules	✓	Approval Step Rules	✓
Field Updates	✓	Custom Buttons & Links	✓
Process Builder	✓	Flow (Visual Workflow)	✓

BLANKVALUE

The BLANKVALUE function checks whether an expression is blank; if it is, it returns specified substitute text. If the expression is not blank, it returns the original expression value.

Format

BLANKVALUE(expression, substitute_expression)

Application Scenarios

Scenario 1: You want to provide feedback or instruction to a user regarding the value of a particular field that resides on a Parent object. In this case, you would either show the Account Site on the Contact being viewed or, if blank, instruct the User to update the Site field. You would use the following field:

> Account.Site (standard field on Account object, Lookup from
> Contact)

The updated function:

```
BLANKVALUE(
Account.Site,
"This Contact's Account does not have a designated Site. Please update the
Site field on the Account record."
)
```

Usability

Table 2-5 shows the areas in which the BLANKVALUE function can be utilized.

Table 2-5. *Allowed BLANKVALUE Function Usage*

BLANKVALUE			
Validation Rules	✓	Escalation Rules	✓
Workflow Rules	✓	Approval Rules	✓
Formula Fields	✓	Assignment Rules	✓
Auto-Response Rules	✓	Approval Step Rules	✓
Field Updates	✓	Custom Buttons & Links	✓
Process Builder	✓	Flow (Visual Workflow)	✓

Other Considerations

This function's use is not terribly extensive. If you want to identify whether a field is blank, you would use ISBLANK, which is also covered in this chapter.

CASE

The CASE function checks an expression against a series of values. If the expression's value matches any of the provided values (e.g., value1), the corresponding result is returned (e.g., result1). If it is not equal to any of the values, the else_result is returned.

Format

```
CASE(expression, value1, result1, value2, result2,...,else_result)
```

Application Scenarios

Scenario 1: You have a custom Customer Survey object within which you want to capture customer feedback related to the handling of a Case. The main field on the Customer Survey object is a score that can range from 1 to 10 or be left blank if not applicable. You want the customer to feel that she can provide granularity in the response, but the ten different values make it difficult to quickly assess and act on the feedback internally. A formula field is built to group some of the values. You will use the following field:

Feedback_Score__c (Custom field on Case object)

The updated function:

```
CASE(
Feedback_Score__c,
1, "Poor",
2, "Poor",
3, "Average",
4, "Good",
5, "Good",
"N/A"
)
```

Scenario 2: You want to show a next step or action item to users based on Opportunity Stage. Here, you'll take each Stage and apply corresponding text to display to users. You would use the following field:

StageName (standard field on Opportunity)

The updated function:

```
CASE(
StageName,
"Prospecting", "Gather Opportunity details.",
"Needs Analysis", "Work with Account Mgmt to solidify approach.",
"Value Proposition", "Communicate value to decision makers.",
```

```
"Decision Makers", "Review related case studies.",
"Perception Analysis", "Submit proposal to customer.",
"Proposal/Price Quote", "Ensure that customer understands quote.",
"Negotiation/Review", "Work with VP to ensure proper approach.",
"Closed Won", "Opportunity won; file proper paperwork.",
"Closed Lost", "Opportunity lost; no further action needed."
"N/A"
)
```

Usability

Table 2-6 shows the areas in which the CASE function can be utilized.

Table 2-6. *Allowed CASE Function Usage*

FUNCTION			
Validation Rules	✓	Escalation Rules	✓
Workflow Rules	✓	Approval Rules	✓
Formula Fields	✓	Assignment Rules	✓
Auto-Response Rules	✓	Approval Step Rules	✓
Field Updates	✓	Custom Buttons & Links	✓
Process Builder	✓	Flow (Visual Workflow)	✓

Other Considerations

Values and results in the Case statement must be of the same return type. For example, value1 and value2 must be of the same return type; however, value1 and result need not be. See the previous example that refers to the Feedback_Score__c field. Also, if you are only dealing with two or three different Case values, you may also want to consider the IF function, which provides additional flexibility.

CASESAFEID

The CASESAFEID function allows a 15-digit Salesforce ID to be converted into a case-insensitive 18-digit ID.

Format

CASESAFEID(id)

Application Scenario

Let's say you are working with a specific application that expects an 18-character ID (yes, this happens), but you only have the 15-character ID. You can use CASESAFEID to automatically generate the necessary value. Relevant fields:

Id (standard field on Case object);

The updated function:

CASESAFEID(Id)

Usability

Table 2-7 shows the areas in which the CASESAFEID function can be utilized.

Table 2-7. *Allowed CASESAFEID Function Usage*

CASESAFEID			
Validation Rules	✓	Escalation Rules	✓
Workflow Rules	✓	Approval Rules	✓
Formula Fields	✓	Assignment Rules	✓
Auto-Response Rules	✓	Approval Step Rules	✓
Field Updates	✓	Custom Buttons & Links	✓
Process Builder	✓	Flow (Visual Workflow)	✓

Other Considerations

Other Considerations. For example:

Formula (number): ABS (Currency_1 - Currency_2) – Difference between Currency_1 and Currency_2 in number format

CEILING, MCEILING, FLOOR, MFLOOR

The CEILING, MCEILING, FLOOR, and MLOOR functions all perform specific rounding functions. Unlike the ROUND function, none allow a specification of desired digits; the numeric argument will simply be rounded to an integer based on which function is used.

- CEILING will round to the nearest integer (away from zero if negative). This function is the most similar to ROUND.

- MCEILING will round up to the nearest integer (toward zero if negative).

- FLOOR will round down to the nearest integer (toward zero if negative).

- MFLOOR will round down to the nearest integer (away from zero if negative).

Format

```
CEILING(number)
MCEILING(number)
FLOOR(number)
MFLOOR(number)
```

Application Scenarios

Scenario 1: A field captures how much an individual owes the organization. The actual amount invoiced, however, needs to be an integer. The amount owed could be positive or negative.

Amount_Owed_to_Organization__c (custom field on Contact object);

The updated function:

CEILING(Amount_Owed_to_Organization__c)

Note   Here, CEILING will ensure that any positive non-integer amount will be rounded *up* to the nearest integer and any negative non-integer amount will be rounded *away from zero* to the nearest integer. $100.01 would become $101.00 AND −$100.99 would become −$101.00.

Scenario 2: A field captures how much an individual owes the organization. The actual amount invoiced, however, needs to be an integer. The amount owed could be positive or negative.

Amount_Owed_to_Organization__c (custom field on Contact object);

The updated function:

MFLOOR(Amount_Owed_to_Organization__c)

Note   Here, MFLOOR will ensure that any positive non-integer amount will be rounded *down* to the nearest integer and any negative non-integer amount will be rounded *away from zero* to the nearest integer. $100.99 would become $100.00 AND −$100.01 would become −$101.00.

Usability

Table 2-8 shows the areas in which the CEILING, MCEILING, FLOOR, and MFLOOR functions can be utilized.

Table 2-8. *Allowed* CEILING, MCEILING, FLOOR, *and* MFLOOR *Function Usage*

CEILING, MCEILING, FLOOR, and MFLOOR			
Validation Rules	✓	Escalation Rules	✓
Workflow Rules	✓	Approval Rules	✓
Formula Fields	✓	Assignment Rules	✓
Auto-Response Rules	✓	Approval Step Rules	✓
Field Updates	✓	Custom Buttons & Links	✓
Process Builder	✓	Flow (Visual Workflow)	✓

Other Considerations

Other Considerations. For example:

Formula (number): ABS (Currency_1 - Currency_2) – Difference between Currency_1 and Currency_2 in number format

CONTAINS

The CONTAINS function checks if identified text contains specified characters, and returns TRUE if it does. Otherwise, it returns FALSE.

Format

CONTAINS(text, compare_text)

Application Scenarios

Scenario 1: You want to capture Leads via Web-to-Lead and you want to identify particular text within the Lead Description field; specifically, if you want to highlight the Lead if the word *compliant* is present. You will use the following field:

      Description (standard field on Lead object)

The updated function:

CONTAINS(Description, "compliant")

Scenario 1: You have Email-to-Case configured and want to flag any Cases that have the word "Cancel" in the subject line so that they can be handled with special attention. You would use the following field:

      Subject (standard field on Case object)

The updated function:

CONTAINS(Subject, "Cancel")

Note   Functions are case sensitive. We will look at how to efficiently handle both cases in some formula field examples in Chapter 3.

Usability

Table 2-9 shows the areas in which the CONTAINS function can be utilized.

Table 2-9. *Allowed CONTAINS Function Usage*

CONTAINS			
Validation Rules	✓	Escalation Rules	✓
Workflow Rules	✓	Approval Rules	✓
Formula Fields	✓	Assignment Rules	✓
Auto-Response Rules	✓	Approval Step Rules	✓
Field Updates	✓	Custom Buttons & Links	✓
Process Builder	✓	Flow (Visual Workflow)	✓

DATE

The DATE function takes the input of day, month, and year separately and returns a Salesforce.com-formatted date value.

Format

```
DATE(Year, Month, Day)
```

Application Scenarios

Scenario 1: The year, month, and day captured from a related record are coming over from a legacy system as separate fields and you want to convert these to a Salesforce-formatted date field. You would use the following fields, all of which are custom number fields on a generic custom object:

>   Year_Captured__c (custom field on generic custom object)

>   Month_Captured__c (custom field on generic custom object)

>   Day_Captured__c (custom field on generic custom object)

The updated function:

```
DATE(Year_Captured__c,Month_Captured__c,Day_Captured__c)
```

Usability

Table 2-10 shows the areas in which the DATE function can be utilized.

Table 2-10. *Allowed DATE Function Usage*

DATE			
Validation Rules	✓	Escalation Rules	✓
Workflow Rules	✓	Approval Rules	✓
Formula Fields	✓	Assignment Rules	✓
Auto-Response Rules	✓	Approval Step Rules	✓
Field Updates	✓	Custom Buttons & Links	✓
Process Builder	✓	Flow (Visual Workflow)	✓

DATETIMEVALUE, DATEVALUE, AND TIMEVALUE

These three related functions return date/time, date, and time values, respectively, from a date/time field or its text representation.

Format

```
DATETIMEVALUE(expression)
DATEVALUE(expression)
TIMEVALUE(expression)
```

Application Scenarios

Scenario 1: You want to programmatically determine whether a Case was closed on the same date as it was opened. You would use the following fields:

> CreatedDate (standard field on Case object)

> ClosedDate (standard field on Case object)

The updated function:

```
DATEVALUE( CreatedDate ) = DATEVALUE( ClosedDate )
```

Scenario 2: You want to display the time that a Case record was created, but you do not care about the date itself.

CreatedDate (standard field on Case object)

The updated function:

TIMEVALUE(CreatedDate)

Usability

Table 2-11 shows the areas in which the DATETIMEVALUE, DATEVALUE, and TIMEVALUE functions can be utilized.

Table 2-11. *Allowed* DATETIMEVALUE, DATEVALUE, *and* TIMEVALUE *Function Usage*

DATETIMEVALUE, DATEVALUE, and TIMEVALUE			
Validation Rules	✓	Escalation Rules	✓
Workflow Rules	✓	Approval Rules	✓
Formula Fields	✓	Assignment Rules	✓
Auto-Response Rules	✓	Approval Step Rules	✓
Field Updates	✓	Custom Buttons & Links	✓
Process Builder	✓	Flow (Visual Workflow)	✓

Note   As of Summer '18, the TIMEVALUE function is not yet available in Process Builder.

DAY, MONTH, YEAR, and WEEKDAY

The DAY function returns the day of the month, a number between 1 and 31. MONTH returns the month, in number format. The values will be between 1 (January) and 12 (December). YEAR returns the year of a date, a number between 1900 and 9999. WEEKDAY returns the day of the week (e.g., "1" for Monday) for a specified date.

Format

```
DAY(Date)
MONTH(Date)
YEAR(Date)
WEEKDAY(Date)
```

Note   The DAY, MONTH, YEAR, and WEEKDAY functions do not accept Date/Time fields; only Date fields can be used.

Application Scenarios

Scenario 1: You have Date Opened on the Case object and you also want to know the month, day, and year in separate fields. You would use the following fields:

> CreatedDate (standard field on Case object)

The updated functions:

```
MONTH(CreatedDate)
DAY(CreatedDate)
YEAR(CreatedDate)
```

Scenario 1: You want to group Opportunities by the weekday of the Close Date. You would use the following fields:

> CloseDate (standard field on Opportunity object)

The updated functions:

```
WEEKDAY(CloseDate)
```

Usability

Table 2-12 shows the areas in which the DAY, MONTH, YEAR, and WEEKDAY functions can be utilized.

Table 2-12. *Allowed* DAY, MONTH, YEAR, *and* WEEKDAY *Function Usage*

DAY, MONTH, YEAR, and WEEKDAY			
Validation Rules	✓	Escalation Rules	✓
Workflow Rules	✓	Approval Rules	✓
Formula Fields	✓	Assignment Rules	✓
Auto-Response Rules	✓	Approval Step Rules	✓
Field Updates	✓	Custom Buttons & Links	✓
Process Builder	✓	Flow (Visual Workflow)	✓

FIND

The FIND function returns the position of the search_text string in text.

Format

FIND(search_text, text [, start_num])

Application Scenarios

Scenario 1: You are using Email-to-Case (or Web-to-Lead) to capture incoming information and you want to glean a phone number, if present, in the description field coming over. You would use the following fields:

Description (standard field on Case or Lead object)

The updated function:

FIND("Phone: ", Description)

Once you have the starting position, you may be able to extract the phone number using a different function.

Usability

Table 2-13 shows the areas in which the FIND function can be utilized.

Table 2-13. *Allowed FIND Function Usage*

FIND			
Validation Rules	✓	Escalation Rules	✓
Workflow Rules	✓	Approval Rules	✓
Formula Fields	✓	Assignment Rules	✓
Auto-Response Rules	✓	Approval Step Rules	✓
Field Updates	✓	Custom Buttons & Links	✓
Process Builder	✓	Flow (Visual Workflow)	✓

HOUR, MINUTE, SECOND, MILLISECOND

The HOUR, MINUTE, SECOND, and MILLISECOND functions return the respective element of a time value. If TIMENOW() returns 12:01:12.471, then the following would be returned for each of these functions:

> HOUR = 12
>
> MINUTE = 1
>
> SECOND = 12
>
> MILLISECOND = 471

Format

```
HOUR(time)
MINUTE(time)
SECOND(time)
MILLISECOND(time)
```

Application Scenarios

Scenario 1: Identifying the hour at which a Case was opened.

      CreatedDate (standard field on Case object);

   The updated function:

HOUR(TIMEVALUE(CreatedDate))

Usability

Table 2-14 shows the areas in which the HOUR, MINUTE, SECOND, and MILLISECOND functions can be utilized.

Table 2-14. *Allowed* HOUR, MINUTE, SECOND, *and* MILLISECOND *Function Usage*

HOUR, MINUTE, SECOND, and MILLISECOND			
Validation Rules	✓	Escalation Rules	✓
Workflow Rules	✓	Approval Rules	✓
Formula Fields	✓	Assignment Rules	✓
Auto-Response Rules	✓	Approval Step Rules	✓
Field Updates	✓	Custom Buttons & Links	✓
Process Builder		Flow (Visual Workflow)	✓

HYPERLINK

The HYPERLINK function produces a hyperlink for the user to use to navigate to a desired page, either within the Salesforce org or outside of it.

Format

HYPERLINK(url, friendly_name [, target])

   Here, url is the URL of the page to which the user will be redirected/linked, friendly_name is the display name of the link, and target specifies where to open the hyperlinked URL.

Application Scenarios

Scenario 1: You want to provide a quick and easy way to access a key Leads report directly from a Lead record. Instead of requiring that users navigate to the Reports tabs and then find the desired report, the hyperlink function can be used to link directly to the report. You would not use any derived fields here but instead add your own values manually.

The updated function:

```
HYPERLINK("/000x0000000hrah", "Today's New Leads", "_self")
```

Scenario 2: You want to provide a hyperlink to a specific reference document to your whole org, but you do not want to replace the "Help with this page" content itself. You can link to a specific page or document with the following function. You would not use any derived fields here; again, you would add your own text.

The updated function:

```
HYPERLINK("https://org62.my.Salesforce/help/doc/en/sf.pdf", "How to be
Successful with Salesforce: PDF from Salesforce")
```

Usability

Table 2-15 shows the areas in which the HYPERLINK function can be utilized.

Table 2-15. *Allowed HYPERLINK Function Usage*

HYPERLINK		
Validation Rules		Escalation Rules
Workflow Rules		Approval Rules
Formula Fields	✓	Assignment Rules
Auto-Response Rules		Approval Step Rules
Field Updates		Custom Buttons & Links
Process Builder	✓	Flow (Visual Workflow)

Other Considerations

The following values can be used in the [, target] attribute:

> _blank: Opens page in new window or tab

> _self: Opens page in same frame in which the link was clicked

> _parent: Opens page in parent frame

> _top: Opens page in full body of same window

> <framename>: Opens page in custom, named frame

If you are referencing a page outside Salesforce, you will need to include http:// or https:// in your URL.

Note   The HYPERLINK function is covered in more detail in Chapter 12 within the topic of user interface development.

IF

IF is a function that will return one of two values conditionally, based on whether the provided logical test is true or false.

Format

IF(logical_test, value_if_true, value_if_false)

Application Scenarios

Scenario 1: You want to provide a simple message to customers regarding the current status and expected next steps of a Case and, based on customer feedback, the Status field itself will not suffice. You would use the following field:

> IsClosed (standard field on Case object)

The updated function:

```
IF(
IsClosed,
"This Case has been closed; please call Support or open a new Case for
further assistance.", "This Case is currently being worked. Please click on
"Add Comment" to post updates."
)
```

Since IsClosed is a Boolean field, you are representing it with its name only in order to derive its stored value; you could also use IsClosed = true.

Scenario 2: You have a custom object capturing student course performance (grade). The field is numeric, containing the raw percentage score and is populated via integration from another system. You want to display the overall pass/fail result, instead of the raw score, on the record detail page. You would use the following field:

Grade__c (custom number field on custom object)

The updated function:

```
IF(Grade__c >= 60, "Pass", "Fail") OR
IF(Grade__c >= 60, true, false)
```

You'll notice the two different approaches just looked at. The appropriate approach depends on the formula field return type you want to use. I will cover return types in depth in Chapter 3, "Formula Fields."

Usability

Table 2-16 shows the areas in which the IF function can be utilized.

Table 2-16. *Allowed IF Function Usage*

IF

Validation Rules	✓	Escalation Rules	✓
Workflow Rules	✓	Approval Rules	✓
Formula Fields	✓	Assignment Rules	✓
Auto-Response Rules	✓	Approval Step Rules	✓
Field Updates	✓	Custom Buttons & Links	✓
Process Builder	✓	Flow (Visual Workflow)	✓

IMAGE

The IMAGE function will result in a specific image being returned/displayed, with the ability to specify alternate text and the height and width of the image.

Format

```
IMAGE(image_url, alternate_text [, height, width])
```

Application Scenarios

Scenario 1: You want to display the logo of each of your accounts. You can assume that you are able to capture a web URL of the image showing the corresponding Account's logo and you store it in a custom field Account_Image_URL__c. Additionally, you want the alternate text to contain the Account's name (e.g., "EDL Consulting, LLC Logo"). You can simply reference the Account Name and display the image at the top of your Account detail page using the following:

```
IMAGE(Account_Image_URL__c, Name & " Logo", 125, 250)
```

   Scenario 2: You want to display an image of your Product on each Product detail page. You can assume that the product images are stored in the same web directory with file names matching the Product SKU. Additionally, you want the alternate text to contain the product name (e.g., "EZ-Twist Wrench"). You would use the following field:

   Product_SKU__c (custom field on Product object)

The updated function:

```
IMAGE("http://www.company.com/images/products/ & Product_SKU__c", Name,
125, 250)
```

Scenario 3: You want to display a banner image at the top of all Opportunity pages that shows a flow of the Opportunity creation and management process. You have uploaded this image as a Document into Salesforce. You will not use any input fields here; all text will be entered manually.

The updated function:

```
IMAGE("/servlet/servlet.FileDownload?file=<DocumentRecordId>", "Opportunity
Banner")
```

Note   The IMAGE function is covered in more detail in Chapter 12 within the topic of user interface development.

Usability

Table 2-17 shows the areas in which the IMAGE function can be utilized.

Table 2-17. *Allowed IMAGE Function Usage*

IMAGE		
Validation Rules		Escalation Rules
Workflow Rules		Approval Rules
Formula Fields	✓	Assignment Rules
Auto-Response Rules		Approval Step Rules
Field Updates		Custom Buttons & Links
Process Builder		Flow (Visual Workflow)

INCLUDES

The INCLUDES function checks a provided text string to see if it is included in the list of selected values within a multiselect picklist. INCLUDES can be seen as the equivalent of ISPICKVAL, but it is used for Multi-Picklists instead of Picklists.

Format

INCLUDES(multiselect_picklist_field, text_literal)

Application Scenarios

Scenario 1: You have an Account field called Present_in_States__c to convey the states in which the organization operates and you want to verify if the account is in Arizona.

INCLUDES(Account.Present_in_States__c, "Arizona")

Usability

Table 2-18 shows the areas in which the INCLUDES function can be utilized.

Table 2-18. *Allowed INCLUDES Function Usage*

INCLUDES			
Validation Rules	✓	Escalation Rules	✓
Workflow Rules	✓	Approval Rules	✓
Formula Fields	✓	Assignment Rules	✓
Auto-Response Rules	✓	Approval Step Rules	✓
Field Updates	✓	Custom Buttons & Links	✓
Process Builder	✓	Flow (Visual Workflow)	

ISBLANK

ISBLANK is a Boolean function that identifies whether a provided expression is blank or not. Although you can use hard-coded text as part of the expression argument, this function is really only useful when using other fields in the expression. In other words,

ISBLANK("String") is a valid use of the function, but it is not valuable. Typically, you would want to use ISBLANK with other functions to return values conditionally (e.g., IF(ISBLANK("Field"), "value_if_true", "value_if_false").

Format

ISBLANK(expression)

Application Scenarios

Scenario 1: A sensitive field containing personal information is hidden from most users via Field-Level Security, but that information is needed at some point during the sales process. It is important for users to identify whether that information has been gathered. You could use ISBLANK to convey this state to users without providing Read access to the sensitive field. You would use the following field:

Personal_Information__c (custom field on Opportunity object)

The updated function:

ISBLANK(Personal_Information__c)

Usability

Table 2-19 shows the areas in which the ISBLANK function can be utilized.

Table 2-19. *Allowed ISBLANK Function Usage*

ISBLANK			
Validation Rules	✓	Escalation Rules	✓
Workflow Rules	✓	Approval Rules	✓
Formula Fields	✓	Assignment Rules	✓
Auto-Response Rules	✓	Approval Step Rules	✓
Field Updates	✓	Custom Buttons & Links	✓
Process Builder	✓	Flow (Visual Workflow)	✓

Other Considerations

You should use ISBLANK() instead of ISNULL() where possible. ISNULL is still supported, but it is considered a legacy function that is less useful than ISBLANK. Avoid using ISNULL if possible.

ISCHANGED

The ISCHANGED function is extremely useful, as it will help you systematically identify whether a field has been modified. It will return TRUE if the field has changed in the current operation; otherwise it returns FALSE.

Format

ISCHANGED(field)

Application Scenarios

Scenario 1: You need to identify when the Amount of an Opportunity has changed programmatically (tracking via field history is not sufficient for you, in this scenario). The values of fields do not matter. You would use the following field:

      Amount (standard field on Opportunity object)

The updated function:

ISCHANGED(Amount)

A second scenario for using this function could be when you want to know if anything on a record has changed. To do this, you can use the Last Modified Date field as the field argument:

      LastModifiedDate (standard field on various objects)

The updated function:

ISCHANGED(LastModifiedDate)

Usability

Table 2-20 shows the areas in which the ISCHANGED function can be utilized.

Table 2-20. *Allowed ISCHANGED Function Usage*

ISCHANGED			
Validation Rules	✓	Escalation Rules	✓
Workflow Rules	✓	Approval Rules	✓
Formula Fields	✓	Assignment Rules	✓
Auto-Response Rules	✓	Approval Step Rules	✓
Field Updates	✓	Custom Buttons & Links	✓
Process Builder	✓	Flow (Visual Workflow)	

> **Note**   ISCHANGED must be manually typed into a formula for a custom button or link.

ISNEW

The ISNEW function checks a record to see if it is new or existing; it will return TRUE if the record is new or FALSE if the record was previously created. No argument is provided.

Format

ISNEW()

Application Scenarios

This function is most effectively used in conditional statements with other functions (e.g., IF) to apply behavior based on whether the record is new or existing. This function will always be formatted as "ISNEW()."

Other Considerations

Some uses of this function will always return FALSE, including

- A workflow rule with a time-based trigger
- A field update for an approval action

Usability

Table 2-21 shows the areas in which the ISNEW function can be utilized.

Table 2-21. *Allowed ISNEW Function Usage*

ISNEW			
Validation Rules	✓	Escalation Rules	✓
Workflow Rules	✓	Approval Rules	✓
Formula Fields	✓	Assignment Rules	✓
Auto-Response Rules	✓	Approval Step Rules	✓
Field Updates	✓	Custom Buttons & Links	✓
Process Builder	✓	Flow (Visual Workflow)	

Note   ISNEW must be manually typed into a formula for a custom button or link.

ISNULL

Refer to the ISBLANK function section.

ISPICKVAL

Many Salesforce functions have known equivalents in other popular applications (e.g., Microsoft Excel). ISPICKVAL is one function that is specific to Salesforce. ISPICKVAL() is a Boolean function that identifies whether a specified field (of type Picklist) on the corresponding record has a certain value. ISPICKVAL can be seen as the equivalent of INCLUDES but for Picklists instead of multi-Picklists.

Format

```
ISPICKVAL(picklist_field, text_literal)
```

Application Scenarios

Scenario 1: You need to identify whether a particular Lead record has a status of "Working - Contacted." You would use the following field:

> Status (standard field on Lead object)

The updated function:

```
ISPICKVAL(Status, "Working - Contacted")
```

Scenario 1: You need to identify whether a particular Opportunity record has a Stage of Qualification. You would use the following field:

> StageName (standard field on Lead object)

The updated function:

```
ISPICKVAL(StageName, "Qualification")
```

Usability

Table 2-22 shows the areas in which the ISPICKVAL function can be utilized.

Table 2-22. *Allowed ISPICKVAL Function Usage*

ISPICKVAL			
Validation Rules	✓	Escalation Rules	✓
Workflow Rules	✓	Approval Rules	✓
Formula Fields	✓	Assignment Rules	✓
Auto-Response Rules	✓	Approval Step Rules	✓
Field Updates	✓	Custom Buttons & Links	✓
Process Builder	✓	Flow (Visual Workflow)	

LEFT, MID, RIGHT

The LEFT, MID, and RIGHT functions return a string of a specified length from identified text. These functions are useful when you a need a subset of the text from a field that has clearly formatted, organized content. For example, you may feel that the "superset" text has unnecessary or redundant text that you'd like to hide, but not delete.

Format

```
LEFT(text, num_chars)
MID(text, start_num, num_chars)
RIGHT(text, num_chars)
```

LEFT returns X characters from the beginning, or left side, of the text. For example, assuming X = 4, LEFT("ExampleText", 4) would return "Exam." MID adds an element of a starting position to allow for the capture of a string that is neither at the beginning nor the end of a larger string of characters. MID("ExampleText", 2, 5), for example, would return "ample." RIGHT returns X characters from the end, or right, of the text. For example, RIGHT("ExampleText", 4) would return "Text."

Application Scenarios

Scenario 1: You have captured a phone number but all you need is the area code for another use in your org. You would use the following field:

Phone (standard field on Lead object)

The updated function:

```
LEFT(Phone,3)
```

Scenario 2: You need to perform some analysis on your zip code data. You have captured Zip Code + 4 for all addresses. Addresses with an unknown "+4" are assigned 0000 for the value (e.g., 12345-0000). You need to split the first five and second five digits for reporting and analysis purposes. You would use the following field:

```
PostalCode (standard field on Contact object)
```

The updated function:

```
LEFT(PostalCode,5)
```

Scenario 3: You have captured a phone number but you need just the middle three digits out of a full ten-digit number for another use in your org. You would use the following field:

Phone (standard field on Lead object)

The updated function:

MID(Phone,3,3)

Other Considerations

The initial start_num is 0. For example, MID("ExampleText", 0, 2) would return "Ex."

Usability

Table 2-23 shows the areas in which the LEFT, MID, and RIGHT functions can be utilized.

Table 2-23. *Allowed* LEFT, MID, and RIGHT *Function Usage*

LEFT, MID, and RIGHT			
Validation Rules	✓	Escalation Rules	✓
Workflow Rules	✓	Approval Rules	✓
Formula Fields	✓	Assignment Rules	✓
Auto-Response Rules	✓	Approval Step Rules	✓
Field Updates	✓	Custom Buttons & Links	✓
Process Builder	✓	Flow (Visual Workflow)	✓

LEN

LEN returns the length, in characters, of a provided text string.

Format

LEN(text)

Application Scenarios

Scenario 1: You require a mailing address for all Contacts that are entered into your system; however, you notice that bogus addresses are being entered with a single character to circumvent the requirement. LEN can identify the length of the field to validate that the entered value is of a reasonable length to be a legitimate address. You would use the following field:

> MailingAddress (standard field on Contact object)

The updated function:

LEN(MailingAddress)

Scenario 1: You ask all users to include an error code for all Cases of Type *Application Error* in the Case Description field, with the code being at least eight characters in length. You can use length to determine whether the Description field could possibly contain an error code (if the length is less than eight characters, you know that no error code is present). You would use the following field:

> Description (standard field on Case object)

The updated function:

LEN(Description)

Usability

Table 2-24 shows the areas in which the LEN function can be utilized.

Table 2-24. *Allowed LEN Function Usage*

LEN			
Validation Rules	✓	Escalation Rules	✓
Workflow Rules	✓	Approval Rules	✓
Formula Fields	✓	Assignment Rules	✓
Auto-Response Rules	✓	Approval Step Rules	✓
Field Updates	✓	Custom Buttons & Links	✓
Process Builder	✓	Flow (Visual Workflow)	✓

MOD

MOD returns the remainder after the number is divided by the specified divisor. Here are examples of values that would be returned by this function:

MOD(3,2) >> 3 can be divided by 2 once, with 1 left as the remainder >> returns 1.

MOD(5,3) >> 5 can be divided by 3 once, with 2 left as the remainder >> returns 2.

MOD(6,3) >> 6 can be divided by 3 twice, with 0 left as the remainder >> returns 0.

MOD(2,2) >> 2 can be divided by 2 once, with 0 left as the remainder >> returns 0.

MOD(1,2) >> 1 can be divided by 2 zero times, with 1 left as the remainder >> returns 1.

This function can be extremely useful when combined with other functions to determine date-related items like the day of the week. I will cover those in more detail in Chapter 3, "Formula Fields."

Format

MOD(number,divisor)

Usability

Table 2-25 shows the areas in which the MOD function can be utilized.

Table 2-25. *Allowed MOD Function Usage*

MOD			
Validation Rules	✓	Escalation Rules	✓
Workflow Rules	✓	Approval Rules	✓
Formula Fields	✓	Assignment Rules	✓
Auto-Response Rules	✓	Approval Step Rules	✓
Field Updates	✓	Custom Buttons & Links	✓
Process Builder	✓	Flow (Visual Workflow)	✓

NOW, TODAY, TIMENOW

NOW, TODAY, and TIMENOW are very simple functions that return the current date (TODAY), the current date/time (NOW), or the current time (TIMENOW). For example, on December 25, 2014, at 8:00 p.m., the following would be returned:

TODAY() >> December 25, 2014

NOW() >> December 25, 2014 8:00 p.m.

TIMENOW() >> 8:00 p.m.

Format

NOW: NOW()

TODAY: TODAY()

TIMENOW: TIMENOW()

Application Scenarios

These functions will be covered further in the chapter on formula fields; they are very useful in time-based calculations that drive business rules and/or automated behavior.

Usability

Table 2-26 shows the areas in which the NOW, TODAY, and TIMENOW functions can be utilized.

Table 2-26. *Allowed NOW, TODAY, and TIMENOW Function Usage*

NOW, TODAY, TIMENOW			
Validation Rules	✓	Escalation Rules	✓
Workflow Rules	✓	Approval Rules	✓
Formula Fields	✓	Assignment Rules	✓
Auto-Response Rules	✓	Approval Step Rules	✓
Field Updates	✓	Custom Buttons & Links	✓
Process Builder	✓	Flow (Visual Workflow)	✓

Note As of Summer '18, the TIMENOW function is not available in Process Builder.

OR

The OR function checks whether at least one of the arguments is true and returns TRUE if at least one argument is true and FALSE if all are false.

Format

OR(logical1,logical2,...)

Application Scenarios

Scenario 1: You want to flag all Opportunities that have an Expected Revenue greater than $100,000 or have a Probability greater than 90 percent. You would use the following fields:

Amount (standard field on Opportunity object)

Probability (standard field on Opportunity object)

93

The updated function:

```
OR(
Amount > 100000,
Probability > 0.9
)
```

Scenario 1: You want to identify all Cases that are Escalated or have an Account Name of ImportantCo. You would use the following fields:

Escalated (standard field on Case object)

AccountName (standard field on Case object)

The updated function:

```
OR(
Escalated,
AccountName = "CloudCraze"
)
```

Usability

Table 2-27 shows the areas in which the OR function can be utilized.

Table 2-27. *Allowed OR Function Usage*

OR			
Validation Rules	✓	Escalation Rules	✓
Workflow Rules	✓	Approval Rules	✓
Formula Fields	✓	Assignment Rules	✓
Auto-Response Rules	✓	Approval Step Rules	✓
Field Updates	✓	Custom Buttons & Links	✓
Process Builder	✓	Flow (Visual Workflow)	✓

Other Considerations

You will notice Escalated in the previous scenario. Since we're dealing with a Boolean field (Checkbox), the value returned is True or False; we can notate it as "Escalated," as opposed to "Escalated = true." So, if you want to evaluate whether a Boolean is true, the field name itself is sufficient. Another approach to evaluate whether one or more arguments are true is by using the || operator. For example:

```
Amount > 100000 || Probability > 0.9
```

The decision to use the function OR or the operator || is purely personal preference. Both can be applied using clicks and there is no advantage to using one vs. the other in terms of how the formula is compiled.

PRIORVALUE

The PRIORVALUE function returns the previous value for the field. For example, if you are changing the Amount from 5000 to 10,000, PRIORVALUE would return 5000.

Format

```
PRIORVALUE(field)
```

Application Scenarios

Scenario 1: You want to validate the previous value of Case Status in your calculation to ensure that users cannot skip certain statuses in the Support process. You would use the following field:

Status (standard field on Case object)

The updated function:

```
PRIORVALUE(Status)
```

Usability

Table 2-28 shows the areas in which the PRIORVALUE function can be utilized.

Table 2-28. *Allowed* PRIORVALUE *Function Usage*

PRIORVALUE			
Validation Rules	✓	Escalation Rules	
Workflow Rules	✓	Approval Rules	
Formula Fields		Assignment Rules	✓
Auto-Response Rules		Approval Step Rules	
Field Updates	✓	Custom Buttons & Links	
Process Builder	x	Flow (Visual Workflow)	

REGEX

The REGEX function checks a provided text string against a regular expression and returns TRUE if a match is found or FALSE if a match is not found.

Format

REGEX(Text, RegEx_Text)

Application Scenarios

Scenario 1: You want to identify if a value in the Social Security field on a custom object is formatted as expected. You would use the following field:

Social_Security_Number__c (custom field on custom object)

The updated function:

REGEX(Social_Security_Number__c, "[0-9]{3}-[0-9]{2}-[0-9]{4}")

Usability

Table 2-29 shows the areas in which the REGEX function can be utilized.

Table 2-29. *Allowed REGEX Function Usage*

REGEX	
Validation Rules	Escalation Rules
Workflow Rules	Approval Rules
Formula Fields ✓	Assignment Rules
Auto-Response Rules	Approval Step Rules
Field Updates	Custom Buttons & Links
Process Builder	Flow (Visual Workflow)

ROUND

The ROUND function performs a rounding to the nearest number away with a specified number of digits.

Format

ROUND(number, num_digits)

Application Scenarios

Scenario 1: An organization allows a cash balance to be converted to points based on a multiplier. A points balance must be an integer.

Balance__c (custom field on User object);

Conversion_Multiplier__c (custom field on User object);

The updated function:

ROUND(Balance__c * Conversion_Multiplier__c,0)

> **Note**   You can provide a number of digits that is greater than the number of digits in the number parameter in the ROUND function. For example, ROUND(12.9,2) would return 12.90.

SUBSTITUTE

The SUBSTITUTE function will replace identified text within a string with alternate text. For example, SUBSTITUTE ("Please contact Tariku about the contract," "Tariku," "Max") would return "Please contact Max about the contract."

Format

SUBSTITUTE(text, old_text, new_text)

Application Scenarios

Scenario 1: You want to share Cases but hide any references to the Account Name field in the Case Subject. You would use the following fields:

> Subject (standard field on Case object)

> AccountName (standard field on Case object)

The updated function:

SUBSTITUTE(Subject, AccountName, "<Account>")

Assuming "<Account>" equal to "Client," "PayCo having issues with TechE application" would become "Client having issues with TechE application."

Scenario 2: Some of your customers have been entering their last name in the Case Description field, but you do not want the last name to be displayed on the Case detail page. You would use the following fields:

> Description (standard field on Case object)

> Contact.LastName (standard field on Case object; looks up to
> Contact object)

The updated function:

```
SUBSTITUTE(Description, Contact.LastName, "<Last Name Removed>")
```

"The XY50 is not operating as expected. Our manager, John Smith, has called Support without success" would become "The XY50 is not operating as expected. Our manager, John <Last Name Removed>, has called Support, without success."

Usability

Table 2-30 shows the areas in which the SUBSTITUTE function can be utilized.

Table 2-30. *Allowed SUBSTITUTE Function Usage*

SUBSTITUTE			
Validation Rules	✓	Escalation Rules	✓
Workflow Rules	✓	Approval Rules	✓
Formula Fields	✓	Assignment Rules	✓
Auto-Response Rules	✓	Approval Step Rules	✓
Field Updates	✓	Custom Buttons & Links	✓
Process Builder	✓	Flow (Visual Workflow)	✓

TEXT

Although simple, TEXT is a very frequently used function within Salesforce. One of the most common uses of this function is to extract the text value from a picklist field.

Format

```
TEXT(value)
```

Application Scenarios

Scenario 1: You want to return the actual value of a Picklist field without using the ISPICKVAL function. You would use the following field:

StageName (Standard field on Opportunity object)

The updated function:

TEXT(StageName)

Scenario 2: You want to return Opportunity Amount (a numeric value) as text. You would use the following field:

Amount (standard field on Opportunity object)

The updated function:

TEXT(Amount)

Usability

Table 2-31 shows the areas in which the TEXT function can be utilized.

Table 2-31. *Allowed TEXT Function Usage*

TEXT			
Validation Rules	✓	Escalation Rules	✓
Workflow Rules	✓	Approval Rules	✓
Formula Fields	✓	Assignment Rules	✓
Auto-Response Rules	✓	Approval Step Rules	✓
Field Updates	✓	Custom Buttons & Links	✓
Process Builder	✓	Flow (Visual Workflow)	✓

TRIM

TRIM is used to remove all spaces from a string except for single spaces in between words.

Format

TRIM (text)

Application Scenarios

Scenario 1: Your customers include extra spaces when submitting Cases via email. You want to strip out extraneous spaces. You would use the following field:

> Subject (standard field on Case object)

The updated function:

TRIM(Subject)

Usability

Table 2-32 shows the areas in which the TRIM function can be utilized.

Table 2-32. *Allowed TRIM Function Usage*

TRIM			
Validation Rules	✓	Escalation Rules	✓
Workflow Rules	✓	Approval Rules	✓
Formula Fields	✓	Assignment Rules	✓
Auto-Response Rules	✓	Approval Step Rules	✓
Field Updates	✓	Custom Buttons & Links	✓
Process Builder	✓	Flow (Visual Workflow)	✓

VALUE

VALUE converts numeric values that are stored as text into a number.

Format

VALUE(text)

Application Scenarios

Scenario 1: You have a legacy field of field-type text in which sales people enter Projected Amount. Additionally, you have cleaned up the records and want to run numeric calculations on the field value. You would use the following field:

Projected_Amount__c (custom field on Opportunity object)

The updated function:

VALUE(Projected_Amount__c)

Usability

Table 2-33 shows the areas in which the VALUE function can be utilized.

Table 2-33. *Allowed VALUE Function Usage*

VALUE			
Validation Rules	✓	Escalation Rules	✓
Workflow Rules	✓	Approval Rules	✓
Formula Fields	✓	Assignment Rules	✓
Auto-Response Rules	✓	Approval Step Rules	✓
Field Updates	✓	Custom Buttons & Links	✓
Process Builder	✓	Flow (Visual Workflow)	✓

Recap

In this chapter, you dove into the world of functions and familiarized yourself with some of the most important functions to be considered when developing within Salesforce. At this point, you should have a fairly solid understanding of function syntax, how to use common functions, and how to properly apply functions to address a specific need within the system. In the next chapter, you will learn more about the application of these functions, specifically within Salesforce formula fields.

CHAPTER 3

All About Formula Fields

The last chapter examined Salesforce formula functions in detail. You familiarized yourself with the anatomy of a function, an approach to declaratively create a function, and the application of simple functions to useful business scenarios. Think of that chapter as *Salesforce Formulas 101: Functions*. Congratulations! Now that you've passed your intro course, you're moving on to *Salesforce Formulas 201: Fields*.

In most, if not all, Salesforce orgs, the majority of fields in a Salesforce org are static. This means that the values present within those fields do not change unless there is a specific update by a user (manually) or the system (via automation and/or code). With formula fields, it's a different ballgame altogether. With some critical thought and the development of the right formula fields in Salesforce, you can add a stroke of intelligence to your records and shift from a list of data points to a rich set of valuable, informational fields.

Note Salesforce defines a *formula field* as a "read-only field that derives its value from a formula expression you define. The formula field is updated when any of the source fields change."

Would purposeful formula fields be valuable to you or your users? Consider a few situations that may guide you to an answer.

- Users review multiple fields to ascertain a record's "true" state.

- Data is not in a desired or ideal format.

- You want to mask, emphasize, or transform certain data points.

- You rely on users to perform calculations to come up with desired metrics (i.e., to export to Excel).

- Users need to be directed or instructed to understand how they should interact with records.

© Philip Weinmeister 2019
P. Weinmeister, *Practical Salesforce Development Without Code*,
https://doi.org/10.1007/978-1-4842-4871-3_3

Formulas themselves are present in many areas of Salesforce (such as validation rules, assignment rules, and workflow rules), but it's safe to say that formula fields come to mind first when thinking of formulas. They are a relatively quick way to get the right data in the right format to the right audience. Don't get me wrong: Formula fields can get extremely complex. However, if you understand how their functions work in conjunction with one another and know how to use them to solve your business problems, you can surprise and delight user within your existing org without writing code.

By the end of this chapter, you will

- Be aware of the preparation needed to make effective, useful formula fields

- Know the different return types of formula fields and when to select each type

- Understand how to combine multiple functions within one formula

- Be able to apply conditional logic to formulas

- Be able to create a formula field from scratch declaratively (using "clicks, not code")

- Solve basic business needs with formula fields

Preparing to Build Your Formula Fields

Before you start to construct a formula field, you should scrutinize your organization's existing data model. Why? Because the source of what you want to convey, calculate, or communicate has to be *somewhere* in the system (even as an external object) before you ever touch a formula. Without relevant source fields, Salesforce formula fields have little or no value.

You might ask yourself: Does the current data model account for all of the necessary data sources? If not, you'll need to make sure to create custom fields for any sources that you might use in your formulas. Remember, the eventual output will be derived from these fields, so don't be too concerned if your data sources aren't in a desired format; we're talking about raw data here. For example, let's say that you need a Contact's emergency phone number for use in a formula field. If you're currently capturing the emergency number as a text field instead of a phone field, that's okay. You can use the formula itself to manipulate and reformat the derived value. The key is that the data is accessible somehow, somewhere within your org.

You should build out the nonformula fields in your data model first; this includes both the fields on the object you will be working with and the fields on any related objects. Any fields that your formulas will reference must be in place up front. With proper planning, you can avoid the frustration that emerges when you realize the need for a nonformula custom field only after you've started building out a formula that depends on that field.

The Structure of Formula Fields

Formula fields have a few key components: values (static and derived), functions, statements, and operators. To ensure that you fully grasp formula fields and how to properly build them, I will walk you through each of these underlying elements.

Static Values

One of the simplest elements that can be inserted within a formula field is a static value. A *static value* could be defined as an unchanging value established by the formula developer. Let's take a look at a few examples.

Any calculation that contains values that are not based on fields would reveal a user-provided static value. For example, assume you want to create a formula that adds 10 days to the date on which a Lead was created. You could represent that calculation like this:

```
CreatedDate + 10
```

In this instance, "10" is our static value. It is provided by the developer and will not change within calculation unless it is edited or removed within the formula itself.

A formula that looks for a specific string would commonly contain a static value, as well. Let's say that you want to identify when a key negative word appears in your Case subject. You would do that with the following:

```
CONTAINS(Subject, "lawsuit")
```

In this instance, you want to know if the Subject ever contains the same, exact string ("lawsuit").

Derived Values

Within formula fields, you can set values directly, as previously described for static values. You can also establish derived values. A *derived value* is a value that is obtained through an existing field within Salesforce. I use "existing" to emphasize that the field from which a value is derived must be created before it is used in a formula. This existing field can be any of the following:

- Any standard or custom field of the same object in which the formula field resides (e.g., any field on the Lead object if you are creating a Lead formula field)

- Any standard or custom field on an object to which the formula field's object relates via a Lookup or Master-Detail relationship (e.g., any field on the Account object if you are creating a Contact formula field)

- A custom field within a hierarchical custom setting

- A custom or standard field on a system object

Note   Static value and derived value are not official Salesforce terms but are used to help in understanding specific elements within formula fields.

I'll start with a formula field on the Contact object and look at examples of each derived field type. All of the examples of fields shown would be valid fields to reference within a custom Contact formula field.

The starting point for derived values is on the object itself (Contact). Within a formula field on the Contact object, you can obtain the value from the Mailing City field with very simple syntax (just the field name): `MailingCity`. Referencing a custom field is similar; the only difference is the way API names are formatted for custom fields. For example, if you want to derive the value from a custom field called "Maiden Name," you would use `Maiden_Name__c`, not `Maiden_Name`.

Note   The *API Name* is a text reference to an element that is used by Salesforce within formula fields, Data Loader, or Apex within API calls; it is not a user-facing string.

Using Lookup or Related Fields

The preceding section examined how to pull in values from fields on the same object as the formula field. Let's expand on that thought and look at pulling in values from *other* objects. As discussed in Chapter 1, Salesforce allows "looking up," or traversing, objects. Think of this approach as inheriting fields from a parent record. Let's say you want to pull in the Date/Time Opened (`CreatedDate`) field from the Account related to a Case and display it on the Contact record. In this case, you need to explicitly capture the Lookup object's name (`Account`). The format is `Account.CreatedDate`.

Let's keep moving up the chain. Assume you also want to use the Entitlement record to which the Case's Account is related. In this case, you'll be looking at a "grandparent" object that lives two lookup levels above the referencing object. Following the format in the last example, you simply add the additional object and an extra period in our syntax: `Account.Entitlement.Name`.

For custom objects, you need to slightly tweak what was done previously for standard objects by using the API Name of the object and replacing the __c with __r ("r" stands for relationship). If you develop declaratively, you don't need to worry about that to build out a formula, since the Formula Builder handles this for you; however, I think it is valuable to know. If you were to look up one level to a standard field on a custom object equivalent to the fields in the previous examples (for standard objects), the syntax would look like this: `Custom_Object_1__r.CreatedDate`.

For two levels, it would look like `Custom_Object_1__r.Custom_Field_2__r.Name`
Following are some additional examples.
For fields on a related object with a single lookup, you would use

- **Lookup to a standard field**: `Account.BillingState`

- **Lookup to a custom field**: `Account.Stock_Ticker_Symbol__c`

For fields on a related object with multiple lookups (via standard object), you would use

- **Lookup to a standard field**: `Account.Owner.LastName`

- **Lookup to a custom field**: `Account.Owner.Twitter_Handle__c`

For fields on a related object with multiple lookups (via custom object):

- **Lookup to a standard field**: `Account.Admin__r.LastName`

- **Lookup to a custom field**: `Account.Admin__r.Twitter_Handle__c`

Custom settings and system objects differ from regular object references. Custom settings of type "Hierarchy" can be referenced within a formula field, which can be extremely useful. Additionally, custom metadata types can now be referenced within a formula field, as well. Chapter 9 will take a closer look at custom settings and custom metadata types. System "objects" contain certain values related to the Salesforce org itself.

For fields on a custom setting:

- **Custom field**: `$Setup.Custom_Setting__c.Config_Value_1__c`

- **Custom field**: `$Setup.Custom_Setting__c.Config_Value_2__c`

For fields on a custom metadata type:

- **Standard field**: `$CustomMetadata.CMT__mdt.Record.DeveloperName`

- **Custom field**: `$CustomMetadata.CMT__mdt.Record.Text_Field__c`

For fields on a system object:

- **Standard field (Organization) – Id**: `$Organization.Id`

- **Custom field (Current User) – ID Number**: `$User.ID_Number__c`

Functions

The preceding chapter dissected Salesforce formula functions, looking at the name, arguments, and optional arguments that come together within a function. That one function, without any added operators, conditions, and or arguments, can serve as a formula, albeit a simple one.

For example, let's say you are using the Web-to-Lead feature to capture Internet Leads and route them directly to your org. Your entire organization is making a huge push to sell one of your newer software products, "IntelliPair," this month. You do capture Product of Interest in your Web-to-Lead form, but you've noticed that customers aren't always successful at communicating their wants and needs and often do not select IntelliPair as a Product of Interest. To that end, you've created a formula field of the Checkbox type to identify whether the Lead description contains "IntelliPair." This formula would be simple, using just the function itself:

```
CONTAINS(Description, "IntelliPair") OR ((TEXT(ProductofInterest) =
"IntelliPair"))
```

Statements and Operators

In addition to deriving values from existing fields, specifying static values, and applying built-in functions, you can assess statements and perform operations to produce the final value to be returned in a formula field. Salesforce provides a number of operators that can be used for these purposes. To comprehend the full scope of what is possible, you'll need to examine the operators that are available, as shown in Table 3-1.

Table 3-1. *Salesforce Operators*

Add	+	Opening parenthesis	(	Greater than	>
Subtract	–	Closing parenthesis	)	Less than or equal to	<=
Multiply	*	Equal to	=	Greater than or equal to	>=
Divide	/	Not equal to	<>	And	&&
Exponentiation	^	Less than	<	Or	||

Add, Subtract, Multiply, and Divide

The Add, Subtract, Multiply, and Divide operators perform basic addition, subtraction, multiplication, and division operations on numeric values, including those of the following field types: Number, Percent, Currency, Date, and DateTime.

Some examples follow:

```
CreatedDate + 2
Amount + 1000
Expected_Resolution_Date__c + Return_Period_in_Days__c

ClosedDate - 3
BudgetedCost - 1000

Probability * 0.85
Units_Requested__c * Unit_Cost__c
Tax * 1.07

Months_Duration__c / 12
```

Note   Think carefully about the data types of the operands and the formula field type when applying Add, Subtract, Multiply, and Divide operators in formula fields. Here is an example of why this is important: `CreatedDate + 3` and `Amount + 3` are both valid, but the 3 in each calculation uses a different unit of measure (days and currency units, respectively).

Exponentiation

The Exponentiation operator performs exponentiation on numeric values, including the following field types: Number, Percent, Currency, Date, and DateTime.

Some examples:

```
ExpectedRevenue ^ 2
Case_Worked_Duration__c ^ 2
```

Opening and Closing Parentheses

The Opening and Closing Parentheses operators allow for certain operations to be prioritized higher in the order of operations. In the following examples, the operation within parentheses will be evaluated first, based on the standard order of operations.

Example 1:
Formula:

```
Expected_Resolution_Date__c - (Return_Period_in_Days__c + 10)
```

Assumption:

```
Expected_Resolution_Date__c = 12/31/2019
Return_Period_in_Days__c = 30
```

Result:
Example 1 will return **11/21/2019** (12/31/2019 - 40).

Example 2:
Formula:

```
(Expected_Resolution_Date__c - Return_Period_in_Days__c) + 10
```

Assumption:

```
Expected_Resolution_Date__c = 12/31/2019
Return_Period_in_Days__c = 30
```

Result:

Example 2 will return **12/11/2019** (12/01/2019 + 10).

Here, you see that a small difference in parenthetical location has a direct impact on the evaluation of the formula.

Here are a couple of other examples of where you might want to use parentheses within a formula:

```
(ClosedDate - CreatedDate) * 2
(Units_Requested__c * Unit_Cost__c) - 500
```

Equal To and Not Equal To

The Equal To and Not Equal To operators evaluate a statement expected to have equivalent values (equal) or different values (not equal) to determine whether it is true or false. If true, the statement will return TRUE; if not, it will return FALSE.

Some examples:

```
CloseDate = DATEVALUE("2015-01-01")
NumberofResponses = 0
Probability = 1
Description = "Test"

Days_Remaining__c <> 0
Quantity <> 2
Subject <> "Test"
```

You can approach the previous statements slightly differently, depending on what type of formula you are trying to build. For example, you can represent a Checkbox (a Boolean field) in the following ways:

```
IsClosed
IsClosed = true
```

You can represent a statement evaluation for a Picklist field in the following ways:

```
ISPICKVAL(Status, "Working")
TEXT(Status) = "Working"
```

Also, for Not Equal, you can use NOT on a corresponding Equal statement:

```
NOT(Probability = 1)
```

Less Than, Greater Than, Less Than or Equal To, and Greater Than or Equal To

The Less Than, Greater Than, Less Than or Equal To, and Greater Than or Equal To operators evaluate a comparative statement to determine whether it is true or false. If true, the statement will return TRUE; if not, it will return FALSE.

Examples:

```
CloseDate < TODAY()
Number_of_Complaints__c < 2

Amount > 1000000
NumberofResponses > 1000

Probability <= 0.5
LastModifiedDate <= ClosedDate

NumberOfEmployees >= 100000
Age_in_Days >= 10
```

And

Like the AND function, the And operator (&&) will check whether all included arguments are true. It returns TRUE if all arguments are true or FALSE if one or more arguments are false.

Examples:

```
Probability > 0.8 && Amount > 10000
ISPICKVAL(Status, "Working") && (Case_Age_in_Days__c + Business_Days__c) <= 10
```

The And operator (&&) and AND function can be used interchangeably. For example, these return the same value.

Using the AND function:

```
AND(
 IsClosed,
 (ClosedDate - CreatedDate) < 15
)
```

Using the And operator:

```
IsClosed && (ClosedDate - CreatedDate) < 15
```

Or

Like the OR function, the Or operator (||) will check whether one or more included arguments are true. It returns TRUE if one or more arguments are true or FALSE if all arguments are false.

Examples:

```
Probability > 0.75 || Amount > 50000
ISPICKVAL(Status, "On Hold") || IsClosed
```

The Or operator (||) and OR function can be used interchangeably. For example, these return the same value:

Using the OR function:

```
OR(
 NOT(IsClosed),
 (TODAY - ClosedDate) < 2
)
```

Using the Or operator:

```
NOT(IsClosed) || (Today - ClosedDate) < 2
```

Note   Since you have different options for evaluating multiple statements (&&, AND), you will want to come up with a thoughtful, systematic approach in your development. Always think about the next person who might come along and maintain what you've built, in case you move on to a different position at your job. When possible, stick with one or the other within a formula.

Creating a Formula Field

It's time to build your first formula field in Salesforce. The remainder of this chapter walks you in detail through the 11 steps in the process of creating a formula field in the program, pointing out your options when appropriate.

Step 1.   Navigate to the corresponding object, as shown in Figure 3-1.

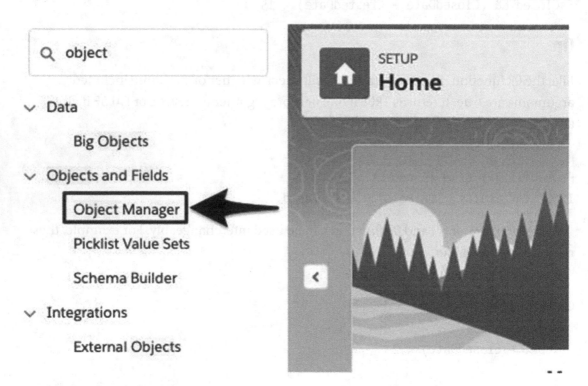

Figure 3-1.   *Location of setup menu item to access custom objects[1]*

To navigate to the appropriate object, use Quick Find in the Setup menu to navigate to the following items:

- **For standard objects (classic):** Setup ➤ Object_Name

- **For custom objects (classic):** Setup ➤ Objects ➤ Object_Name

- **For all types (LEX):** Setup ➤ Object Manager ➤ Object_Name

---

[1]All Salesforce screenshots in this chapter © copyright Salesforce, Inc. Used with permission.

From there, navigate to the "Fields" section for that object.

Step 2. Click on the "New" button in the custom fields section, as shown in Figure 3-2.

SETUP > OBJECT MANAGER
Case
Details
Fields & Relationships
Case Page Layouts
Case Close Page Layouts
Fields & Relationships
40+ Items, Sorted by Field Label
Quick Find
New
Field Dependencies
Set History Tracking
FIELD LABEL
FIELD NAME
DATA TYPE
CONTROLLING FIE...
INDEXED
Account Name
AccountId
Lookup(Account)
Asset
AssetId
Lookup(Asset)

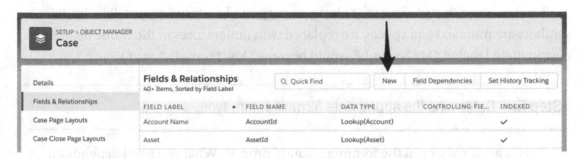

Figure 3-2. The "New" button allows you to create a new formula field

Step 3. Select "Formula" for the field type and click the "Next" button, as shown in Figure 3-3.

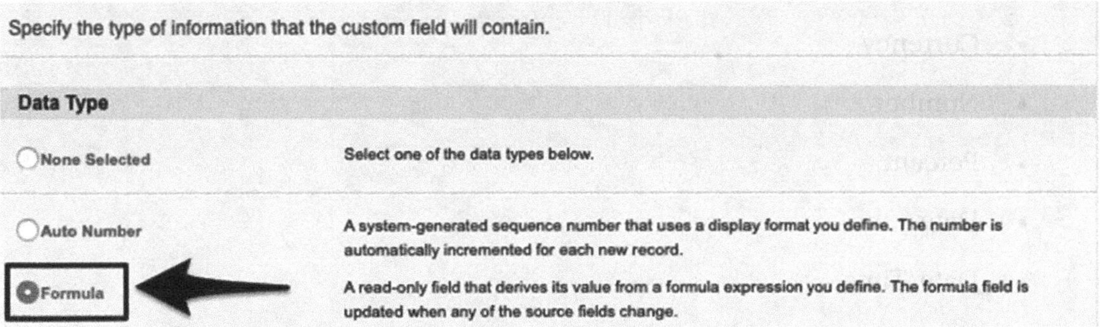

Specify the type of information that the custom field will contain.
Data Type
None Selected
Select one of the data types below.
Auto Number
A system-generated sequence number that uses a display format you define. The number is automatically incremented for each new record.
Formula
A read-only field that derives its value from a formula expression you define. The formula field is updated when any of the source fields change.

Figure 3-3. Selection of the formula field type

Step 4. Label and name the field, as shown in Figure 3-4.

Field Label	My Custom Field		Field Name	My_Custom_Field	i

Figure 3-4. *The formula's "Field Name" will autopopulate after you populate the "Field Label" and hit the tab key*

I recommend that you use the Salesforce-suggested name when possible. By default, symbols are removed and spaces are replaced with underscores in the Name field. A custom field labeled "My Formula" would become "My_Formula," as in Figure 3-4.

Step 5.   Determine the appropriate formula return type.

This is a critical step in the formula creation process. What you need depends on how your data should be displayed and/or how you intend your users or the system to interact with the field. Much of what you will do with formula fields will center on the Text return type, but I'll cover the others as well.

Let's walk through the options and review when it makes sense to use each of them. The current formula return type options are

- Checkbox
- Currency
- Number
- Percent
- Date
- Date/Time
- Text
- Time

Checkbox

The clearest way to understand the value of the Checkbox and how it can be used is to focus on the fact that it serves as a Boolean operator rather than thinking of it as an actual checkbox. The Checkbox will simply tell us if our formula is true or false, regardless of the complexity of the formula itself. Here are some basic examples of when you might select Checkbox for the return type:

- **Contract object**: You can use this object to determine whether a particular contract is still in effect based on a Start Date and Contract Term by entering the following: `TODAY() > StartDate + (ContractTerm * 12)`

- **Lead object**: This can be used to flag a potentially valuable lead if her organization has a hundred thousand or more employees or brings in a revenue of $100,000,000 or more, as follows: `NumberOfEmployees >= 100000 || AnnualRevenue >= 100000000`

- **Campaign member object**: A checkbox return type on this object could determine if the Campaign to which the Campaign Member is related is inactive or was created over 1 year ago as such: `NOT(Campaign.Active) || (TODAY() - CreatedDate) > 365`

A Checkbox formula can also be very useful within other formulas (such as formula fields, validation rules, and workflow rules). If you need to determine whether a specific formula is true in multiple areas of your system, consider creating a Checkbox formula field. You'll be able to quickly and easily reference it once the field is set up.

Currency, Number, and Percent

Currency, Number, and Percent are numeric return types that behave similarly when building the corresponding formula field. As long as your formula corresponds to a number, any of these three return types will work; it's simply a matter of how you want the data to be displayed and used throughout the system.

Here are some examples of formulas with a return type of Currency:

- **Opportunity object**: You could use this object to determine what the Expected Revenue would be with an additional upsell of 10 percent of the current Expected Revenue as follows: `ExpectedRevenue * 1.1`

- **Case object**: You could use this object to display the related Account's annual revenue as such: `Account.AnnualRevenue`

Here are some examples of formulas with a return type of Number:

- **Lead object**: This object is used to calculate the age of a Lead: `TODAY() - CreatedDate`

- **Contact object**: This object displays the number of total Contacts associated with the Contact's Account via a custom field on the Account object: `Account.Total_Number_Of_Contacts__c`

Here are some examples of formulas with a return type of Percent:

- **Opportunity object**: This object calculates the ratio of the ClosedAmount to the initial Amount at the time of Opportunity creation: `Amount / Initial_Amount__c`

- **Quote object**: This object displays the ratio of the Quote's Grand Total to the related Opportunity's Amount (assume the Quote is not the primary one): `GrandTotal / Opportunity.Amount`

Date, Date/Time, and Time

Date, Date/Time, and Time formula fields are used to calculate a date, a time, or a date and time and can be extremely valuable for an organization. Time is a relatively new addition to the mix. While Time is fairly straightforward, the decision of selecting Date or Date/Time may require more thought. The obvious benefit of Date/Time is the additional detail; however, it can be a problem if the time is irrelevant. Showing "12:00:00" or even a seemingly random time can confuse your users. If you need to capture the time an event occurred or convey a strict deadline that needs to be precise down to the minute, Date/Time is the right return type. For anything else that doesn't require a specific time, it is better to just create a Date field.

Date:

- **Opportunity object**: This is used to calculate a date that precedes the CloseDate by 10 days, serving as a "reminder" date to increase efforts to close the open Opportunity as follows: `CloseDate - 10`

- **Case object**: This calculates a "Follow-up Date" one week after Case closure: `ClosedDate + 7`

Date/Time:

- **Case object**: Calculates an expected first contact date/time 1 hour from the time of Case creation: `CreatedDate + (1 / 24)`

- **Custom Event object**: Calculate an exact date/time by which event payment must be received (24 hours before the event): `Event_Date__c - 1`

Time:

- **Contact object**: Calculates the last time a rep should place an outbound call to the contact each day: `Workday_End__c - 1`

Note   Operations with Date and Date/Time fields are identical within formula fields; integers are interpreted as days. For example, adding 1 would add 1 day to either a Date or a Date/Time field within formula field calculations. In Time fields, integers are handled as hours.

Text

Formulas with a Text return type are arguably the most flexible and are my personal favorites. With all other return types, the returned value is always in the same format, whereas a formula field with a return type of Text can contain more than just text; you can include text strings, hyperlinks, and even images. Think of it like a rich-text field. Here are some examples:

- **Lead object**: This object identifies Leads with high Annual Revenues and Ratings as high priority as follows: `IF(AnnualRevenue > 1000000 && ISPICKVAL(Rating, "Hot"), "High Priority", "Standard")`

- **Opportunity object**: This displays a link to the chapter in the Salesperson Guidebook that corresponds to the current Stage: `CASE(StageName, "Prospecting", "http://www.company.com/collateral/salesguidebook#2.1", "Qualification", "http://www.company.com/collateral/salesguidebook#2.3", "Needs Analysis", "http://www.company.com/collateral/salesguidebook#3.1", "http://www.company.com/collateral/salesguidebook#4")`

- **Case object**: This displays an informational message if the Subject field contains certain keywords, such as "Cancel" or "Quit":
  ```
  IF(CONTAINS(Subject, "Cancel") || CONTAINS(Subject,
  "Quit"), "Case may be related to cancellation; please
  review ASAP" , "")
  ```

See Figure 3-5 for examples of text formula fields displaying images.

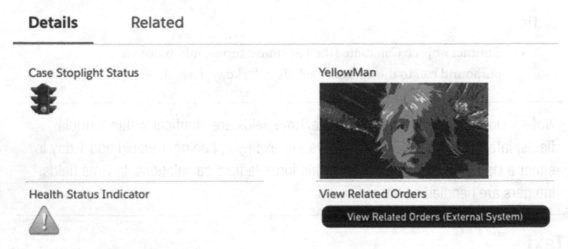

Figure 3-5. *Four text formula fields that display images*

Some of your formulas may require extra thought when deciding on a return type. For example, assume you want to display the Account's five-digit Billing Zip Code on the Contact object. Although five-digit zip codes are numeric, your formula return type must be Text. This will handle zip codes that start with zero. Additionally, you don't need to use zip codes in any statements or operations.

Step 6.   Select the applicable "Formula Return Type" and click "Next," as in Figure 3-6.

Case
New Custom Field

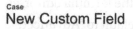

Help for this Page ❓

Step 2. Choose output type	Step 2 of 5

Previous | Next | Cancel

Field Label [My Formula]   Field Name [My_Formula] [i]

Formula Return Type

○ None Selected	Select one of the data types below.
○ Checkbox	Calculate a boolean value
	Example: [TODAY() > CloseDate]
○ Currency	Calculate a dollar or other currency amount and automatically format the field as a currency amount.
	Example: [Gross Margin = Amount - Cost__c]
○ Date	Calculate a date, for example, by adding or subtracting days to other dates.
	Example: [Reminder Date = CloseDate - 7]
○ Date/Time	Calculate a date/time, for example, by adding a number of hours or days to another date/time.
	Example: [Next = NOW() + 1]
○ Number	Calculate a numeric value.
	Example: [Fahrenheit = 1.8 * Celsius__c + 32]
○ Percent	Calculate a percent and automatically add the percent sign to the number.
	Example: [Discount = (Amount - Discounted_Amount__c) / Amount]
◉ Text	Create a text string, for example, by concatenating other text fields.
	Example: [Full Name = LastName & ", " & FirstName]
○ Time	Calculate a time, for example, by adding a number of hours to another time.
	Example: [Next = TIMEVALUE(NOW()) + 1]

Figure 3-6. *Selecting a return type for your formula*

Step 7.   Select the advanced formula editor if necessary, as shown in Figure 3-7.

Simple Formula	**Advanced Formula**

[Insert Field]   [Insert Operator ▾]

My Formula (Text) =

Figure 3-7. *The advanced formula editor tab*

Once you select your formula return type, you'll be presented with the formula editor, as discussed in Chapter 2. If your formula editor does not automatically default to "Advanced Formula," click on that tab to select this editor, which will then serve as the default going forward. You will select the advanced formula editor through the remainder of this book.

Step 8.   Build your formula.

This step is where all the magic (and fun) occurs. You'll take a formula of midlevel complexity and methodically build it out. The scenario is that you're creating a new Case formula field to provide some additional information to agents about the Case. The formula looks at a few Case attributes, including whether the Case is escalated, whether it is closed, and what the Created Date is.

If the Case is escalated, a direct phone call to the customer is required. Closed cases are automatically de-escalated at your business, so you don't need to add a qualification that the Case is open. You will display the following to agents: "Contact customer directly by phone to address customer needs."

If the Case is not escalated, but it is at least 7 days old and it is still open, you will display "Handle Case with urgency; Case has been open over one week."

If neither of those conditions matches the record, then no text will be displayed. Continue to build out this formula step by step. You will build this formula declaratively, or by using the clickable user interface that Salesforce has provided. However, as you feel more comfortable, you can feel free to type out your formulas. It is completely personal preference whether you use clicks or code when building a formula.

Step 8.1.   Select and insert the IF function to start building the formula as in Figure 3-8.

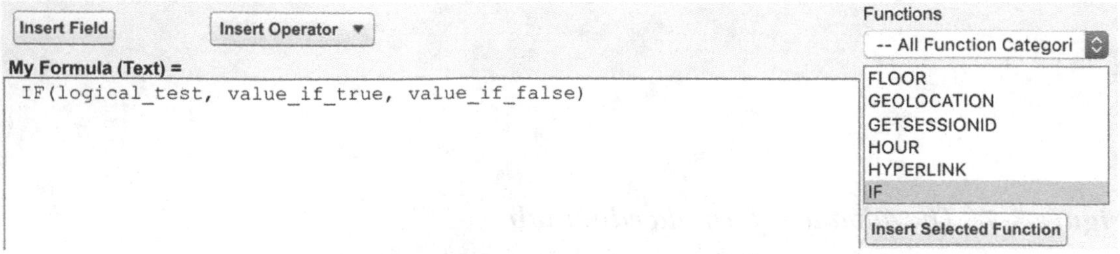

Figure 3-8. *The IF function after being inserted into the formula*

Step 8.2.   You have the option to reformat your IF statement for a cleaner view, as done in Figure 3-9.

Figure 3-9. *Reformatting the default placement of formula elements*

Step 8.3.   Select and double-click "logical_test" in preparation for replacing the text with the actual test statement, as shown in Figure 3-10.

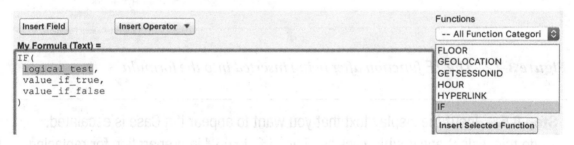

Figure 3-10. *Selecting the text to be replaced*

Step 8.4.   Insert the Escalated field to determine whether a particular record has been escalated or not, as in Figure 3-11. To do this, click the "Insert" button, select the Case object and the Escalated field, and then click on the "Insert" button to inject the field into your formula, replacing the "logical_test" text, as shown in Figure 3-12.

Insert Field

Select a field, then click Insert. Labels followed by a ">" indicate that there are more fields available.

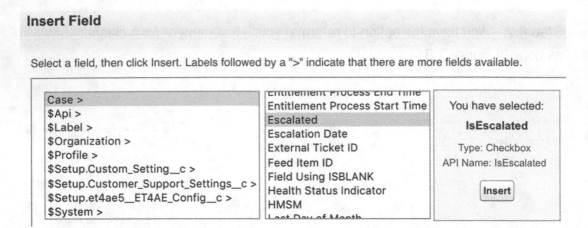

Figure 3-11. *The "Insert Field" menu*

Figure 3-12. *The* IF *function after being inserted into the formula*

Step 8.5.   Input the display text that you want to appear if a Case is escalated. To do this, select and double-click "value_if_true," in preparation for replacing the text with the text to be displayed, as in Figure 3-13.

Figure 3-13. *Selecting the text to replace with the second* IF *function*

Step 8.6.   Paste in the text you would like to display for escalated Cases, as shown in Figure 3-14.

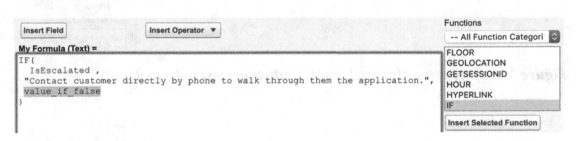

Figure 3-14. Field that appears after inserting the text to be displayed

Step 8.7.   Build a detailed IF statement to answer the question, What if my logical test is false? First, highlight the "`value_if_false`" text, as shown in Figure 3-15, and replace it with the `IF` statement, as done in Figure 3-16. Reformat the formula, as shown in Figure 3-17.

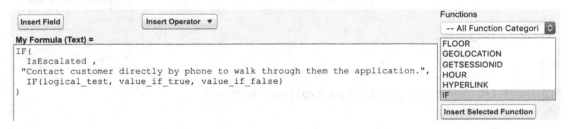

Figure 3-15. Highlighting the text to be replaced

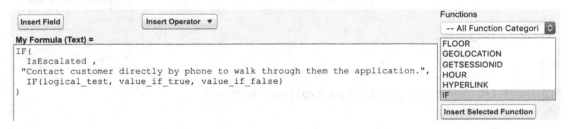

Figure 3-16. Field that appears after inserting the second IF function

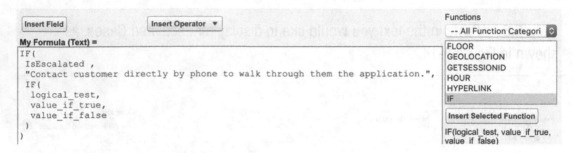

Figure 3-17. *Build your formula and continue to reformat, as needed*

Step 8.8. To establish the logical test for the second IF statement, highlight "`logical_test`," as in Figure 3-18, and insert the NOT function, as done in Figures 3-19 and 3-20.

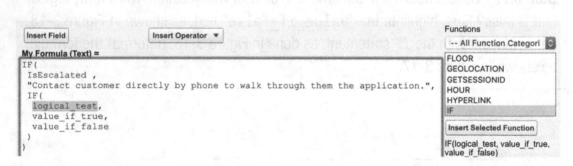

Figure 3-18. *Selecting "`logical_test`," indicating text to be replaced*

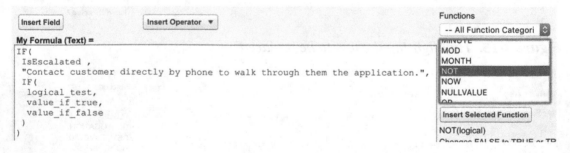

Figure 3-19. *Selecting the NOT function (on the right)*

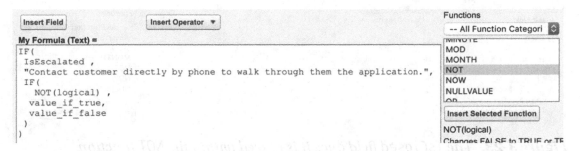

Figure 3-20. *Screen that appears after the NOT function has been inserted*

Step 8.9.   Select the text within parentheses in the NOT function, as in Figure 3-21, and replace it with the Closed field, as is done in Figures 3-22 and 3-23.

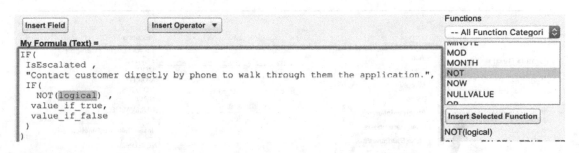

Figure 3-21. *Selecting the text to be replaced within the NOT function*

Insert Field

Select a field, then click Insert. Labels followed by a ">" indicate that there are more fields available.

Case >	Case Owner (User) >	You have selected:
$Api >	Case Pending Time	**IsClosed**
$Label >	Case Reason	
$Organization >	Case Resolution Details	Type: Checkbox
$Profile >	Case Reviewed Date	API Name: IsClosed
$Setup.Custom_Setting__c >	Case Stoplight Status	
$Setup.Customer_Support_Settings__c >	Closed	**Insert**
$Setup.et4ae5__ET4AE_Config__c >	Closed by Self-Service User	
$System >	Closed When Created	

Figure 3-22. *Selecting the Closed field within the "Insert Field" menu*

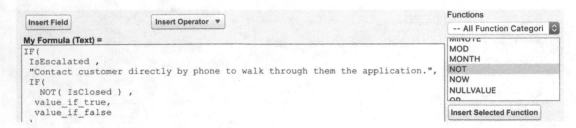

Figure 3-23. *The* IsClosed *field once it is placed within the* NOT *function*

Step 8.10. You have added the condition that the Case is not closed in our second IF statement. Now, continue and add the age aspect of the condition. First, you need to establish that this needs to be an AND statement by inserting the && operator, as shown in Figure 3-24.

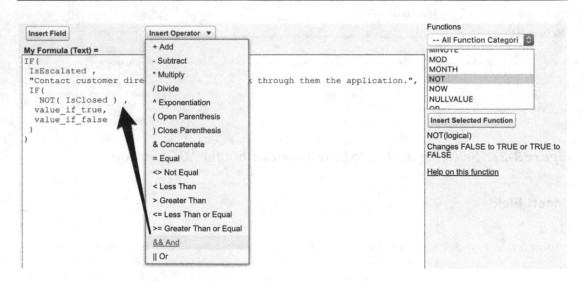

Figure 3-24. *Selecting "&&" and inserting the operator into the formula*

In this case, you could use the AND function instead of the double ampersands. However, with just two statements in the logical test, it's simpler and cleaner to use "&&."

Step 8.11. To determine whether the Case is over 7 days old, you'll need to build a calculation that takes the difference between the current date and the Case Created Date and assesses whether that value is greater than 7. First, add some parentheses for clarity, per Figures 3-25 and 3-26.

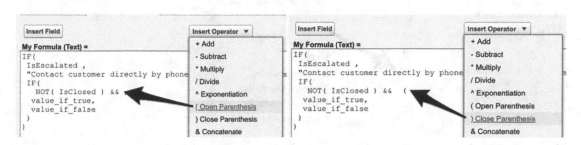

Figure 3-25. *Adding open and close parentheses*

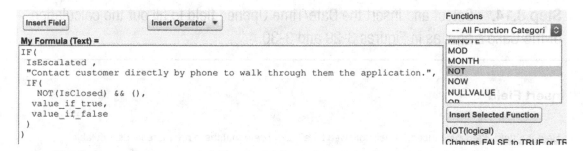

Figure 3-26. *The parentheses, after insertion*

Step 8.12. Insert the current date/time by selecting the NOW function and clicking "Insert Selected Function," as in Figure 3-27.

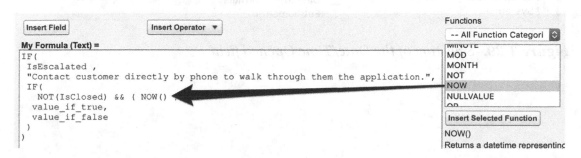

Figure 3-27. *Inserting the NOW function*

Step 8.13.   Select and insert a minus sign, as done in Figure 3-28.

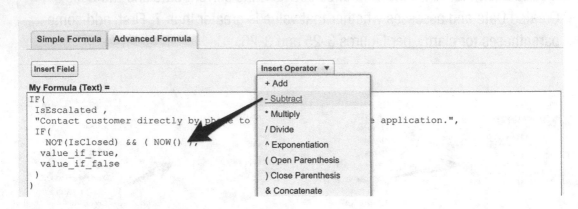

Figure 3-28. *Inserting the Subtract operator*

Step 8.14.   Select and insert the Date/Time Opened field to fill out the calculation of the Case's age, as in Figures 3-29 and 3-30.

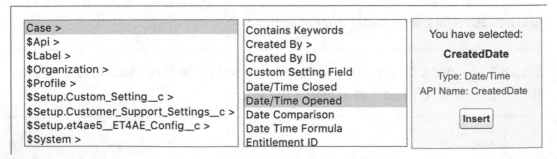

Figure 3-29. *Selection of the Date/Time Opened field*

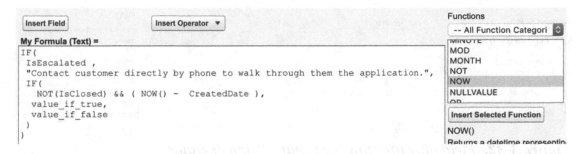

Figure 3-30. *Formula view after* CreatedDate *has been inserted into the formula*

Step 8.15.   Optionally, clean up the formula and place the cursor after "CreatedDate)". You are now going to set up the check of whether the Case Age is greater than seven. You'll first need a greater than symbol, as in Figures 3-31 and 3-32.

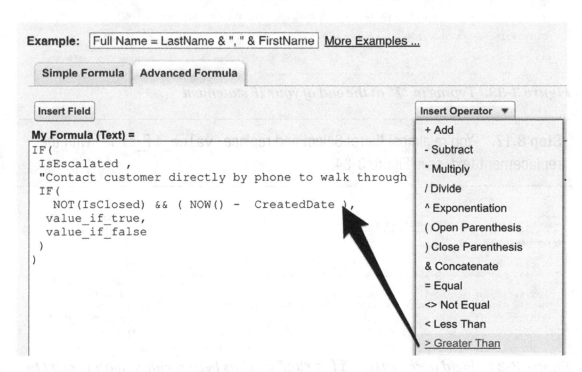

Figure 3-31. *Selecting the Greater Than operator*

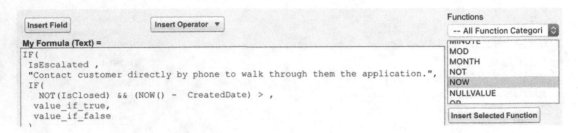

Figure 3-32. *Field after inserting the Greater Than operator*

Step 8.16.   Type in "7" manually at the end of the IF statement to complete the "logical_test," as done in Figure 3-33.

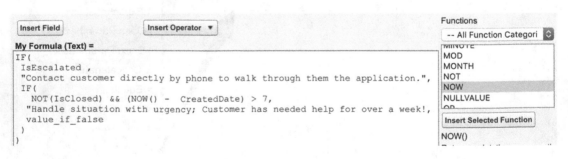

Figure 3-33. *Typing in "7" at the end of your IF statement*

Step 8.17.   You're almost there! Select and replace "value_if_true" with the replacement text, as in Figure 3-34.

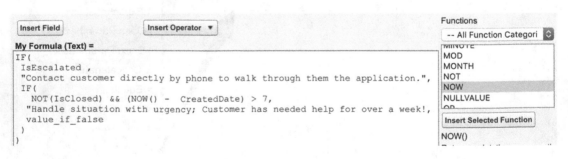

Figure 3-34. *Field once "value_if_true," text has been replaced with the text to display*

Step 8.18. Replace "value_if_false" with double quotations since you do not want any text to display in this scenario, as shown in Figure 3-35.

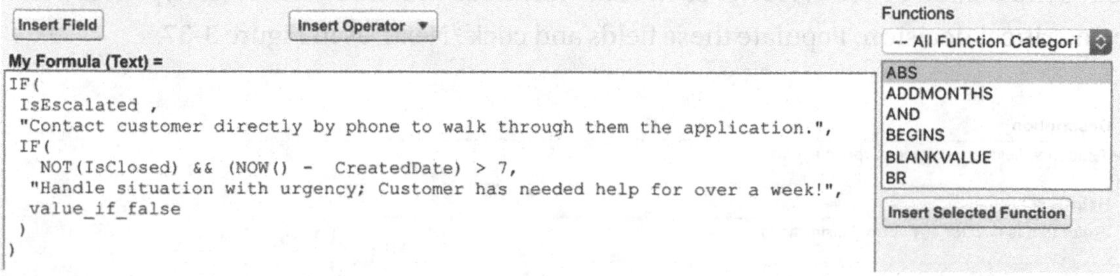

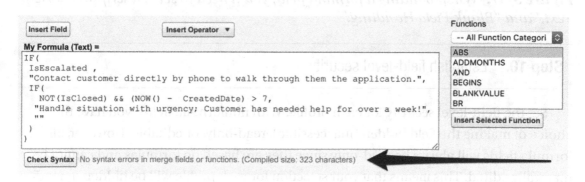

Figure 3-35. *Field after replacing the "value_if_false" text with double quotations*

Step 8.19. The formula has been built. Now comes the moment of truth. Click the "Check Syntax" button at the bottom of the page to find out if it was built properly, as in Figure 3-36.

Figure 3-36. *Clicking "Check Syntax" to find out if our formula was built properly*

Congratulations, you have successfully built a meaningful formula field! Give yourself a pat on the back. Make it quick, though, because you have a few more steps left to complete and save the field.

Step 9. Finalize field attributes.

You have completed the formula, but you will still want to populate the Description field; optionally, you can populate the Help Text field. There is one additional choice as well: blank field handling. Within a formula, you can set any derived fields that are blank with a value of zero or leave them blank. In this formula, it does not matter, so you'll leave the default of zeros. However, in some formulas with numeric return types, this can be a critical decision. Populate these fields and click "Next," as in Figure 3-37.

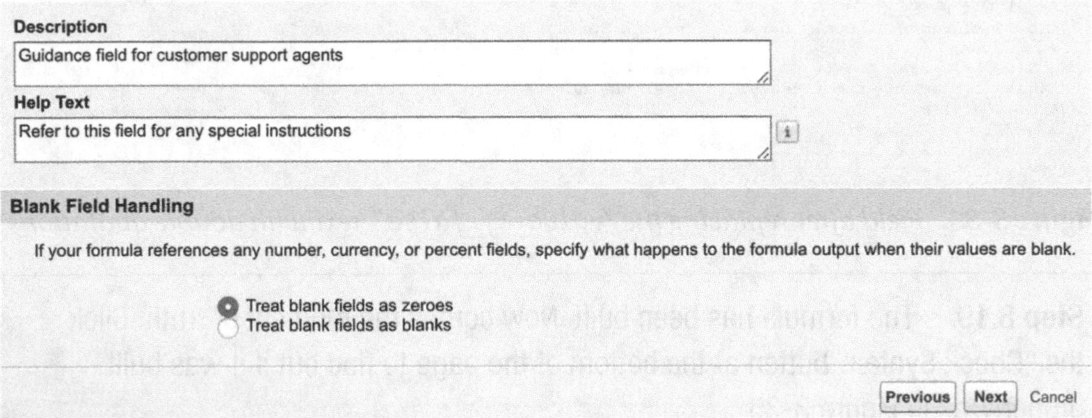

Figure 3-37. *When building a formula field, you'll need to set "Description," "Help Text," and "Blank Field Handling."*

Step 10.   Establish field-level security.

Set the field-level security for each profile. With nonformula fields, you have the choice of making the field hidden (inaccessible), read-only, or editable. However, all formula fields will always be read-only since they are based on formulas and cannot be manually edited. This means that your selection for each profile will be hidden or read-only. See the chapter on security in this book for additional details on considerations when making this decision. Click the "Next" button, shown in Figure 3-38, to proceed to the final step.

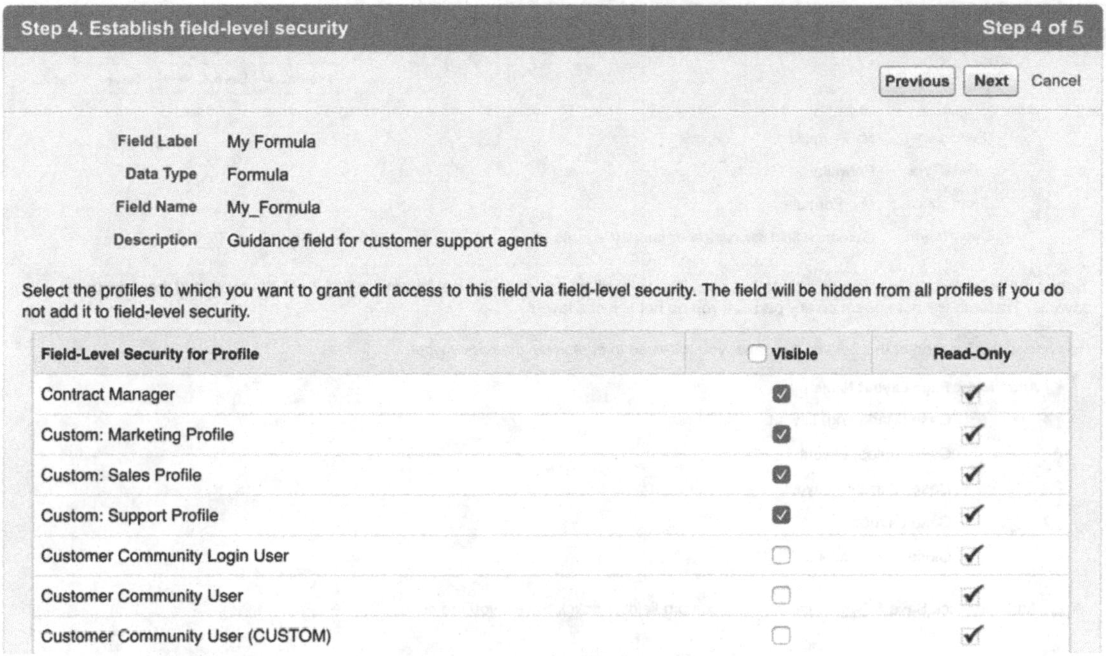

Step 4. Establish field-level security		Step 4 of 5

Previous | Next | Cancel

Field Label   My Formula
Data Type   Formula
Field Name   My_Formula
Description   Guidance field for customer support agents

Select the profiles to which you want to grant edit access to this field via field-level security. The field will be hidden from all profiles if you do not add it to field-level security.

Field-Level Security for Profile	Visible	Read-Only
Contract Manager	☑	✓
Custom: Marketing Profile	☑	✓
Custom: Sales Profile	☑	✓
Custom: Support Profile	☑	✓
Customer Community Login User	☐	✓
Customer Community User	☐	✓
Customer Community User (CUSTOM)	☐	✓

Figure 3-38. *Field-level security for the formula field*

Step 11. Add to page layouts.

Select the page layouts to which your new formula field should be added, as shown in Figure 3-39. Click the "Save" button. Your formula field is now complete!

Figure 3-39. *For the last step, identify which page layouts should display the new formula field*

Recap

It's a fair statement to stay that there's quite a bit to Salesforce formula fields. Fortunately, you have just taken a very detailed look at the elements of formula fields, when they can be used in a real-world, business context, and how to properly build them from start to finish. Formulas are used extensively within Salesforce, and what you have just learned will come in extremely handy as you learn about other areas of the platform in subsequent chapters.

CHAPTER 4

Automating Your Business with Workflow

At this point in our journey to build solutions without code, you have added a nice variety of tools to your Salesforce development tool belt. You have learned how to establish a meaningful and effective data model using objects, fields, and relationships; how to utilize functions; and how to build formula fields based on calculations, statements, and derived values from other fields. Next, you will take your org to a new place altogether by automating your business processes. Let's start with an understanding of what business process automation means in the context of Salesforce.

The one thing you're guaranteed to find in every active instance of Salesforce is interaction. It is a given that your users (and even other systems) will add, edit, and/or remove data from your org on a regular basis. Consider these updates to Salesforce as the first step in your automation efforts. The second step is making Salesforce do what you want *based on that initial interaction* with no further manual activity from users.

The original business process automation tool, known as Workflow, is an extremely powerful way to take one of these regular, everyday interactions and allow it to drive your business forward without spending the time or money to have additional people or systems make the change happen. At the simplest level, I can describe workflow rules as operating as follows:

1. Workflow rules "look for" a particular state of specific data (i.e., your criteria).

2. The workflow rules "fire" (i.e., are triggered/become active) if the current state of the data satisfies the configured criteria.

3. The workflow rules execute one or more designated, automated actions to occur.

© Philip Weinmeister 2019
P. Weinmeister, *Practical Salesforce Development Without Code*,
https://doi.org/10.1007/978-1-4842-4871-3_4

Through this process, your organization will have taken an additional step forward using process automation. Whether you use workflow rules to notify a colleague that further action is needed or you update a field to reflect the current state of data, you ensure that some desired action will happen and can do it all with a small, one-time investment of your cerebral efforts as opposed to an ongoing, manual activity.

With the potential value that lies in workflow rules comes a critical need for a solid understanding of these rules and a strategic approach when building them. You will quickly find that there are numerous ways to automate one business process; you will also discover that there is usually a best option. To that end, I will dissect each component of this functionality to help guide you through the decision-making process as you automate your own organization's processes.

After going over the workflow rule framework and how to use it effectively, I will examine four scenarios and demonstrate how to take real-world business processes and automate them in Salesforce via workflow rules. Knowing how to create a workflow rule is critical, but our end goal is actually satisfying a business need through the workflow rules. By the end of this chapter, you will

- Recognize scenarios warranting business process automation

- Know how to properly apply evaluation criteria to workflow rules

- Be able to develop rule criteria for workflow rules

- Understand how and when to create workflow actions, including time-based actions

- Grasp key considerations when working with workflow rules

Workflow in the Proper Context

One of the most significant additions to *Practical Salesforce Development without Code* since the first edition is undoubtedly the inclusion of Process Builder as an additional declarative business process automation tool. Chapter 7 will be fully dedicated to that tool and provide guidance on its use and application. This new scope begs the million-dollar question, "When should I still use Workflow?"

First, let me say that justice is not being done by anyone who has an absolute blanket response to that question (e.g., "Do not use Workflow anymore." or "Always use Workflow for task creation instead of Process Builder.") It's not quite that black and white. I will dive into more of the Workflow vs. Process Builder topic in Chapter 7. For now, understand that there are contexts in which Workflow is still not only a viable, but a preferred, tool.

In 2018, I was fortunate to see a presentation by David K. Liu titled, "Clicks versus Code! ...Which one should you choose?" at the Tahoe Dreamin' Salesforce community event. In that session, David articulated some key, data-driven takeaways on the topic of choosing Workflow, Process Builder, Flow, or Apex to optimally deliver a solution. Here, I'll include some of the findings and recommendations from that session regarding Workflow along with some additional, personal input. There are definitely some limiting factors that might deter you from using Workflow; for example:

- Scope of functionality (very limited)

- Order of execution (no control among workflow rules)

- Extensibility/scalability (cannot call other tools)

- Innovation (Salesforce is not investing in Workflow)

At the same time, there are reasons why Workflow should still be considered:

- Simplicity

- Limits

- Debugging/Error handling

- Speed

- Development Time

- Risk

In seeing the number of bullet points, you might immediately conclude that Workflow remains a front-runner among the development tools on the platform. However, you must also understand that the four points identified as weaknesses (functional scope, order of execution, extensibility, and innovation) are absolutely critical to many organizations. Solutions built on Salesforce or on any other platform are becoming more complex by the day due to ever-evolving business needs around the world. The main points here are

- There are definitely still solutions that can greatly benefit from a Workflow-driven approach.

- Workflow has a very defined scope; there is quite a bit in the arena of business process automation that it cannot support.

139

- Each solution warrants some thought process around the ideal delivery tool, whether Workflow or something else.

- The skill sets available when a solution is to be handed off must be considered, whether built with Workflow or not.

The Elements of a Salesforce Workflow Rule

Before you create a workflow rule, you'll need to make sure you clearly understand each piece of the proverbial puzzle. It is very easy to create a workflow that does *not* do what you want it to do, and that is no fault of Salesforce. My goal is to prepare you so that you can minimize adjustments and tweaks after you create workflow rules. Once you have an understanding of the workflow rule elements, I will walk you through each step of the creation process for workflow rules. By building upon a solid foundation and delivering your solutions with precision, you can enjoy the lovely silence of satisfied users after putting this chapter into practice.

"Base" Object

The base object – which is my term, not Salesforce's – is the object on which the initial data change will occur; Workflow waits for a database change on a record of a specific object. For example, assume you have a custom object called Property that has a Master-Detail relationship to the Account object. If you wanted to make a change to a Property record to drive an automated application, you would identify the Property object as your base object. That may seem obvious, but it is important to note that the object that is automatically updated through a workflow rule may differ from the base object.

In Figure 4-1, I have identified the object being updated as the "action" object. Note that a change to Object 1 may trigger an automated update to Object 2; this is called *cross-object workflow* and will be covered later in this chapter.

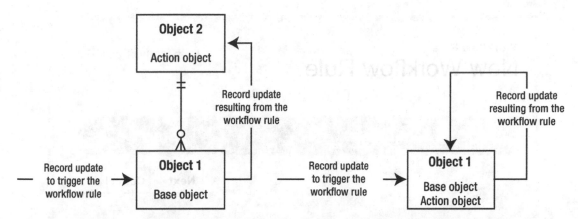

Figure 4-1. *The "base" object can update a Parent record with which it has a Master-Detail relationship (left side of diagram). Most commonly, workflow rules drive an update of the record that triggered the rule (right side).*

The *base object* refers to the object where the initial activity occurs, not necessarily where the update takes place. On the left side of the diagram, Object 1 has a Master-Detail relationship with Object 2 that allows configuring a workflow rule to update an object different than the base object.

From the Setup menu, use Quick Find (typing a value in the Setup search field without clicking the Enter button) and search for "Workflow." Click on Workflow Rules and then click on the "New Rule" button. From there, you will select your base object from the available Picklist of objects shown in Figure 4-2.

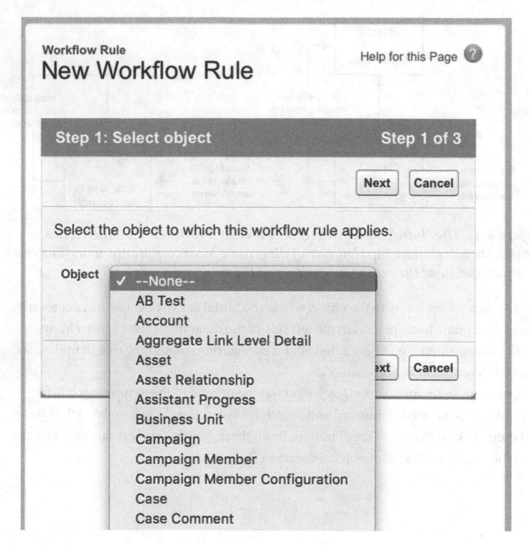

Figure 4-2. *Base object selection in your workflow rule*[1]

Evaluation Criteria

Once you identify your base object, you will need to configure its evaluation criteria. By establishing the evaluation criteria, you are setting the conditions in which the workflow rule should be considered or evaluated. You can think of it as the first "gate" that needs

---

[1]All Salesforce screenshots in this chapter © copyright Salesforce, Inc. Used with permission.

to be passed through for your automated business process to fully execute. The choices are fairly straightforward; you must select one of the three available evaluation criteria options identified and described in Table 4-1.

Table 4-1. *Evaluation Criteria Options Within a Workflow Rule*

Workflow Rule: Evaluation Criteria	
Criteria	**Description**
Created	The workflow rule will be evaluated *only* at the point of record creation. Regardless of the rule criteria you specify, the rule will never fire for an existing record.
Created, and every time it's edited	The workflow rule will be evaluated upon every single change to the record, whether at the time of creation or after.
Created, and any time it's edited to subsequently meet criteria	The workflow rule will be always evaluated at record creation. For existing records, it will be evaluated only when the new/current state of the record satisfies the rule criteria *and* the previous state did not satisfy the rule criteria.

The "Created, and any time it's edited" option in Table 4-1 trips some people up. Table 4-2 and Figure 4-3 exemplify real-life scenarios and the resulting outcomes when using this option.

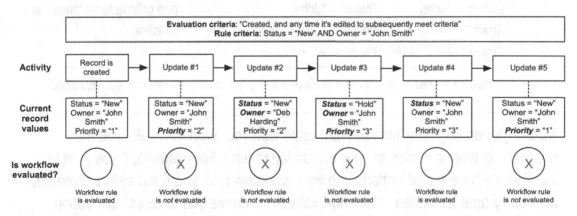

Figure 4-3. *Because the evaluation criteria setting includes "Created, and any time it's edited to subsequently meet criteria," the workflow rule will only be evaluated if the rule criteria are satisfied AND they were not already satisfied before the most recent update.*

Figure 4-3 looks at a different scenario than Table 4-2 but also uses the same evaluation and rule criteria. Note that bolded text signifies a field that had its value change in the specified step.

Table 4-2. *A Workflow Rule Using the "Created, and Any Time It's Edited" Option*

Workflow Rule Example

Evaluation criteria: "Created, and any time it's edited to subsequently meet criteria"

Rule criteria: Status = "New" *and* Owner = "John Smith"

Scenario	Previous State	Current State	Evaluated	Details
1	Status = "New" Owner = "John Smith" Product SKU = "A1A"	Status = "New" Owner = "John Smith" **Product SKU = "B2B"***	No	Only Product SKU changed. The rule criteria was already satisfied before update to the record.
2	Status = "Working" Owner = "John Smith" Product SKU = "A1A"	**Status = "New"** Owner = "John Smith" Product SKU = "A1A"	Yes	Update to Status causes rule criteria to be satisfied as a direct result of the change.
3	Status = "New" Owner = "John Smith" Product SKU = "A1A"	**Status = "Closed"** Owner = "John Smith" Product SKU = "A1A"	No	Update to Status causes rule criteria to no longer be satisfied.

*Bolded field labels and values signify that the value has been modified from the previous state

Note   Depending on what you want to do with your workflow rule, you may not actually have a choice of your evaluation criteria. For example, if you plan to incorporate time-based actions into your workflow rule, you must select "Created, and every time it's edited." Although Salesforce forces you to select this option when using time-based actions, knowing this in advance will help you build solutions via workflow rules more quickly and efficiently.

Rule Criteria

Unlike evaluation criteria, which are comprised of three predefined options, rule criteria are completely wide open and allow for significant flexibility and creativity. Rule criteria equate to the second "gate" in Figure 4-4, which provides an overview of whether corresponding workflow actions are fired by a particular record update.

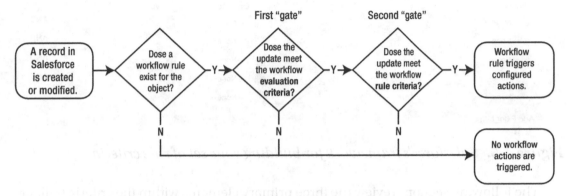

Figure 4-4. *The multiple "gates" that the creation or modification of any record has to pass through before a workflow action will occur*

The rule criteria come into play if and only if one or more active workflow rules exist for the object of the record being updated *and* the evaluation criteria of the workflow rule(s) have been met. The rule criteria that you configure will then be evaluated; if the evaluation deems them to be true, the associated workflow actions will be triggered. Rule criteria can be built by using one of the following tools:

- Criteria builder
- Formula editor

Criteria Builder

The first and probably most commonly used tool available to you when establishing your rule criteria is the standard "criteria builder." There is actually no official name for this element; I am coining the term for the purpose of quickly identifying this option in the workflow rule creation process. You will find the criteria builder used throughout Salesforce, not just in workflow rules. You will see this criteria builder reappear in upcoming chapters for such topics as list views, assignment rules, and escalation rules.

This tool allows you to create one or more statements that can be evaluated as true or false. Figure 4-5 is a view of the criteria builder within the workflow rule framework.

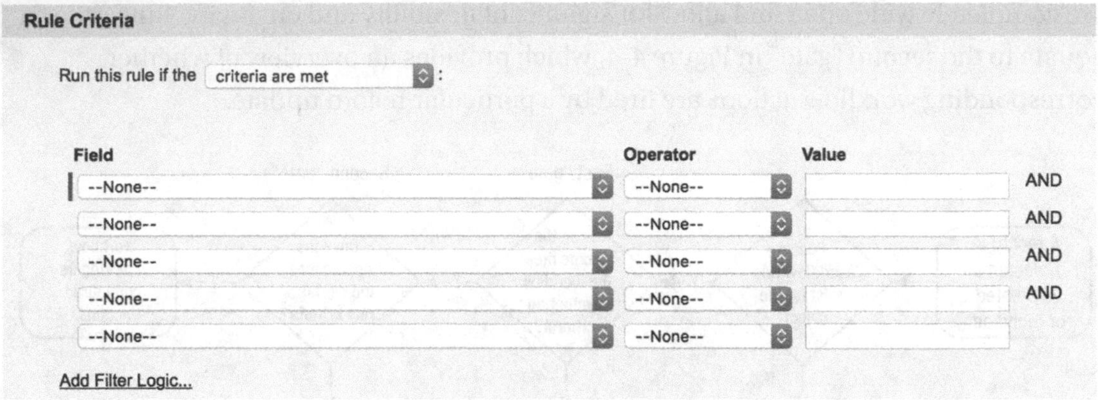

Rule Criteria

Run this rule if the [criteria are met ◊] :

Field	Operator	Value	
--None-- ◊	--None-- ◊		AND
--None-- ◊	--None-- ◊		AND
--None-- ◊	--None-- ◊		AND
--None-- ◊	--None-- ◊		AND
--None-- ◊	--None-- ◊		

Add Filter Logic...

Figure 4-5. *Salesforce's framework for building your set of rule criteria*

The following sections review the three primary elements within the criteria builder tool: *field*, *operator*, and *value*. These will come together to establish one or more statements that will ultimately determine whether or not the workflow actions should occur.

Field

There is more to a rule criteria field selection than you might think. You would be correct to assume that all of the fields on the workflow rule's object would be available for selection. For example, if you are creating a workflow rule for the Opportunity object, you could choose Amount as your field; you could also choose any of the other standard or custom fields on the Opportunity object.

However, there are a number of additional fields that may be available depending on your object and your organization's data model. When creating a workflow rule for a standard object, you may use fields from any objects to which your workflow rule object is related via relationship fields. For example, the Contact object has a standard field (Account Name) that is a Lookup relationship from Contact to Account. As a result, you may use an Account field for selection in your rule criteria statement. Figure 4-6 shows the lookup objects fields available for some of the most commonly used standard objects in Salesforce.

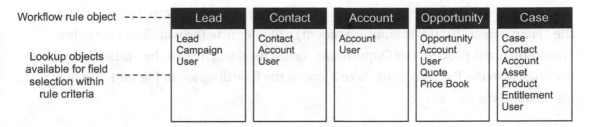

Workflow rule object	Lead	Contact	Account	Opportunity	Case
Lookup objects available for field selection within rule criteria	Lead Campaign User	Contact Account User	Account User	Opportunity Account User Quote Price Book	Case Contact Account Asset Product Entitlement User

Figure 4-6. *Lookup objects available for standard objects. Depending on the object you are using for your workflow rule, you may be able to establish rule criteria from fields on related objects.*

The selection availability differs for custom objects. When creating a workflow rule for a custom object, you may use fields from

1. The object selected for the workflow rule

2. The User object (see the following note)

3. Any object that is the Master object in a Master-Detail relationship with the object selected for the workflow (#1)

Note   The User object is available for selection as the field when using the workflow rule criteria builder. In this context, User represents the Current User (i.e., the User making the actual change to the record).

When you select a field from the same object used for the workflow rule in the criteria builder, the mode of operations is straightforward. Assume you are using the Opportunity object, you would select "Opportunity: Amount" in the Field column and establish that the amount of the Opportunity is less than 100. Your workflow actions will fire if the evaluation criteria are met and the Opportunity amount in the most recent update is less than 100.

However, the flow is not quite the same when you are dealing with related objects, and it is critical to understand the difference. If you select a field from a related object for the field in the workflow rule criteria builder, you are now no longer dealing solely with the workflow rule object. Again, I will use a hypothetical scenario for you to create a workflow rule for the Opportunity object. This time, however, assume your field is the Annual Revenue field on the (Parent) Account object and that your rule criterion is (Account) Annual Revenue > 1,000,000. Obviously, an update to the Account record

147

must take place for the workflow rule to fire. Unlike in the last example, the update to the "Field object" (in this scenario, Account) will *not* cause the workflow rule to fire. To complete the process, the Opportunity record itself will need to be updated to pick up the change to the Parent record. Take a look at the flow diagram in Figure 4-7 to help understand the process.

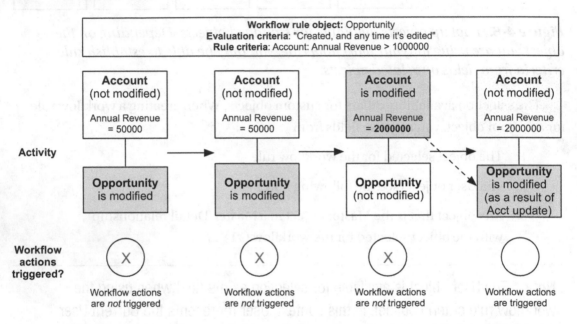

Figure 4-7. *An opportunity workflow rule based on the Annual Revenue field*

It is important to understand how a workflow rule operates when the rule criteria involves a field on a related object. Here, we see that the Opportunity's rule criteria is based on an Account field. Although the rule criteria is technically met when the Account field value is edited accordingly, the workflow actions will not fire until those changes are picked up via an edit of the Opportunity record itself.

The Child Opportunity record does not "know" that the Parent Account record has been updated. As a result, there must be a subsequent update to the Opportunity record to pick up the relevant changes to the Parent Account record. The workflow actions will be triggered at that point.

Note   One difference between the available fields for standard and custom objects in the workflow criteria builder (but not the formula editor) is that Lookup relationship objects on custom objects are *not* available for use; these are only available on standard objects. For example, Account is available in the criteria builder tool when creating a workflow rule for the Contact object; however, Account would not be available in the criteria builder for a workflow rule on a custom object if the Account were related as the Master in a Master-Detail relationship.

Operator

When using the criteria builder, you are provided with an operator list and must select one value from that list to build out a given statement to be evaluated as part of the rule criteria. The list generally overlaps with the operators found within the formula editor with five exceptions: **Starts With**, **Contains**, **Does Not Contain**, **Includes**, and **Excludes**. These operators can be found in the criteria builder but are not present in the formula editor as operators.

However, these operators do have equivalents with the formula editor if you take into consideration individual formula functions and combinations of formula functions. The five exceptions previously mentioned can be represented in formulas. Here is a mapping of the criteria builder operators that are listed earlier and the formulas that can be used in place of them:

- **Starts With:** BEGINS()

- **Contains:** CONTAINS()

- **Does Not Contain:** NOT(CONTAINS())

- **Includes:** INCLUDES()

- **Excludes:** NOT(INCLUDES())

See Chapter 2 for more detail on formula functions. Table 4-3 is a breakdown of operators available in the Picklists in the formula editor and the criteria builder tools.

Table 4-3. *Operators for Building Workflow Rule Criteria Available via the Formula Editor and Criteria Builder*

Comparison of Operator Availability		
Operator	**Formula Editor**	**Criteria Builder**
Add	+	
Subtract	-	
Multiply	*	
Divide	/	
Exponentiation	^	
Open Parenthesis	(	
Close Parenthesis	)	
Concatenate	&	
Equal	=	✓
Not Equal	<>	✓
Less Than	<	✓
Greater Than	>	✓
Less Than or Equal	<=	✓
Greater Than or Equal	>=	✓
And	&&	
Or	||	
Starts With		✓
Contains		✓
Does Not Contain		✓
Includes		✓
Excludes		✓
Within		✓

Value

Once you have selected your field and operator, you'll need to enter a value to complete your statement, which will be evaluated in your evaluation criteria. There are a few considerations you will need to keep in mind when you complete your statement:

1. You do not need to include quotes around text if the string itself does not include a comma, as shown in Figure 4-8.

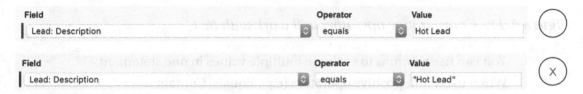

Figure 4-8. *Proper use of quotes in the value field when commas are not present. Quotes around text are unnecessary, unlike within the formula editor, where they are required.*

2. Text is not case sensitive – that is, typing in "Mgr" will also match "mgr," as shown in Figure 4-9.

Field	Operator	Value
Lead: Title	contains	Manager

Title   manager

Figure 4-9. *Evaluation of "manager" is identical to "Manager" within workflow rule criteria*

3. Date format is MM/DD/YYYY (leading zeroes are not required), as in Figure 4-10. The Date/Time format is MM/DD/YYYY HH:MM AM/PM; however, HH:MM AM/PM can be omitted and 12:00 AM will be used.

Field	Operator	Value
Lead: Date Field	equals	10/17/1979

Figure 4-10. *Formatting a date in the criteria builder*

151

4. Comparative operators (e.g., Greater Than) will work with text (e.g., "zebra" would satisfy "greater than aardvark"). Figure 4-11 shows a similar statement applied to the Lead Description field.

Field	Operator	Value
Lead: Description	greater than	a

Description   b   ◯

Figure 4-11. *Comparative operators will work with text*

5. You can use commas to evaluate multiple values in one statement. When used with positive operators (e.g., Equals, Contains, Includes), a comma-separated list of values actually causes the statement to behave differently. For example, take this statement: Last Name = Weinmeister. If I change "Weinmeister" to "Wein,Meister" (disregard the quotes, they would not be included), the statement would not be evaluated as Last Name = "Wein,Meister". Instead, it is evaluated as Last Name = Wein OR Last Name = Meister. Figure 4-12 displays three statements that use commas and their equivalents.

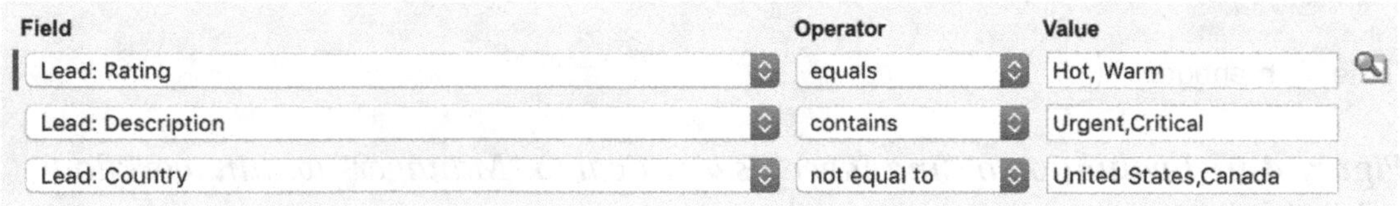

Field	Operator	Value	
Lead: Rating	equals	Hot, Warm	🔍
Lead: Description	contains	Urgent,Critical	
Lead: Country	not equal to	United States,Canada	

Figure 4-12. *Criteria with a comma-separated list of values. Omitting quotes evaluates the comma-separated values as a list; including quotes evaluates the string as one value, even if it includes commas.*

The following statements are pseudo code equivalents for the criteria statements shown in Figure 4-12. Note: "∗" is a wild card.

1. Rating = "Hot" OR Rating = "Warm" (Note: these are picklist values, not freeform text)

2. Description = "∗Urgent∗" OR Description = "∗Critical∗"

3. Country <> "United States" AND Country <> "Canada"

You can and should use quotes within your value in some situations. If you are trying to evaluate a text string that contains a comma, you must surround the full string with quotes. For example, take a hypothetical status field with two values: "Submitted" and "Submitted, Awaiting Payment". Using an input of "Submitted, Awaiting Payment" (in quotes) would only pick up the second of the two values. To consider both Picklist values when using *equals* as the operator, you would enter Submitted, "Submitted, Awaiting Payment" in the Value column. This highlights the need to be very careful with your syntax and pay close attention to detail.

In addition to understanding how the field, operator, and value work together, you should be aware of two additional features: First, you may add rows to the default five that are displayed. You may have up to 25 rows of criteria, although this number may increase at some point in the future.

Next, Salesforce offers what is referred to as "filter logic" to provide even more granularity to your criteria. By default, you are creating AND statements. For example, if you create five criteria, they are interpreted as 1 AND 2 AND 3 AND 4 AND 5. If one of the five statements is not true, then the workflow actions will not be triggered. However, with filter logic, you can replace the ANDs with ORs and combine the statements in logical groupings for evaluation. Figure 4-13 applies filter logic to these criteria.

Filter Logic:
(1 AND 3) OR 2

Figure 4-13. *Filter logic applied to rule criteria*

Figure 4-14 shows the criteria in Figure 4-13 from a visual perspective.

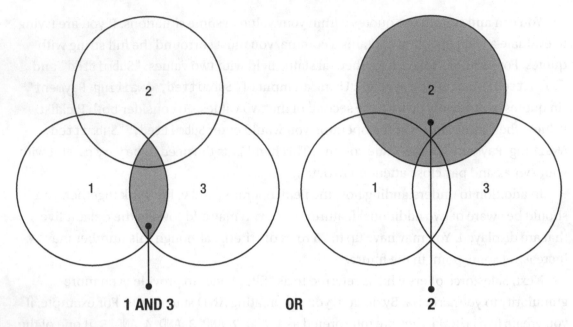

Figure 4-14. *A visual interpretation of rule criteria in Figure 4-13: (1 AND 3) OR 2*

Formula Editor

Workflow rules are one of many features that utilize the formula editor that was covered in previous chapters. All of the fundamentals about formulas and the corresponding formula editor apply to the formula editor associated with workflow rules, although there are some differences between what is available in this tool for formula fields and workflow rules. When building a formula for a workflow rule, you may only use the previously mentioned advanced formula editor; the basic formula editor is not an option. Additionally, some functions that are available for formula fields are not available for workflow rules.

By switching to the formula editor, you potentially gain access to additional fields. If you use the criteria builder, you cannot access fields via Lookup relationships from standard to custom objects, or Lookup relationships from custom objects to any other objects. There is no way around this restriction and that factor could be fairly limiting depending on what you need to include as criteria. Fortunately, you can access both if you decide to use the formula editor.

Another significant difference in how the formula editor is used for workflow rules (and many other areas of the platform) compared to formula fields is that the formula you build here *must be a Boolean statement*; the evaluation must produce a true or false result. If your formula evaluates to true, your workflow actions will be triggered, but they will not be triggered if your formula evaluates to false. You cannot select from the slew of return types that are available when creating a Formula field; you are essentially forced to select "Checkbox," which is the only Boolean option. For example, if you tried to create a non-Boolean formula with a return type of Text, you would see this error message:

```
Error: Formula result is data type (Text), incompatible with expected data
type (true or false).
```

The following formula *would not* be valid for use as the criteria in a workflow rule:

```
IF(
Account.AnnualRevenue > 1000000 && Amount < 100,
"Review Opportunity for potential upsell",
""
)
```

The following formula *would* be valid for use as the criteria in a workflow rule:

```
IF(
Account.AnnualRevenue > 1000000 && Amount < 100,
true,
false
)
```

Once you understand how to create your criteria for a workflow rule, you will need to decide whether to use the criteria builder or the formula editor. Part of the decision will be based on your comfort level, as the criteria builder is definitely easier to use. However, since formulas are such an integral part of Salesforce development without code, creating a workflow rule may be a good opportunity to explore the formula editor. Take a look at Table 4-4 for suggestions on which tool to use to develop criteria.

Table 4-4. *Guideline for Selecting Which Tool to Use for Developing Workflow Rule Criteria*

Tools for Developing Workflow Rule Criteria		
Criteria Characteristics	**Criteria Builder**	**Formula Editor**
Statements/conditions are simple and clear	✓	
Statements include a list of values for the same field/operator	✓	
Requires access to a field via Lookup from a standard to custom object		✓
Requires access to a field via Lookup from a custom object		✓
Data manipulation/transformation required		✓
Use of Salesforce functions		✓

Criteria developed via the criteria builder are generally easier to maintain; however, your decision should be primarily based on your ability to meet business needs, not the ability to easily maintain the solution. If your solution does not achieve what your business requires, the ease of maintenance becomes irrelevant.

Workflow Actions

The last, but certainly not least, element of workflow rules is the resulting action or actions that occur. Everything you have done up to this point has determined whether an action will be triggered. Workflow actions determine what will actually occur; these handy helpers give you the automation in business process automation. Like with so many other features, Salesforce provides options and significant flexibility here, as well. You can configure what type of action is automated, when the action will occur, and where in the data model it will take place.

Action Types

When you build a workflow rule, you have the option of creating any of a few unique types of actions:

- Field Update
- Task

- Email Alert
- Outbound Message

Field Update

Based on my personal experience, I would say that the Field Update action is undoubtedly the most commonly utilized workflow action type. From a development perspective, you have the most to gain by learning about this type of workflow action; as a result, I will spend much more time diving into the details of Field Updates than I will on the details of the other action types. A Field Update allows you to automatically modify a newly created record or an existing record based on the state of the record data and your workflow rule criteria. Figures 4-15 and 4-16 are examples.

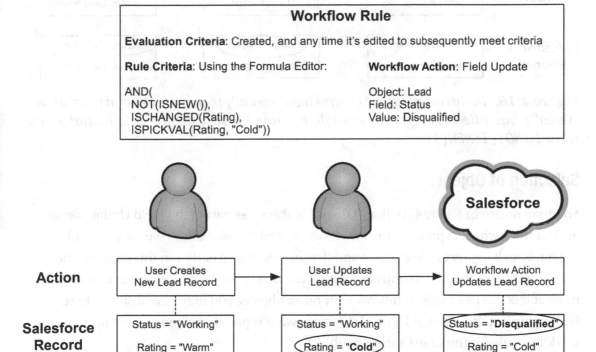

Figure 4-15. *An example of the Status field being updated automatically via a workflow rule*

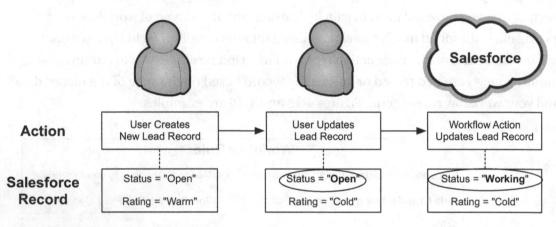

Figure 4-16. *In this example, the criteria were partially met upon creation (Status =* *"Open"), but failed to trigger the workflow action because the formula excludes new records: NOT(ISNEW())*

Selection of Object

You may notice in Figure 4-16 that "Object" is shown as part of the Field Update details and wonder why it is present since we have created this workflow rule for the Lead object. Recall my terms *Base object* and *Action object* from earlier in this chapter; the selection here is the Action object, not the Base object. In the case of the Lead object, you must select the Lead object; however, for other objects, you may have a choice here. For example, take a look at Figure 4-17 to see what is possible when you create a workflow rule for the Case Comment object.

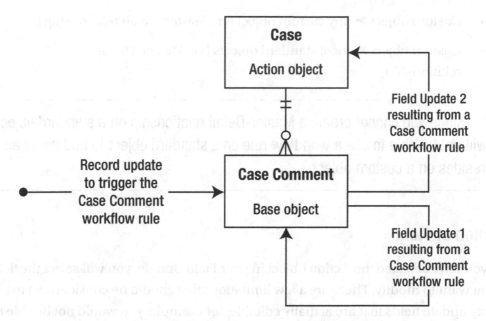

Figure 4-17. *Depending on the object you are using and the relationship fields that exist on it, you may be able to update multiple records within one workflow rule.*

Not only can you have multiple workflow actions occur based on the same update, you can actually update two different objects: Case Comment *and* Case. As you would expect, this is only available on objects that have eligible relationships with other objects. Specifically, the base object must have a specific relationship with the Action object. If a standard object is your Base object, certain standard objects may be available, as shown in the following workflows. If a custom object is your Base object, only objects to which your Base Object is related via a Master-Detail relationship are available. This functionality is referred to by Salesforce as "Cross-object workflow" and can be extremely powerful in automating your business. Cross-object workflows are available for the following object relationships:

- Case Comment ➤ Case

- Email ➤ Case

- Opportunity Product ➤ Opportunity

- Opportunity ➤ Account

- Custom object ➤ any custom object (via Master-Detail relationship)
- Custom object ➤ most standard objects (via Master-Detail relationship)

Note   Since you cannot create a Master-Detail relationship on a standard object, you will not be able to use a workflow rule on a standard object to update a field that resides on a custom object.

Selection of Field

Once you have selected the Action object in your Field Update, you will select the field that you want to modify. There are a few limitations that should be considered. First, you can only update fields that are actually editable; for example, you would not be able to update a formula field. Second, a workflow rule trumps object and field-level security settings. In other words, a workflow rule configured to update Field B based on a change to Field A will not be prevented if the acting user does not have the ability to directly edit Field B. Likewise, a Read-Only setting on a page layout for a particular field will not prevent a workflow rule from updating that field if that page layout is invoked.

Configuration of Field Value

This is where things get very interesting. In Figures 4-15 and 4-16, I used simple scenarios to show how a Field Update could be used to change the Status field on the Lead object from "New" to "Disqualified" or "Working." In those examples, I would set one of the Picklist values as the value for the Field Update and be done. As you previously learned, there are numerous field types in Salesforce; each of these has its own particular behavior when it comes to Field Updates. Field update options differ by field type. Table 4-5 conveys the type of updates that are possible for each field type.

Table 4-5. *Field Update Options by Field Type*

Field Type	Ways to Update
Numeric (all)	Set the field as blank OR update via formula.
Text (all)	Set the field as blank OR update via formula.
Date (all)	Set the field as blank OR update via formula.
Phone	Set the field as blank OR update via formula.
Email	Set the field as blank OR update via formula.
Checkbox	Set the field to True or False.
Picklist	Select the preceding or following value in the list OR specify a value from the list.
Picklist (Multi-Select)	Cannot update.
Formula	Cannot update.
Owner	Specify the Owner.
Lookup	Cannot update, with the exception of Owner.
Master-Detail	Update a field on the Master object according to the previous update options.

Reevaluation of Workflow Rules

Selecting "Reevaluate Workflow Rules After Field Change" (see Figure 4-18) will cause Salesforce to reevaluate your workflow rules.

Field Update Edit	Save	Save & New	Cancel	

Identification   **I** = Required Information

Name	Set Case to Escalated
Unique Name	Set_Case_to_Escalated [i]
Namespace Prefix	pwtest
Description	
Object	Case
Protected Component	☐
Field to Update	Case: Escalated
Field Data Type	Checkbox
Re-evaluate Workflow Rules after Field Change	☐ [i]

Figure 4-18. *"Re-evaluate Workflow Rules after Field Change" can be an extremely useful setting*

You will first want to check if one of your workflow rules is dependent on a workflow action from another workflow rule. In that scenario, leaving this field unchecked will prevent the dependent workflow rule from meeting the configured criteria. "Workflow #2" in Figure 4-19 shows an example of what can result from checking this field (i.e., setting it to "true").

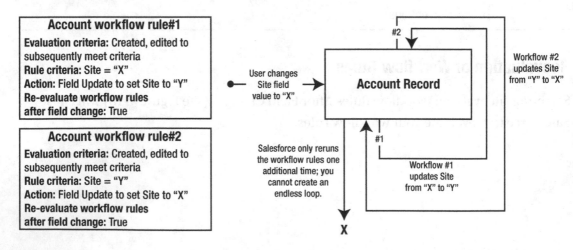

Figure 4-19. *Although it may seem like creating an endless loop is very simple to do with workflow rules, Salesforce has built-in protection against doing so. Workflow rules can be reevaluated only one additional time based on the original event or action.*

Additional Thoughts on Field Updates

As you take in an inordinate amount of information related to Field Updates, it may be a challenge to see how powerful your options really are. The fact that you can use a formula to set a number of the field types gives you extreme flexibility in your business process automation, and you don't need a line of code to make it happen. Think about this: you can determine if an automated action occurs based on the state of your record and then you can configure a dynamic update based on a formula. You have already seen what formulas can do – they allow you to pull from other fields or even other objects and return a value based on a defined condition. Put this all together and you can perform quite a bit of automation in your Field Update.

New Task

The second type of automated action you can create via workflow rules is significantly different than the Field Update I previously discussed. Here, you can trigger the creation of a new task record, as shown in Figure 4-20. This is fairly straightforward: you specify the values of a number of task fields to be populated in the new task record. There are a couple fields worth calling out, specifically:

- **Due Date**: Like a Time Trigger, you can set the Due Date relative to any Date or Date/Time field on the record.
- **Protected Component**: Selecting this field prevents the component from being referenced or linked to by components created in a subscriber org. It allows a developer to delete the component in a future release without adversely affecting any Apex test results.

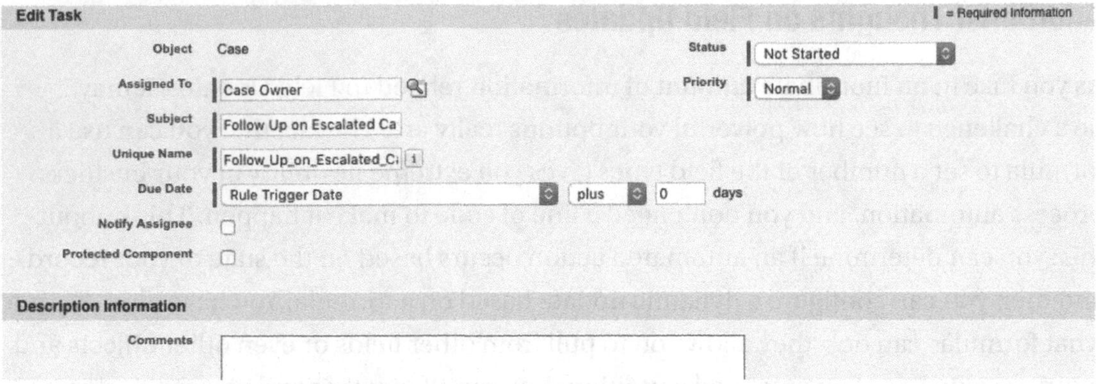

Edit Task				**I** = Required Information
Object	Case	Status	Not Started	
Assigned To	Case Owner 🔍	Priority	Normal	
Subject	Follow Up on Escalated Ca			
Unique Name	Follow_Up_on_Escalated_C ⓘ			
Due Date	Rule Trigger Date	plus	0	days
Notify Assignee	☐			
Protected Component	☐			
Description Information				
Comments				

Figure 4-20. *Options when creating a new task via a workflow rule*

Email Alert

The Email Alert action allows you to automate the sending of an email to one or more recipients within a workflow rule. This is a simple, but very useful, feature to utilize within Salesforce. You will find that modifications to your records will often require notifying someone of the change. One aspect of Email Alerts that is particularly beneficial is that you can send an Email Alert to an email address directly; in other words, the recipients do not have to be Salesforce Users. Of course, Salesforce has provided a simple way to reference contacts related to the applicable record. You can reference any email field (standard or custom) or even reference a contact in a particular role (e.g., a Case Team Member).

To build out your Email Alert, you'll have to create your Email Template in advance. Once it's completed, you can configure an Email Alert to be triggered as part of your workflow rule. Figure 4-21 shows the Email Alert configuration screen.

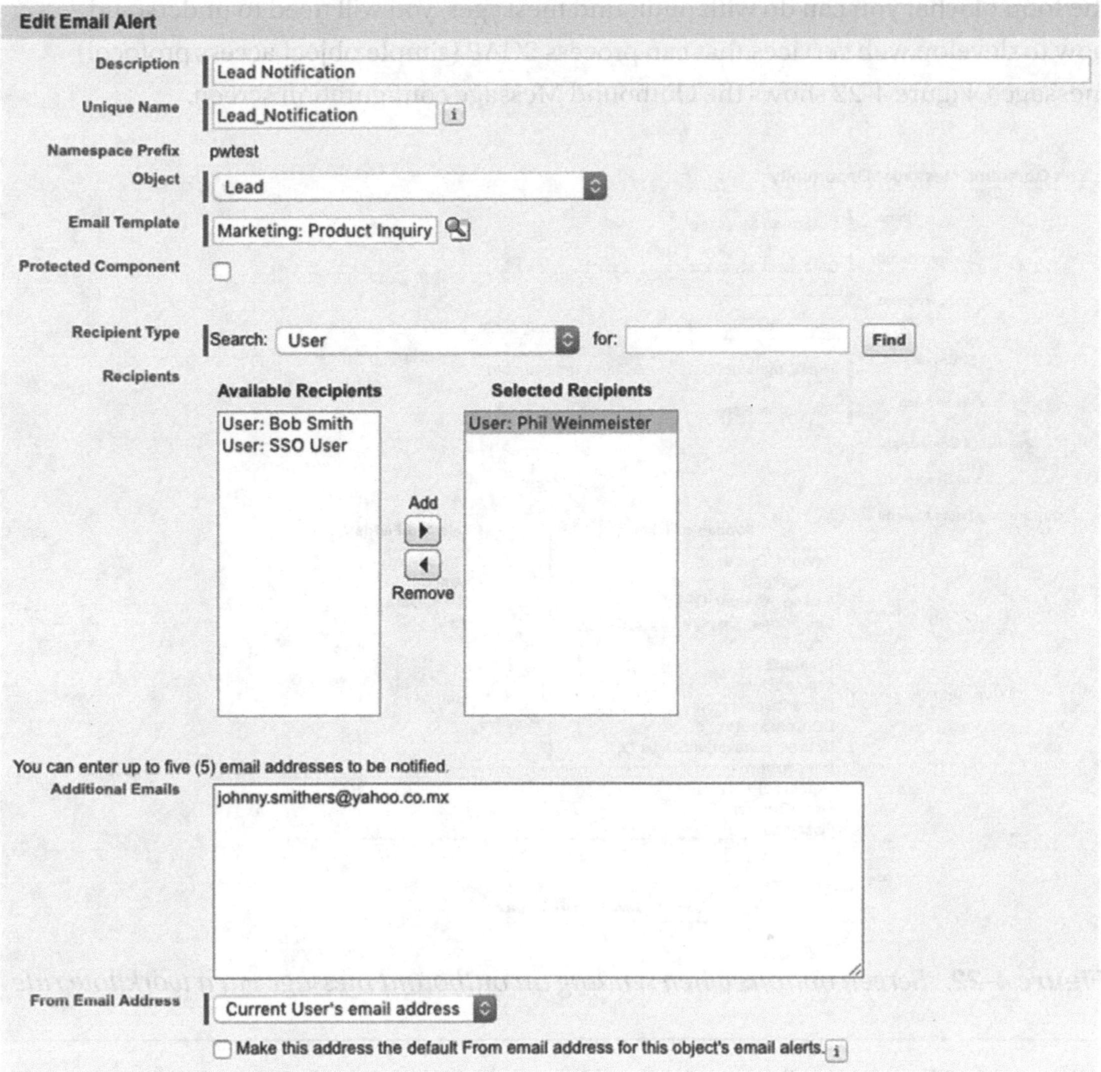

Edit Email Alert

Description	Lead Notification
Unique Name	Lead_Notification [i]
Namespace Prefix	pwtest
Object	Lead
Email Template	Marketing: Product Inquiry [🔍]
Protected Component	☐
Recipient Type	Search: User for: [Find]

Recipients

Available Recipients		Selected Recipients
User: Bob Smith User: SSO User	**Add** [▶] [◀] Remove	User: Phil Weinmeister

You can enter up to five (5) email addresses to be notified.

Additional Emails

johnny.smithers@yahoo.co.mx

From Email Address   Current User's email address

☐ Make this address the default From email address for this object's email alerts. [i]

Figure 4-21. Screen options for creating an Email Alert via a workflow rule

Outbound Message

Outbound Message is a workflow action type that allows you to send data from your record to an outside system for processing. From a Salesforce perspective, this is essentially a "send and forget" function; the actual processing of the sent data, including any responses, acknowledgements, logs, and so on, will be developed outside of your Salesforce org. Here, we decide whether an outbound message will be sent (via the evaluation and rule criteria) and what the content of that message will be. To complete the loop of what you can do with outbound messages, you will need to understand how to develop web services that can process SOAP (simple object access protocol) messages. Figure 4-22 shows the Outbound Message configuration screen.

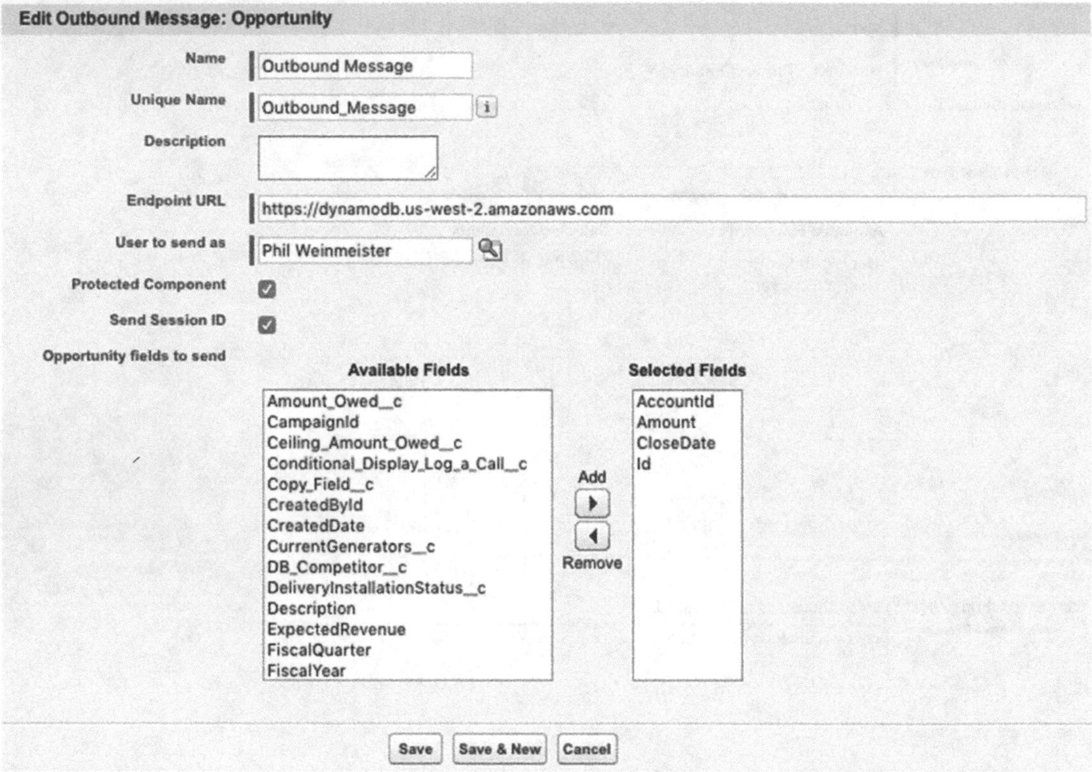

Edit Outbound Message: Opportunity

Name	Outbound Message
Unique Name	Outbound_Message [i]
Description	
Endpoint URL	https://dynamodb.us-west-2.amazonaws.com
User to send as	Phil Weinmeister
Protected Component	☑
Send Session ID	☑

Opportunity fields to send

Available Fields
- Amount_Owed__c
- CampaignId
- Ceiling_Amount_Owed__c
- Conditional_Display_Log_a_Call__c
- Copy_Field__c
- CreatedById
- CreatedDate
- CurrentGenerators__c
- DB_Competitor__c
- DeliveryInstallationStatus__c
- Description
- ExpectedRevenue
- FiscalQuarter
- FiscalYear

Add ▶
◀ Remove

Selected Fields
- AccountId
- Amount
- CloseDate
- Id

[Save] [Save & New] [Cancel]

Figure 4-22. *Screen options when sending an outbound message via a workflow rule*

Note   A "Flow Trigger" was introduced as a pilot Workflow Action a few years ago. However, the pilot is now closed and the feature never saw a GA release.

Action Timing

So far, I have spoken about field updates in the context of immediate activity: a record is modified and that modification triggers a system update that immediately follows the original action. However, there is another option called "time-based workflow actions" that completely changes that paradigm. Time-based workflow actions allow you to control *when* your configured actions occur; this is defined as your "time trigger." You can configure the following within a time trigger:

- Any Date or Date/Time field

- Whether the action will occur before or after the corresponding Date or Date/Time field

- The time gap between the Date field value and the action; from 1 hour to 999 days

Figure 4-23 explains each of the available time trigger options.

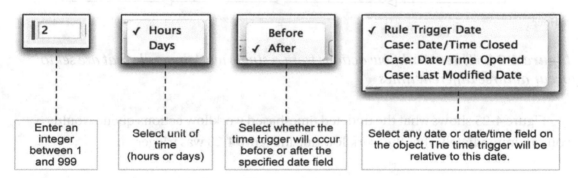

Time Trigger Options

Figure 4-23. *You can configure four settings that establish how your time triggers will behave*

Note   A time-based workflow action will not be created if the time trigger is based on a Date or Date/Time field that is blank on the modified record. For example, let's assume I have a time trigger that performs an action 5 days before my custom "Expected Completion Date" field value. If the Expected Completion Date field value is blank, no action will be created.

In the example shown in Figure 4-24, one workflow rule has three resulting actions taking place: field update #1 immediately, field update #2 an hour after the action, and email alert #1 3 hours after the original action.

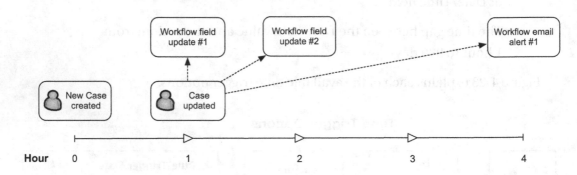

Figure 4-24.   *Three Workflow actions from a single workflow rule that are set to occur at three different times*

Figure 4-25 shows what the updated time-based workflow actions queue would contain immediately after the workflow rule in Figure 4-23 was triggered.

	Record Name	Object	Workflow Rule Name	Scheduled Date	Created By	Created Date
☐	00001029	Case	Case Workflow with Time Triggers	8/14/2018 10:30 AM	Weinmeister, Phil	8/14/2018 9:30 AM
☐	00001029	Case	Case Workflow with Time Triggers	8/14/2018 12:30 PM	Weinmeister, Phil	8/14/2018 9:30 AM

Figure 4-25.   *Time-based workflow actions queue where a Case workflow rule has been triggered on 8/14/18 at 9:30 AM*

Figure 4-26 also has multiple future updates. However, in this case, they are not based on the time of the update; they are based on a Date/Time field on the object, which takes place 1 hour and 1 day before the corresponding Date/Time value.

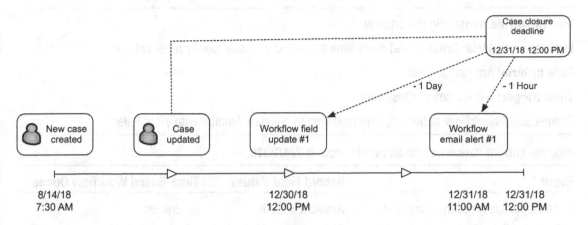

Figure 4-26. *This workflow rule uses a time trigger based on a Date/Time field that is on the record instead of the Rule Trigger Date value*

Figure 4-27 shows what the time-based workflow queue actually looks like while the actions are pending.

Record Name	Object	Workflow Rule Name	Scheduled Date	Created By	Created Date
00001024	Case	Case Workflow Rule with Time Triggers	12/30/2018 12:00 PM	Weinmeister, Phil	8/14/2018 8:38 AM
00001024	Case	Case Workflow Rule with Time Triggers	12/31/2018 11:00 AM	Weinmeister, Phil	8/14/2018 8:38 AM

Figure 4-27. *Time-based workflow queue showing the pending actions from the example in Figure 4-26*

You have seen what happens initially with a time-based workflow rule; the corresponding time-based actions are created and scheduled relative to the time trigger. However, you should also be familiar with the rule's behavior after the actions are first created. Table 4-6 presents an example of a time-based workflow rule that goes through multiple modifications.

Table 4-6. *Breakdown of How Changes to a Record Are Handled by a Workflow Rule*

Example of Opportunity Workflow Rule with Time-Based Workflow Action

Workflow rule name: Big Opportunity

Evaluation criteria: Created, and every time it's edited to subsequently meet criteria

Rule criteria: Amount > 1000

Time trigger: 5 Days before Close Date

Time-based workflow action: Update next step to "Review Amount with VP of Sales"

Assume current date on which all events occur is **7/4/2019**.

Event	Record Field Values	Time-Based Workflow Queue
1. An Opportunity record is created. The workflow rule's evaluation criteria and rule criteria ***are not*** satisfied.	**Amount** = 500 **Close date** = 7/31/2019	No entries
2. The Amount on the Opportunity record is modified. The workflow rule's evaluation criteria and rule criteria ***are*** now satisfied.	**Amount** = 3300 **Close date** = 7/31/2019	Automatically added entry: **Workflow rule name:** Big Opportunity **Scheduled date:** 7/26/2019 12:00 AM
3. The Close Date on the Opportunity record is modified. The workflow rule's evaluation criteria and rule criteria ***are still*** satisfied.	**Amount** = 3300 **Close date** = 8/31/2019	Automatically updated entry: **Workflow rule name:** Big Opportunity **Scheduled date:** 8/26/2019 12:00 AM
4. The Close Date on the Opportunity record is modified. The workflow rule's evaluation criteria and rule criteria ***are still*** satisfied.	**Amount** = 3300 **Close date** = 7/6/2019	Automatically updated entry: **Workflow rule name:** Big Opportunity **Scheduled date:** 7/1/2019 12:00 AM
5. The Amount on the Opportunity is modified. The workflow rule's evaluation criteria and rule criteria ***are no longer*** satisfied.	**Amount** = 800 **Close date** = 7/6/2019	Entry removed

To explain why the time-based workflow queue was updated as described in Table 4-6, here are some additional details:

1. The created Opportunity does not meet the workflow rule criteria, so no action is triggered.

    The created Opportunity now meets the criteria. Since this workflow rule has a time-based workflow action, the corresponding action is added to the time-based workflow queue based on the configured time trigger (5 days before Close Date, or "7/31/2019 12:00 AM – 5 days").

2. Since the time trigger's Date field was modified, the entry in the time-based workflow queue is also updated accordingly. The entry will now be set to 5 days before 8/31/2019, instead of 5 days before 7/31/2019.

3. Since the time trigger's Date field was modified, the entry in the time-based workflow queue is also updated accordingly. The entry will now be set to 5 days before 7/6/2019, instead of 5 days before 8/31/2019. Note here that the time trigger is actually in the past (current date is assumed to be 7/4/2019). The action will occur the next time a batch is executed (see "Note" for additional details).

4. If a record with a pending time-based workflow action is modified and no longer satisfies the original evaluation and rule criteria, the corresponding time-based workflow queue entry will be removed completely and the previously pending action will not occur.

Note   It is critical to be aware of how time-based workflow actions are processed. These actions are executed in batches, not individually. This means that your time-based workflow actions will likely not occur precisely at the configured time. Salesforce does not publish how frequently batches are processed. In my experience, batches have been executed every 15 minutes starting on the hour (that is not official and may change at any time). Consider the practical impact to your rules. If you have an action queued for 1:14 PM, it would occur one minute later at 1:15 PM. However, if you have an action queued for 1:16 PM, it will likely not occur for 14 additional minutes (at 1:30 PM). Make sure to thoroughly test what you've built and do not use time-based workflow rules if absolute precision is a business requirement.

Building a Workflow Rule and Actions: Step by Step

You have learned the low-level details of workflow rules, but the main goal is to put this knowledge into practice. To help you piece it all together, I will provide a quick recap of the steps to create an effective workflow rule.

Preparation Step: Create Relevant Custom Fields

As is the case with formula fields, you will need to have your data model properly established before you begin creating workflow rules. Most important, any relevant Lookup or Master-Detail relationships fields will need to be created. Additionally, you will need to create any custom fields that you want to update via workflow actions or use as part of your criteria. As a reminder, you'll need to use the following navigation path:

- **For standard objects**: Setup ➤ Customize ➤ [Your Object]} ➤ Fields ➤ New

- **For custom objects**: Setup ➤ Create ➤ Objects ➤ [Your Object] ➤ New Custom Field

It's time to create the actual workflow rule. Navigate to **Setup ➤ Create ➤ Workflow & Approvals ➤ Workflow Rules ➤ New Rule**. The process is as follows:

1. **Create the workflow rule**: To do so, you'll need to take four additional steps:

   a. Identify the Base object.

   b. Provide a name and description for the workflow rule.

   c. Select the evaluation criteria.

   d. Establish the rule criteria, whether via the criteria builder or the formula editor.

2. **Add time triggers**: Do you plan on having any actions that occur at some point in the future? If so, you'll need to create the corresponding time triggers. If you're still in the workflow rule creation process, you'll simply need to click "Add Time Trigger." Create one or more of these time triggers and proceed.

3. **Add workflow actions**: Add your desired workflow actions to your workflow rule. You'll first need to determine whether the actions need to be immediate or time based and then click on the corresponding button. From there, you'll need to select which type of workflow action you want to create. Select your action and follow the steps to completely build it out.

Note   Once you have created a Field Update, New Task, Email Alert, or Outbound Message action, you can reuse it in future workflow rules. To do so, select "Add Existing Action" for your action type and select your desired action.

---

4. **Activate**: Click on the Activate button to make your workflow rule live!

Workflow Rules: Real-World Examples

Let's look at some hypothetical real-world scenarios in which you might want to utilize workflow rules.

Scenario 1: Lead Assessment

Let's say your organization sells consulting services and manages its business through Salesforce, and some of your leads come in from the Web. Since web leads are manually qualified before they are created, they do not initially have a rating value. However, say you wanted to automatically set the rating on certain leads that come in through the Web, specifically to identify web leads that communicate a near-future project start. The following components would be needed:

- **Custom fields**

    - *Projected Project Start (Picklist)*

    - *Picklist values*: 0–1 month, 1–3 months, 3–6 months, 6–12 months, 12–24 months, 24+ months.

        - You create the "Projected Project Start" field to convey the likely timing of the need for consulting services.

- **Evaluation criteria:** Evaluate the rule when a record is: Created

- **Rule criteria:** Run this rule if the following criteria are met:

  - *Lead*: Lead Source *equals* Web

  - *Lead*: Projected Project Start *equals* 0-1 month

- **Immediate workflow actions**

  - *Field update*: Update Rating

  - *Object*: Lead

  - *Field to update*: Lead: Rating

  - *New field value*: Hot

- **Time-dependent workflow actions:** None

Summary

You just created a workflow rule that looks for any web-sourced leads that inquire about engaging your consulting services in the next few weeks. If a lead meets the specified criteria, the rule automatically increases the rating to "Hot"; this will allow users to see this new lead via a list view of open leads with a rating of "Hot" and take action quickly.

Scenario 2: Opportunity Probability

Say you have configured your sales process and set an appropriate Probability percentage for each corresponding Opportunity Stage. However, you feel that some sales situations warrant a higher probability than what you have assigned. One scenario in particular is an open Opportunity associated with an Account within a certain industry (government) with which an Opportunity has closed in the past year. These variables point to a higher probability of closure. As a result, you set up a custom field to track your "True Probability" and update it based on a workflow rule.

This Opportunity Probably scenario involves multiple objects, so read carefully. Both workflow rules are based on the Opportunity object. The first workflow rule updates the Parent Account record and the second rule includes the related Account record in the rule criteria. The following components apply:

Part I: Workflow Rule to Update Custom Date Field on Account

- **Custom fields**

  - *Last Won Opportunity Date (Date)*: You create this field to capture the date of the most recent Closed/Won Opportunity. Note: This custom field should be on the Account object, not the Opportunity object.

- **Evaluation criteria**: Evaluate the rule when a record is: Created, as well as any time it's edited to subsequently meet criteria

- **Rule criteria**: Run this rule if the following criterion is met:

  - *Opportunity*: Won **equals** true

- **Immediate workflow actions**

  - *Field update*: Update Last Won Opportunity Date

  - *Object*: Opportunity

  - *Field to update*: Account: Last Won Opportunity Date

  - Use a formula to set the new value: CloseDate

- **Time-dependent workflow actions:** None

Part II: Workflow Rule to Update True Probability on Opportunity

- **Custom fields**: *True Probability (Percent)*: You create this field to convey a more accurate probability of the Opportunity (without overwriting or removing the standard Probability field).

- **Evaluation criteria**: Evaluate the rule when a record is: Created, as well as any time it's edited.

- **Rule criteria**: Run this rule if the following formula evaluates to true:

```
AND(
  ISPICKVAL(Account.Industry, "Government"),
  Amount > 1000,
  (TODAY() - Account.Last_Won_Opportunity_Date__c) < 365
)
```

- **Immediate workflow actions**

  - *Field Update*: Update Last Won Opportunity Date

  - *Object*: Opportunity

  - *Field to Update*: Opportunity: True Probability

  - Use a formula to set the new value: MAX(0.9, Probability *1.2)

Note   In Scenario 2, assume that you don't want the probability of an open Opportunity to exceed 90 percent so you cap it accordingly. You can achieve this limit by utilizing the MAX( ) function in your workflow action.

- **Time-dependent workflow actions**: None

Scenario 3: Case Escalation

Perhaps your customers do not always accurately communicate the real reason for submitting a Case and your organization has, unfortunately, had an issue with certain urgent Cases slipping through the cracks as a result. You have noticed a correlation between the presence of a few certain keywords in the Description field and requests for subscription cancellations. To address the issue, you want to escalate Cases with any of those particular keywords in the Description field. Additionally, you want to provide a custom visual indicator to appear on the Case Detail page that will show a different image for Open/Non-Escalated, Open/Escalated, and Closed Cases. Additionally, if the Case is still open, you want an email to be sent out 2 hours after the Case is created as a follow-up to make sure that the Case is closed promptly. The following elements apply

- **Custom fields**: Health Status Indicator (formula):

```
IF(
 IsClosed,
 IMAGE("img/msg_icons/confirm32.png", "Closed"),
 IF(
 IsEscalated,
 IMAGE("/img/msg_icons/error32.png", "Escalated"),
```

```
IMAGE("/img/msg_icons/warning32.png", "Open")
 )
)
```

This formula will display a visual indicator to represent Case status, as in Figure 4-28.

Health Status Indicator

Figure 4-28. *Your Health Status Indicator field*

Note   You may notice that the images in your formula are not external.
They are actually from a little-known library of built-in icon images that you can
use. However, the images are not guaranteed to always be around, so keep that
in mind.

- **Evaluation criteria**: Evaluate the rule when a record is Created, as well as any time it's edited to subsequently meet criteria.

- **Rule criteria**: Run this rule if the following criteria are met:

  - Case: Description *contains* Cancel,Quit,Sue,Refund.

  - Case: Closed *equals* false.

- **Immediate workflow actions**

  - *Field Update*: Update Escalated

  - *Object*: Case

  - *Field to Update*: Case: Escalated

  - *Set to*: True

- **Time triggers**: Two hours after rule trigger date

- **Time-dependent workflow actions**

  - *Email Alert*: `Alerts escalations team`

  - *Email Template*: `Potential Cancellation Case`

  - *Recipients*: `Director, Customer Service AND Escalations Queue`

Recap

In this chapter, you have learned how to automate your business processes within Salesforce by leveraging Workflow. As you can see, you have a significant amount of flexibility to build efficiency and productivity into your applications using "clicks, not code." With the right preparation, some creativity, and a little hard work, you can ease the burden on your employees and make your system data much more meaningful. Make sure to plan out your workflow rules carefully and test them extensively and you'll be able to move your business forward with a notable degree of efficiency.

CHAPTER 5

Supporting Your Business with Validation Rules

To be a successful system administrator, consultant, analyst, or developer, you must keep the needs of your users at the forefront of your decision-making and provide them with the ability to effectively carry out their job. However, while users should retain a critical position in your thought process, they are not perfect, either. A reality with which you are probably all too familiar is that the users of any system, including `Salesforce`, don't always follow the rules. Whether purposeful or not, users' actions within the system sometimes fail to align with their expected behavior. Fortunately, `Salesforce` provides validation rules to support a meaningful, synergistic existence of users and the real-world system that they use. Validation rules are specified conditions that allow you to enforce your business rules of operation and guide your users to interact with the system in a beneficial way.

Thus far, I have discussed a number of possibilities and tools available to you when building solutions within `Salesforce`; I've covered objects, fields, relationships, functions, formulas, and workflow rules and the role they play in declarative development. Now it's time to shift gears and discuss how to keep your users on the right track when using the system. When you don't use validation rules, you grant your users the ability to openly create and modify records without restriction, within the parameters of their configured security and system settings. When you do use validation rules, you can enforce your business rules and provide helpful feedback to users along the way. By the end of this chapter, you will

- Understand the basics of validation rules within Saleforce and why they are valuable
- Know when to apply validation rules to your business processes

179

© Philip Weinmeister 2019
P. Weinmeister, *Practical Salesforce Development Without Code*,
https://doi.org/10.1007/978-1-4842-4871-3_5

- Be able to create relevant and effective validation rules within your Salesforce org

- Be familiar with various considerations that should be made when creating validation rules

A Clear Definition of Validation Rules

Before diving into the details of creating effective validation rules, I want to help you understand exactly what they are . . . and what they are not. Validation rules are defined criteria-based error conditions of specified data. When configured as a validation rule, a once-allowed data state immediately becomes invalid. Take a look at the following example (Figure 5-1). We see a sequence of actions, including the creation of a validation rule with the following criteria: Field X = "ABC." At first, Field X on the Contact object does not have a validation rule; this allows for a field value of "ABC." However, once the validation rule is created for Field X, the field value is restricted across all Contact records. In this case, the rule prevents a value of "ABC."

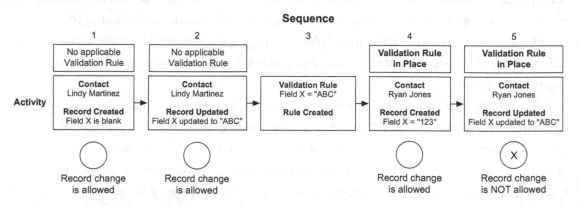

Figure 5-1. *Here, the addition of a validation rule to the Contact object prevents an action that was previously allowed by identifying a particular field value as invalid.*

Figure 5-1 shows a simple validation rule that identifies one specific value as invalid for a particular field. This is about as basic as it gets; as you'll see, the formula editor can be used to define your criteria, significantly opening up your options when creating rules.

You may be wondering about the format of the validation rule in the figure: Shouldn't it be Field X <> "ABC" to capture the fact that Field X should not equate to the banned value of "ABC"? This observation leads us to the first key takeaway in understanding validation rules: They are error conditions and define the *disallowed* "space" within your system. They are not a description of your proper business modus operandi. Figure 5-2 shows a comparison of two similar validation rules and how they correspond to a real-world business rule.

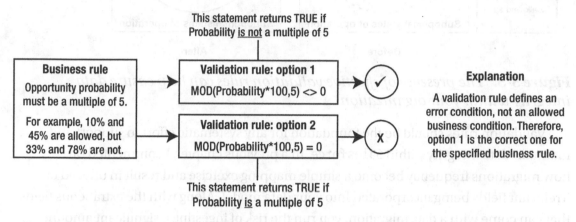

Figure 5-2. *Two opposite validation rules for the same business rule. While the second may appear to be what is desired, as it mirrors your business rule, the first is correct. You define the error condition, not the business rule.*

To solidify this concept, I'd like to take a step back and look at a Salesforce org as a whole and how validation rules come into play. Take a look at the image in Figure 5-3. The squares contain all possible states of your data based on the data model that you have created. The inside of the circles represent the desired states of your data based on your business processes, and the outside represents the undesired states of your data that go against your organization's business rules. The validation rules you build will allow you to prevent those undesired states by invalidating them with applicable criteria.

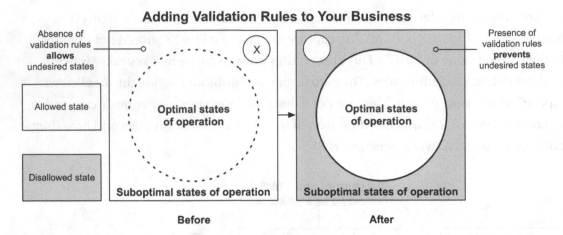

Figure 5-3. *The presence of effective validation rules can help ensure data integrity within your organization*

Validation rules should be the foundation for any systematic effort to support and maintain data integrity within Salesforce. In a previous chapter, I commented on how migrations frequently become a simple mapping exercise and result in unused or irrelevant fields being incorporated into your data model. Along with the extraneous fields that can come with a data migration, you run the risk of ingesting a significant amount of irrelevant, incorrect, or unproductive data in the process. Properly created validation rules can prove extremely valuable when importing data. While it may increase the effort required to carry out the import process, having clean data in your Salesforce org will pay off in spades for your users and for you. See Figure 5-4 for a visualization of this concept.

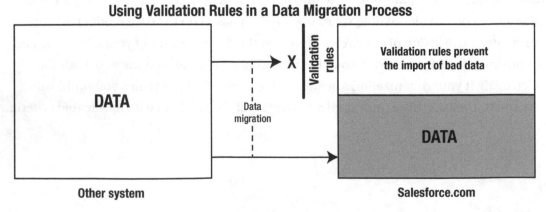

Figure 5-4. *In this scenario, an organization is migrating data from a system to their Salesforce org. The presence of validation rules can serve as a filter to prevent bad data from being transmitted.*

In the context of a migration, it's important to understand that you shouldn't depend your validation rules to "clean up" the data mid-migration. Validation rules are to maintain data integrity and prevent invalid states of data; they won't actively "clean up" anything for you.

Building an Effective Validation Rule

Before I break down some key considerations that warrant your attention when establishing validation rules within Salesforce, I will cover the steps involved in creating a validation rule. If you have read the chapters on formulas and workflow rules, you have a great head start. There's actually a fair amount of overlap between how validation rules and some other Salesforce elements are created. Following are the steps to create a validation rule.

Step 1: Define the Scenario and Corresponding Business Rules

For this exercise, I will use a specific scenario to illustrate how to create a relevant validation rule for your business. Let's say your business sells subscription-based software services to medium-to-large corporations in a highly competitive space. The sales life cycle typically lasts months and requires a number of conversations in order to come up with an agreed-upon set of features and a corresponding price. You use Marketing Cloud to capture incoming Leads via telephone and the Web; qualified, converted Leads then become Opportunity records, which the sales team utilizes in the hopes of generating eventual subscriptions.

The VP of Sales has noticed a recent drop-off in Opportunity win percentage coupled with an increase in Opportunities being closed as a result of the potential client being a poor fit. Although these clients have an initial interest, they rarely end up signing a deal, finding the price tag, large scope, and maintenance needs that come with the software subscription to be overwhelming. After a few discussions, the VP of Sales agrees to a new business rule that would aim to increase the quality of Opportunities, specifically those that are created via a Lead conversion. This new business requirement indicates that for *converted Leads*

1. The Annual Revenue field must be populated.

2. The Annual Revenue field value must be greater than or equal to $100,000.

3. The Number of Employees field must be populated.

4. The Number of Employees field value must be greater than or equal to 50.

5. An exception process will exist to allow circumvention of the rules, represented by a custom Checkbox field called Approved Exception.

Step 2: Enter Basic Rule Information

In Lightning Experience, you'll need to first access "Object Manager," which you can find via Quick Find within Setup. From there, select the relevant object and click the "Validation Rules" tab on the left. In Classic, the path is a bit different. You can use Quick Find for standard objects by searching for "Validation Rules"; for custom objects, navigate to "Objects," click the relevant object, and then find Validation Rules on the object setup page. Click the "**New**" button to get started. You'll begin by identifying information, as shown in Figure 5-5. Like always, put some thought into the rule name and description to facilitate a quick understanding of the rule and expedite future knowledge-transfer requirements.

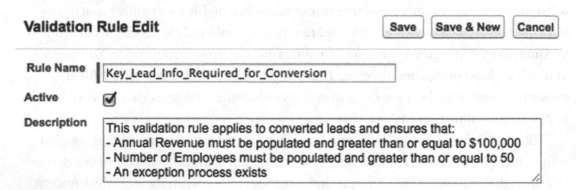

Figure 5-5. *It's important to enter a meaningful name and description for your validation rule*

Step 3: Establish the Error Condition Formula

The core tool of the validation rule process is the formula editor that was covered in detail in Chapters 3 and 4. With this editor, you will establish the error condition that will be prevented within your Salesforce org. It is critical to understand that you are defining the invalid or disallowed state here; you are not simply translating real-world business rules into a Salesforce-friendly format. For example, if your business rules required the standard Opportunity field **Quantity** to be less than or equal to 50, the corresponding Error Condition formula would be: Quantity > 50, not Quantity <= 50. You'll need to translate each of your business rules into error conditions in a similar fashion. Table 5-1 lays out the requirements for creating error conditions for specific business rules.

Table 5-1. *Requirements for Creating Error Conditions for Specific Business Rules When Building Your Overall Error Condition Formula*

#	Business Rule	Error Condition (Description)	Error Condition Formula
1	The **Annual Revenue** field must be populated.	**Annual Revenue** is not populated.	ISBLANK(AnnualRevenue)
2	The **Annual Revenue** field value must be greater than or equal to $100,000.	**Annual Revenue** is less than $100,000.	AnnualRevenue < 100000
3	The **Number of Employees** field must be populated.	**Number of Employees** is not populated.	ISBLANK(NumberOfEmployees)
4	The **Number of Employees** field value must be greater than or equal to 50.	**Number of Employees** is less than 50.	NumberOfEmployees < 50
5	Exceptions can be captured via custom Checkbox: **Is Approved Exception**.	**Is Approved Exception** is false.	NOT(Is_Approved_ Exception__c)

When establishing your error condition criteria, you may feel more comfortable combining the NOT() function with the allowed condition instead of explicitly defining the error condition, as shown in Table 5-1. The fourth rule requires that the Number of Employees field value must be greater than or equal to 50. To achieve this, I have built the following statement for my formula: `NumberOfEmployees < 50`. However, it is completely valid to use the following format instead: `NOT(NumberOfEmployees >= 50)`. Ultimately, this is your choice and should reflect the factors impacting your personal situation (e.g., how you most effectively read code, the likelihood of a future handoff or knowledge transfer) or your company's standards. I take and recommend the approach of building a cleaner, simpler formula. That means avoiding the extraneous NOT() in this case. Table 5-2 points out alternative approaches for two of the error conditions from the previous table. The fifth rule is another good example of where an alternative approach can be used. With Booleans (Checkboxes), there is no need for "= true" or "= false", although using each will work. In this case, you could use Is_Approved_Exception__c = false instead of the NOT(Is_Approved_Exception__c) that I produced.

Table 5-2. *Alternative Approaches for Two Error Conditions from Table 5-1*

#	Business Rule	Error Condition Formula	Alternative Approach
1	The **Number of Employees** must be greater than or equal to 50.	`NumberOfEmployees < 50`	`NOT(NumberOfEmployees >= 50)`
2	Exceptions can be captured via custom Checkbox: **Is Approved Exception**.	`NOT(Is_Approved_Exception__c)`	`Is_Approved_Exception__c = false`

You now have the elements to use within your error condition formula representing a failure to satisfy a required business rule. The next step is to establish the logic that will allow you to complete the formula. Since you know that the error condition only applies to converted Leads, you know that the system field Converted must be present and must be true. Since this is a Boolean field, the starting point is simply the field name:

IsConverted

Next, you'll need to augment the formula to ensure that the Is Approved Exception field is FALSE. This will prevent circumvention of the business rules:

IsConverted **&& NOT(Is_Approved_Exception__c)**

Third, you'll need to address the error conditions that were established in Table 5-1 to systematically capture unsatisfied business rules. You will want to build your validation rule to halt activity in which *any* of these error conditions are found. In other words, you want to display an error message if error conditions 1, or 2, or 3, or 4 occur. Add the bolded text to the existing formula:

IsConverted && NOT(Is_Approved_Exception__c) **&& (ISBLANK(AnnualRevenue) || AnnualRevenue < 100000 || ISBLANK(NumberOfEmployees) || NumberOfEmployees < 50)**

Figure 5-6 gives a view of the formula in the error condition formula screen.

Error Message

Example: | Discount percent cannot exceed 30% |

This message will appear when Error Condition formula is **true**

Error Message | Qualified Leads typically require at least $100,000 of annual revenue and at least 50 employees. If you feel that this Lead is validly qualified, request that "Approved Exception" is checked by the VP of Sales and retry once the exception is granted. |

This error message can either appear at the top of the page or below a specific field on the page

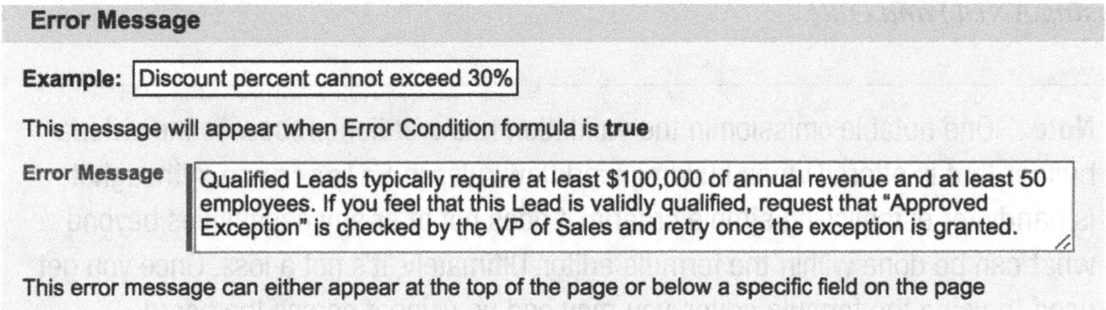

Figure 5-6. *Completed Error Condition Formula screen for our Lead qualification validation rule scenario*[1]

I previously discussed the options available when establishing AND/OR logic within formulas. You have the AND() and OR() functions as well as the && and || operators at your disposal. Either approach is acceptable when building validation rules. The decision whether to select the functions or the operators is up to you. Figure 5-7 shows how this validation rule would appear if you were using the AND() and OR() functions.

---

[1]All Salesforce screenshots in this chapter © copyright Salesforce, Inc. Used with permission.

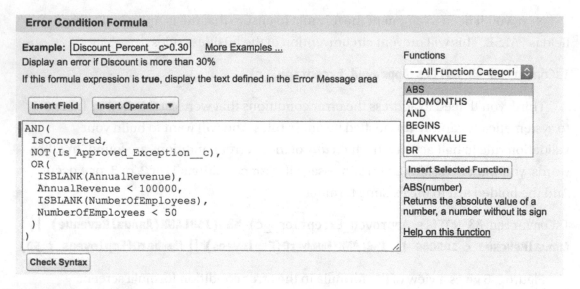

Figure 5-7. *An alternative approach for building your error condition formula using AND() and OR()*

Note   One notable omission in the validation rule creation process is the criteria builder that is offered when building workflow rules in Salesforce. Although it is handy for establishing simple criteria, it does not offer any capabilities beyond what can be done within the formula editor. Ultimately, it's not a loss. Once you get used to using the formula editor, you may end up using it across the board.

Step 4: Formulate the Error Message

Once you've completed the formulation of your error condition, you will need to determine what message will be displayed when that condition is encountered. While this is admittedly straightforward, you may be surprised at the prevalence of error messages present in Salesforce orgs today that are ambiguous or simply not useful. Being presented with a less-than-helpful error message from a validation rule is something that many of you can probably relate to. Here are few suggestions of content to include in your error messages:

1.   The business rules that are being broken

2.   The fields at play in the error condition

3. The objects at play in the error condition if multiple objects exist
    in the criteria or update

4. The actions required to proceed without triggering the error
    Condition again

5. The individuals (e.g., system administrator, developer) needed
    to resolve the issue if the condition can't be fixed by the end user
    him or herself

That may seem like it adds up to a verbose error message, but that's typically not the case. You should be able to capture these items within two or three sentences. In this case, you have multiple business rules involved. An effective error message might look like this: "Qualified Leads typically require at least $100,000 of annual revenue and at least 50 employees. If you feel that this Lead is validly qualified, request that "Approved Exception" is checked by the VP of Sales and retry once the exception is granted." See Figure 5-8 for an example.

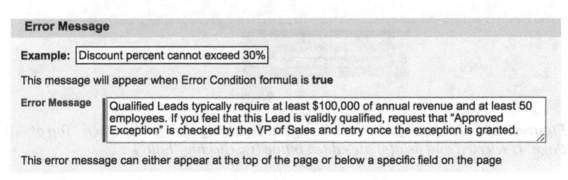

Figure 5-8. *Provide an error message that has sufficient meaning to your users*

Step 5: Determine the Error Message Location

Now that you have put together a meaningful error message, you'll have to determine where it will be displayed when invoked. As shown in Figure 5-9, Salesforce gives you two choices: **Top of Page** or **Field**.

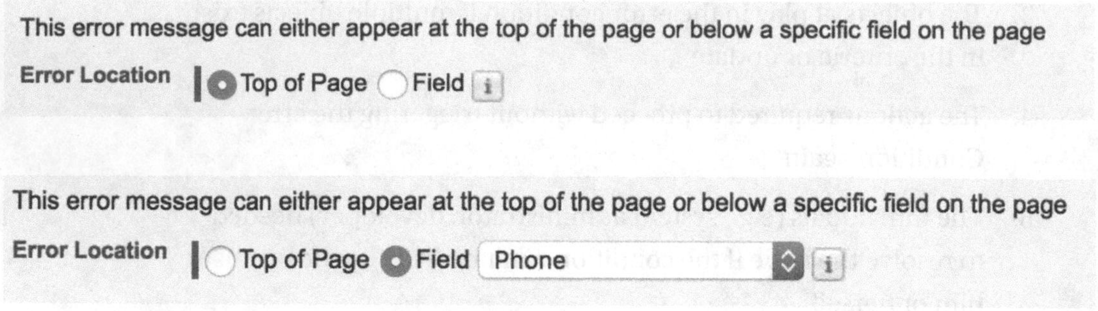

This error message can either appear at the top of the page or below a specific field on the page

Error Location | ● Top of Page ◯ Field [i]

This error message can either appear at the top of the page or below a specific field on the page

Error Location | ◯ Top of Page ● Field Phone [⇕] [i]

Figure 5-9. *Choice between the top of the page or a specific field for the location of the error message*

Both options in the figure will show an error message such as, "Error: invalid data. Review all error messages below to correct your data." However, the field choice will result in the specific validation rule error message appearing just below the selected field instead of at the top with generic error text, as shown in Figures 5-10, 5-11, and 5-12.

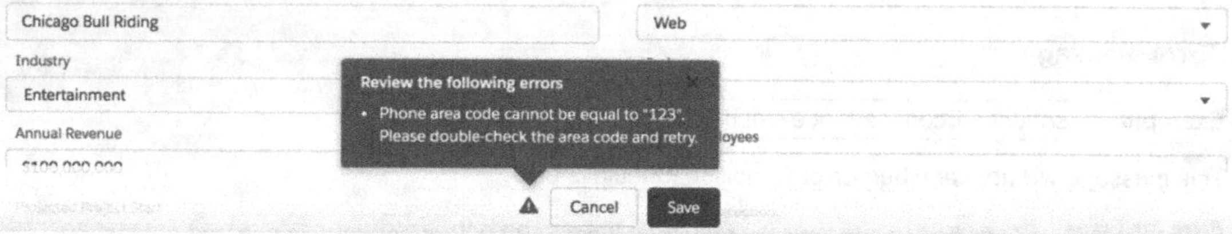

Chicago Bull Riding		Web	▼
Industry			
Entertainment			▼
Annual Revenue			

Review the following errors ✕
- Phone area code cannot be equal to "123". Please double-check the area code and retry.

⚠ Cancel Save

Figure 5-10. *The displayed error message in Lightning Experience when "Top of Page" is selected and field(s) are edited inline (vs. clicking "Edit")*

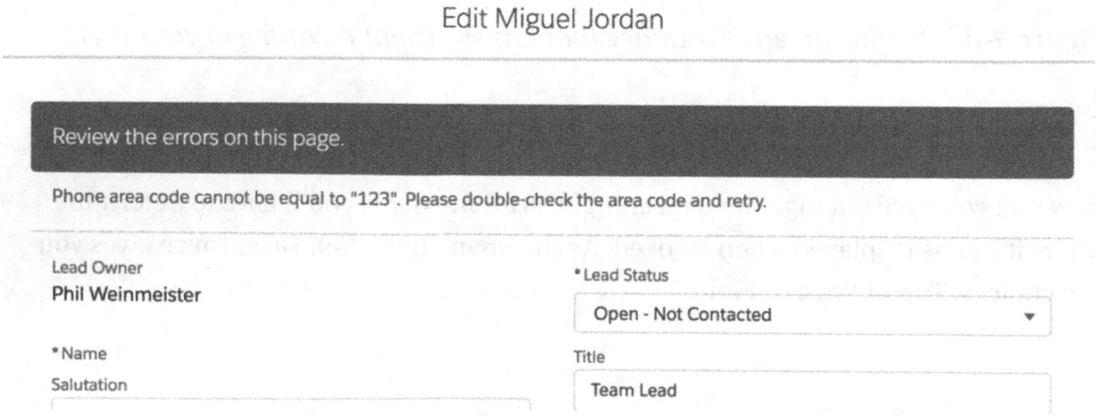

Edit Miguel Jordan

Review the errors on this page.

Phone area code cannot be equal to "123". Please double-check the area code and retry.

Lead Owner	* Lead Status
Phil Weinmeister	Open - Not Contacted ▼
* Name	Title
Salutation	Team Lead

Figure 5-11. *The displayed error message in Lightning Experience when "Top of Page" is selected and "Edit" button is clicked for editing*

Edit Miguel Jordan

Contact Information

Email
mjordan@chibullriding.org.1

Phone
(123) 123-1234

Phone area code cannot be equal to "123". Please double-check the area code and retry.

Website
www.bullriderz4life.com.1

Mobile
(123) 123-1235

Figure 5-12.   *The displayed error message in Lightning Experience when "Field" is selected and "Edit" button is clicked for editing*

Salesforce recommends that you use the Field option if your validation rule includes only one field; otherwise, it suggests that you choose Top of Page. For the most part, that is the right approach. However, there may be occasions where multiple fields are involved, yet only one of those fields would require a modification by the end user. In that case, you may decide to break from the official suggestion and show the error message next to the corresponding field.

In the case of the Lead qualification example being used in this chapter, the selection of the location is actually irrelevant. If the record update occurs anywhere other than the detail page of the validation rule's object, you will have no control over its display. In the Lead qualification validation rule, we are dealing with the conversion of a Lead, which will occur via the Lead conversion page and not on the Lead detail page itself, as shown in Figure 5-13.

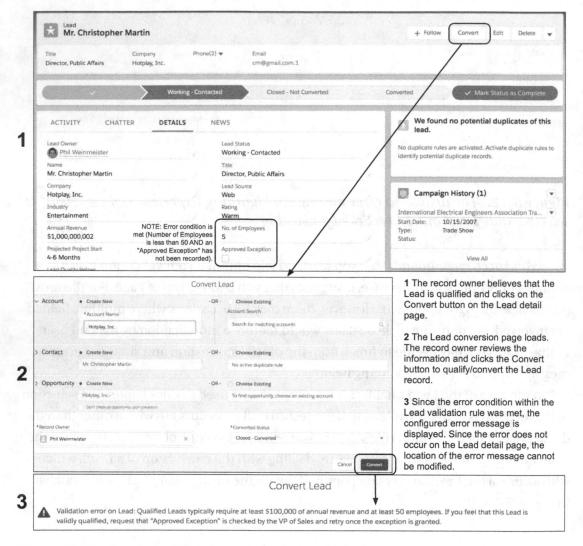

Figure 5-13.   *Lead qualification example in which the error message does not appear on the Lead detail page but rather on the Lead conversion page*

A similar situation occurs if a validation rule includes a related object in its error condition formula. Take Figure 5-14, an example that uses the Opportunity Product object, on which the rule criteria exists. However, the Opportunity field included in the criteria (Quantity) is directly impacted by the Opportunity Products that have been added to the corresponding Opportunity record. If we have a validation rule that limits the Opportunity Quantity to one, we will encounter the error condition when trying to add a second Opportunity Product record. Like in the example from Figure 5-11, the error message does not appear on the detail page of the validation rule's object.

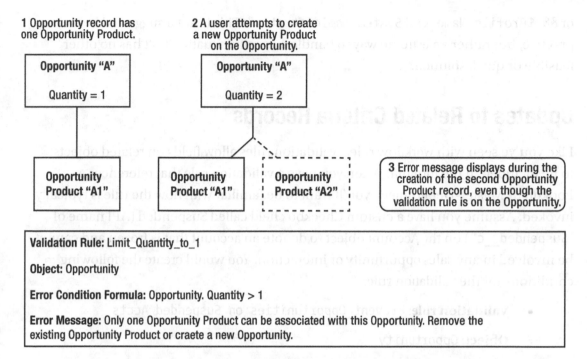

Figure 5-14. *An Opportunity validation rule for Opportunity Products displayed on the "Add Product(s) to Opportunity" page*

Considerations for Validation Rule Creation

There are a few additional factors to take into account when constructing validation rules, and I will go over the important considerations here.

Security Model Impact

While validation rules are not typically heralded as a Salesforce security feature, they may impact some of your security-related requirements. It is critical to understand that the error conditions present in an active validation rule cannot be circumvented. They apply to all users, including those with a system administrator profile, they are invoked via all interfaces (i.e., through actions occurring via the standard user interface or API calls), and they are never trumped by any traditional user permission setting. Any exceptions have to be directly established in the validation rule itself. For example, if you want to exempt a User or Profile from being impacted by a validation rule, you would have to include something like, && $User.Username <> "bunker.jones@salesforce.com" or `&& $Profile.Name <> "System Administrator"`. This is not a suggested best practice, but rather an extreme way to handle a specific situation that has no other feasible or quick solution.

Updates to Related Criteria Records

Like you've seen with workflow rules, validation rules allow fields on related objects to be included in the formula. When you have a validation rule that references a Lookup or Master-Detail object, you'll want to be familiar with how the rule is typically invoked. Assume you have a custom Checkbox field called Suspended (API name of `"Suspended__c"`) on the Account object to denote an account that is frozen and cannot be involved in any sales opportunity or interaction. You would create the following conditions for the validation rule:

- **Validation rule**: `Prevent_Opportunities_on_Suspended_Accts`

- **Object**: `Opportunity`

- **Error condition formula**: `Account.Suspended__c`

- **Error message**: `You may not add an Opportunity to a suspended Account. Please contact the Finance Manager for additional information.`

In this case, the only field included in the error condition formula is a field on a related object (Account). This changes the order of operations to invoke the validation rule. Unlike a rule that only includes fields from the "base object," the error condition can be satisfied on the related object. Here, an Account can have its Suspended flag updated to true and be saved successfully. Don't miss this key point: an Account can have its Suspended flag set to true, but an Opportunity *cannot be added* to an Account with a Suspended flag set to true. This can occur because the validation rule is not on the related object (Account). The validation rule only fires when a record of the object type identified in the rule validation rule's object is created or edited. In this example, that would have to occur on the Opportunity. Figure 5-15 shows this series of events.

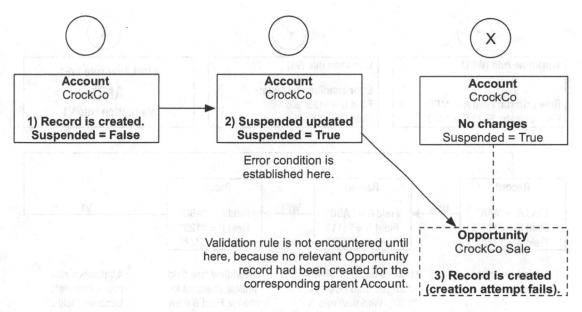

Figure 5-15. *An error condition that is satisfied before a validation rule is encountered*

It is important to understand the difference between this scenario and the one referenced in Figure 5-14. In Figure 5-14, the creation of a Child Opportunity Product record is prevented as a result of a validation rule on the Parent Opportunity record. In that case, the creation of the Opportunity Product directly updates a field on the Parent Opportunity record ("Quantity"). When the Quantity field's value changes on the Opportunity record and satisfies the error condition, the validation rule fires and produces an error message for the user. Since the action originated with an attempt to create an Opportunity Product record, the error will appear on the "Add Product(s) to Opportunity" screen.

Coexistence of Validation Rules with Automation

You will need to give special attention to Flows, workflow rules, Apex triggers, and processes when validation rules are present. It is very easy to create an output from one of these tools and, separately, validation rules in silos and fail to foresee how they overlap and impact each other. In Figure 5-16, you can see an example of a conflict between a workflow rule and a validation rule.

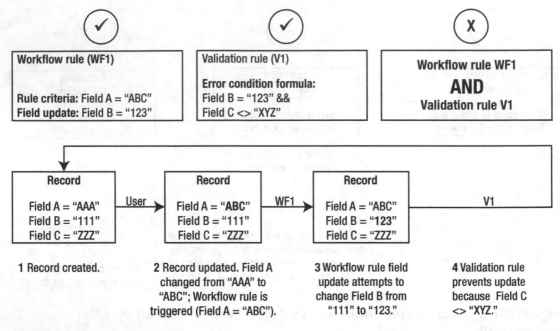

Figure 5-16. *Proceed with caution when you combine validation rules and workflow rules. It is easy to encounter an overlap where a validation rule unexpectedly prevents a Field Update. Make sure that you thoroughly test everything you develop (and in a sandbox, prior to production).*

In this case, the workflow rule and validation rule "collide." Fortunately, you do have options, and you'll need to decide which route you want to take. To minimize the deviation from the original intention of your workflow rule and validation rule, you may want to consider one of the following approaches:

- Add an additional Field Update to WF1 that sets Field C to "XYZ."

- Leave WF1 and V1 as is but communicate in the error message that Field C will need to be manually updated to "XYZ" before Field A can be set to "ABC."

Deployments and Integrations

While we typically tend to think about a solution within the org in which it is being developed, we must give special attention to potential destination orgs when thinking about validation rules. First, we must consider how a validation rule could potentially impact an existing integration. If an integration is expecting a type of value from a particular field and your validation rule prevents that value from being accessed as needed, your integration might break. Additionally, when deploying any solution (whether including validation rules or not), you must consider the active validation rules that might be present in the destination org. This has caused many people many hours of frustration as they go to deploy a solution from a sandbox to another org, only to have test classes inexplicably fail. Many times, it turns out that existing validation rules impact the logic of the test classes. Make sure to check this when you have test classes fail for an unknown reason.

Error Condition Grouping

When you build validation rules, you have the ability to group error conditions together. This can very beneficial, as it potentially minimizes both the initial development effort and the effort required to modify each of the individual error conditions. However, as you add specific error conditions into your overall error condition formula, keep in mind that the granularity of your error message will inevitably decrease. Take a look at Figure 5-17 to see how this can happen. Here, three fields are included in corresponding error conditions. You can choose to group these into one larger validation rule or to break them out as individual rules. The decision is not one to be made according to a broad generalization. You'll need to review your particular situation and consider your development and maintenance costs and your users' needs as well. Note that Salesforce will check all validation rules, even if the rules are separated; this means that either scenario will display the results of all rules, whether separated or grouped.

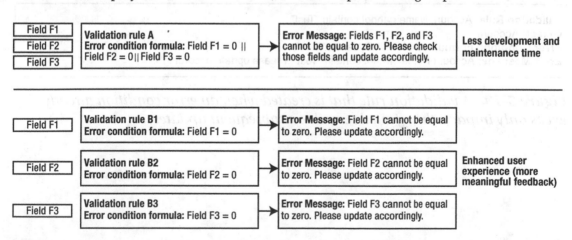

Figure 5-17. *When building validation rules, you can group the rules together (top) or separate them (bottom)*

Existing Error Conditions

It is critical to understand that a newly created or activated validation rule will not directly modify a record that already satisfies the error condition. In other words, validation rules only prevent configured error conditions that exist in updates that occur after that validation rule is in place. In the example in Figure 5-18, an Account was created before a corresponding validation rule was created. The Account record actually satisfies the validation rule's error condition; however, since the Account already existed, it remains intact after the rule is created and activated. The key here is that any *subsequent* modifications to the Account will take the validation rule into consideration, which means that in the next update, the record will need to be modified to *not* meet the error condition.

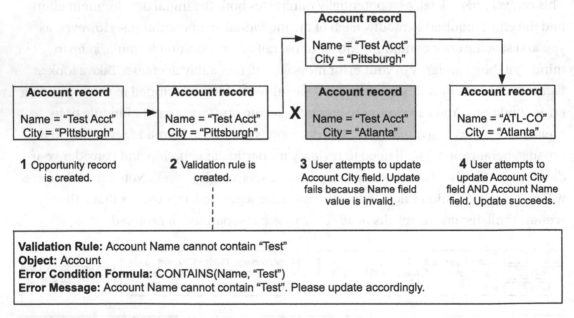

Figure 5-18.   *A validation rule that is created when an error condition already exists only impacts the affected records on subsequent updates*

Unavailable Functions

Not all formula functions are available when using the formula editor for validation rules. The following functions cannot be used with validation rules:

- HYPERLINK

- IMAGE

- URLFOR

Note   While there are some unavailable functions within validation rules, VLOOKUP is one function that is *only* available within validation rules. See Chapter 2 for details on this function.

Recap

In this chapter, you have delved into the world of validation rules and gained an understanding of their value for your organization, their relation to business rules, and when to utilize them. You have walked through each step of the rule creation process and identified how to build rules to satisfy related requirements within your organization. To achieve success through creating effective validation rules, make sure that you weigh the key considerations in this chapter and test everything you build thoroughly.

CHAPTER 6

Building Effective Approval Processes

When I introduced the previous chapter on validation rules, I made the shocking statement that users of your system are not always perfect; they don't always behave as expected and they occasionally make mistakes. To help combat a loss of data integrity and prevent general, widespread chaos throughout your org, we reviewed how to build validation rules to disallow error conditions. It's an excellent skill to have. However, the scenarios you'll encounter in the real world are not always so cut and dried. While certain conditions can be established in advance as invalid and blocked via validation rules, some conditions still require that special human touch. That's where approval processes come into the picture.

At the most basic level, approval processes allow for the manual review and approval of a particular state or condition. Excluding a possible "recall" of the review request, the outcome of that request must ultimately emerge as an approval or a rejection. Various real-world scenarios exist that may warrant an approval process. Here are a few examples:

- A sales opportunity that bears an elevated discount beyond a preapproved level

- A new product that is added/submitted and is pending public visibility/consumption

- A support case in an industry with valuable and highly sensitive clients that is pending closure

- A contract that is compiled and prepared for a client's signature

- A new account that is added with certain financial information that warrants confirmation

© Philip Weinmeister 2019
P. Weinmeister, *Practical Salesforce Development Without Code*,
https://doi.org/10.1007/978-1-4842-4871-3_6

Like many other facets of Salesforce, approval processes can be deceptive because of the speed with which they can be assembled. It's true that Salesforce has done an outstanding job of building a framework that significantly eases what could be an overwhelmingly burdensome process. However, your burden still remains – to build an approval process that accurately and efficiently addresses a corresponding business need. You have a number of options when developing an approval process, and I want to make sure you understand all of them clearly. Even for those of you who have experience in this arena, by reading this chapter you'll likely pick up something new that you can bring to the table when working with your customers or fellow employees. By the end of it, you will

- Understand the guiding metadata that serves as the "wrapper" for an approval process

- Be familiar with how to limit who can invoke an approval process and under what circumstances

- Know how to build a dynamic approval process that is relationship based, not person based

- Have learned how to establish a proper flow of the approval process routing

- Have walked through a fully detailed, end-to-end review of each step in the creation of an approval process

- Comprehend the considerations that should be made when building approval processes

The Flow of a Salesforce Approval Process

Before I jump into Salesforce-specific terminology and configurations, let me break down the general flow of a Salesforce approval process. You should understand each step of the process in detail in order to assist in making it accurate and thorough for your business or your clients. A few questions to ask yourself might be

- What am I trying to prevent from occurring by implementing this approval process?

- What am I trying to automate as a result of this approval process?

Figure 6-1 gives a visual overview of this flow.

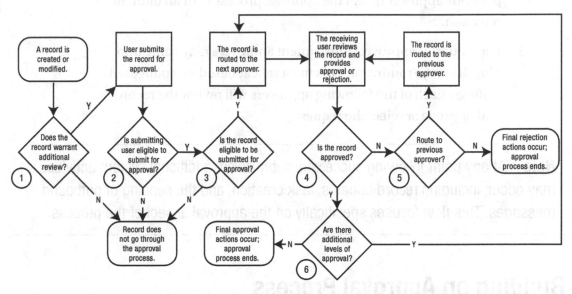

Figure 6-1. *Visual interpretation of flow of general approval process*

I should clarify some considerations about the decision points in Figure 6-1. For each decision point:

1. This decision point should determine whether the record needs to be reviewed (i.e., whether it should be submitted for approval).

2. The user manually submitting the record for approval must be eligible to do so based on the configured criteria. For example, it may be required that the User has a specific Role or is a part of a configured Public Group.

3. The record itself that is submitted for approval must be eligible for submission. The eligibility will be determined based on whether the record meets the configured criteria or, if a formula is used, whether the evaluation for the formula shows that it is true.

4. Once the record is submitted to an approver, that approver will need to make a decision to approve or reject the request.

5. If the request is rejected, the request will either "roll back" to the previous approver or exit the approval process with an ultimate rejection.

6. If a request is approved, subsequent approvers may come into play. If so, the routing process must repeat based on configured settings. Each of the following approvers will review the record and approve or reject the request.

Note   At any point following successful submission, additional system activities may occur, including record updates, task creation, and the sending of outbound messages. This flow focuses specifically on the approval aspect of the process.

Building an Approval Process

With so many elements making up the overall approval process framework, the variety in the processes that you will create can be extreme. It wouldn't take long to fill up a separate book strictly covering the possible processes that could be built across standard and custom objects. I will set the stage with one specific scenario that could be analogous to what you might encounter in the real world. This will keep the volume of information palatable while avoiding a purely theoretical understanding of approval processes.

Brokerage Support Scenario Overview

Say you work for a brokerage that handles extremely wealthy (and demanding) clients. These clients have a significant amount of money to invest and they do not have the time or patience to deal with ongoing or repeated issues related to their investments. As a result of their sensitivity, improperly or partially resolved issues are seen as completely unacceptable. A Case that is closed without being fully resolved could potentially cost your brokerage millions of dollars. To ensure that Cases are properly resolved, they must go through an approval process immediately preceding their closure. Throughout the chapter, I'll refer to this scenario as the "brokerage support scenario."

Scenario Requirements

In this scenario, I'll assume you've met with stakeholders and gathered the relevant requirements. The following configuration settings establish the primary requirements that will drive the setup of and behavior within the approval process. As I proceed through each key area of the process, I will address a number of other configuration settings not listed here as well.

- **Entry criteria for a Case to be eligible for the approval process**

    - **Status** must equal "Pending Closure Approval."

    - **Type** must not equal "Online Password Reset."

    - **Migrated from Legacy System** (a custom Checkbox field) must not equal TRUE.

- **Initial submitters for Case Closure Approval**

    - The creator of the Case

    - The owner of the Case

    - Users with a Role associated with the customer support organization

    - Users in the Public Group "After-Hours Support"

- **Initial actions**

    - The internal status of a record in the review process will be set to "Closure Review" upon entry into the approval process.

- **Approval steps**

    - The manager of the Case owner (the User identified in the Manager field on the User record associated with the Case owner) must approve the closure of the Case.

    - Case Closure queue members (only if the manager in Step 1 does not have a Role associated with the customer support organization) must approve it.

- Any of the two directors within the customer support organization must approve it.

- Users in the queue containing C-level officers perform the final approval. (Note that if the request is rejected by the chief officers, the Case should be resubmitted to the customer support directors.)

- **Other requirements**

  - A submitted record may not be modified during the approval process, with the exception of changes by Users with the System Administrator profile.

  - Appropriate email notifications will be sent throughout the process.

Initiation of the Approval Process

To start the approval process, you'll first need to kick off its creation. To do so, navigate to Approval Processes in the Setup menu by searching for "Approval Process" using Quick Find. The first decision you'll have to make when building your approval process will be selecting the appropriate object. Click "Manage Approval Processes For:" and select the applicable object (in this example, Case). You can see this drop-down field at the top of Figure 6-2.

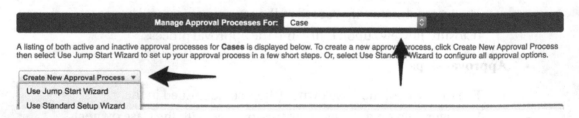

Figure 6-2. *After selecting the primary object for your approval process (top), you will be presented with two wizard options (bottom-left) when kicking off the creation of your approval process.*[1]

---

[1]All Salesforce screenshots in this chapter © copyright Salesforce, Inc. Used with permission.

Once you have selected the Case, you'll initiate the creation of a Case-specific approval process on the screen shown at the bottom-left of Figure 6-2. Salesforce provides two choices: a Jump Start Wizard and a Standard Setup Wizard. For this example, which has a number of intricacies, you will need to use the Standard Setup Wizard.

Note   While the Jump Start Wizard does provide the means to get an approval process up and running very quickly, it is worthwhile to get accustomed to the more robust, thorough Standard Setup Wizard, as a number of settings are not available in the Jump Start Wizard. Ultimately, ensuring that you don't bypass a useful step is preferable to skipping one that you see as unnecessary.

Process Definition Detail

Salesforce refers to the primary attributes and metadata belonging to an approval process as the "process definition detail." When you initiate the creation process by selecting the Standard Setup Wizard, you are immediately presented with the configuration settings that comprise the process definition detail. Follow these steps for configuration.

Step 1. Enter Name and Description

As trivial as it may seem, I have to mention that you need to first provide a Process Name (user-facing label), a Unique Name (referenced in the API/Apex), and a Description, as shown in Figure 6-3. As always, resist the temptation to leave the Description field blank; instead, add at least one descriptive sentence that clarifies the process for other users.

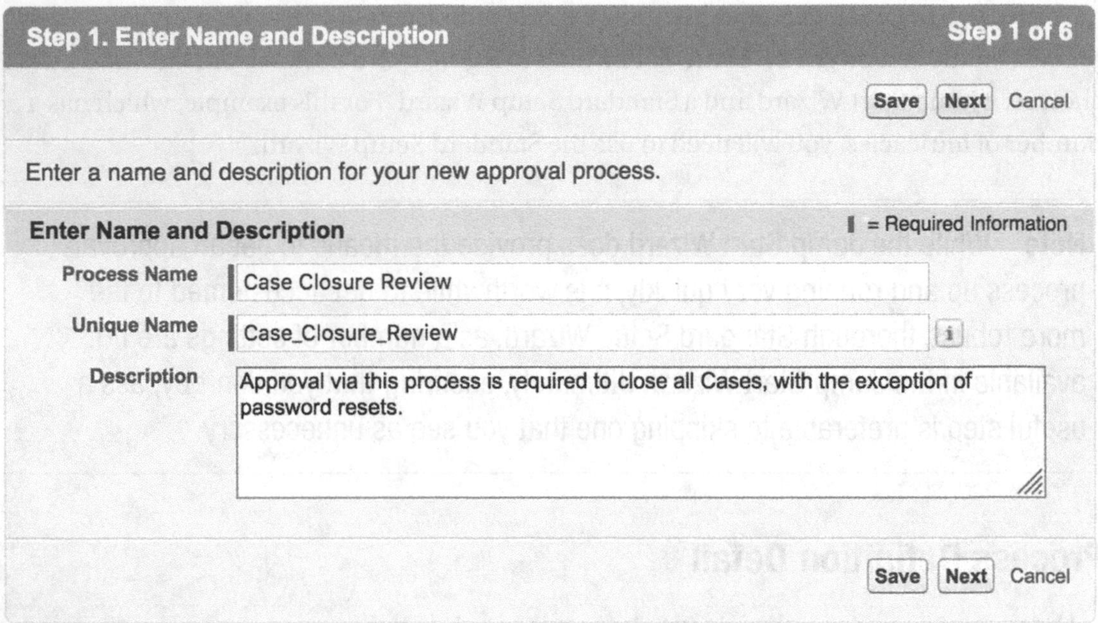

Step 1. Enter Name and Description   **Step 1 of 6**

Save Next Cancel

Enter a name and description for your new approval process.

Enter Name and Description   ▌ = Required Information

Process Name	Case Closure Review
Unique Name	Case_Closure_Review
Description	Approval via this process is required to close all Cases, with the exception of password resets.

Save Next Cancel

Figure 6-3. *"Enter Name and Description" section for specifying details of your approval process*

Step 2. Specify Entry Criteria

As with the workflow rule criteria, you have a choice of tools when establishing the entry criteria for approval processes: you can use either what I have been referring to as the "criteria builder" or the formula editor. Many times, the choice comes down to personal preference. However, it may be beneficial to reiterate that the spectrum of criteria combinations you can establish with the criteria builder is only a subset of what can be established with the formula editor. Simple criteria with only a few included statements are best developed with the criteria builder, while anything with complexity is probably best served with the formula editor. I'll go over both options here based on our three requirements for entry criteria. The criteria builder option is shown in Figure 6-4.

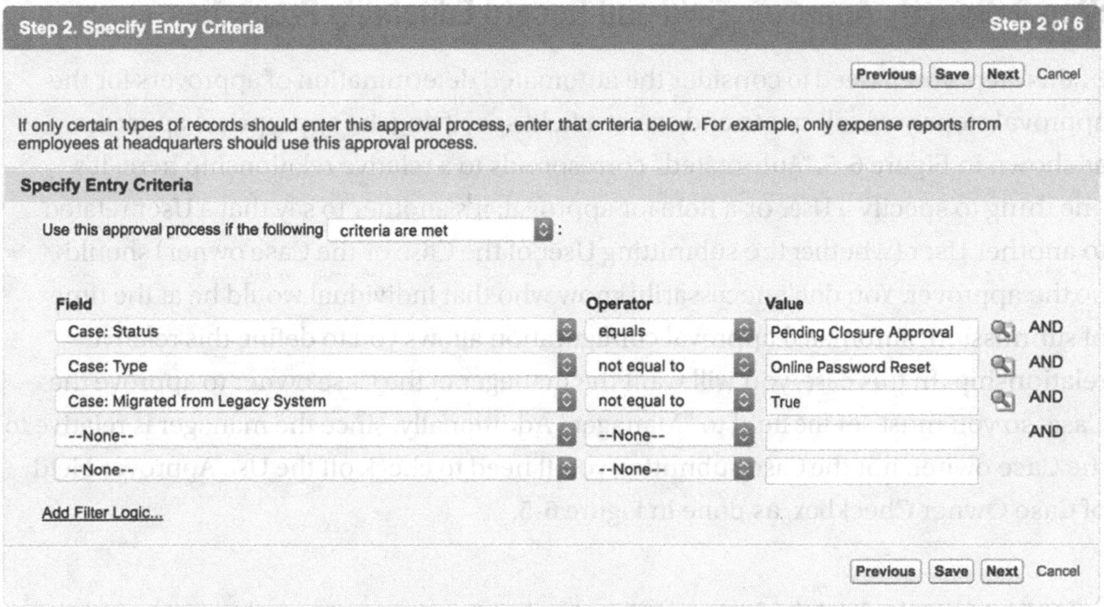

Figure 6-4. *You can specify criteria to restrict record entry into the approval process in the "Specify Entry Criteria" section*

Alternatively, if you wanted to use the formula editor as an option, you could establish the entry criteria via a formula like this:

```
AND(
 ISPICKVAL(Status, "Pending Closure Approval"),
 TEXT(Type) <> "Online Password Reset Request",
 NOT(Migrated_from_Legacy_System__c)
)
```

You may notice that I am not using ISPICKVAL() for both picklists (Status and Type), but only one of them. Since one of the statements involving a picklist is exclusive, NOT() would have to be used in conjunction with ISPICKVAL(). To simplify the formula and avoid the function combination, I used TEXT() with <> instead. For this example, the criteria builder will be sufficient for configuring the entry criteria, so that will be used as the active criteria tool.

Step 3. Specify Approver Field and Record Editability Properties

In this step, you'll need to consider the automated determination of approvers for the approval steps you will create and select a field specifying the appropriate approver, as shown in Figure 6-5. "Automated" corresponds to a relative relationship here. It's one thing to specify a User or a Role for approval; it's another to say that a User related to another User (whether the submitting User of the Case or the Case owner) should be the approver. You don't necessarily know who that individual would be at the time of submission; automated approval configuration allows you to define this relative relationship. In this case, you will want the manager of the Case owner to approve the Case, so you must set the field to "Manager." Additionally, since the manager is relative to the Case owner, not the Case submitter, you'll need to check off the Use Approver Field of Case Owner Checkbox, as done in Figure 6-5.

Figure 6-5. *In this chapter's example, you want to have the Case Owner's manager approve the request, so select "Manager" for Automated Approver and check the box for Case Owner.*

In the same step, you'll determine the "editability" of the record being submitted for approval. You have two choices: Users with a profile of "System Administrator" only, or System Administrators and the current approver. In this example, you want to restrict this to System Administrators only (see Figure 6-6).

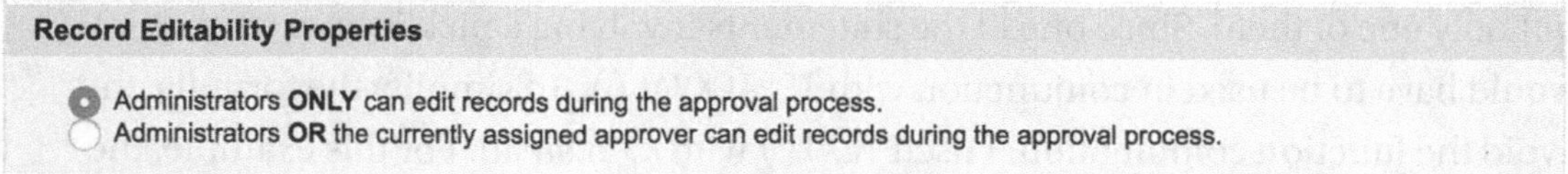

Figure 6-6. *You may choose whether System Administrators only or both admins and the current approver can edit the record during the approval process*

Step 4. Select Notification Templates

For a truly thorough approval process, you will need to ensure that the proper communication occurs to notify the individuals involved in the process. While I'm not dedicating a chapter solely to the creation of notification templates in this book, I'll cover them here at a basic level to get you started. In Lightning Experience, multiple options exist for creating a template; here, I'll use the "classic" approach, as it works for both Lightning Experience and Classic UX. In this scenario, you will need to create a custom notification template to be sent to potential approvers that contains key information about the request. Not only does this notification expedite the process by providing immediate awareness of the request, but also it allows the individual to start the decision-making process by conveying the request details via email.

Note   If you decide not to build a custom notification template, a default template will be sent to the approver(s). This template will contain a link that takes the approver(s) to a page where the approval or rejection can be completed.

In order to create a new custom Email Template via the Classic method (whether you are using LEX or Classic), search for "Email Template" using Quick Find. Here, you will be presented with four choices: Text, HTML (using letterhead), Custom (without using letterhead), and Visualforce. When done correctly, HTML and Visualforce will always be more aesthetically pleasing than simple text notifications. However, you must weigh your business needs with the estimated level of effort required any time you are building solutions in Salesforce. In this case, you're dealing with an internal notification; corresponding beautification of an internal Email Template will infrequently be considered a hard requirement. If you already have a letterhead or you are quick with HTML/Visualforce, go for it. Here, you will be creating a simple text-based email notification.

The next part of creating a template is to configure the metadata (Template Name, Folder, etc.). Make sure that the template is marked as "Available for Use" and in a nonprivate folder. Once you've taken care of that, it's on to the Subject and Body of your Email Template. To provide the approver with the most relevant information possible, you will want to take advantage of merge fields to pull in information from the Case record dynamically.

The Subject field text should be clear and contain some identifying information. For example, the message "Case 1234 is pending closure and requires your review" provides a unique piece of data and clearly communicates what is needed from the recipient. Since Case Number is Case specific, a merge field will be needed. Figure 6-7 shows the "Available Merge Fields" section. Select "Case Fields" for the Field Type, then "Case Number" for the Field.

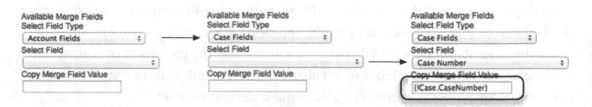

Figure 6-7. *The Available Merge Fields section allows you to select the Field Type and Field to generate a Merge Field Value that you will include in your Email Template*

Once you've generated the merge field value, you can then set the subject line of your Email to the following: `Case {!Case.CaseNumber} is pending closure and requires your review.` In the Email body, you'll need to provide more detail. You can include the following fields:

1. **Case Owner:** `{!Case.OwnerFullName}`

2. **Case Subject:** `{!Case.Subject}`

3. **Case Account:** `{!Case.Account}`

4. **Case Contact:** `{!Case.Contact}`

5. **Case Type:** `{!Case.Type}`

6. **Case Reason:** `{!Case.Reason}`

7. **Case Resolution Details (custom field):** `{!Case.Case_Resolution_Details__c}`

8. **Case URL:** `{!Case.Link}`

The final template body might look something like this:

```
Case {!Case.CaseNumber} is pending closure and requires your review. Please
note the following:

Case Owner: {!Case.OwnerFullName}
Case Subject: {!Case.Subject}
Case Account: {!Case.Account}
Case Contact: {!Case.Contact}
Case Type: {!Case.Type}
Case Reason: {!Case.Reason}
Case Resolution Details: {!Case.Case_Resolution_Details__c}

To further review the Case and provide your approval decision, please click
here: {!Case.Link}.
```

Assuming you use a template name of "Case Closure Approval," you will set the Email Template as shown in Figure 6-8.

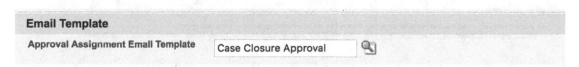

Figure 6-8. *The "Email Template" section allows you to select the template to be used to notify each approver of the pending request*

Step 5. Select Fields to Display on Approval Page Layout

When an approver initiates the process to approve or reject a request, he or she is presented with a page that contains information corresponding to the record submitted for approval. While you don't want to add the kitchen sink to the layout of the page, you want to add a sufficient amount of data in order to provide enough information for the reviewer to be able to make a decision on the approval request without having to navigate to the record directly. There's nothing wrong with the reviewer accessing the record directly to gain additional context; however, a streamlined process that does not require an approver to step outside the intended flow will save time and bring a little more happiness to your users. The fields you'll use will closely resemble those included in the Email Template you just created. Here is a suggested list of fields you may want to consider including Case Number, Case Owner, Account Name, Contact Name, Subject, Description, Type, Case Reason, and Case Resolution Details.

Additionally, you will have to decide whether to show the history of all previous approval decisions for this record. Typically, there is no reason to omit this information and it can prove to be helpful. The example shown in Figure 6-9 is set to include the approval decision history.

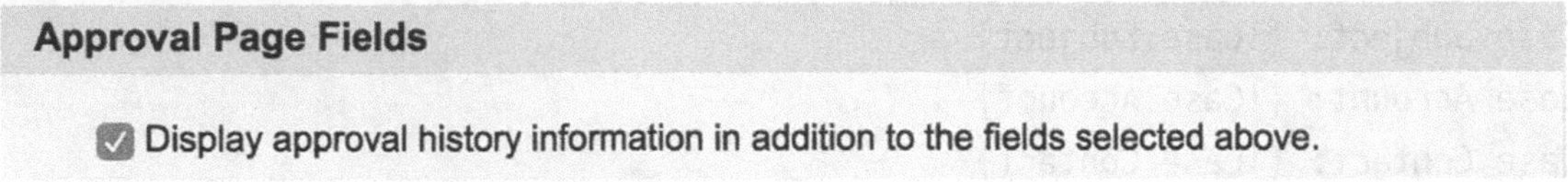

Approval Page Fields

☑ Display approval history information in addition to the fields selected above.

Figure 6-9. *The "Approval Page Fields" section gives you the option to include the approval history on the approval page layout*

As the final piece in the Definition Detail process, you're required to identify the security settings of the approval page, as shown in Figure 6-10. If you need to provide mobile access, you'll have to select the second option. Do keep in mind that you cannot combine this selection with the ability to manually identify an approver.

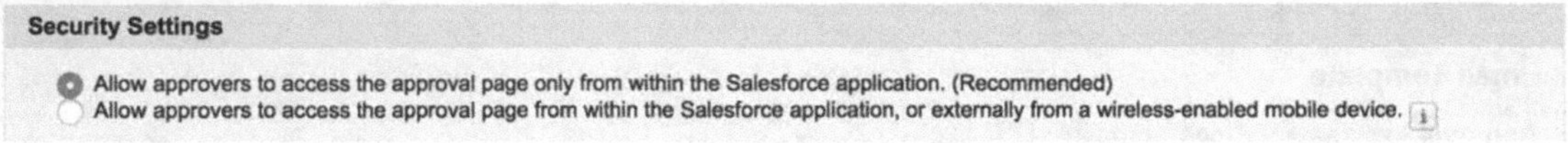

Security Settings

◉ Allow approvers to access the approval page only from within the Salesforce application. (Recommended)
◯ Allow approvers to access the approval page from within the Salesforce application, or externally from a wireless-enabled mobile device. ⓘ

Figure 6-10. *The "Security Settings" section allows you to limit access to the interface to those in the Salesforce application (desktop) or to extend access to wireless devices*

Step 6. Specify Initial Submitters

When building an approval process, it is critical to identify who should be able to submit the record for approval. Granting this ability to all internal users will definitely be the exception. You may even want to limit the potential users to as few as one (possibly the Case owner). In this case, the requirements listed earlier in the chapter warrant selection of a few different users and groups. Figure 6-11 shows the Available Submitters and Allowed Submitters lists, giving you the option to limit who will be allowed to submit for approval.

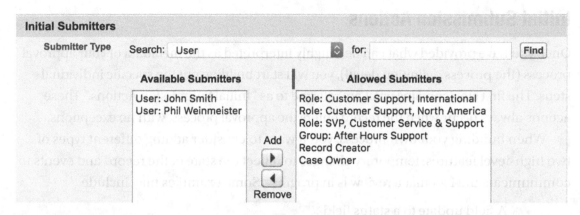

Figure 6-11. Configured list of initial submitters that will be allowed to submit the Case for approval

You will also have to decide whether to allow recalls of the approval request. Many times, you will want to do this. In this case, the process is tight and there should not be a reason to recall a request once submitted. Do not provide the ability to recall the request in this example; however, this will be driven by your organization's requirements in your own real-world scenarios.

Recap of Process Definition

Let's take a breather and review what has been completed so far. All of the routing and resulting actions are yet to come. Figure 6-12 gives a view of the process definition that was just configured.

Process Definition Detail   Edit ▼ Clone Delete Activate View Diagram

Process Name	Case Closure Review	Active ☐
Unique Name	Case_Closure_Review	Next Automated Approver Determined By — Manager of Record Owner
Description	Approval via this process is required to close all Cases, with the exception of password resets.	
Entry Criteria	(Case: `Status` EQUALS Pending Closure Approval) AND (Case: `Type` NOT EQUAL TO Online Password Reset) AND (Case: `Migrated from Legacy System` NOT EQUAL TO True)	
Record Editability	Administrator **ONLY**	Allow Submitters to Recall Approval Requests ☐
Approval Assignment Email Template	Case Closure Approval	
Approval Post Template		
Initial Submitters	Role: Customer Support, International, Role: Customer Support, North America, Role: SVP, Customer Service & Support, Group: After Hours Support, Record Creator, Case Owner	

Figure 6-12. A view of the "Process Definition Detail" screen after configuration

215

Initial Submission Actions

Once you have provided what can be roughly interpreted as the metadata of your approval process (the process definition detail), you will start building out the specific individual steps. The first step contains what are referred to as "Initial Submission Actions." These actions always occur when the record enters the approval process, with no exceptions.

When building your own process, you'll want to consider adding different types of two high-level features: temporary changes to reflect the state of the record and events to communicate the fact that a review is in progress. Some examples may include

- A field update to a status field

- An Email Alert sent to the Case owner or another interested party

- A call-out to another system to reflect the event

To meet the requirements in the brokerage support scenario previously described, you will be updating the Status field from "Pending Closure Approval" to "Closure Review" to ensure that the current state is clear to all parties. Figure 6-13 shows the initial configuration of the "Field Update Edit" screen, which is followed by "Initial Submission Actions," which comes after the update in Figure 6-14.

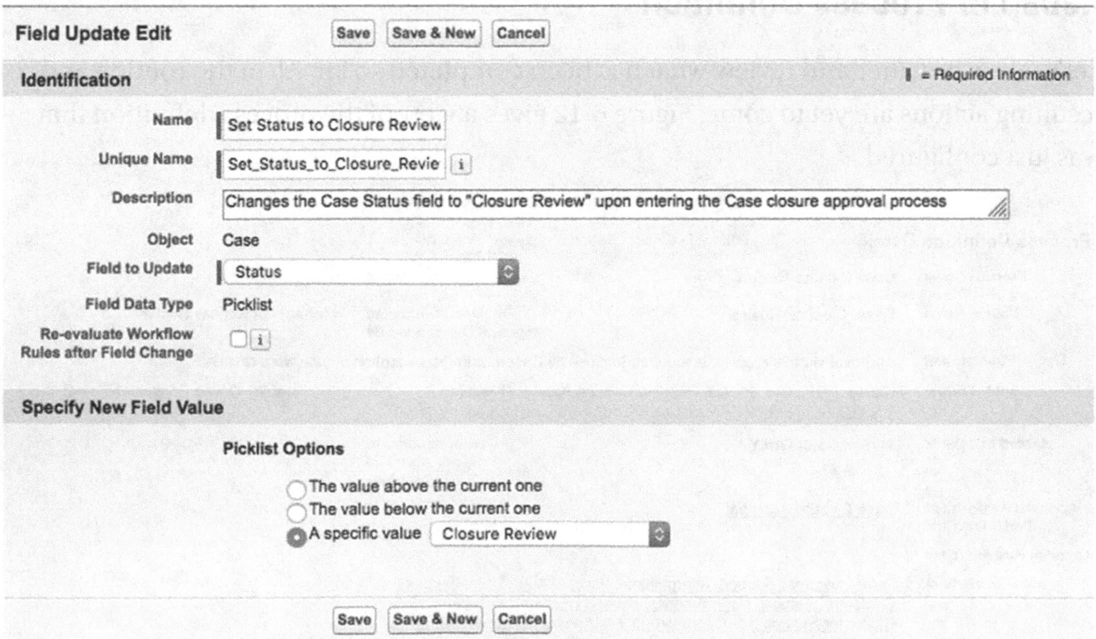

Figure 6-13. *Configuration of the "Field Update Edit" screen associated with the Initial Submission action*

Initial Submission Actions Add Existing Add New

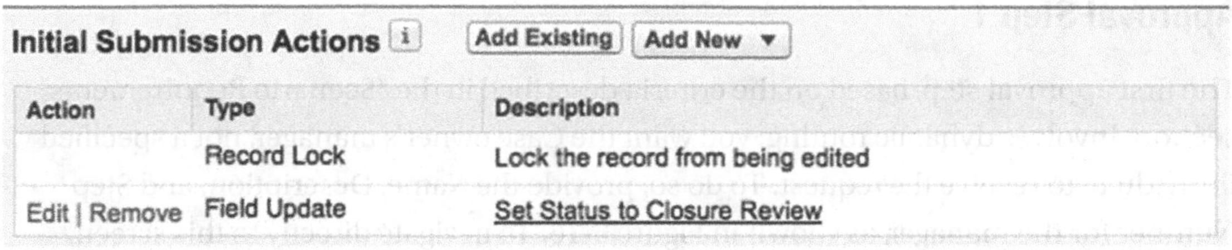

Action	Type	Description
	Record Lock	Lock the record from being edited
Edit | Remove	Field Update	Set Status to Closure Review

Figure 6-14. *"Initial Submission Actions" section following completion of configuration*

Approval Steps

Before diving in to the approval steps, I want to point out how much has already been covered before ever touching them. While the approval steps are the crux of the Salesforce approval process, there's much more to think about than simply who approves the process and in what order. Without the right foundation for your process, the approval steps won't achieve their full potential in terms of organizational value. I will walk through each of the previously established requirements to identify the approval sequence and recipients, and explain the configuration approach and reasoning along the way. Figure 6-15 presents an overview of the approval flow.

Approval Process Flow
Manager of the Case owner
1
Case Closure queue
2
Director, International Customer Support
3
OR
Director, North American Customer Support
C-Level queue
4
If manager in step 1 does not have a customer support-related Role, proceed to step 2. Otherwise, skip to step 3.
Proceed to step 4 if Case is escalated. If Case is not escalated, closure is approved.

Figure 6-15. *Approval flow for the brokerage support scenario*

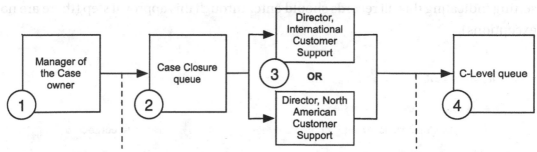

Approval Step 1

The first approval step, based on the criteria described in the "Scenario Requirements" section, involves dynamic routing; you want the Case owner's manager, not a specified individual, to receive the request. To do so, provide the Name, Description, and Step Number for the manager, as shown in Figure 6-16. To navigate directly to this screen, click the "New Approval Step" button on the main Approval Process screen.

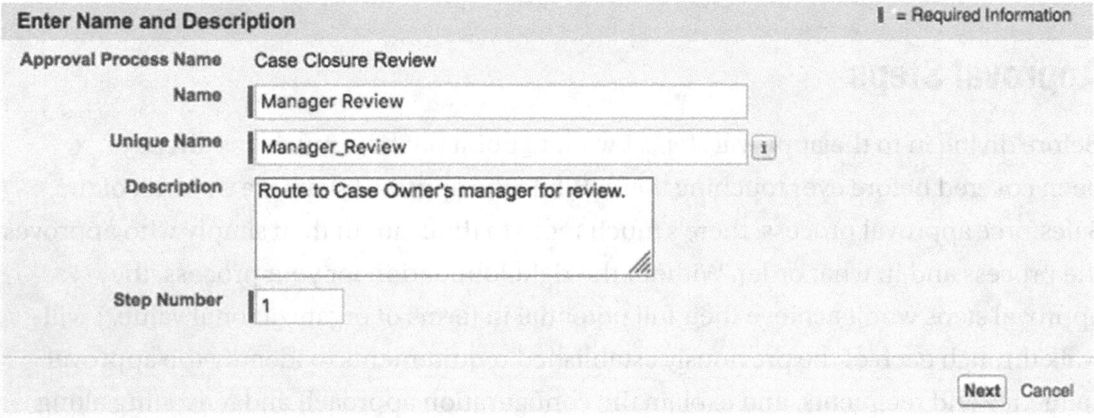

Figure 6-16. *Providing Name, Description, and Step Number for dynamic routing*

When you get to "Specify Step Criteria," shown in Figure 6-17, leave the default setting indicating that all records should enter through this approval step (there are no exceptions).

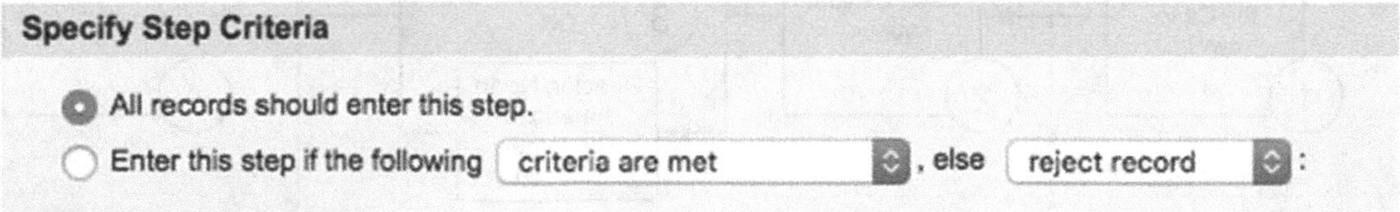

Figure 6-17. *Specifying step criteria*

Your previous work pays off in the next part of the step. Since you already set the Case owner's manager as the dynamic approver, you simply have to select the provided option for this choice. You don't have any requirements to provide access to delegates so you can leave that unchecked throughout this chapter. This is shown in Figure 6-18.

218

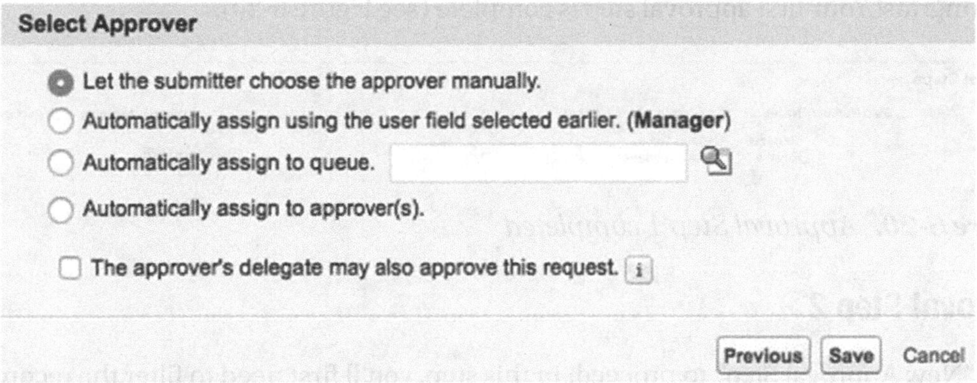

Select Approver

○ Let the submitter choose the approver manually.

○ Automatically assign using the user field selected earlier. (**Manager**)

○ Automatically assign to queue. [   ] 🔍

○ Automatically assign to approver(s).

☐ The approver's delegate may also approve this request. [i]

[Previous] [Save] Cancel

Figure 6-18. *Selection of approver*

Your approval step is complete. You are then prompted to associate an action with an approval or a rejection corresponding to this step. I'll assume you want to create an action associated with an approval to communicate each of your approval process updates to the Case owner to keep him informed. You can build an Email Template to do this and configure it for each approval step by following the prompt in Figure 6-19.

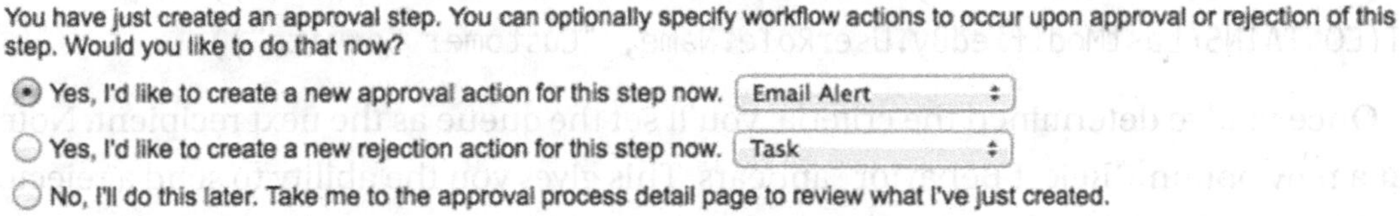

You have just created an approval step. You can optionally specify workflow actions to occur upon approval or rejection of this step. Would you like to do that now?

⦿ Yes, I'd like to create a new approval action for this step now. [Email Alert   ⇅]

○ Yes, I'd like to create a new rejection action for this step now. [Task   ⇅]

○ No, I'll do this later. Take me to the approval process detail page to review what I've just created.

Figure 6-19. *Next steps after creating the approval step*

Your Email Alert settings might look something like this:

- **Description:** "Notify Case Owner of incremental approval."

- **Unique name:** "Notify_Case_Owner_of_Incremental_Approval"

- **Email Template:** "Additional Closure approval received."

- **Recipient type:** Owner

- **Selected recipients:** Case Owner

- **From Email Address:** Current User's Email Address

Congrats! Your first approval step is complete (see Figure 6-20).

Action	Step Number	Name	Description	Criteria	Assigned Approver	Reject Behavior
Show Actions | Edit	1	Manager Review	Route to Case Owner's manager		Manager	Final Rejection

Approval Steps [i]

Figure 6-20. *Approval Step 1 completed*

Approval Step 2

Click "New Approval Step" to proceed. In this step, you'll first need to filter the records that will be allowed to proceed through this step, routing some of them directly to this step. The criteria established for this step in the "Scenario Requirements" section is that if the Case owner's manager does not have a Role associated with the customer support organization, the Case would need to be reviewed by a User in the Case Closure queue. The format is just like you saw with workflow rules – you have a choice of using the criteria builder or the formula editor. I would suggest using the formula editor here. You can set your formula to this for the brokerage support scenario example:

```
NOT(CONTAINS(LastModifiedBy.UserRole.Name, "Customer Support")) &&
NOT(CONTAINS(LastModifiedBy.UserRole.Name, "Customer Service"))
```

Once you've determined the criteria, you'll set the queue as the next recipient. Note that a new option, "Reject Behavior," appears. This gives you the ability to send a rejected record back a level. However, based on the requirements, you should leave the default setting set to perform all rejection action and final rejection actions. See Figure 6-21 for a view of the "Select Approver" and "Reject Behavior" sections.

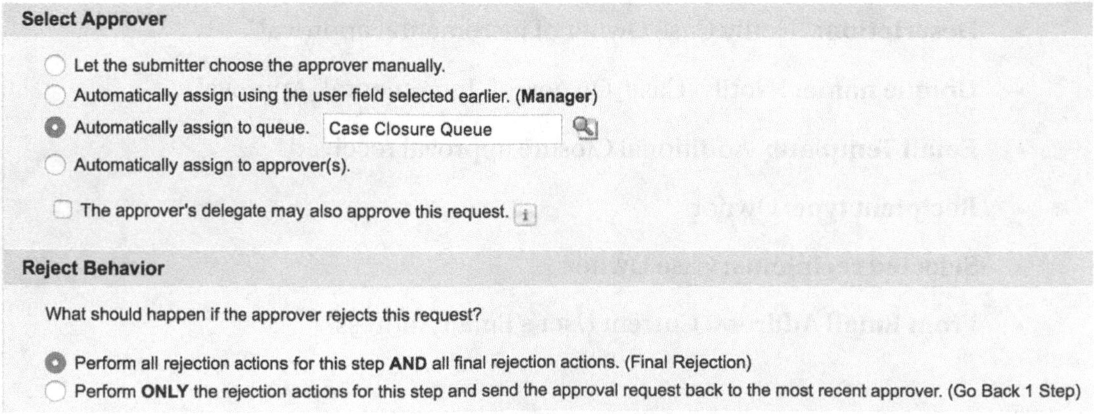

Select Approver

○ Let the submitter choose the approver manually.
○ Automatically assign using the user field selected earlier. (**Manager**)
◉ Automatically assign to queue.   Case Closure Queue   [🔍]
○ Automatically assign to approver(s).

☐ The approver's delegate may also approve this request. [i]

Reject Behavior

What should happen if the approver rejects this request?

◉ Perform all rejection actions for this step **AND** all final rejection actions. (Final Rejection)
○ Perform **ONLY** the rejection actions for this step and send the approval request back to the most recent approver. (Go Back 1 Step)

Figure 6-21. *Approval Step 2: "Select Approver" and "Reject Behavior" options*

Just associate the existing Email Alert with Step 2, and you're all done!

Approval Step 3

Step 3 involves routing to two individuals at one time, as outlined in the "Scenario Requirements" section in this chapter. One great option that Salesforce provides is the ability to choose whether both of these approvers are required or only one (in which case, the first one to review the record makes the call). Let's go with the latter option and only require approval from one of the two Customer Support directors.

For the "Select Approver" option, select "Automatically assign to approver(s)" and click the lookup icon, as done in Figure 6-22. One at a time, select each director. Since you don't require unanimous approval, you'll leave the default option selected allowing the first response to determine the overall decision for this step.

Figure 6-22. *Approval Step 3: Selection of multiple approvers using only one response*

Approval Step 4

Step 4 reintroduces the need for prequalification. You want to determine whether the Case is escalated or not; if it is, it requires an additional approval from one of your c-level officers. Since the criterion is singular and straightforward, the criteria builder will be sufficient. Figure 6-23 shows the section in which you will enter the step criteria.

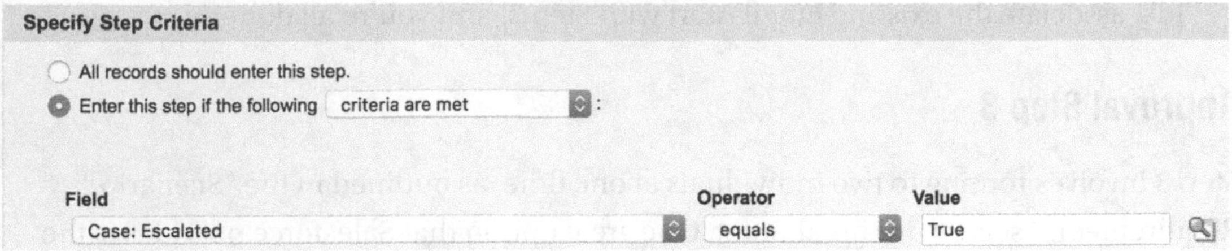
Specify Step Criteria
◯ All records should enter this step.
◉ Enter this step if the following criteria are met :
Field
Operator
Value
Case: Escalated
equals
True

***Figure 6-23.** Approval Step 4: Specifying step criteria*

While you've seen the queue selection in a previous approval step, you will change the reject behavior here. You will indicate that, if the C-level officers reject this request, it will need to go back down one level for further review. You can configure this by selecting the second option in the "Reject Behavior" section in Figure 6-24.

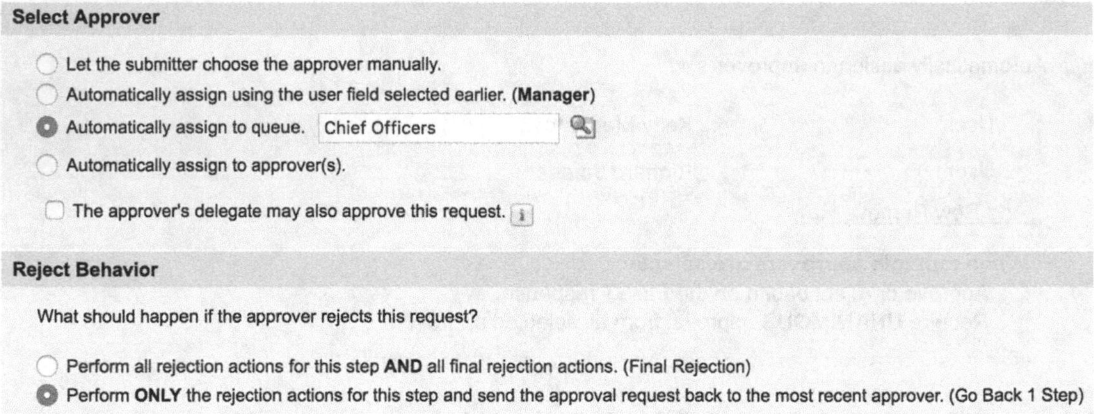
Select Approver
◯ Let the submitter choose the approver manually.
◯ Automatically assign using the user field selected earlier. (Manager)
◉ Automatically assign to queue. Chief Officers
◯ Automatically assign to approver(s).
☐ The approver's delegate may also approve this request.
Reject Behavior
What should happen if the approver rejects this request?
◯ Perform all rejection actions for this step AND all final rejection actions. (Final Rejection)
◉ Perform ONLY the rejection actions for this step and send the approval request back to the most recent approver. (Go Back 1 Step)

***Figure 6-24.** Filling in Approval Step 4: "Select Approver" and "Reject Behavior" sections*

You have completed your four approval steps! Figure 6-25 is a view from the approval process detail page.

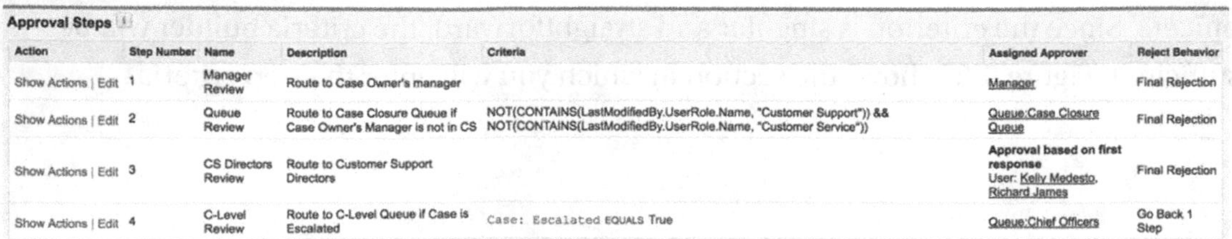

Approval Steps

Action	Step Number	Name	Description	Criteria	Assigned Approver	Reject Behavior
Show Actions | Edit	1	Manager Review	Route to Case Owner's manager		Manager	Final Rejection
Show Actions | Edit	2	Queue Review	Route to Case Closure Queue if Case Owner's Manager is not in CS	NOT(CONTAINS(LastModifiedBy.UserRole.Name, "Customer Support")) && NOT(CONTAINS(LastModifiedBy.UserRole.Name, "Customer Service"))	Queue:Case Closure Queue	Final Rejection
Show Actions | Edit	3	CS Directors Review	Route to Customer Support Directors		**Approval based on first response** User: Kelly Medesto, Richard James	Final Rejection
Show Actions | Edit	4	C-Level Review	Route to C-Level Queue if Case is Escalated	Case: Escalated EQUALS True	Queue:Chief Officers	Go Back 1 Step

***Figure 6-25.** Completed approval steps*

Final Actions

It is critical to properly establish the actions that will correspond to specific events in your approval process once it's underway. In specific, there are three actions to consider:

- Final Approval Actions

- Final Rejection Actions

- Recall Actions

For some organizations, the stamp of approval itself may be sufficient. However, I would recommend also considering both status updates and communication via email, at the very least. You will want to clear the Case Resolution Details field we used in this example, since this information is no longer relevant or accurate. Figure 6-26 gives a view of the flow of these final actions and Figure 6-27 shows the configuration steps necessary to implement them. To navigate to the appropriate configuration screen, click the "Add Existing" button in either the "Final Rejection Actions" or "Final Approval Actions" section on the record detail page of the approval process.

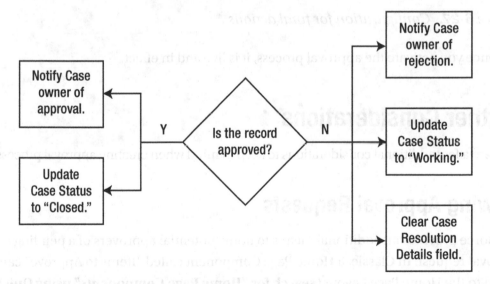

Figure 6-26. *Flow of actions related to final decisions*

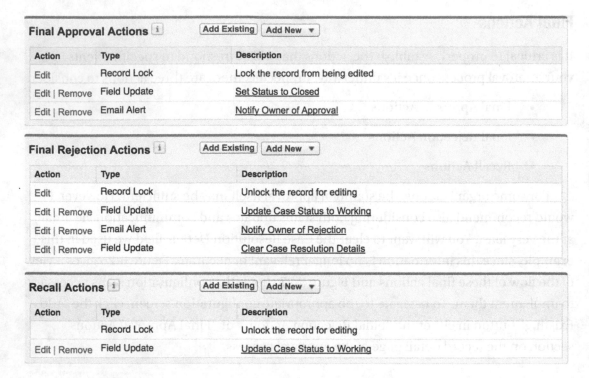

Figure 6-27. *Configuration for final actions*

Once you activate the approval process, it is live and in effect.

Further Considerations

Here are a few additional considerations to keep in mind when creating approval processes.

Viewing Approval Requests

Salesforce provides an additional means to notify potential approvers of a pending approval request. In Classic, a Home Page Component called "Items to Approve" can be added to the Home Page Layout (**search for "Home Page Components" using Quick Find**). In Lightning Experience, a Lightning Component called "Items to Approve" is available for drag 'n' drop onto the LEX home page. Either option is a great complement to the Email Template, as neither requires any action or visibility outside of Salesforce. I would definitely suggest adding the appropriate component if you utilize approval requests within your organization.

Submit for Approval Button

When dealing with the approval processes, the "Submit for Approval" button can catch you off guard. Even once your approval process is activated, you must add this button to the corresponding Page Layout(s). Without it, users cannot manually initiate the approval process. To add the button, enter the Page Layout editor, select "Buttons" on the left, and drag the "Submit for Approval" button down to the "Standard Buttons" section, as shown in Figure 6-28.

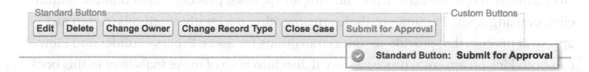

Figure 6-28. *Adding the "Submit for Approval" button to all applicable page layouts*

Note   The Spring '17 release brought a valuable enhancement to the proverbial approval process table. A new setting, "Add the Submit for Approval button and Approval History related list to all Object page layouts," was introduced. When checked, you no longer need to think about manually adding the Submit for Approval button to each page layout! Consider enabling this if you frequently use approval processes.

Invalid Submission Details

Unfortunately, Salesforce does not provide specific instructions for users who submit a record that does not meet the entry criteria. So, if a particular field needs to be set properly, the user would not be told how to do so when encountering an error. To complicate the situation, the error message applies not only to records with invalid entry criteria but also to submitters not included in the valid list of initial submitters. The vague error message you get when the program is unable to submit a record for approval is shown in Figure 6-29.

Unable to Submit for Approval

This record does not meet the entry criteria or initial submitters of any active approval processes. Please contact your administrator for assistance.

Click here to return to the previous page.

Figure 6-29. *Error message that appears when you haven't met entry criteria or when you're not included in the list of allowed initial submitters*

Initiation of Process

Originally, two options existed for initiating an approval process: either manual button click or using Apex. Fortunately, there are now other declarative methods to start an approval process that provide seamless transitions for users. Process Builder and Flow can both kick off approval processes; we'll dive into both of those tools later in this book.

Validation Rules

Status is typically a critical aspect of any effective approval process. Your entry criteria will allow you to restrict the allowed Status field values for users at the time of submission, which is very useful. However, you'll need to think through the overall process and may need to supplement it with one or more validation rules to ensure proper flow. For example, in the example scenario used in this chapter, you would want to restrict users from manually changing the status to "Closed," as that would defeat the purpose of the approval process. Think through your flow and add validation rules as needed.

Workflow Rules

Since field updates are commonly an element of approval processes, you will want to make sure that any overlaps with existing workflow rules are expected and desired. An approval process may work perfectly as configured; however, if you forget about a workflow rule related to one of the field updates that occurs at the point of final approval, you will likely have some undesired updates and unhappy users.

Recap

In this chapter, we reviewed the bulk of what Salesforce offers for declaratively building approval processes for records that warrant some special handling. We walked through a real-life scenario in order to bring some life to the various steps and settings, including entry criteria, initial submitters, notification Emails, Initial Submission actions, approval steps, implementing approval steps, and final actions. To round out the chapter, I offered some tips and additional considerations that might come in handy when building out your own approval processes.

Building Powerful Declarative Solutions with Process Builder

Prior to 2015, those looking to automate business processes on the Salesforce platform without using code depended almost solely on Workflow. Sure, a few functional prodigies out there were using Flow, but that was definitely the exception. If you wanted to send an e-mail when a specific Case field changed from X to Y, you would combine a Workflow rule with an Email Alert and be on your way. For that simple scenario, Workflow always worked well. However, as the desire and need for more advanced and varied automation grew, Workflow couldn't quite keep up. While it continues to serve as an automation stalwart to this day, it has been enhanced very infrequently and the scope of its capabilities have stagnated. Enter Process Builder.

In 2015, Process Builder was introduced to the Salesforce ecosystem and was immediately embraced as the missing link between creative declarative developers and the applications (of ever-increasing complexity and scope) that they were seeking to build. Unbeknownst to many, Process Builder was built on top of the core engine powering Flow (see next chapter for more on Flow), but with different capabilities and a different user interface. We've now had a few years to see significant advancements from Salesforce as well as powerful applications from partners and customers, giving us a much better understanding of the tool and its capabilities.

I would imagine that anyone familiar with this history is asking or has already asked, "Which tool should I use?" or "Is there any reason to still use Workflow?" I will dive into some comparative analysis in this chapter, but let me start off by making a few very clear

© Philip Weinmeister 2019

P. Weinmeister, *Practical Salesforce Development Without Code*,
https://doi.org/10.1007/978-1-4842-4871-3_7

and important statements that are critical for proper perspective of automation tools on the Salesforce platform. First, regarding Workflow:

- Workflow is alive and well. There are no known public plans to retire/sunset Workflow.

- Workflow "works"; it is known for its predictability and reliability.

- There is no inherent issue with maintaining existing Workflows.

That being said, let's face reality:

- Salesforce is not investing in Workflow.

- Salesforce has invested heavily in Process Builder since its inception in 2015 and continues to do so years later.

- Process Builder's capabilities are much more expansive than those of Workflow.

- Essentially all Workflows could, in theory, be rebuilt in Process Builder.

Ultimately, you will need to make the right decision for your organization and/or your clients when it comes to deciding on a strategy for using Workflow vs. Process Builder. In this chapter, I will try to give you the information you need to decide when to leverage Process Builder for building declarative solutions.

Understanding Process Builder

While Process Builder is, in my opinion, fairly intuitive, it can only help to have a thorough understanding of the tool before diving in. Even if you have used Process Builder for some time, it's unlikely you have utilized (or are even aware of) all the enhancements the process automation product team at Salesforce has delivered. My preceding statement about Salesforce's investment in and commitment to process automation means rapid change, emphasized through the volume and impact and process-related changes on the platform contained in the triannual release notes.

Let's start at the beginning though. At the highest level, Process Builder monitors specific changes/activity in Salesforce and automates other actions based on those particular changes. See Figure 7-1.

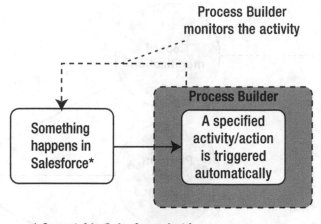

Figure 7-1. *Process Builder automates actions based on certain activities occurring in Salesforce*

Process Invocation

Let's dive a bit deeper into the "something happens" piece from Figure 7-1. Naturally, we want to start the beginning of the lifecycle of a Process, which is its invocation. A process has no value without an ability to invoke it. In other words, something on the platform must "kick off" a Process to evaluate it and, potentially, drive automated activities. Figure 7-2 shows the following invocation methods visually:

- A record is changed (record creation is considered a change).

- A platform event occurs.

- A Process invokes another Process.

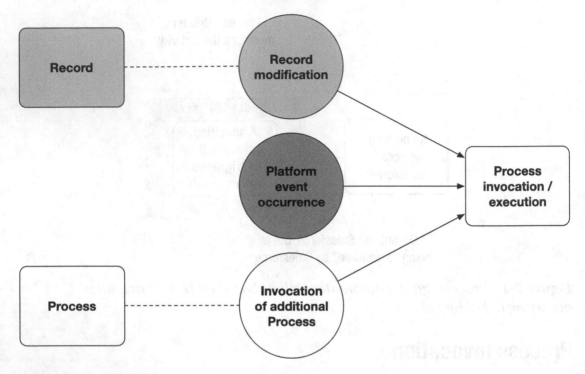

Figure 7-2. *Process invocation methods*

By far, record modifications serve as the most common method to invoke a process, but the other two methods do multiply the power of Process Builder and should be considered when building an automated solution with this tool.

Record Modification

Record modification-driven process invocation is fairly straightforward. If a record of a specified object is created or modified, you can automate an action as a result. For example, you might want to automate an action based on the creation of an opportunity or the update of a case. Let's look at the process – no pun intended – when working with record modification, as shown in Figure 7-3.

1. **Specify a standard or custom object**: Record-driven Processes must be associated with one and only one object for invocation.

2. **Identify the modification scope**: Whether the Process should look at record creation or record creation/edit (any change).

3. **Establish recursion behavior**: Establishes whether the automated change from a Process causes the same record to execute the flow more than once.

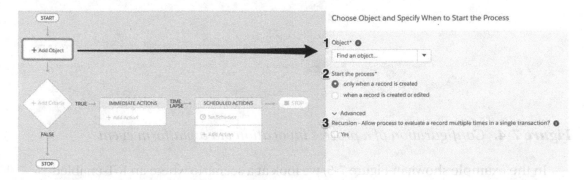

Figure 7-3. *Initiating automated actions within Process Builder through record modification*

Note   Record modification is the sole option that allows you to access data via trigger.old/priorvalue, as processes invoked by other processes can only access trigger.new/current data.

Platform Event

When they were introduced to the Salesforce platform around 2016, Platform Events significantly upped the ante in terms of value provided by Process Builder. With Platform Events, Process Builder can subscribe to events produced outside Salesforce and, in real-time, automate an action based on an occurrence of that event. Upon initial creation of a process, "A platform event occurs" can be selected for "The Process starts when." In that scenario, the process admin will select the event that triggers the process (1), as well as the record on which to act (2). See Figure 7-4.

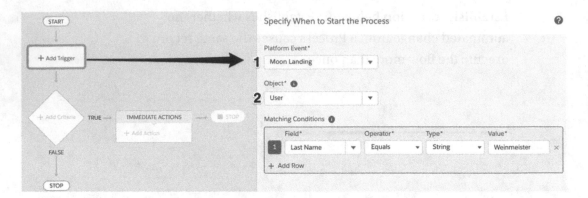

Figure 7-4. *Configuration of a process invocation via a platform event*

In the example shown in Figure 7-5, we look at a scenario where an IoT-enabled device hooked up to a water heater produces a platform event upon detecting water.

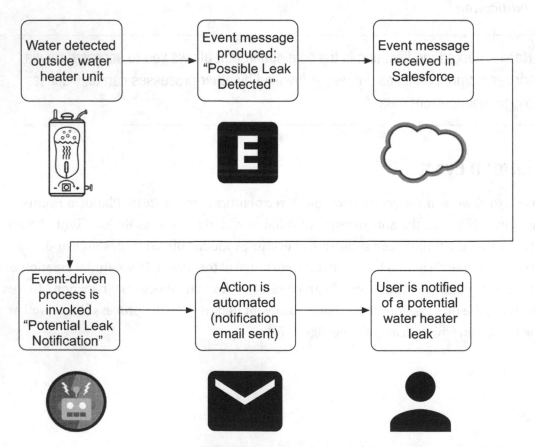

Figure 7-5. *In this example, a Salesforce Event (a signal from an IoT-enabled device) invokes a Process*

Process-to-Process Invocation

A final option for invoking a Process is associating it with another process as an automated action. This is an explicit activity; process 1 specifically identifies a second process. Process 2 is then associated with an object, similar to how a Process is triggered by record modification (see Figure 7-6).

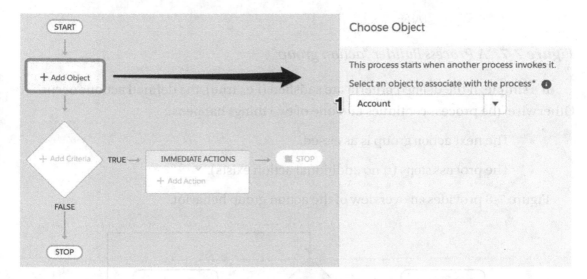

Figure 7-6. *Configure a Process that is invoked by another Process; the setup is similar to when record modification invokes a Process*

Action Groups

Once a process has been invoked or initiated, the action groups take over. An action group has a two-part structure (see Figure 7-7):

1. Action group criteria

2. Action group action

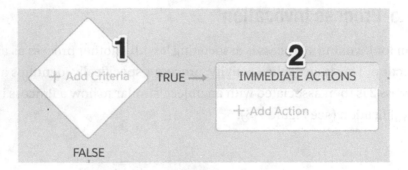

Figure 7-7. *A Process Builder "action group"*

It's simple. If the defined criteria are satisfied (i.e., true), the defined actions occur. Otherwise, the process continues and one of two things happens:

- The next action group is assessed.

- The process stops (if no additional action exists).

Figure 7-8 provides an overview of the action group behavior.

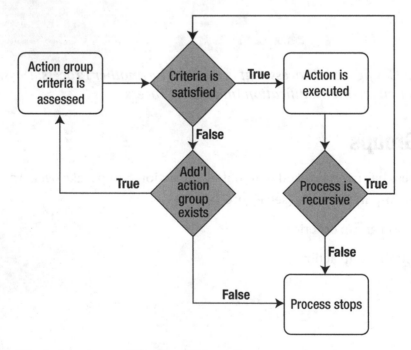

Figure 7-8. *The behavior and logic within a Process action group*

Action Group Criteria

Action group criteria determines whether a specific action is executed. The structure is almost identical across all types of processes. The only difference in criteria definition between record-driven, process-driven, and event-driven processes is that event-driven processes allow for the selection of either the event or the associated object for criteria definition. Figure 7-9 shows the user interface for the first two scenarios; Figure 7-10 covers the slight difference in the event-driven interface.

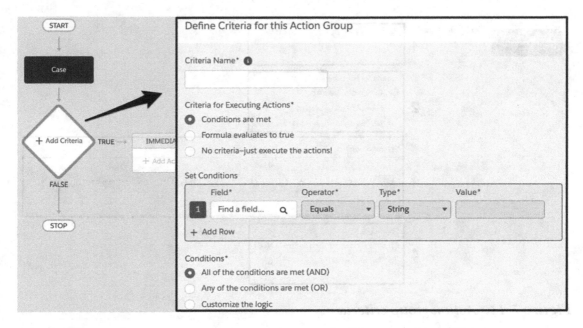

Figure 7-9. *Defining criteria for Processes invoked by record modification or another Process*

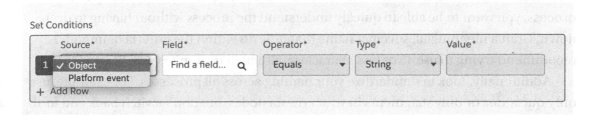

Figure 7-10. *The setting of conditions varies for Processes triggered by Events*

Four elements exist within Action Group Criteria (see Figure 7-11):

1. Name

2. Execution threshold/behavior

3. Criteria (via conditions or formula)

4. Conditional logic (if applicable)

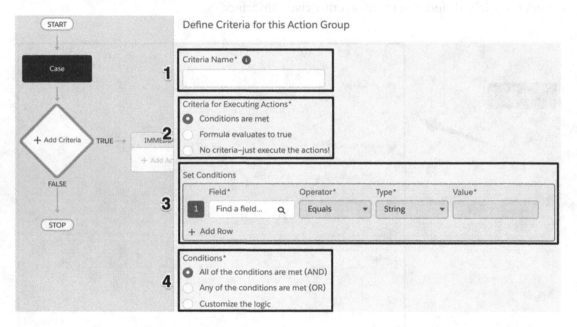

Figure 7-11. *Action group criteria*

Criteria Name

The name for your criteria matters more than you might realize. When you open a process, you want to be able to quickly understand the process without having to drill down. Craft a meaningful, succinct name that *fully fits* within the criteria diamond. I recommend trying to use 40 or less characters, although the limit is well beyond that.

Additionally, look to standardize your naming across all processes. For example, use only questions or only statements in your criteria nodes, but don't switch back and forth between the two.

Execution Threshold/Behavior

When it comes to the determination of whether your process actions should be executed your first choice is deciding if criteria should exist at all. That's right, you can completely bypass any conditional aspects of execution by selecting "No criteria..." You would select this option if you *always* wanted in-scope records to drive an action based on creation and/or updates.

For the more common scenario where conditional logic does exist, you have another choice: use what I have previously referred to as "criteria builder" or use Formula Builder. How do you choose? First, let's break down the main pros and cons of using each, as shown in Table 7-1. While there is some subjectivity in these factors, I can say with confidence that the majority of administrators would agree with this assessment.

Table 7-1. *Using Conditions vs. Formulas in Process Builder*

	Criteria/Condition Builder	Formula Builder
Easier to use	Yes	No
Easier to maintain	Yes	No
More powerful/functional	No	Yes

Based on the preceding assessment, I would suggest using criteria builder, if possible. If it cannot support your required conditions, then explore Formula Builder to solve your needs. For use of formulas, review Chapters 2 and 3, which are focused on formula functions and fields. Here, we will take a closer look at creating conditions through use of the criteria builder provided within Process Builder.

Conditions with Criteria Builder

Building conditions within Process Builder is very similar to the same activity for Workflow, but it is not identical and warrants a review. There are four parts to building conditions, as shown in Figure 7-12.

1. Field

2. Operator

3. Type

4. Value

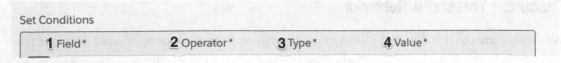

Figure 7-12. *Condition configurations*

Field

To set the proper context for Operator, Type, and Value, the Field must first be selected. First, you click "Find a field…," which brings up a "Select a Field" modal. See Figure 7-13.

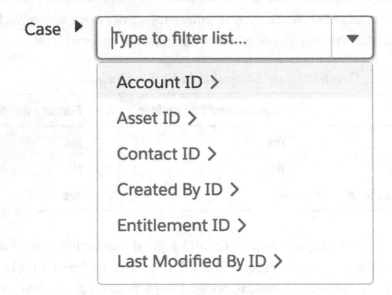

Figure 7-13. *Selecting a field*

Now, you select the appropriate field. Typing prefilters the list to expedite the process. Note that anything shown with a right arrow (e.g., "Account ID >") signifies a lookup to another object. Once a lookup is selected, you will select a field or another lookup. If you select another lookup, you're in the same boat: select your field or keep "going up the chain." Once you have selected your field, you will see a summary of the selection, as shown in Figure 7-14.

Case ▶ Account ID ▶ Account Name

You have selected the following field:

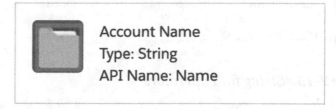

Account Name
Type: String
API Name: Name

Figure 7-14. *Here, "Account Name" from the Account object was selected for the Case object by traversing through the Account lookup on Case*

Operators

Once the field is selected, the corresponding operator values are populated within the picklist. Here are examples of some common field types and the operators that are made available:

- **String**: Equals, Does not equal, Starts with, Ends with, Contains, Is null, Is changed

- **Picklist**: Equals, Does not equal, Starts with, Ends with, Contains, Is null, Is changed

- **Boolean**: Equals, Does not equal, Is null, Is changed

- **Date/Time**: Equals, Does not equal, Greater than, Greater than or equal, Less than, Less than or equal, Contains, Is null, Is changed

- **Currency**: Equals, Does not equal, Greater than, Greater than or equal, Less than, Less than or equal, Contains, Is null, Is changed

- **Number**: Equals, Does not equal, Greater than, Greater than or equal, Less than, Less than or equal, Contains, Is null, Is changed

Figure 7-15 shows the values for a string field.

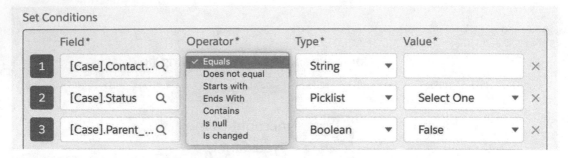

Figure 7-15. *String field operators*

Type

Type gets pretty darn interesting. This is one area whether Process Builder leaves Workflow in the rear-view mirror. Four types exist:

- **Field Type**: Enter the static value to be used in evaluating the condition. For example, string, picklist value, Boolean, date/time, currency, number, and so on.

- **Field Reference**: A reference to another field related to the same object record. This is immensely powerful and is not available in Workflow. Let's say you want to make sure your Contact's phone number matches the phone number on the Contact's Account (but the number could change at any time); you can use field reference to compare the value of the Contact phone field to the Account phone field.

- **Global Constant**: For example, $GlobalConstant.EmptyString.

- **Formula**: Any custom formula. See chapters on formulas to fully harness the power of formulas.

Value

Your final step is to specify the value to be assessed in your condition.

- **String, Currency, Number, Date/Time**: Enter the appropriate value as free-form text.

- **Picklist/Boolean**: Select from the provided list (True/False for Boolean).

- **Global Constant**: Select from the list of available global constants.

- **Formula**: Build a formula; this will return a value to your condition to be assessed.

Conditional Logic

As with the use of criteria builders elsewhere on the platform, you can configure the logic that is leveraged when determining whether conditions have been met. Let's say you create five conditions (C1–C5). Your choices are

- All conditions are met (C1 AND C2 AND C3 AND C4 AND C5 = true).

- At least one condition is met (C1 OR C2 OR C3 OR C4 OR C5 = true).

- Custom logic rules. For example:

  - (C1 OR C2) AND C3 AND C4 AND C5

  - C1 AND (C2 OR (C3 AND C4)) AND C5

  - (C1 OR C2 OR C3 OR C4) AND C5

Action Group Actions

Once your criteria have been established, you will configure the action(s) that are executed (dependent on the satisfaction of conditions).

Action Types

The available actions are best shared in context alongside the capabilities of Workflow. Table 7-2 will help illuminate the true, full power of Process Builder and why it has become so popular.

Table 7-2. *Comparing Workflow and Process Builder Actions*

	Workflow	Process Builder
Call Apex	No	Yes
Create a record	No	Yes
Update records	Partial	Yes
Email alerts	Yes	Yes
Invoke flows	No	Yes
Invoke processes	No	Yes
Post to Chatter	No	Yes
Trigger quick actions	No	Yes
Submit for approval	No	Yes

Note   Process Builder is "bulkified." That means that multiple records can be changed together (e.g., through Data Loader) and Process Builder will look at all records, not just the first in the list. You will encounter standard limits on the platform, so do be aware of those before releasing a Process into production to handle large sets of records kicking off a Process at the same time.

Creating a Process: A Step-by-Step Guide

Let's create a process together! This process is Service Cloud-oriented and will provide an example of multiple areas within Process Builder. Please note that it is built for an illustration. Any real-world use of this process would require a full, thorough review of other requirements that might come into play.

The Scenario

Our organization, VltLkr (pronounced "Vault Locker"), provides B2B data encryption services to other corporations. The services require an extremely responsive support organization. An area of difficulty has been with VltLkr's management of parent and child cases, resulting in inaccurate statuses and manual work.

Fortunately, you've been brought in to bring some much-needed organization and optimization to the case management process. You're tasked with the following goals to build out what is shown in Figure 7-16:

- **Establish a process** to close master cases

- **Automate submission of an approval request** to make that happen

- **Trigger various actions** when a master case is closed, (e.g., record updates/new record creation)

- Automate all of these **without a single line of code!**

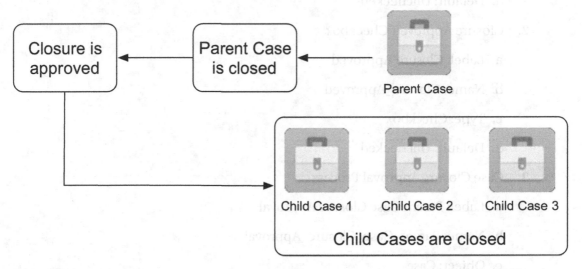

Figure 7-16. *A high-level view of what will be automated with Process Builder*

Process Creation

It's time to create the process. However, before diving straight in, we will first look at related dependencies.

Pre-Exercise Setup: Add Custom Fields and Relationships

To establish the appropriate data model to support our functionality, we will need to first create a few custom fields on the Case object:

1. Parent Checkbox

    a. Label: Parent

    b. Name: Parent

    c. Type: Checkbox

    d. Default: Unchecked

2. Closure Approved Checkbox

    a. Label: Closure Approved

    b. Name: Closure_Approved

    c. Type: Checkbox

    d. Default: Unchecked

3. Case Closure Approval Process

    a. Label: Parent Case Closure Approval

    b. Name: Parent_Case_Closure_Approval

    c. Object: Case

    d. Details: The critical behaviors of this approval process are

       • Send to specified approvers for approval (choose whomever you want as approver(s)).

       • Upon (final) approval, update Closure Approved custom field to True/Checked.

       • Make sure the Field Update for Closure Approved in the last step has the following set to true (checked): "Re-evaluate Workflow Rules after Field Change."

4. Case Status Value

    a. Add additional Status picklist value, "Pending Closure Approval."

5. Case Reason Value

    a. Add additional Case Reason picklist value, "Outage."

6. Close Case Quick Action

    a. Follow the steps in the help article at this URL: `https://help.salesforce.com/articleView?id=cases_set_up_lex_close_case.htm`

    b. Display only the Status and Case Reason fields.

7. Data setup

    a. Create a new Case called "Parent Case" and check the "Parent" checkbox.

    b. Create at least two new Cases that look up to "Parent Case" via the Parent Case lookup relationship field.

Exercise 1: Create New Process and Define Criteria for First Action Group

Here is an overview of Exercise 1:

-   **Goal**: Create a new process to be used for the purpose of automating specific Service Cloud-related operations. Establish the criteria that will trigger the first set of corresponding actions.

-   **Scenario**: VltLkr wants to be able to identify whether related cases should be closed based on the concept of a parent/master case and cascading a parent case closure down to the child cases. Additionally, VltLkr would like to ensure accuracy with a manual approval during the process.

-   **Tasks**:

    -   Create a new process within Process Builder.

    -   Configure the new process to be used with case records.

    -   Name the criteria for your first action group and define the criteria type.

    -   Set criteria conditions and condition logic.

Instructions:

Step 1: Create a new process for your Service Cloud automation.

1. Navigate to **Process Builder**.

2. Click **New**.

3. Create your new process.

    a. **Process Name:** Child Case Auto-Closure

    b. **API Name:** (This field auto-populates if you use tab.)

    c. **Description:** Process to close all child cases upon parent case closure and automate related actions.

    d. **The process starts when:** A record changes

4. Click **Save.**

Step 2: Add an object to your process.

1. Click + **Add Object.**

2. Click **Find an object... and select** Case.

3. For **Start the process, select** when a record is created or edited.

4. Click **Save.**

Step 3: Name the criteria for your first action group and define the criteria type.

1. Click + **Add Criteria** within your newly created process.

2. Click below **Criteria Name** and enter "Parent Case Set to Closed"

3. Under **Criteria for Executing Actions**, select Conditions are met.

Step 4: Set criteria conditions and condition logic.

1. Add a condition that Parent is checked.

    a. Under **Set Conditions, click Find a field....**

    b. **Scroll down and click Parent.**

    c. **Click Choose.**

    d. Click the **Value** drop-down and select True.

2. Add a condition that Closed is true.

   a. Click + **Add Row**.

   b. Click **Find a field...**.

   c. **Scroll down and click Closed**.

   d. **Click Choose**.

   e. Click the **Value** drop-down and select True.

3. Add a condition that Closure Approved is false.

   a. Click + **Add Row**.

   b. Click **Find a field...**.

   c. **Scroll down and click Closure Approved**.

   d. **Click Choose**.

4. Click **Advanced** and check the Yes checkbox next to Do you want to execute the actions only when specified changes are made to the record?

5. Click **Save** at the bottom of the page.

See Figure 7-17.

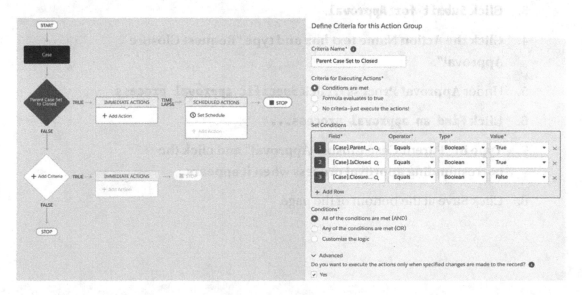

Figure 7-17. *Our Process after completing Exercise 1*

Exercise 2: Add Actions Within First Action Group

Here is an overview of Exercise 2:

- **Goal**: Build and use a custom report type to retrieve data that spans multiple object types.

- **Scenario**: VltLkr wants to automate the submission of an approval request to ensure that the parent case is truly closed. During the approval process, all child cases will be updated to reflect the pending closure.

- **Tasks**:

  - Configure an action to automatically submit the case record for approval.

  - Configure an action to update the status of child case records.

Instructions:

Step 1: Add an action to automatically submit the opportunity for approval.

1. Click **+ Add Action, to the right of the criteria defined in Exercise 1**.

2. **Click the Action drop-down**.

3. **Click `Submit for Approval`**.

4. **Click the Action Name text box and type "Request Closure Approval"**.

5. Under **Approval Process∗**, click **`Specific approval process`**.

6. Click **`Find an approval process...`**

7. **Type in "Parent Case Closure Approval" and click the corresponding approval process when it appears.**

8. Click **Save** at the bottom of the page.

Step 2: Configure an action to automatically update Status field based on the previously defined criteria.

1. Click + **Add Action, to the right of the criteria defined in Exercise 1.**

2. **Click the Action drop-down.**

3. **Click Update Records.**

4. **Click the Action Name text box and type "Update Child Cases".**

5. **Under Select a Record to Update, click Select a record related to the Case.**

6. **Click the text box showing "Type to filter list...".**

7. **Type "Cases" and click Cases when it appears (it should show API Name as ParentId.**

8. **Click Choose.**

9. Under Criteria for Updating Records, select Updated records meet all conditions.

10. Under Filter the records you update based on these conditions, click Find a field....

11. Scroll down and click Closed.

12. Under Set new field values for the records you update, click Find a field....

13. **Scroll down and click Status.**

14. Click the **Value** drop-down and select Pending Closure Approval.

15. Click **Save** at the bottom of the page.

A view of our process after Step 1 in Exercise 2 is shown in Figure 7-18.

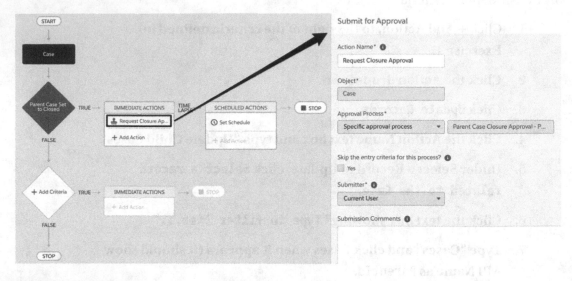

Figure 7-18. *Our action to automatically submit a request for approval*

A view of our process after Step 2 in Exercise 2 is shown in Figure 7-19.

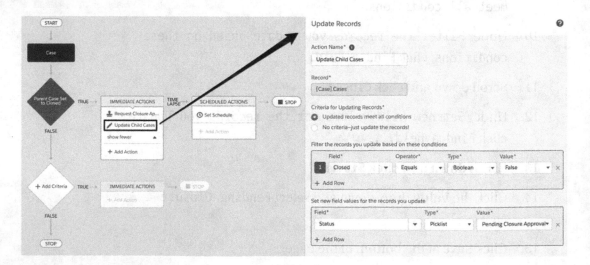

Figure 7-19. *Our action to automatically update the Status field*

Exercise 4: Add Actions Within Second Action Group and Activate Your Process

Here is an overview of this exercise:

- **Goal**: Automate actions based on previously defined criteria.

- **Scenario**: VltLkr wants to kick off a number of automated actions when a parent case is closed.

- **Tasks**: Configure an action to automatically close child cases that look up to the updated parent case.

  - Configure an action that will automatically create a new task on the case.

  - Configure an action that will automatically post to Chatter about the parent case closure.

  - Activate your process.

Instructions:

Step 1: Configure an action that will update all of the child cases associated with this case.

1. Click **+ Add Action, to the right of the criteria defined in Exercise 3**.

2. **Click the Action drop-down**.

3. **Click `Update Records`**.

4. **Click the Action Name text box and type "Close Child Cases"**.

5. Under **Select a Record to Update, click `Select a record related to the Case`**.

6. Click **`Type to filter list...`**, type "Cas", then click **`Cases`**.

7. **Click Choose**.

8. Make sure `No criteria—just update the records!` is selected.

9. Under **Set new field values...**, click **`Find a field...`**.

10. **Scroll down and click `Case Reason`**.

11. Click the **Type** drop-down for Case Reason and select Field Reference.

12. Click **Type to filter list...**.

13. **Scroll down and click Case Reason**.

14. **Click Choose**.

15. Click + **Add Row**.

16. Click **Find a field...**.

17. **Scroll down and click Status**.

18. **Click the Value drop-down and select Closed**.

19. Click **Save** at the bottom of the page.

Step 2: Configure an action to automatically create a task related to the parent case.

1. Click + **Add Action, to the right of the criteria defined in Exercise 3**.

2. **Click the Action drop-down**.

3. **Click Create a Record**.

4. **Click the Action Name text box and type "Create Task for Case Owner"**.

5. Under **Record Type∗, click Find a record...**.

6. **Scroll down and click Task**.

7. Click the **Value** drop-down for Priority and select High.

8. Click the **Value** drop-down for Status and select In Progress.

9. Click the **Type** drop-down for Assigned To ID and select Field Reference.

10. Click **Find a field...**.

11. **Scroll down and click Owner ID**.

12. **Click Choose**.

13. Click + **Add Row**.

14. Click **Find a field...**.

15. **Scroll down and click Related To ID**.

16. Click the **Type** drop-down and select Field Reference.

17. Click Find a field... **under Value∗**.

18. **Scroll down and click Case ID**.

19. **Click Choose**.

20. Click + **Add Row**.

21. Click **Find a field...**.

22. **Scroll down and click Subject**.

23. **Click the Value text area and type "Post-mortem work".**

24. Click **Save** at the bottom of the page.

Step 3: Configure an action that will automatically post to Chatter about the auto-closed child cases.

1. Click + **Add Action, to the right of the criteria defined in Exercise 4**.

2. **Click the Action Type drop-down.**

3. **Click Post to Chatter**.

4. **Click the Action Name text box and type "Post to Chatter".**

5. Under **Post to∗, click This Record**.

6. Under **Message∗, click the text area box and type** "All child cases have been closed!"

7. Click **Save** at the bottom of the page.

Step 4: Activate your process.

1. Click **Activate at the top-right of the screen**.

2. **Click Confirm**.

See Figure 7-20 for a view of Step 1 after being completed.

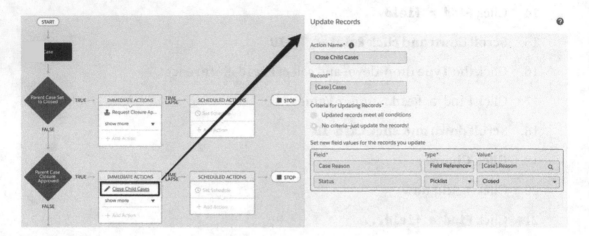

Figure 7-20. *Configure child case update*

See Figure 7-21 for a view of Step 2 after being completed.

Figure 7-21. *Configure task creation*

See Figure 7-22 for a view of Step 3 after being completed.

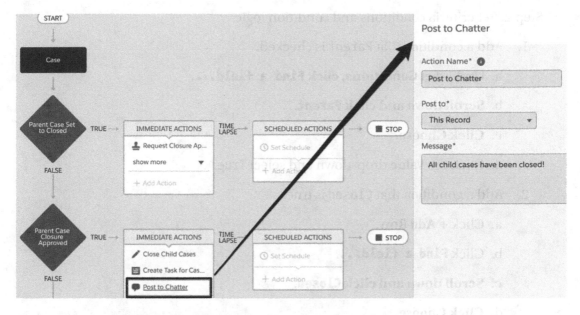

Figure 7-22. Configuration Chatter post activity

Exercise 3: Define Criteria for Second Action Group

Here is an overview of Exercise 3:

- **Goal**: Establish the criteria that will trigger the second set of corresponding actions.

- **Scenario**: Your organization wants to trigger a set of automated actions when a parent case is closed.

- **Tasks**:
  - Name the criteria for your second action group and define the criteria type.

  - Set criteria conditions and condition logic.

Instructions:

Step 1: Name the criteria for your first action group and define the criteria type.

1. Click + **Add Criteria** within your newly created process.

2. Click below **Criteria Name** and enter "Parent Case Closure Approved."

3. Under **Criteria for Executing Actions**, select Conditions are met.

Step 2: Set criteria conditions and condition logic.

1. Add a condition that Parent is checked.

   a. Under **Set Conditions, click `Find a field...`**.

   b. **Scroll down and click `Parent`**.

   c. **Click Choose.**

   d. Click the **Value** drop-down and select True.

2. Add a condition that Closed is true.

   a. Click + **Add Row.**

   b. Click **`Find a field...`**.

   c. **Scroll down and click `Closed`**.

   d. **Click Choose.**

   e. Click the **Value** drop-down and select True.

3. Add a condition that Closure Approved is true.

   a. Click + **Add Row.**

   b. Click **`Find a field...`**.

   c. **Scroll down and click `Closure Approved`**.

   d. **Click Choose.**

   e. Click the **Value** drop-down and select True.

4. Click **Advanced** and check the Yes checkbox next to `Do you want to execute the actions only when specified changes are made to the record?`

5. Click **Save** at the bottom of the page.

Figure 7-23 shows a view of the criteria for the second action group.

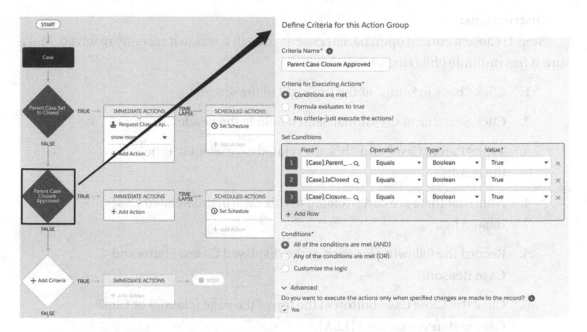

Figure 7-23. *Criteria configuration for our second action group*

Exercise 5: Run (and Validate) Your Process

Here is an overview of this exercise:

- **Goal**: Validate the process that you just created.

- **Scenario**: A parent case is resolved that automatically closes a few child cases. Validate all of the expected automated behaviors that should be triggered.

- **Tasks**:

  - Update a parent case for as though it was just recently resolved.

  - Approve a related approval request that was triggered by your process.

  - Validate the actions resulting from the "Service Cloud Automation" process.

Instructions:

Step 1: Close a current open parent case as though it was just recently resolved. Make sure it has multiple child cases related to it.

1. Click "Back to Setup" at the top-right of the screen.

2. Click Search... in the Global Search field in the header.

3. Type "Parent Case" and click the related case when it appears in the results.

4. Note that there are cases related to this Case in the Related Cases related list.

5. Record the following for each of the displayed Cases: Status and Case Reason.

6. Click the Close Case button at the top of the page (classic) or Close Case action you created (LEX).

7. Set Status to Closed.

8. Set Case Reason to Outage.

9. Click Save.

Step 2: Validate values of child Cases.

1. Child Cases should have a status value of "Pending Closure Approval."

Step 3: Validate and approve the automatically submitted approval request. Make sure to be logged in as the specified approver or a system administrator.

1. Scroll down to Approval History and note the new approval request.

2. Click the "Approve/Reject" link associated with the approval request and then click Approve (classic only).

3. Click the Approve button (2×) (LEX only).

Step 4: Validate automatic actions previously configured in the process.

1. Scroll down to the Related Cases related list.

2. Note that related cases have a Status of Closed and a Case Reason of Outage.

3. Scroll down to the Open Activities related list.

4. Note a newly created task, created with the details set in the process.

5. Scroll up to the top of the Case page.

6. Click the Feed tab to expose the Chatter feed.

7. Confirm that a Chatter post was automatically created through your process with the text of "All child cases have been closed."

Figure 7-24 shows the action of closing the parent case in Lightning Experience.

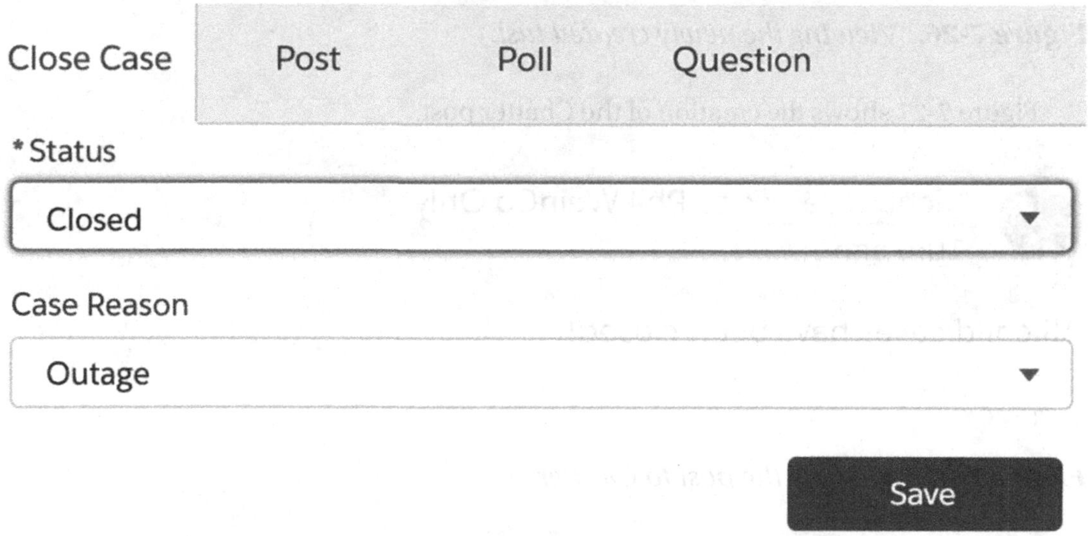

Figure 7-24. Closing the parent case

Figure 7-25 shows the approval of the approval request.

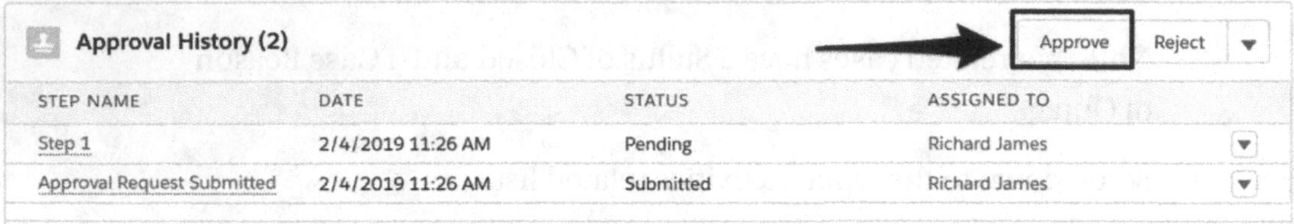

STEP NAME	DATE	STATUS	ASSIGNED TO	
Step 1	2/4/2019 11:26 AM	Pending	Richard James	▼
Approval Request Submitted	2/4/2019 11:26 AM	Submitted	Richard James	▼

📤 **Approval History (2)**   [Approve] [Reject] [▼]

Figure 7-25. *Approving the request to close the parent case*

Figure 7-26 shows the creation of the new task.

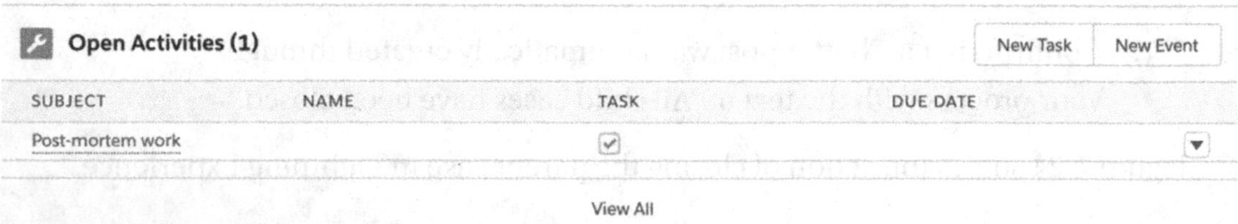

🔧 **Open Activities (1)**   [New Task] [New Event]

SUBJECT	NAME	TASK	DUE DATE	
Post-mortem work		✓		▼

View All

Figure 7-26. *Viewing the newly created task*

Figure 7-27 shows the creation of the Chatter post.

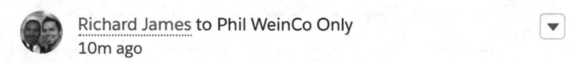

Richard James to Phil WeinCo Only
10m ago   [▼]

All child cases have been closed!

1 view

Figure 7-27. *Viewing the post to Chatter*

Figure 7-28 shows Status and Case Reason of a child case following the closure of the parent case.

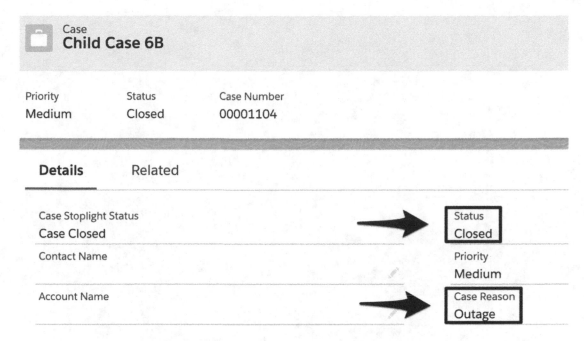

Figure 7-28. *The child case reflects the desired values in Status and Case Reason following the closure of the parent case*

Taking Our Process Further

This process was built for clarification and demonstration purposes. Feel free to expand on it for your own needs. However, if you do, make sure to think through all related requirements in detail before going live!

Recap

In this chapter, we covered what has become Workflow's successor for many in the Salesforce ecosystem. We discussed when you might use a process (including when considering the use of Workflow), walked through the different elements of a process, and built our very own process from scratch. This should be plenty to get you up and on your way to building powerful and valuable processes for your organization or clients.

CHAPTER 8

Producing Advanced Automation with Flow

If you are getting the sense that Salesforce has a strong focus on business process automation, you are absolutely correct. I have dedicated separate chapters to automation via the utilization of Workflow and Process Builder, yet another key automation tool still needs to be discussed: Flow. Flow has had quite a history and has held a variety of previous titles. It resides in a space that offers significant value for developers and nondevelopers alike: it allows for significantly more intricacy and complexity than the other automation solutions I have discussed and it does so without requiring code. I will be the first to say that the power of Flow can absolutely be extended with custom code, but that is not the focus of this book. Flow is not simply a different means to achieve the same results that you saw with workflow rules and processes; it covers additional different use cases. It is critical to understand when and why you would choose to use Flow to create flows for your business before getting into the details of how it works.

Flows, the output of the Flow tool, can involve a large number of components and can be extremely complex. This chapter is not intended to be a complete resource on every aspect of flows but instead to provide guidance and walk you through a real-life business scenario for which a flow can be developed. A few Flow experts ("flownatics") have authored books dedicated to process automation via Flow, and those can serve as an excellent supplement for those of you looking to go even deeper into the world of this tool.

In this chapter, you will

- Understand the differences between flows, processes, and workflow rules

- Learn when Flow can be used to effectively solve a business need

- Become familiar with both Flow tools, including Cloud Flow Designer and the newer Flow Builder

- Build your own flow from the ground up

© Philip Weinmeister 2019
P. Weinmeister, *Practical Salesforce Development Without Code*,
https://doi.org/10.1007/978-1-4842-4871-3_8

Why Flow?

While Flow clearly offers more functionality than workflow rules, it would likely be short-sighted to use Flow for 100 percent of your Salesforce automation. Workflow rules and Process Builder allow you to create event-triggered actions that occur immediately or at some specified point in the future. While they may possess some level of complexity, managing and/or enhancing them is often a relatively straightforward task once you are familiar with the tools. Although possible, using Flow instead of workflow rules to update Field B when Field A changes would be overkill. While I feel obliged to provide this warning to not exclude workflow rules, it is true that Flow does cover a number of scenarios that cannot be satisfied by workflow rules alone. We will look at some of these scenarios in the following sections.

Event-Triggered and User-Triggered Flows

Years ago, a primary factor in the decision between using workflow rules and using Flow in order to employ an automated solution was whether you wanted an action to be driven by an event (as it would be with workflow rules) or by a user (as happens with Flows). In the absence of writing custom code to supplement a configuration-based solution, actions resulting from workflow rules continue to be limited to event-triggered activity. A user doesn't manually make the decision to "activate" a workflow rule; rather the user's behavior is subject to the configured business rules and his system actions determine whether or not automation occurs.

However, flows can be triggered by either a system event or a user action. Previously, flows sat opposite from workflow rules, requiring the user to initiate the process. However, "auto-launched" flows were introduced, drastically changing the game. Along with the traditional types of actions that can be driven by a workflow rule (e.g., Email Alerts, Field Updates, Tasks, and Outbound Messages), there are now declarative to kick off a Flow without human intervention.

Note   Although this book focuses on development without code, it must be pointed out that the capabilities with Flow can be significantly extended using Apex, Lightning Components, and/or Visualforce.

User Input and Decision Points

With a single workflow rule, once the initial user input kicks off a rule, all remaining actions are automated; no additional user input will be elicited. One powerful feature of Flow is the "Screen" element, which provides the ability to capture user input *during* the workflow process. The input can be tied to a particular field or not. For example, you could use a flow to "fill out" a customer's Contact record in a logical or strategic sequence that differs from the standard Contact detail page. Alternatively, you could ask questions that would help determine how to handle a particular customer situation. Specifically, these questions could be associated with one or more decision points, another standout feature of Flow. Using either existing data or data captured during an executed workflow, you can configure different outcomes to occur.

Additionally, the data captured as input from a customer could then be used as query criteria to identify additional details specific to the customer or her situation. Figure 8-1 shows a short flow that involves both input and output on each page.

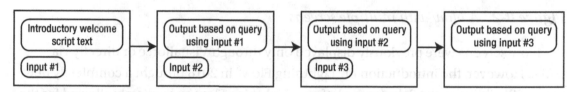

Figure 8-1. *You can capture input and display output on Flow screens*

Screen Output, UI Output, and Lightning Flow

With workflow rules, the only notable impact on the user interface has been the automated changes made to the modified record(s). However, with Flow, custom pages showing customized combinations of text and existing data can be displayed to the user through the Salesforce user interface. These pages could be used to capture user input, as I previously mentioned, or depending on your organization's needs, they could instead be used to display useful information to the user. For example, a customized set of fields showing key contact, account, and subscription information could be displayed to aid the user in confirming a customer's identity. See Figure 8-2 for a conceptual view of a Flow with multiple screens.

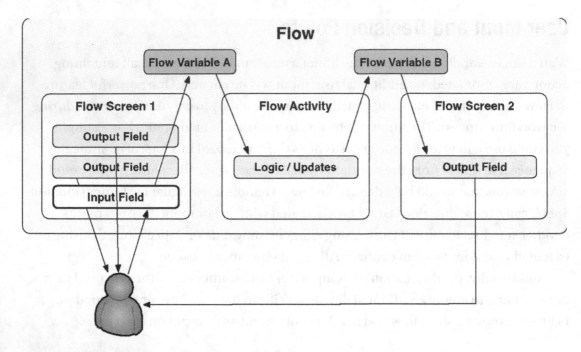

Figure 8-2. *A Flow with multiple screens*

Flow screens were previously displayed only through Visualforce or directly via URLs. However, the introduction of "Lightning Flow" in 2018 brought a completely new level of flexibility to the Salesforce platform. Lightning Flow immediately allowed for the drag 'n' drop of Flows onto Lightning interfaces, including in both Lightning Experience and Lightning Communities. Figure 8-3 shows the Flow component within a Lightning community.

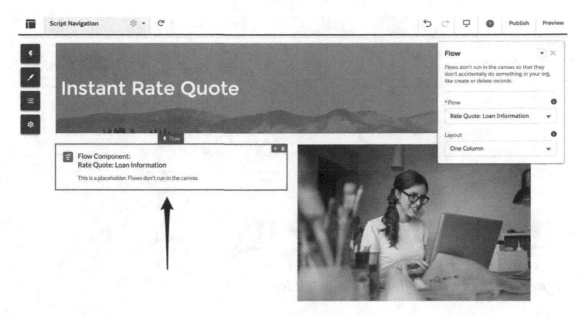

Figure 8-3. *Lightning Flow within a community*

Multiple Steps/Cohesive View of Process

Although it is possible to "chain" more than one rule to trigger an action when using workflow rules, doing so adds significant risk and complexity to your system's behavior. While some use cases may exist that could benefit from chaining workflow rules, the sensitivity of this approach prevents me from recommending it as a broad approach for a solution. The fact alone that your chained rules have no direct association that is visible within the Setup menu is a potential challenge that warrants thinking twice before utilizing that approach. Process Builder does address this, at least to a degree, and could potentially serve as the right solution in this case.

We must also bring Flow into the conversation here. Flow is ripe for multiple updates or steps within an automated process. The visual aspect of this tool provides a major boost. If you create a sequence of updates within a flow, you can get a visual representation of the process and see what happens along the way. Additionally, the flow is designed for these sequential updates. Workflow rules are very limited in this regard, in that a workflow rule-driven action that modifies the originally updated record can't trigger a second update to that same record. With Flow, you can update the same record multiple times without an issue. Figure 8-4 gives a look at a completed end-to-end flow.

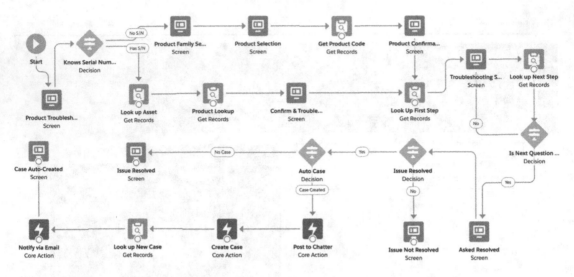

Figure 8-4. *A look at a flow in Flow Builder*

Subflows and Advanced Flow Topics

Flows are not only the containers of the overall process automation, they can be modular pieces of process automation that are referenced from within a flow. While I won't get into subflows in detail in this chapter, it's important to know about the concept of subflows (shown in Figure 8-5).

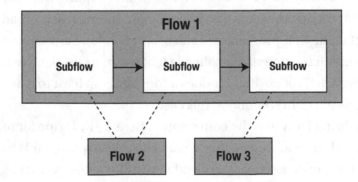

Figure 8-5. *The concept of subflows*

There other additional topics that I would consider advanced that can truly push the limits of what is possible with Flow without using a line of code. The ability to loop through collections of records, store related variables, and then reuse those variables later in a Flow, for example, is something that goes well beyond the scope of Process

Builder. Flow "actions" and "templates" are driving a grow third-party library of modular solutions that can be downloaded and used within a flow...again, without any code. Make sure to consider what AppExchange has to offer when thinking about developing Flow solutions declaratively. Figure 8-6 shows a Flow solution that is available on AppExchange.

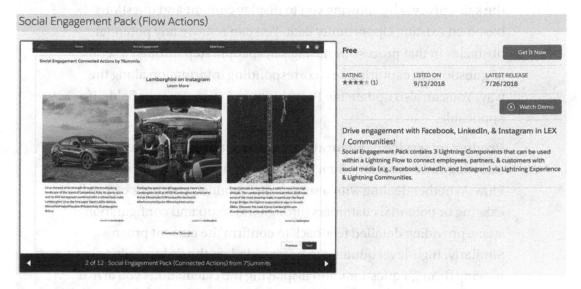

Figure 8-6. *A Flow solution that can be downloaded from AppExchange*

Effective Application of Flow

Flow applies to a number of applicable real-life scenarios. Generally, it is most valuable when those scenarios involve interaction between the user and the presented interface. You can build workflows that have no user-facing components once kicked off; however, depending on the exact requirements, a solution based on Visualforce, Apex, and/or other code may better satisfy your organization's needs. Some examples of when it is most effective to apply Flow include

- **Lead qualification**: Flow allows you to walk a potential contact through a series of questions to determine the prospect's qualification level. Newly captured data will be saved to the Lead record, and data you have already captured can be displayed on the screen to help reassure the individual that you know him/her and have listened to him/her during what can be a fairly cold and impersonal process. Ultimately, you can have the Lead marked as unqualified or follow up the call with a conversion to an Opportunity for qualified Leads.

- **Sales strategy/methodology**: The tool enables you to provide your sales team with a script to guide them through the ins and outs of the sales process by allowing you to display content and questions based on existing Opportunity data. You can remove any potential obstacles in that process by having salespeople step through a series of questions to capturing key, corresponding information along the way. You can also update the Probability and even Amount fields, if applicable.

- **Product or service configuration/sales quotations**: The idea of selecting various options for a service or product plays very well in Flow. Whether dealing with a service or a product, your reps can walk existing or potential customers through the setup and configuration steps, providing detailed feedback to confirm the current progress. Similarly, high-level quotes can be provided on the fly by easily moving through questions and displaying the calculations you arrive at from the flow.

- **Triaging**: Flow allows reps to ask a series of questions to better understand and address a customer's needs. Based on the customer input, the rep can appropriately send the customer to the right individual or team for additional assistance. Of course, Salesforce offers assignment rules, but there may be circumstances where user input is needed to accurately determine the assignment.

- **Product or service troubleshooting**: A flow could be developed with a decision tree that would provide both the scripting to ask the right questions and the potential answers that could resolve a customer's issue with her product or service.

- **Form population**: Any general data entry process that is used on a regular basis could be inserted into a flow to make the process more efficient. Only the necessary input fields would be displayed, and dependencies and decision points could be handled in a multistep process.

Cloud Flow Designer

The original tool that Salesforce provided to create flows is called "Cloud Flow Designer." The "cloud" part might seem redundant, with Salesforce being a fully cloud-based platform, but it makes sense when you know that the only tool originally able to create flows was a desktop application. While this tool may technically still be available for use while you are reading this book, its days are likely numbered. I highly recommend that you dive in head-first with the new tool, Flow Builder. See Figure 8-7 for a view of Cloud Flow Designer and Figure 8-8 for a look at the permission that allows you to use it (while it is available).

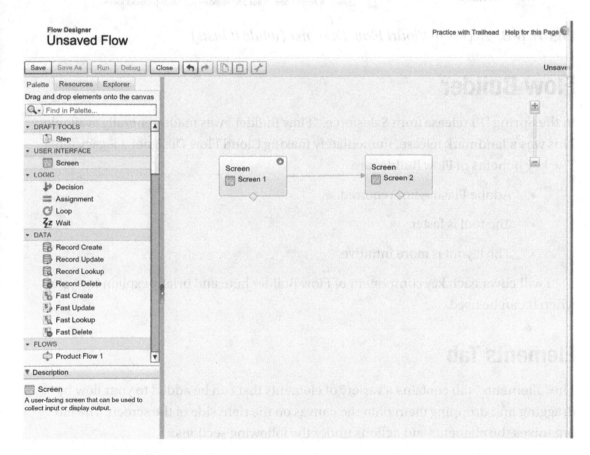

Figure 8-7.   *Cloud Flow Designer*

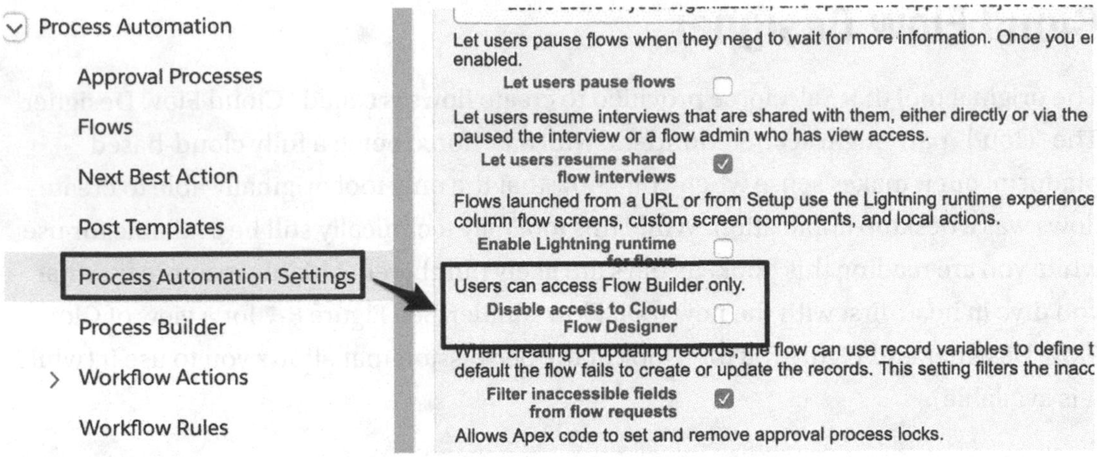

Figure 8-8. *Access to Cloud Flow Designer (while it lasts)*

Flow Builder

In the Spring '19 release from Salesforce, "Flow Builder" was made generally available. This was a landmark release, immediately making Cloud Flow Designer a legacy tool. The key benefits of Flow Builder are

- Adobe Flash is not required.

- The tool is faster.

- The layout is more intuitive.

I will cover each key component of Flow Builder here and briefly explain how and when it can be used.

Elements Tab

The "Elements" tab contains a variety of elements that can be added to your flow by dragging and dropping them onto the canvas on the right side of the screen. The tab organizes the elements and actions under the following sections:

- **User Interface**: In this section, you will find the Screen element, which allows the creation of a screen to capture data input and/or display specified text.

  - Screen

- **Logic**: This section includes Decision, Assignment, Pause, and Loop elements. The Decision element allows the creation of a decision point to allow for different workflow behavior based on either input or existing data. Assignment is used to update variables you have created in the flow. Pause allows the Flow to be paused and wait for an additional event to occur. With Loop, you can "loop" through values in a collection.

  - Assignment

  - Decision

  - Pause

  - Loop

- **Data**: The Data element included here allows you to look up, create, update, or delete a record. Standard and Fast options are provided for each function.

  - Create Records

  - Update Records

  - Get Record

  - Delete Records

- **Actions**: In this section, you will find a variety of actions that can be utilized within a Flow to trigger some kind of action, including

  - Email Alerts

  - Apex Action (Legacy)

  - Apex Action

  - Email Alert

  - Subflow

Figure 8-9 shows a partial view of the "Palette" tab.

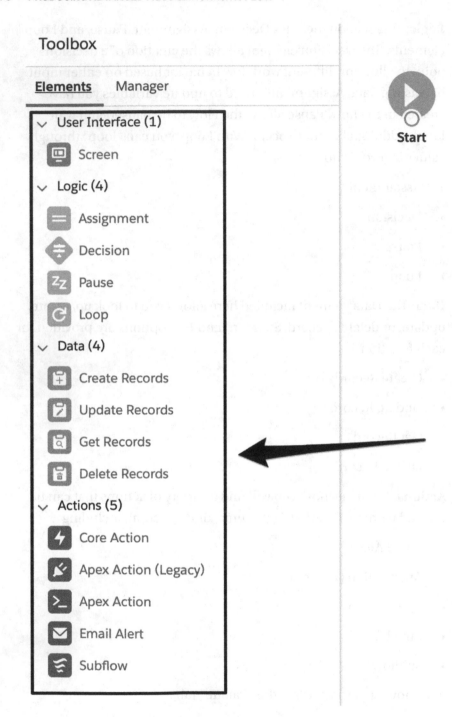

Figure 8-9. *"Elements" tab within the Flow Builder*

Manager Tab

The elements under the "Manager" tab are distinctly different from those under the Elements tab and reference "resources." While elements are focused on system actions, logic, or display behavior, resources represent actual values that can be referenced, manipulated, displayed, or reused in your flow – these include resource templates and actually used resources. Upon creating a new resource via clicking "New Resource" as shown in Figure 8-10, the following types of resources can be created:

- **Variable**: A value that can be updated or referenced in the flow (note that this value is not tied to a specific record or object)

- **Constant**: A fixed value that can be referenced in the flow

- **Formula**: A calculation of a value that can be referenced in your flow

- **Text Template**: Formatted text that can include any other created resources and can be referenced in your flow

- **Choice**: A selection option that can be set when a choice is presented

- **Record Choice Set**: Dynamic choices from an object

- **Picklist Choice Set**: Dynamic choices from a picklist field

- **Stage**: Progress within a flow

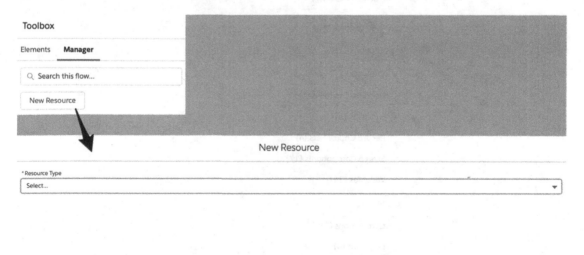

Figure 8-10. *Creating a new resource within Flow Builder*

A view of the available resources to create from within the Manager tab is shown in Figure 8-11.

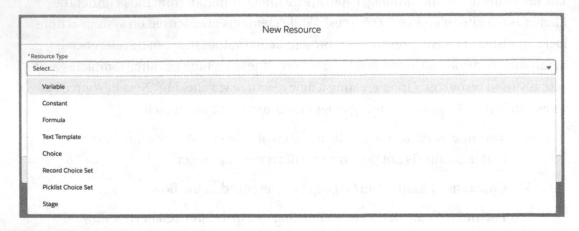

Figure 8-11. *Resource types*

Within the Manager tab, you can take a look at all resources and elements available in the flow (see Figure 8-12).

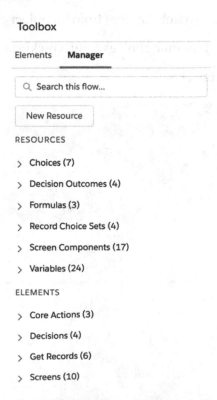

Figure 8-12. *Manager tab with some resources and elements displayed*

Status Indicator

At the top right of the Flow Designer screen, you'll notice some text in the navigation bar. You should see "Draft," "Inactive," or "Active." These are overall flow status indicators. See Figure 8-13.

Figure 8-13. Flow status indicator, at the top right of Flow Builder

Flow Administration Options

Navigate to Flows in the Setup menu to view and/or manage existing flows. Your options here are

- **Links**

  - **Open**: Launches the corresponding flow for editing of the flow itself

  - **Edit**: Allows you to edit the Name and Description of the flow (not the flow itself)

  - **Del**: Deletes the flow

  - **Flow Name**: Displays all versions of the flow; provides you with the ability to run/execute it

- **Buttons**

  - **New Flow**: Opens Flow Builder

  - **New Flow in Cloud Flow Designer**: Opens Cloud Flow Designer (you must enable Cloud Flow Designer in Process Automation Settings)

In Figure 8-14, you can see existing flows and available administrative options.

Action	Flow Label ↑	Type	Is Active
	New Flow New Flow in Cloud Flow Designer		
Open | Edit | Del	7Summits Onboarding - Guided Profile Setup	Screen Flow	☐

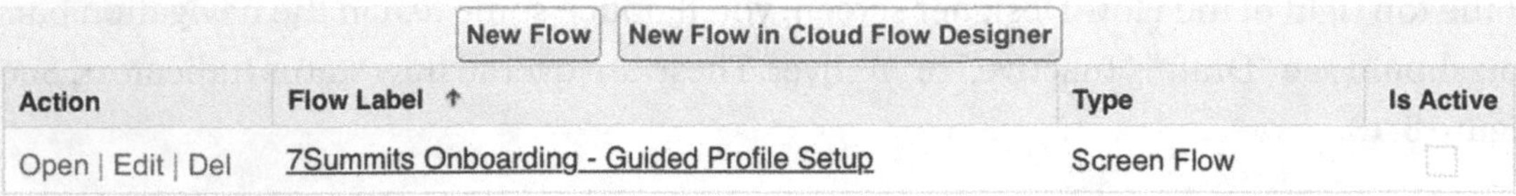

Figure 8-14. *Your administrative options with a flow*

When you click a flow's name, you will be taken to its corresponding detail page, as shown in Figure 8-15. There, you will see the "Run" button. This button executes the flow as a user would experience it. Also, notice the "Template" field; this field will allow you to create a flow to be included in a managed package that can be cloned by the end user for modification.

Figure 8-15. *Flow Detail page*

Additionally, you can run or debug a flow as an admin. Running a flow simply executes it (if auto-launched) or presents it (if screen-based). From there, you can interact with the flow and verify it is doing what you expect. See Figure 8-16.

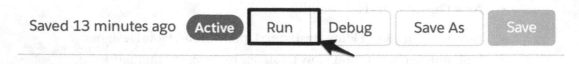

Figure 8-16. *Run a flow from Flow Builder by clicking the "Run" button*

The last – and very powerful – option you have to administer Flows is the ability to debug them. By clicking debug, you can control the input variables to be used in the Flow. This is extremely useful for robust testing of a Flow without going back and forth between Flow Builder and the page on which the Flow resides. See Figure 8-17 for the initial debug settings screen and Figure 8-18 for the actual debug UI.

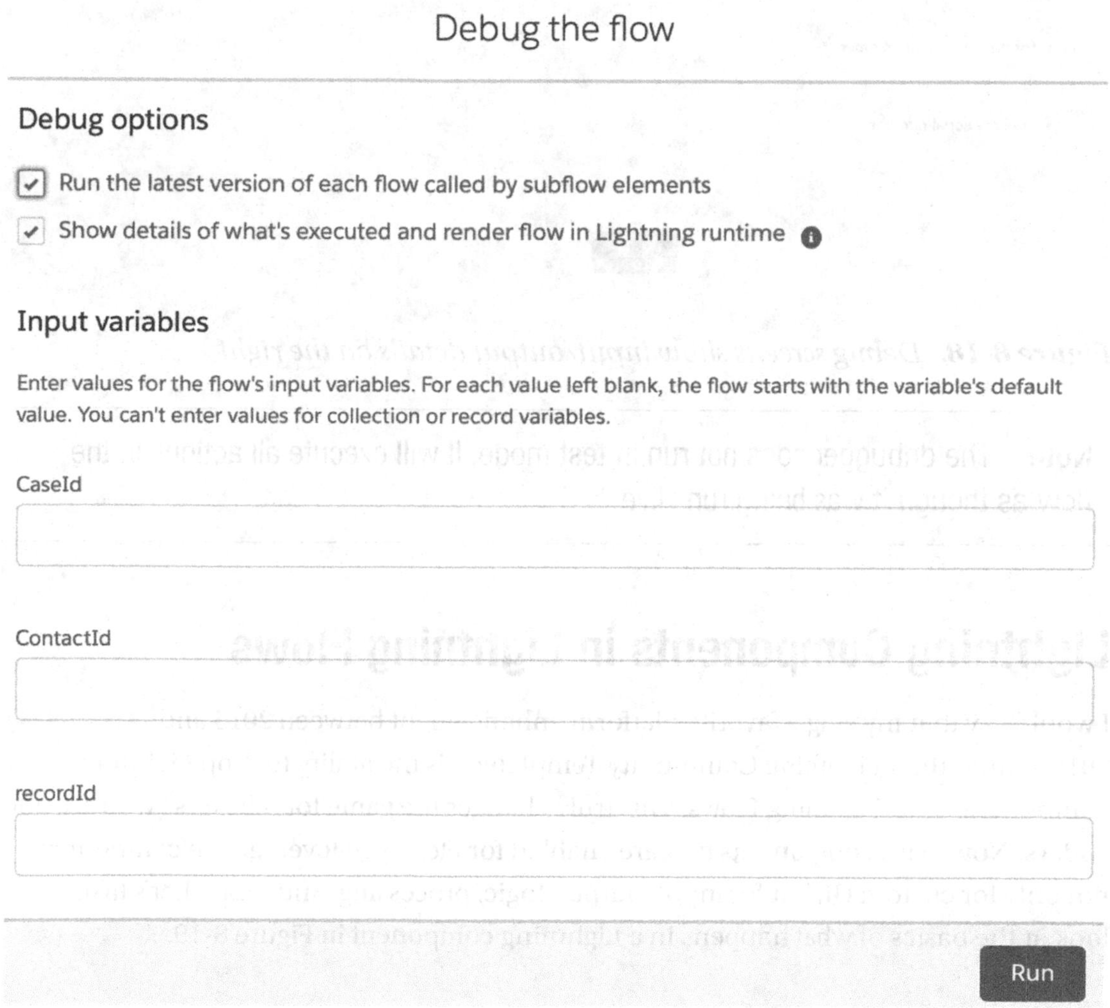

Debug the flow

Debug options

☑ Run the latest version of each flow called by subflow elements

☑ Show details of what's executed and render flow in Lightning runtime ⓘ

Input variables

Enter values for the flow's input variables. For each value left blank, the flow starts with the variable's default value. You can't enter values for collection or record variables.

CaseId

ContactId

recordId

Run

Figure 8-17. *Flow debug options*

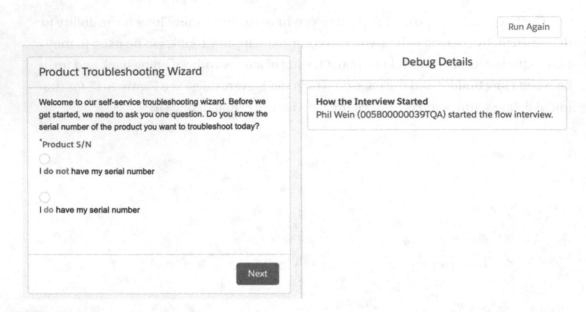

Figure 8-18. *Debug screens show input/output details on the right*

Note The debugger does not run in test mode. It will execute all actions in the flow as though it was being run "live."

Lightning Components in Lightning Flows

I would say that my single favorite platform enhancement between 2015 and 2018 – other than Lightning Community Templates – is the ability to drop Lightning components into Lightning Flows. This truly changes the game for "clickers" who are not coders. Now, with components that are enabled for Flow, you leverage the component not only for custom UI, but for input, output, logic, processing, and more. Let's take a look at the basics of what happens in a Lightning component in Figure 8-19.

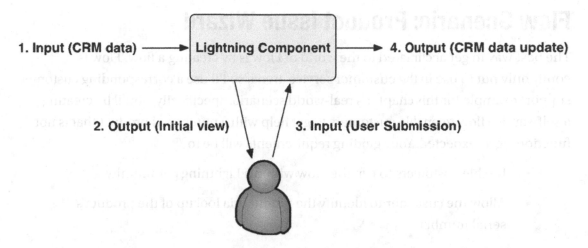

Figure 8-19. *The mechanisms of a Lightning component*

Figure 8-19 shows how a user interacts with a component and how that component interacts with the rest of Salesforce. Now, let's look at a component within a flow (Figure 8-20).

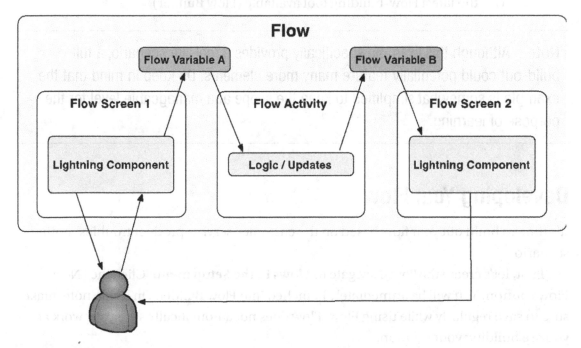

Figure 8-20. *Now, Lightning components can be included within Flows, providing additional functionality for users*

Flow Scenario: Product Issue Wizard

The best way to get acclimated to the world of Flow is by creating a flow. Flow is commonly put to use in the customer service arena, so I'll use a corresponding customer support example for this chapter's real-world scenario. Specifically, you'll be creating a self-service flow to enable customers to get help with a purchased product that is not functioning as expected. Your guiding requirements will be to

- Enable customers to run the Flow within a Lightning community

- Allow the customer to identify the product via lookup of the product's serial number

- Provide common steps for possible resolution

- For customers whose problem has not been addressed, auto-create a case to initiate the replacement process

- Notify internal stakeholders of the issue via email

- Use the latest Flow-building tool available (Flow Builder)

Note   Although this example specifically provides a real-life scenario, a full build-out could potentially feature many more elements. Do keep in mind that the example is somewhat simplified to keep the scope at a manageable level for the purpose of learning.

Developing Your Flow

It's time to build out your flow based on the customer-service-product troubleshooting scenario.

First, let's create the flow. Navigate to **Flows in the Setup menu**. Click the "New Flow" button. You will be immediately launched into Flow Builder. On a side note, make sure to save regularly while using Flow. Flow does not automatically save your work as you are building your solution.

1. Formula: User Information

When you are designing your flow, it's critical to know exactly where it will fit within your business process. For the customer service troubleshooting scenario, you'll need to identify the contact record and email address associated with the "running user" who is stepping through the flow in your community. This will allow you to quickly access key data and output it onto the screen.

Contact Id

Navigate to the "Manager" tab and click "New Resource." Create a resource of type "Formula" and Data Type of "Text." The API Name should be "Running_User_Contact". The Formula itself will be "{!$User.ContactId}". The corresponding screen is shown in Figure 8-21.

Figure 8-21. *Create the Running_User_Contact formula*

Email

Repeat the process for creating a new process. Navigate to the "Manager" tab and click "New Resource." Create a resource of type "Formula" and Data Type of "Text." The API Name should be "Running_User_Email". The Formula itself will be "{!$User.Email}".

2. Screen: Enter Serial No.

After you name your screen (e.g., "Enter Serial No."), you'll want to cover the following items on this first screen to be displayed to the user:

- General introductory text
- Capture of product serial number

Screen

First, you'll need to drag the Screen element onto the canvas (Figure 8-22).

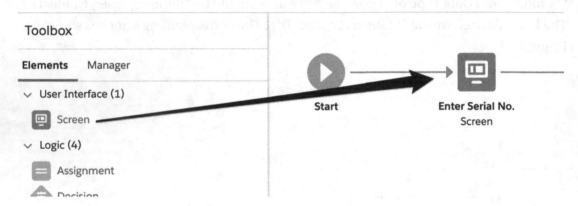

Figure 8-22. *Create a screen to allow the user to enter a serial number*

Display Text: Intro_Text

Click the "Display Text" screen component on the left. Name it "Intro_Text" and provide the following for the text itself:

Welcome to our self-service troubleshooting wizard!

Before we get started, please enter the serial number of the product you want to troubleshoot today in the space provided below.

Text: My_Serial_Number

Next, you'll provide a way for users to provide their product serial number for lookup. Label the text component "Product Serial Number" and require value entry.

Summary

Figure 8-23 shows the Enter_Serial_No screen.

Figure 8-23. "Enter Serial No." screen

3. Get Records: Asset Lookup

To access and display details about the product the customer purchased, you'll first need to look up the asset.

Variables

Create two text variables by clicking New Resource for each. They should be named "AssetId" and "ProductId" and be both of type "Text."

Get Records

In this step, you'll use the provided serial number to find the Asset record, create new variables for display, and set those variables based on the identified Asset record that was found. Here are the specific steps:

- Drag a "Get Records" element onto the canvas.
- Label the Record Lookup "Asset Lookup."
- Set the API Name to "Asset_Lookup."

- In the "Get Records of This Object" section, set the object to "Asset."

- In the "Filter Asset Records" section, set Condition Requirements to "Conditions are Met."

- Set Field to "SerialNumber," Operator to "equals," and Value to the variable in which the serial number was previously captured ("My_Serial_Number").

- In the "Sort Asset Records" section, sort ascending by Id. Store only the first record and store values in separate variables.

- In the "Select Variables to Store Asset Fields," store the following fields as the corresponding variables:

  - Id > {!AssetId}

  - Product2Id > {!ProductId}

Figure 8-24 gives an abridged view of the Get Records element.

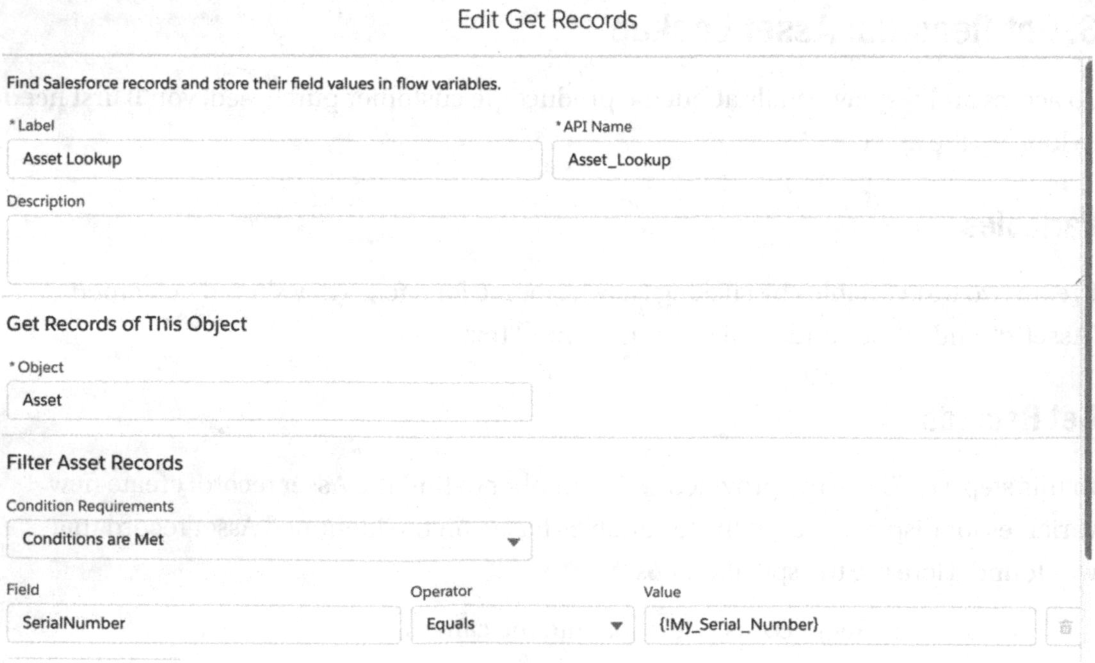

Edit Get Records

Find Salesforce records and store their field values in flow variables.

* Label

Asset Lookup

* API Name

Asset_Lookup

Description

Get Records of This Object

* Object

Asset

Filter Asset Records

Condition Requirements

Conditions are Met

Field	Operator	Value	
SerialNumber	Equals	{!My_Serial_Number}	🗑

Figure 8-24. *Our "Asset Lookup" Get Records element*

Current View

Figure 8-25 shows a current view of the flow.

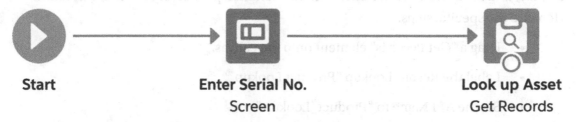

Start

Enter Serial No.
Screen

Look up Asset
Get Records

Figure 8-25.   *Current state of our flow*

4. Get Records: Product Lookup

Now that the asset record information has been looked up and stored, you'll need to look up the product.

Custom Fields

Create two rich text fields on the Product object first (outside of Flow):

- Product Image (Product_Image__c) – will contain an image in the body of the rich text field

- Troubleshooting Help (Troubleshooting_Help__c) – will contain FAQs and answers regarding product issues

Variables

Create four text variables by clicking New Resource for each:

- ProductCode
- ProductHelp
- ProductImage
- ProductName

Get Records

In this step, you'll use the product id to find the Product record, create new variables for display, and set those variables based on the identified product record that was found. Here are the specific steps:

- Drag a "Get Records" element onto the canvas.

- Label the Record Lookup "Product Lookup."

- Set the API Name to "Product_Lookup."

- In the "Get Records of This Object" section, set the object to "Product."

- In the "Filter Product Records" section, set Condition Requirements to "Conditions are Met."

- Set Field to "Id," Operator to "equals," and Value to the variable {!ProductId}.

- In the "Sort Product Records" section, sort ascending by Id. Store only the first record and store values in separate variables.

- In the "Select Variables to Store Product Fields," store the following fields as the corresponding variables:

  - Name > {!AssetId}

  - ProductCode > {!ProductId}

  - Product_Image__c > {!ProductImage}

  - Troubleshooting_Help__c > {!ProductHelp}

Note   With Flow Builder, this last step can be done in a different and, arguably, more efficient way going forward. You can now use the "Record" variable and store multiple field values that can be accessed later.

Figure 8-26 gives an abridged view of the Get Records element.

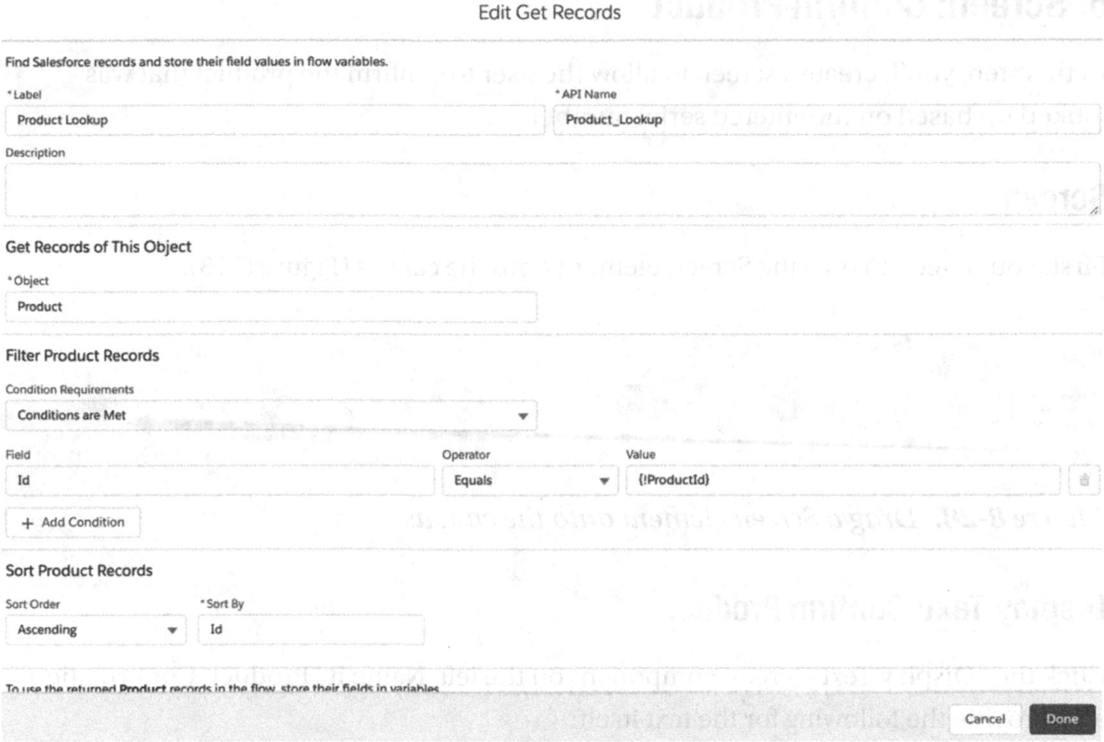

Edit Get Records

Find Salesforce records and store their field values in flow variables.

* Label

Product Lookup

* API Name

Product_Lookup

Description

Get Records of This Object

* Object

Product

Filter Product Records

Condition Requirements

Conditions are Met

Field	Operator	Value
Id	Equals	{!ProductId}

+ Add Condition

Sort Product Records

Sort Order

Ascending

* Sort By

Id

To use the returned Product records in the flow, store their fields in variables

Cancel   Done

Figure 8-26. *Our "Product Lookup" Get Records element*

Current View

Figure 8-27 shows a current view of the flow.

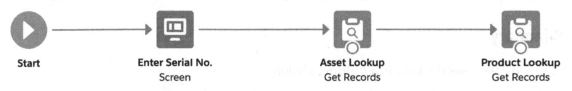

Start — Enter Serial No. Screen — Asset Lookup Get Records — Product Lookup Get Records

Figure 8-27. *Current state of our flow*

5. Screen: Confirm Product

In this step, you'll create a screen to allow the user to confirm the product that was looked up based on the entered serial number.

Screen

First, you'll need to drag the Screen element onto the canvas (Figure 8-28).

Figure 8-28. *Drag a Screen element onto the canvas*

Display Text: Confirm Product

Click the "Display Text" screen component on the left. Name it "Product_Confirmation" and provide the following for the text itself:

```
Please confirm that this is your product:
```

```
{!ProductName}
{!ProductCode}
{!ProductImage}
```

```
If not, please re-enter your serial number
```

Summary

Figure 8-29 shows the Confirm Product screen.

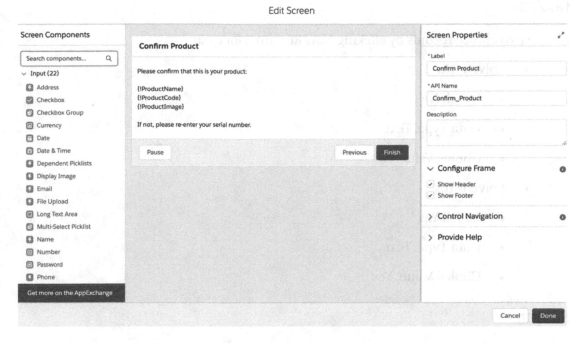

Figure 8-29. *Our "Confirm Product" screen confirms the queried product with the user*

Current View

Figure 8-30 shows a current view of the flow.

Figure 8-30. *Current state of our flow*

6. Screen: Issue Help

In this step, you'll create a screen that shows troubleshooting steps to the user and confirms whether the information helped to resolve the issue.

Choices

Create two choice records by clicking New Resource for each:

- Solved_No
    - Label: No
    - Data Type: Text
    - Choice Value: No
- Solved_Yes
    - Label: Yes
    - Data Type: Text
    - Choice Value: Yes

Screen

Once you've created the choices, you'll need to drag the Screen element onto the canvas (Figure 8-31).

Figure 8-31. *Drag a Screen element onto the canvas*

Display Text: Confirm Product

Click the "Display Text" screen component on the left. Name it "Product_ Troubleshooting_Details" and provide only the Product Help variable for the text itself:

{!ProductHelp}

Picklist: Choose One

Click the "Picklist" screen component on the left. Name it "Issue_Solved_Question" and provide the following for the settings:

- **Label**: "Choose one:"
- **API Name**: "Issue_Solved_Question"

- **Require**: True

- **Data Type**: Text

- **Default Value**: None

- **Select Choices**

  - Choice: {!Solved_Yes}

  - Choice: {!Solved_No}

Summary

Figure 8-32 shows the Issue Help screen.

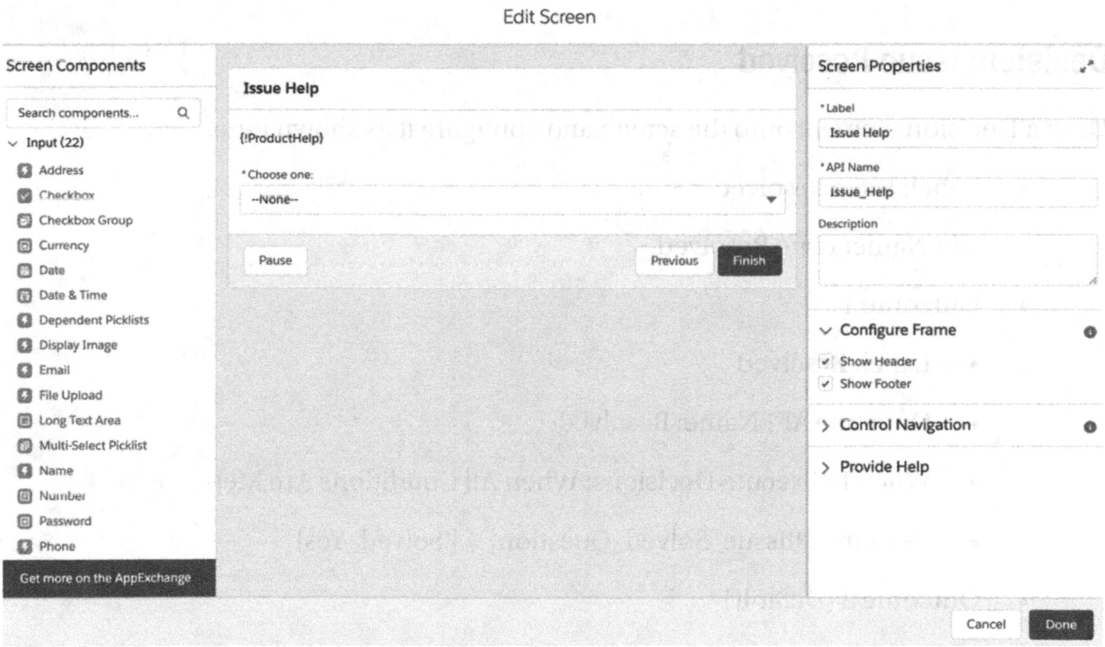

Figure 8-32. *A look at our "Issue Help" screen*

Current View

Figure 8-33 shows a current view of the flow.

Figure 8-33. *Current state of our flow*

7. Decision: Issue Resolved

Once the troubleshooting steps are displayed to the user, we need to determine whether that information helped him or her to resolve the issue.

Decision: Issue Resolved

Drag a Decision element onto the screen and configure it as shown here:

- Label: Issue Resolved

- API Name: Issue Resolved

- Outcome 1

    - Label: Resolved

    - Outcome API Name: Resolved

    - When to Execute Decisions: When All Conditions Are Met

    - Resource: {!Issue_Solved_Question} = {!Solved_Yes}

- Outcome 2 (Default)

    - Label: Not Resolved

Figure 8-34 shows the decision element, as configured.

Edit Decision

*Label
Issue Resolved

*API Name
Issue_Resolved_Decision

Description

Outcomes For each path the flow can take, create an outcome. For each outcome, specify the conditions that must be met for the flow to take that path.

OUTCOME ORDER ⊕ +	OUTCOME DETAILS

≡ Resolved

Not Resolved

*Label
Resolved

*Outcome API Name
Resolved

When to Execute Outcome
All Conditions Are Met ▾

Resource	Operator	Value
{!Issue_Solved_Question}	Equals ▾	{!Solved_Yes}	🗑

+ Add Condition

Cancel   Done

Figure 8-34. *Our "Issue Resolved" decision element*

Current View

Figure 8-35 shows a current view of the flow.

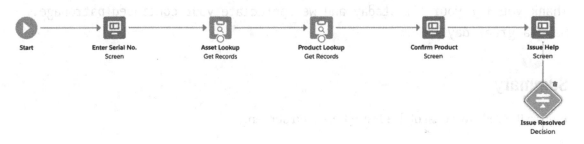

Figure 8-35. *Current state of our flow*

8. Screen: Issue Resolved

In this step, you'll create a screen to wrap things up for users who are all set.

Screen

First, you'll need to drag the Screen element onto the canvas (Figure 8-36).

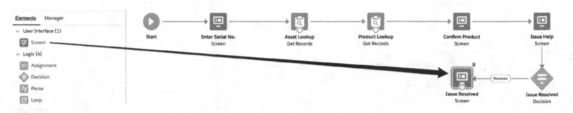

Figure 8-36. *Drag a screen element onto the canvas*

Display Text: Issue Resolved Text

Click the "Display Text" screen component on the left. Name it "Issue_Resolved_Text" and provide the following for the text itself:

```
Thank you for your time today and we appreciate your continued patronage.
Have a great day.
```

Summary

Figure 8-37 shows part of the Issue Resolved screen.

Edit Screen

Issue Resolved	Screen Properties
Thank you for your time today and we appreciate your continued patronage. Have a great day.	* Label Issue Resolved
Pause Previous Finish	* API Name Issue_Resolved

Figure 8-37. *A look at our "Issue Resolved" screen*

Current View

Figure 8-38 shows a current view of the flow.

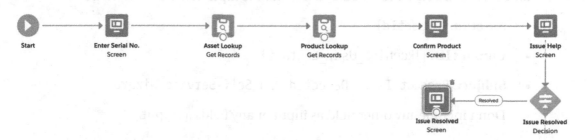

Figure 8-38. *Current state of our flow*

9. Core Action: Create Case

In this step, you'll auto-create a case for users whose issue has not been resolved.

Screen

First, you'll need to drag the Core Action element onto the canvas (Figure 8-39).

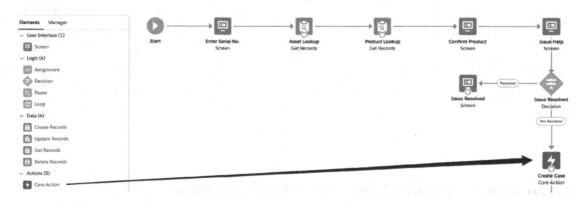

Figure 8-39. *Drag a Core Action onto the canvas*

Core Action: Self-Service Wizard Case

Select "Self-Service Wizard Case" for the type of core action. Label the core action "Create Case" and set the API Name to "Create_Case." Set the input values as shown here:

- **Asset Id**: {!AssetId}

- **Contact ID**: {!Running_User_Contact}

- **Subject**: Product Issue Detected via Self-Service Wizard

- Don't include any other field as input or any fields as input.

Summary

Figure 8-40 shows the core action setup screen.

Figure 8-40. *Setup screen for our "Create Case" core action*

Current View

Figure 8-41 shows a current view of the flow.

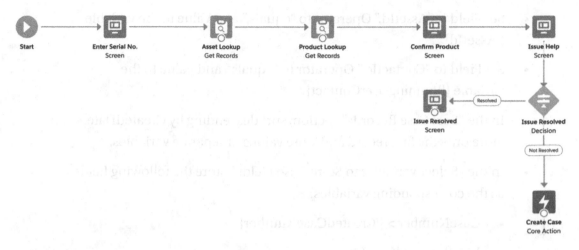

Figure 8-41. *Current state of our flow*

10. Get Records: Case Lookup

We'll need to access a few key case details once the case is created.

Variables

Create two text variables by clicking New Resource for each:

- CreatedCaseNumber

- CreateCaseId

Get Records

In this step, you'll use the product id to find the Product record, create new variables for display, and set those variables based on the identified product record that was found. Here are the specific steps:

- Drag a "Get Records" element onto the canvas.

- Label the Record Lookup "Case Lookup."

- Set the API Name to "Case_Lookup."

- In the "Get Records of This Object" section, set the object to "Case."

- In the "Filter Case Records" section, set Condition Requirements to "Conditions are Met."

- Set Field to "AssetId," Operator to "equals," and Value to the variable {!AssetId}.

- Set Field to "ContactId," Operator to "equals," and Value to the variable {!RunningUserContact}.

- In the "Sort Case Records" section, sort descending by CreatedDate. Store only the first record and store values in separate variables.

- In the "Select Variables to Store Case Fields," store the following fields as the corresponding variables:

  - CaseNumber > {!CreatedCaseNumber}

  - Id > {!CreatedCaseId}

Figure 8-42 gives an abridged view of the Get Records element.

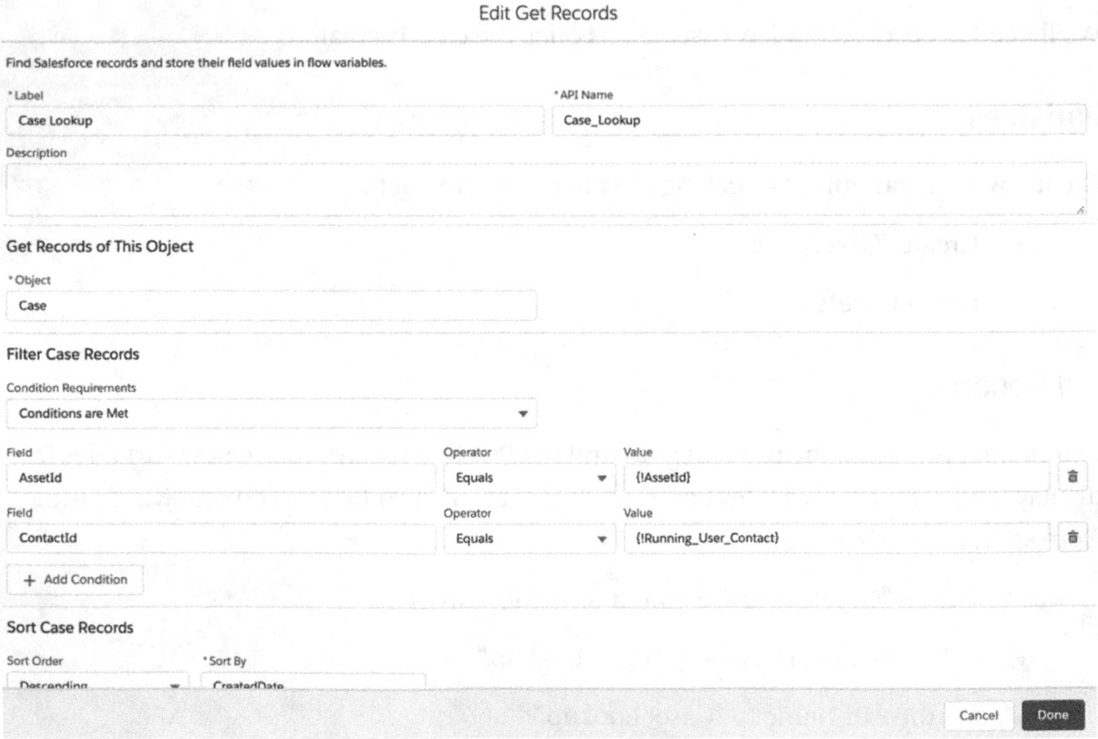

Edit Get Records

Find Salesforce records and store their field values in flow variables.

* Label	* API Name
Case Lookup	Case_Lookup

Description

Get Records of This Object

* Object

Case

Filter Case Records

Condition Requirements

Conditions are Met

Field	Operator	Value	
AssetId	Equals	{!AssetId}	🗑
Field	Operator	Value	
ContactId	Equals	{!Running_User_Contact}	🗑

+ Add Condition

Sort Case Records

Sort Order	* Sort By
Descending	CreatedDate

Cancel   Done

Figure 8-42. *The "Case Lookup" Get Records element*

Current View

Figure 8-43 shows a current view of the flow.

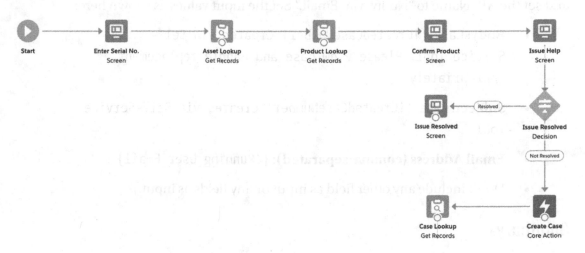

Figure 8-43. *Current state of our flow*

11. Core Action: Notify via Email

In this step, you'll send an email to a stakeholder to let them know about the product issue so they can start the process to deliver a replacement product.

Screen

First, you'll need to drag the Core Action element onto the canvas (Figure 8-44).

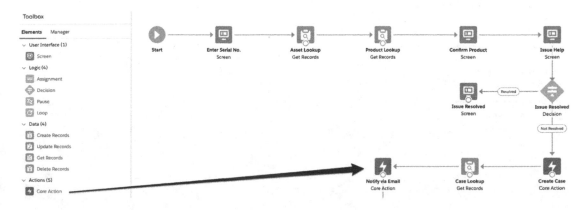

Figure 8-44. *Drag another Core Action onto the canvas*

Core Action: Self-Service Wizard Case

Select "Send Email" for the type of core action. Label the core action "Notify via Email" and set the API Name to "Notify_via_Email." Set the input values as shown here:

- **Body**: Case {!CreatedCaseNumber} Created via Self-Service Tool. Please view Case and handle replacement appropriately.

- **Subject**: Case {!CreatedCaseNumber} Created via Self-Service Tool

- **Email Address (comma-separated)**: {!Running_User_Email}

- Don't include any other field as input or any fields as input.

Summary

Figure 8-45 shows the core action setup screen.

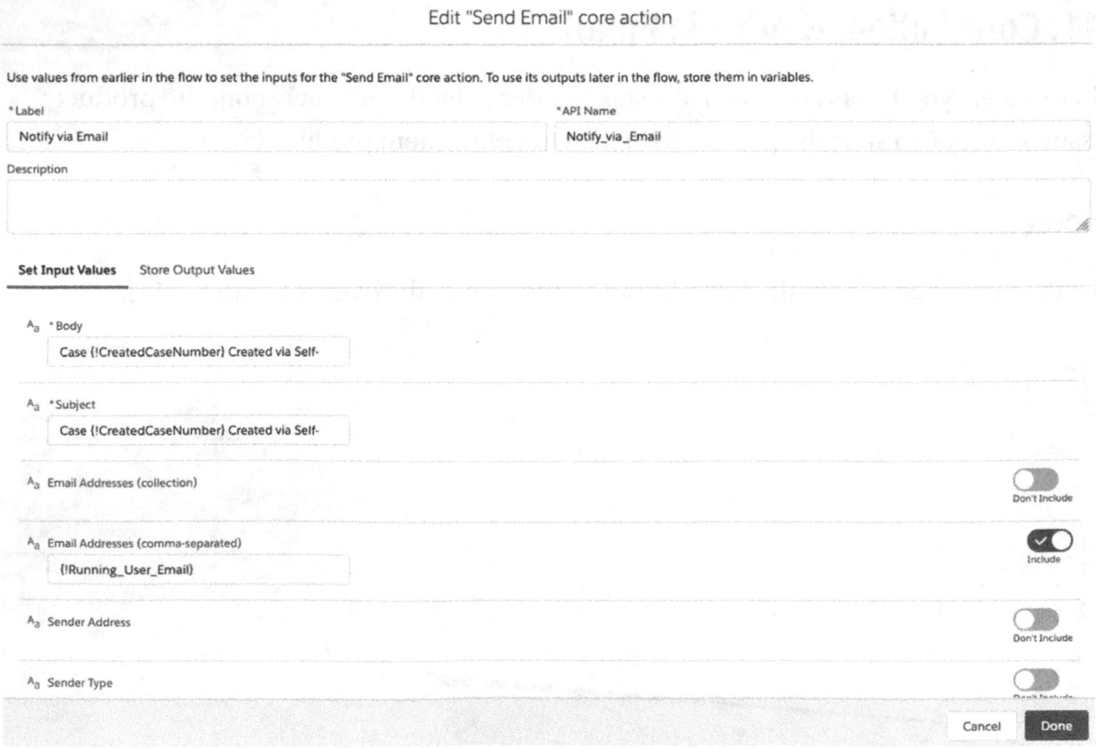

Edit "Send Email" core action

Use values from earlier in the flow to set the inputs for the "Send Email" core action. To use its outputs later in the flow, store them in variables.

* Label
Notify via Email

* API Name
Notify_via_Email

Description

Set Input Values   Store Output Values

A₂ * Body
Case {!CreatedCaseNumber} Created via Self-

A₂ *Subject
Case {!CreatedCaseNumber} Created via Self-

A₂ Email Addresses (collection)
Don't Include

A₂ Email Addresses (comma-separated)
{!Running_User_Email}
Include

A₂ Sender Address
Don't Include

A₂ Sender Type

Cancel   Done

Figure 8-45. *The setup screen for our "Notify via Email" Core Action*

Current View

Figure 8-46 shows a current view of the flow.

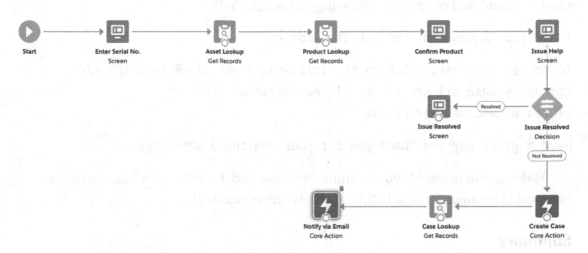

Figure 8-46. *Current state of our flow*

12. Screen: Case Auto-Created

In this step, you'll create a screen to wrap things up for users who had a case auto-created for them.

Screen

First, you'll need to drag the Screen element onto the canvas (Figure 8-47).

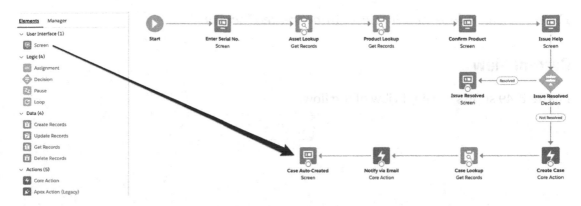

Figure 8-47. *Drag the final Screen onto the canvas*

Display Text: Issue Resolved Text

Click the "Display Text" screen component on the left. Name it "Case_Creation_
Confirmation" and provide the following for the text itself:

Thank you. A case has been created for you.

To access the case, click on the following link: <A HREF="https://<your_
community_base_url_here>/case/{!CreatedCaseId}"><B>Case
{!CreatedCaseNumber}</B></A>

Have a great day and thank you for your continued patronage.

Make sure to replace "<your_community_base_url_here>" with a formula or your
hardcoded community base URL (formula is recommended).

Summary

Figure 8-48 shows part of the Issue Resolved screen.

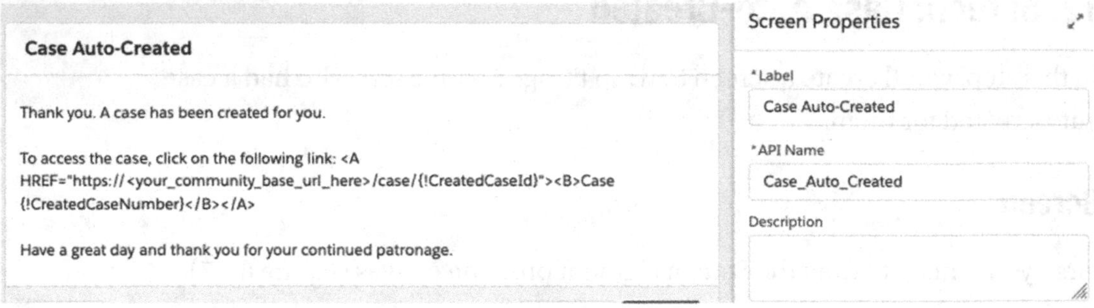

Figure 8-48. *A look at our "Case Auto-Created" screen*

Current View

Figure 8-49 shows the final view of the flow.

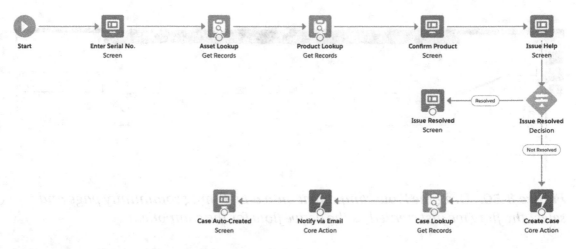

Figure 8-49. *Final state of our flow*

Preparing the Flow for Use

We'll now need to do the following to prepare the Flow for use:

- Save the Flow.

- Activate the latest version of the Flow.

- Open Community Builder for the Lighting Community that will use this Flow.

- Drag and drop the "Flow" component onto a page.

- Select the Product Issue Wizard Flow as the Flow to be used in the component.

- Publish the community.

Figure 8-50 shows the Community Builder setup steps.

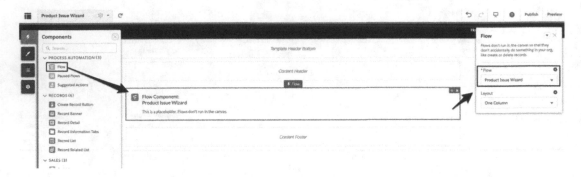

Figure 8-50. *Drag the Flow component onto a Lightning community page and select the flow we just created as the active flow for the component*

Your Flow: Live and in Effect

It wouldn't be any fun to create a Flow and leave it there. Let's take a look at it in action! First, you must log in to your community as an external user to walk through the Flow. Once you are logged in and on the relevant community page, you should see what is shown in Figure 8-51.

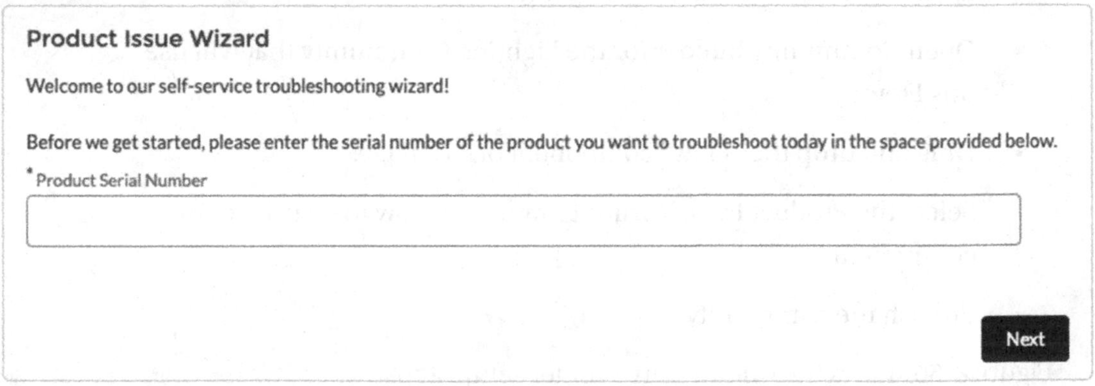

Product Issue Wizard

Welcome to our self-service troubleshooting wizard!

Before we get started, please enter the serial number of the product you want to troubleshoot today in the space provided below.

* Product Serial Number

[   ]

`Next`

Figure 8-51. *Our first screen: eliciting user input (serial number)*

Next, enter your existing product serial number in the area shown in Figure 8-52. Note that you will need to have at least one Asset record and one Product record set up in your instance of Salesforce to make this work. Enter the serial number from your Asset record as shown in Figure 8-52 (your S/N will differ, of course).

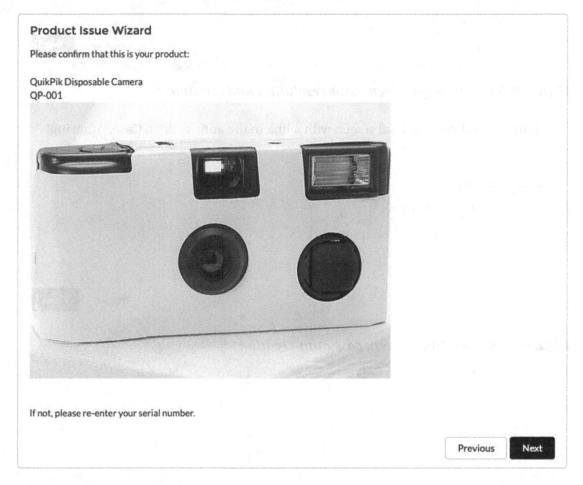

Product Issue Wizard

Welcome to our self-service troubleshooting wizard!

Before we get started, please enter the serial number of the product you want to troubleshoot today in the space provided below.

* Product Serial Number

SN55021492

Next

Figure 8-52. *Our first screen: user input received*

Next, confirm that this is your product. See Figure 8-53 for the corresponding screen.

Product Issue Wizard

Please confirm that this is your product:

QuikPik Disposable Camera
QP-001

If not, please re-enter your serial number.

Previous   Next

Figure 8-53. *Our second screen: product confirmation*

Then, confirm whether the provided steps resolved the issue. Assume they did not and select "No" for the answer, as shown in Figure 8-54.

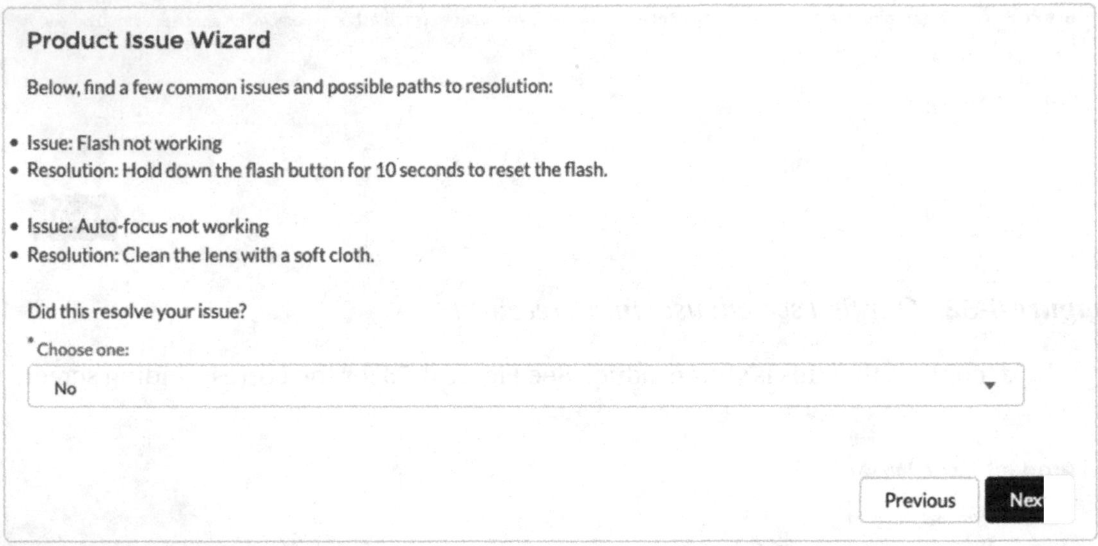

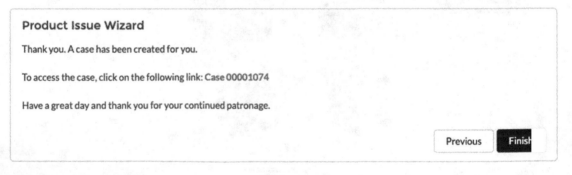

Figure 8-54. *Our third screen: issue resolution and question*

Figure 8-55 shows the final screen with a link to the auto-created Case. Amazing!

Figure 8-55. *Our final screen: case auto-creation*

Recap

In this chapter, you learned how to deliver business automation via Flow. Flow is more difficult to use than other tools such as workflow rules and escalation rules, but it is significantly more powerful than either. Additionally, with the introduction of Flow Builder, the tool has become much more intuitive. I covered the key parts of Flow, including proper application, elements of the Cloud Flow Designer and Flow Builder, and the creation of a flow from scratch. At this point, you should be able to clearly see that "development without code" within Salesforce is no small topic!

CHAPTER 9

Create Flexible Solutions with Custom Settings and Metadata Types

One of Salesforce's most valued characteristics is its ability to be tailored to meet an organization's needs rather extensively without requiring a single line of code. Salesforce has provided a number of powerful tools – including workflow rules, validation rules, and formula fields – that depend on formulas for the purpose of declarative development. However, with the high level of control that is granted to noncoders through formulas comes a potential trade-off with configurability. Fortunately, you can mitigate what you have to give up by taking advantage of custom settings and custom metadata types in your solution development.

Both of these entities provide a container for applications or solutions that require top-level configuration with the highest level of flexibility. They are integral to delivering architecturally sound, forward-looking solutions on the Salesforce platform, helping developers to minimize code and allowing noncoders to have more control. In this chapter, you will learn

- The basic structure of custom settings and custom metadata types

- How to create custom settings and custom metadata types

- How to reference custom settings and custom metadata types in various formula-driven tools

© Philip Weinmeister 2019
P. Weinmeister, *Practical Salesforce Development Without Code*,
https://doi.org/10.1007/978-1-4842-4871-3_9

Custom Settings

The best way to explain the trade-off between formula-based control and overall configurability, along with the related role of custom settings, is with an example. Let's assume that you are creating a workflow rule. You have a choice of using the criteria builder or the formula editor to determine whether the workflow rule should apply to a particular update. The criteria builder has some key limitations (e.g., you cannot choose from the full list of functions), but it's relatively easy to maintain and update. Each criteria entry is distinct and can be modified or removed without a deep knowledge of advanced Salesforce functionality.

Assume that a workflow rule needed to be updated and the original developer/administrator was not available for the task. Figure 9-1 shows the criteria for the associated workflow rule. If one of the criteria entries needed to be removed or edited, the task is straightforward: remove the line or change the field, operator, or value, as needed. It's an intuitive interface that can be picked up by others who are not necessarily familiar with the specific workflow rule.

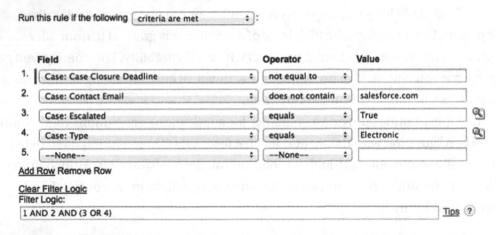

Figure 9-1.   The criteria option typically makes for easy understanding and maintenance of the rule(s)[1]

When you decide to go with the formula editor, your control over the operations within Salesforce significantly increases. However, the speed and ease at which a formula can effectively and accurately be updated decreases. For example, take a look at a formula that serves as workflow rule entry criteria in Figure 9-2. If this formula were

---

[1]All Salesforce screenshots in this chapter © copyright Salesforce, Inc. Used with permission·

not producing the expected results based on current business processes, some analysis would be needed to determine and resolve the source of the discrepancy. The time and effort required to refactor the formula would very likely exceed what might be expected for a reworking of criteria created with the criteria builder.

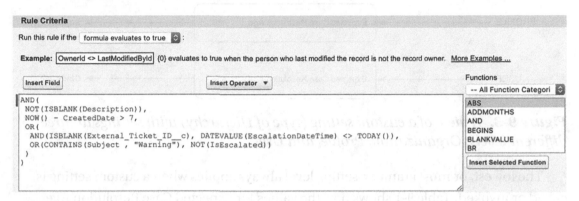

Figure 9-2. *Using the formula editor is not as conducive to simple, quick changes as using the criteria builder*

This is when custom settings come into the picture. They are somewhat analogous to custom objects and allow you to separate key variables within your business rules and logic from the "code" you have created through configuration. Take a look at the formula editor in the previous figure; it includes the following statement: NOW() - CreatedDate > 7. This statement establishes whether a Case was created at least 7 days ago. With custom settings, you can reference the value in your formula; this allows you to minimize the direct modification to your formulas and make maintenance much easier.

Custom Setting Types

Custom settings provide a means to manage and access your custom data. There are two types: List and Hierarchy. Both have a number of applicable use cases. However, I will only focus on the Hierarchy custom-setting type in this chapter, as the List type cannot be used in configuration-based settings (i.e., it requires custom development).

With Hierarchy custom settings, you can manage data at one of three levels: "Organization," "Profile," and "User." This allows you to create different sets of data specific for individual Users or sets of Users. If doing so is not a requirement, you can simply manage the data at the highest level (Organization). In that scenario, the data applies to all Users and Profiles. Figure 9-3 provides an example of a custom setting of the Hierarchy type that has values managed at all three levels.

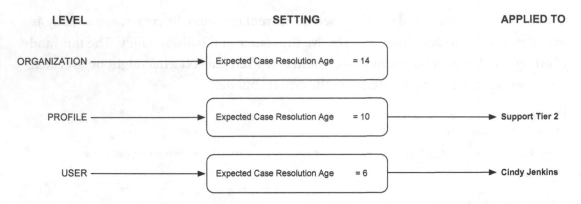

Figure 9-3. *A view of a custom setting (type of Hierarchy) with settings at three different levels: Organization, Profile, and User*

The lowest, or most granular, setting level always applies when a custom setting is called or invoked. Table 9-1 shows how the values for Expected Case Resolution Age shown in Figure 9-3 would apply to the three Users referenced in Table 9-1.

Table 9-1. *A Look at Three Users and How the Custom Setting Configuration in Figure 9-3 Applies to Them*

User	Profile	Applicable Hierarchy Level	Applicable Hierarchy Field Value
Cindy Jenkins	Support Tier 1	User	6
Bunker Jones	Support Tier 2	Profile	10
Johnny Smithers	Support Tier 3	Organization	14

The reasoning behind this table is as follows:

- Cindy has a User setting, so any Profile or Organization setting is disregarded. The value associated with her User-level setting is "6."

- Bunker does not have a User setting but does have a Profile setting, since he has a profile of "Support Tier 2" with a value of "10." Any Organization setting will not apply as a result.

- Johnny does not have an applicable hierarchy setting at the User or Profile level. The Organization-level value of "14" will apply to him.

Creating a Custom Setting and Corresponding Fields

To create a new custom setting, use Quick Find in the Setup menu to find "Custom Settings" and click the "New" button. Figure 9-4 shows the initial screen you will see when creating a custom setting.

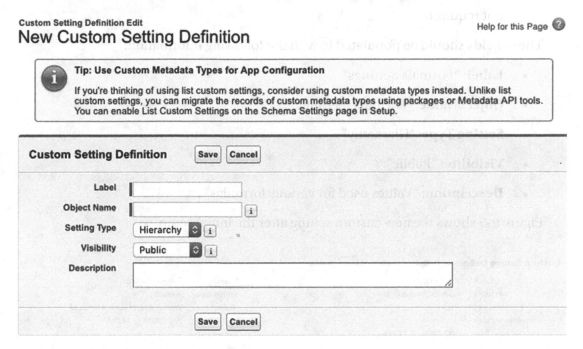

Figure 9-4. *A look at the new custom setting screen*

When creating a custom setting, the following fields are available to populate:

- **Label**: (Required) The user-friendly name to be used within the Salesforce user interface

- **Object Name**: (Required) The name value to be referenced by other applications or formulas within Salesforce

- **Setting Type**: (Required) Hierarchy or List. (See previous section for details on the Hierarchy setting.)

317

- **Visibility**: (Required) Protected or Public. This field impacts the visibility of the custom setting within a managed package. Managed packages are not covered in depth in this book, so this value can be disregarded for now. The default of Public will be acceptable.

- **Description**: (Optional) Like always, this field is recommended, but not required.

These fields should be populated in with the following information:

- **Label**: "Formula Settings"

- **Object Name**: "Formula_Settings"

- **Setting Type**: "Hierarchy"

- **Visibility**: "Public"

- **Description**: "Values used for various formulas"

Figure 9-5 shows the new custom setting after the initial setup.

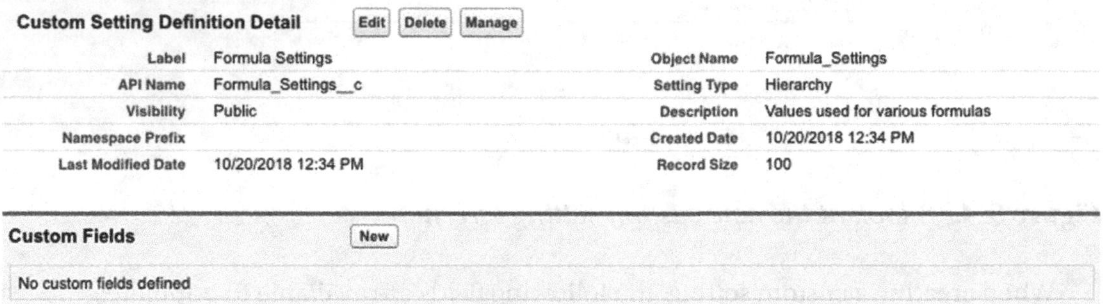

Custom Setting Definition Detail	Edit Delete Manage		
Label	Formula Settings	Object Name	Formula_Settings
API Name	Formula_Settings__c	Setting Type	Hierarchy
Visibility	Public	Description	Values used for various formulas
Namespace Prefix		Created Date	10/20/2018 12:34 PM
Last Modified Date	10/20/2018 12:34 PM	Record Size	100

Custom Fields	New
No custom fields defined	

Figure 9-5. *A newly created custom setting (fields have not yet been created)*

You can loosely think of your custom setting as an object. Once you create the skeleton of the setting, you'll need to create the corresponding fields. Click the "New" button after the custom setting has been created. It is important to note a limitation here. You cannot create fields with the following types: Lookup Relationship, Roll-Up Summary, or Formula. The values you will store cannot be dependent on Users or other fields in the system. In Figure 9-6, a custom setting field of type "Number" is displayed.

Field Label | Maximum Age | [i]

Please enter the length of the number and the number of decimal places. For example, a number with a length of 8 and 2 decimal places can accept values up to "12345678.90".

Length | 4 | Decimal Places | 2 |
Number of digits to the left of the decimal point   Number of digits to the right of the decimal point

Field Name | Maximum_Age | [i]

Description | Maximum Case age allowed at the time of Case Closure |

Help Text | (In Days) | [i]

Required   ☑ Always require a value in this field in order to save a record
Unique   ☐ Do not allow duplicate values
External ID   ☐ Set this field as the unique record identifier from an external system

Default Value   Show Formula Editor
| 7 |
Use formula syntax: Enclose text and picklist value API names in double quotes : ("the_text"), include numbers without quotes : (25), show percentages as decimals: (0.10), and express date calculations in the standard format: (Today() + 7)

Figure 9-6. *The new field screen is identical to the new field screen for objects*

Note a couple of the field settings for this custom setting (of the Number type):

- **Required**: This setting is important if you have processes that are dependent on the custom setting. The box should be checked off if that is the case.

- **Default Value:** This setting can provide some peace of mind for future use of the custom setting. If a user is creating a custom setting and she is not aware of the correct value, the default value can be used.

For each custom setting field, you'll need to confirm and save before the field is available. Once you have created your fields, the data model for your custom setting is complete. The next step will be the creation of data that can be referenced.

Managing Your Custom Setting

To use your custom setting, you will need to set up the necessary records based on the fields you just established. Salesforce refers to this as "managing" your custom setting. Click the "Manage" button to start the process. Figure 9-7 shows its location.

Custom Setting Definition Detail | Edit | Delete | **Manage** |

Label	Formula Settings	Object Name	Formula_Settings
API Name	Formula_Settings__c	Setting Type	Hierarchy
Visibility	Public	Description	Values used for various formulas
Namespace Prefix		Created Date	10/20/2018 12:34 PM
Last Modified Date	10/20/2018 12:34 PM	Record Size	106

Figure 9-7. *The "Manage" button for creating or editing your custom setting data*

I will follow the hierarchical example earlier in the chapter and set up three levels of data for this custom setting. Figure 9-8 shows the placement of the two "New" buttons that will facilitate the creation of the fields for this example.

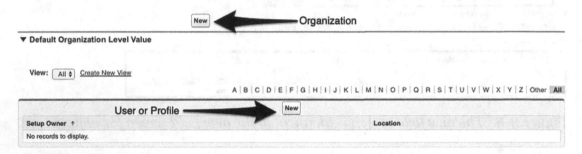

Figure 9-8. *The top "New" button is for the organization-wide custom setting; the bottom "New" button is for a setting specific to a User or a Profile*

Note   The layout for managing custom settings is not very intuitive. Make sure you pay attention to which "New" button you click to create a record for your custom setting.

Click the "New" button above the "Default Organization Level Value" line to set the custom setting for your entire organization (top of Figure 9-8). Recalling the details from earlier in our example, "Maximum Age" is required and has a default value of 7. In this case, leave "7.00" as the set value and click "Save." Figure 9-9 shows this screen. Note that "Location" is blank; that is because this is for the organization as a whole.

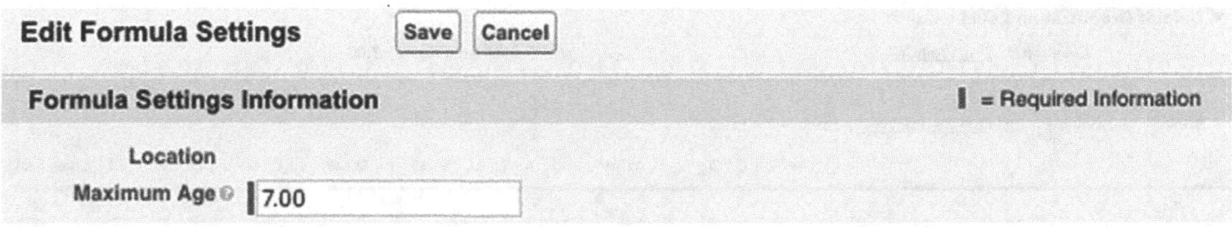

Edit Formula Settings   Save   Cancel

Formula Settings Information   ❙ = Required Information

Location
Maximum Age ⊘ | 7.00

Figure 9-9. *Setting the Maximum Age at Closure value at the Organization Level*

Now, move on to the Profile-level setting. Click the "New" button *below* the "Default Organization Level Value" line on the screen we looked at in Figure 9-8. You'll need to configure the location by identifying the level type ("Profile," in this case), and the Profile or User to which you want to apply the setting. You can create a custom Profile ("Custom: Support Profile") and set the Maximum Age at Closure value to "6." Figure 9-10 shows how to set up the corresponding configuration.

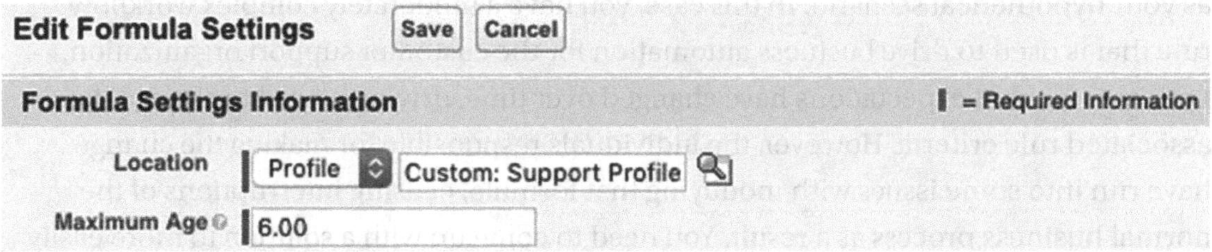

Edit Formula Settings   Save   Cancel

Formula Settings Information   ❙ = Required Information

Location | Profile ◇ | Custom: Support Profile 🔍
Maximum Age ⊘ | 6.00

Figure 9-10. *Setting the Maximum Age at Closure value at the Profile Level*

Finally, repeat the steps for creating a Profile-level setting, but this time create a User-level setting instead. Set the custom setting value to "5." See Figure 9-11 for the User-specific setting value.

Formula Settings Information   ❙ = Required Information

Location | User ◇ | Richard James 🔍
Maximum Age ⊘ | 5.00

Figure 9-11. *Setting the Maximum Age at Closure value at the User Level*

You'll end up with three records, as shown in Figure 9-12.

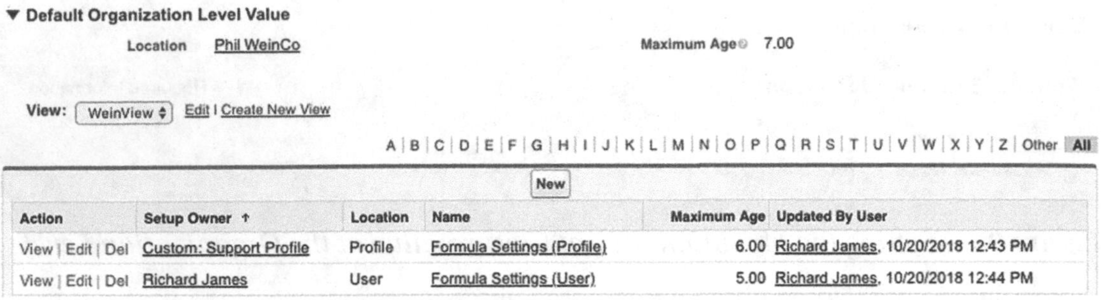

▼ **Default Organization Level Value**

        Location   Phil WeinCo   Maximum Age⊙ 7.00

View: [WeinView ⬦] Edit | Create New View

A | B | C | D | E | F | G | H | I | J | K | L | M | N | O | P | Q | R | S | T | U | V | W | X | Y | Z | Other | **All**

New

Action	Setup Owner ↑	Location	Name	Maximum Age	Updated By User
View	Edit	Del Custom: Support Profile	Profile	Formula Settings (Profile)	6.00	Richard James, 10/20/2018 12:43 PM
View	Edit	Del Richard James	User	Formula Settings (User)	5.00	Richard James, 10/20/2018 12:44 PM

Figure 9-12. *A view of the data at multiple levels (Organization, Profile, and User)*

Referencing a Custom Setting

Now that you've set up your custom setting, its fields, and the corresponding records, you can put it to work. Take a look again at Figures 9-4 through 9-12; I will use these as your hypothetical scenario. In this case, you have a moderately complex workflow rule that is used to drive business automation for the customer support organization. Let's assume that expectations have changed over time, driving a need to change the associated rule criteria. However, the individuals responsible for making the change have run into some issues with modifying that formula, causing interruptions of the normal business process as a result. You need to come up with a solution to more easily manage the formula. That's where a custom setting comes into play.

To make one, navigate to the relevant object (Case, in this example) and click "Edit" next to the formula field. Once you are in the formula editor, highlight the "7" in this line: `NOW() - Created > 7`. See the full formula as follows:

```
AND(
 NOT(ISBLANK(Description)),
 NOW() - CreatedDate > 7,
 OR(
 AND(ISBLANK(EngineeringReqNumber__c), DATEVALUE(EscalationDateTime) <> TODAY()),
 OR(CONTAINS(Subject , "Warning"), NOT(IsEscalated))
 )
```

Next, replace the highlighted value ("7") with the configurable custom setting. To do so, click the "Insert Field" button in the formula editor and follow the steps shown in Figures 9-13 and 9-14.

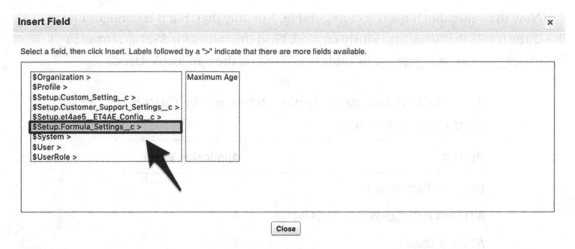

Figure 9-13. *Clicking the custom setting that you created to find the appropriate field*

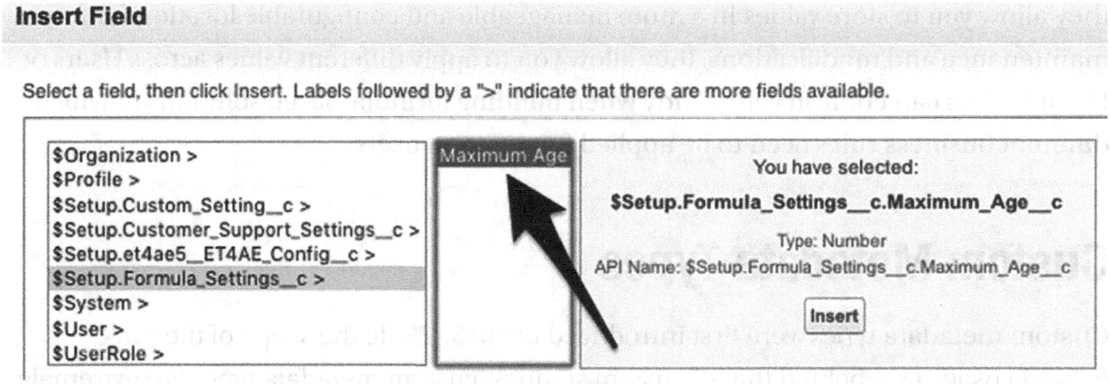

Insert Field

Select a field, then click Insert. Labels followed by a ">" indicate that there are more fields available.

Figure 9-14. *Selecting the corresponding field and clicking "Insert"*

Your end result will be

```
AND(
 NOT(ISBLANK(Description)),
 NOW() - CreatedDate > $Setup.Formula_Settings__c.Maximum_Age__c,
 OR(
  AND(ISBLANK(EngineeringReqNumber__c), DATEVALUE(EscalationDateTime) <>
  TODAY()),
  OR(CONTAINS(Subject , "Warning"), NOT(IsEscalated))
 )
)
```

Now the value that is used is configurable. Not only that, but it is configurable at the three levels that were previously created. Find the values for $Setup.Formula_ Settings__c.Maximum_Age__c in Table 9-2 based on the applicable User.

Table 9-2. *Values to Be Applied Based on the Custom Setting in the Example*

User(s)	Applicable Value
User: "Richard James"	5
All Users with "Custom: Support Profile"	6
All other Users	7

It is important to understand the usefulness of custom settings here. Not only do they allow you to store values in a more manageable and configurable location for future maintenance and modifications, they allow you to apply different values across Users or Profiles. This can come in very handy when building formula-based solutions in which different business rules need to be applied for different users.

Custom Metadata Types

Custom metadata types were first introduced in 2015. While the scope of their in-formula usage lags behind that of custom settings, custom metadata types are extremely useful and even preferred over custom settings where both elements are available for use. As of the close of 2018, custom metadata types are only available in two declarative formula-based areas: validation rules and formula fields. I would suspect that this will expand, so keep an eye out on changes in this area. Table 9-3 shows where both custom settings and custom metadata types are available for use.

Table 9-3. Potential Usage of Custom Settings and Custom Metadata Types

Custom Settings		Custom Metadata Types	
Lightning Components	✓	Lightning Components	✓
Apex	✓	Apex	✓
Validation Rules	✓	Validation Rules	✓
Workflow Rules	✓	Workflow Rules	
Formula Fields	✓	Formula Fields	✓
Auto-Response Rules	✓	Auto-Response Rules	
Field Updates	✓	Field Updates	
Process Builder	✓	Process Builder	
Escalation Rules	✓	Escalation Rules	
Approval Rules	✓	Approval Rules	
Assignment Rules	✓	Assignment Rules	
Approval Step Rules	✓	Approval Step Rules	
Custom Buttons and Links	✓	Custom Buttons and Links	
Flow	✓	Flow	✓

The concept of custom metadata types is similar to that of custom settings. They store data that be referenced from various places within an org and allow centralized management of certain reusable variables. Their structure is more like that of an object than a custom setting, however. There is no concept of level (e.g., organization, profile, user) or type (hierarchy, list) within custom metadata types. The largest difference between custom settings and custom metadata types, however, is the fact that custom metadata type record data *can be included in a change set or a metadata API-driven deployment*. That is huge! This allows admins to include referenceable configuration data in a deployment instead of doing it as a postdeployment step. Figure 9-15 visualizes this advantage over custom settings.

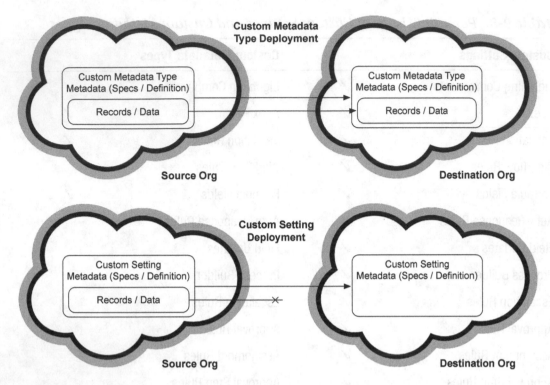

Figure 9-15. *Deployment of custom metadata types vs. custom settings*

As a result of their familiar data model structure and the ease in which they can be deployed, custom metadata type data are preferable over custom settings...*where available*. Personally, I would recommend using custom metadata types in validation rules and formula fields instead of using custom settings.

To create a custom metadata type, search for "custom metadata" using Quick Find in the Setup menu, then click the "New" button (see Figure 9-16).

All Custom Metadata Types

Help for this Page ⓘ

Custom metadata types enable you to create your own setup objects whose records are metadata rather than data. These are typically used to define application configurations that need to be migrated from one environment to another, or packaged and installed.

Rather than building apps from data records in custom objects or custom settings, you can create custom metadata types and add metadata records, with all the manageability that comes with metadata: package, deploy, and upgrade. Querying custom metadata records doesn't count against SOQL limits.

Action	Label	Installed Package	Namespace Prefix	Visibility	Api Name	Record Size	Description
Del | Manage Records	My Custom Metadata Type			Public	My_Custom_Metadata_Type__mdt	141	

Figure 9-16. *Click "New Custom Metadata Type" to start the creation process*

326

The next step is populating the necessary data to establish the custom metadata type. The following is available for setup, as shown in Figure 9-17:

- **Label**: (Required) The user-friendly name to be used within the Salesforce user interface

- **Plural Label**: (Required) The user-friendly name to be used within the Salesforce user interface when referencing multiple records

- **Starts with vowel sound**: (Optional) Check if the word starts with a vowel sound. Default is unchecked.

- **Object Name**: (Required) The name value to be referenced by other applications or formulas within Salesforce

- **Description**: (Optional) Like always, this field is recommended, but not required.

- **Visibility**: (Required) "All Apex code and APIs can use the type, and it is visible in Setup" or "Only Apex code in the same managed package can see the type..." This field impacts the visibility of the within a managed package. The default (first setting) is fine to use in most situations.

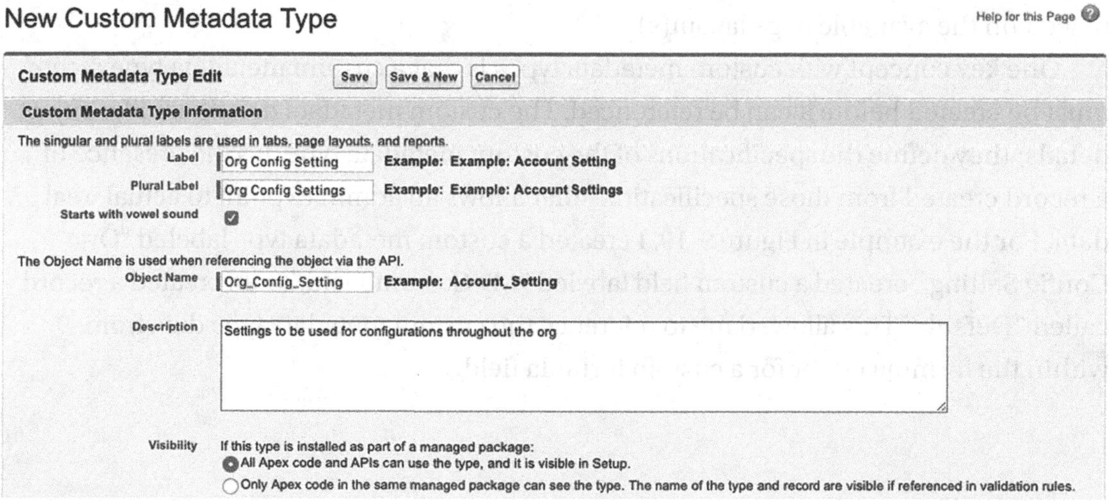

New Custom Metadata Type

Figure 9-17. *Populate label, plural label, and object name (at a minimum) of your custom metadata type*

Once the type has been created, it can be further customized. On the custom metadata type detail page, an admin can manage custom fields, validation rules, and page layouts. When creating a custom metadata type field, a few key points need to be noted:

- Not all field types are present. For example, Time, Text Area (Rich), and Lookup Relationships are not present, among others.

- A unique "Metadata Relationship" type exists (see Figure 9-18). This allows references from a custom metadata type to another type. This is extremely useful in complex app that uses a hierarchy of custom metadata types that need to reference each other.

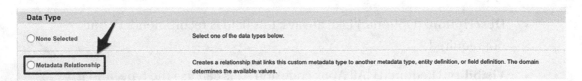

Figure 9-18. *"Metadata Relationship" is a field type unique to custom metadata type fields*

Field setup is a three-part journey. After selecting the field type, you add the key details (label, name description, etc.) and then you decide whether the field should be placed on the available page layout(s).

One key concept with custom metadata types is that a custom metadata type *record* must be created before it can be referenced. The custom metadata details are like object details; they define the specifications of the custom metadata type. It's the presence of a record created from those specifications that allows an admin to point to actual, real data. For the example in Figure 9-19, I created a custom metadata type labeled "Org Config Setting," created a custom field labeled "My Custom Field," then created a record called "Default." This allowed me to reference the custom metadata type data from within the formula editor for a custom formula field.

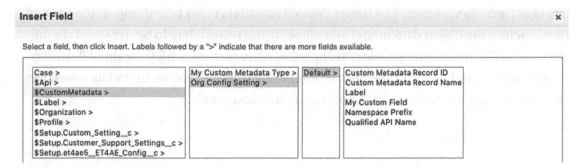

Figure 9-19. *Referencing a custom metadata type declaratively*

While there is absolutely value in referencing custom metadata types in validation rules and formula fields, the functionality can go a step further through the formula fields. A custom metadata type field value from a specified record can be referenced in a formula field; that formula field, in turn, can be referenced in Process Builder. Figure 9-20 shows this concept.

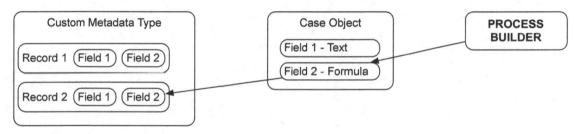

Figure 9-20. *A custom metadata type-based formula field can be referenced by Process Builder to drive extreme configurability in automated processes*

Recap

In this chapter, we revisited formulas and explored a way to more effectively and efficiently manage the data referenced within them. By utilizing custom settings and custom metadata types, you can avoid placing specific hard-coded values within formulas; instead, you can manage the data separately. Custom setting values can be associated with specific users, profiles, or the organization as a whole, potentially simplifying the complexity within your formulas and allowing you to more easily manage formula variables. The newer custom metadata types take things a step further by modeling the object data model and allowing the record data to be deployed via the metadata API. You should consider using these constructs to achieve optimal flexibility in your solutions. I made the recommendation to prioritize custom metadata types over custom settings, when they can support your business needs.

CHAPTER 10

Create Efficient User Experiences with Actions

While some features are introduced with fanfare (e.g., Einstein), others are added to the platform more quietly. Actions, known by different monikers – publisher actions, quick actions, global actions, and so on – are an example of this. Actions have been brought into the fold without much of a stage presence over the past few years, but carry potentially significant implications for both developers and users.

Historically, the means for a user to manually create or update a record or log an activity within the traditional Salesforce user interface have been limited; you could configure a page layout for a particular object or take a custom route with Visualforce (or, now, Lightning components). While page layouts do allow a particular presentation of a record to be modified, multiple page layouts cannot be shown to the same profile (for the same record type, if applicable). This means that, without customization, you cannot display a different layout in a different circumstance without changing the record type or the user's profile. As for Visualforce and Lightning components, they dramatically expand your options and doing so is an optimal approach for many projects. However, this assumes that you have the means to write (or pay for someone to write) custom code as well as the capability to maintain it indefinitely. Enter actions as our solution for this challenge.

In my opinion, actions stand out from the crowd of available interface-related features (such as case feed and consoles) that allow you to provide more meaningful and efficient ways. With actions, you can help your users avoid wasteful scrolling, applying unnecessary thought to optional fields, and cumbersome navigation from tab to tab throughout their workday. Not only can they be applied with a high level of flexibility, actions can be extended with Visualforce, Apex, Flow, and Lightning components. Fortunately, they do not require code to perform any of the core functionality. It is important to point out that, for some uses of actions, Chatter must be enabled.

331

© Philip Weinmeister 2019
P. Weinmeister, *Practical Salesforce Development Without Code*,
https://doi.org/10.1007/978-1-4842-4871-3_10

In this chapter, you will

- Review the different categories and types of actions

- Understand where actions can potentially reside

- Examine how to configure predefined fields and layouts for actions

- Learn how to effectively build and apply actions to meet business needs

- Cover certain considerations that should be made when working with actions

Action Labels

I will be the first to say that, while individual actions are straightforward, there is a quite a breadth to the overall scope of this "feature" and the related terms and descriptive language can be confusing at times. I will do my best to address this in this chapter to make actions as clear as possible.

To start our journey, we will first consider action "labels" (my term, not Salesforce's). When looking into actions, you will find multiple action labels referenced within the platform:

- Quick actions

- Publisher actions

- Mobile actions

- Lightning (Experience) actions

- Global actions

The first four items simply refer to an action's user interface home. These are not various "types" of actions in the sense that they are inherently different. You can create an action and, from there, make it either a "mobile action" or a "publisher action" (or both); that depends on where you configure it in a page layout and which Salesforce interface you are using (Classic or Lightning Experience). We will explore these action homes in more detail throughout this chapter.

A "global action" is a bit different. The "global" indicates that the action is not bound to an object and, therefore, can be used throughout the platform (i.e., "globally"). Think about it this way: an action to update a case must be on a case record page (since the case to update must be known), but a global action to create a case could be global and placed anywhere since there is no need for data binding to execute the action.

Action Categories

Regardless of label (as described in the previous section), there are six primary *categories* of actions that can be created with Salesforce:

- Standard actions

- Nonstandard actions

- Default actions

- Mobile smart actions

- Custom actions

- Productivity actions

Standard Actions

Salesforce has created a baseline set of standard actions that are available for all objects. Together, they make up the default Global Action layout that resides within a Chatter feed. These actions cannot be edited or deleted and are specific to their corresponding feed; they include

- **Question**: Posts a question (two-part post: question and additional/supporting detail)

- **Post**: Posts a comment

- **File**: Uploads a file from Salesforce or your computer and, optionally, an accompanying comment

- **Link**: Posts a URL and, optionally, an accompanying comment

- **Poll**: Posts a description of a poll along with two to ten choices

- **Thanks (if Work.com is enabled):** Posts a note recognizing someone in your organization

Figure 10-1 provides a view of the first five standard actions that are available, even if you do not have Work.com enabled.

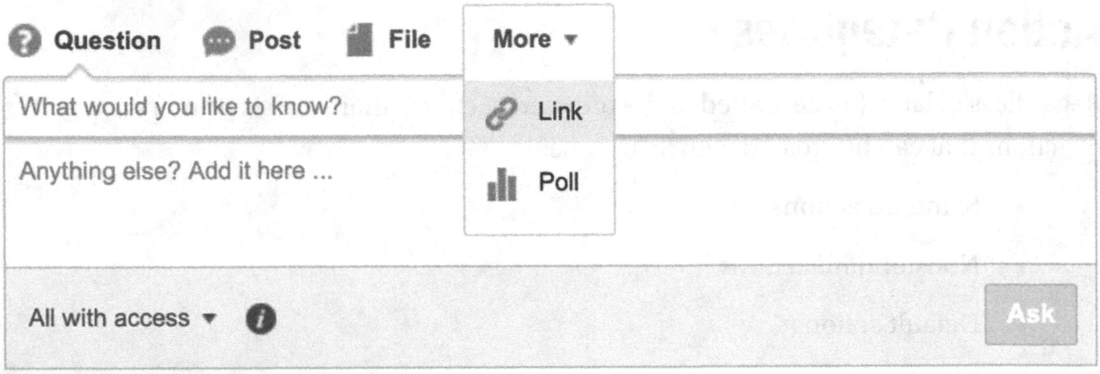

Figure 10-1. *The default set of standard actions in an org when Work.com is not enabled*

You cannot modify how these actions behave although you can reorder them or hide them altogether.

Nonstandard Actions

Nonstandard actions are actions that you can set up for your own organization's or your client's specific needs. There are a few primary types of actions that you can configure within the nonstandard action category:

- Create actions

- Send email actions

- Log a call actions

- Update actions

Create Actions

Create actions allow users to quickly create records with a custom abbreviated layout. Related validation rules and required fields still apply, although later in this chapter, I will cover how Salesforce has provided a way to minimize their impact on the user's experience by using predefined values. You can develop a create action for any standard or custom object. For standard objects, default actions and corresponding layouts are available. Alternatively, you can establish a custom layout and modify the displayed fields and their sequence. For custom objects, you'll always have to create the action and the corresponding layout. Figure 10-2 shows a (Create) New Case Action layout.

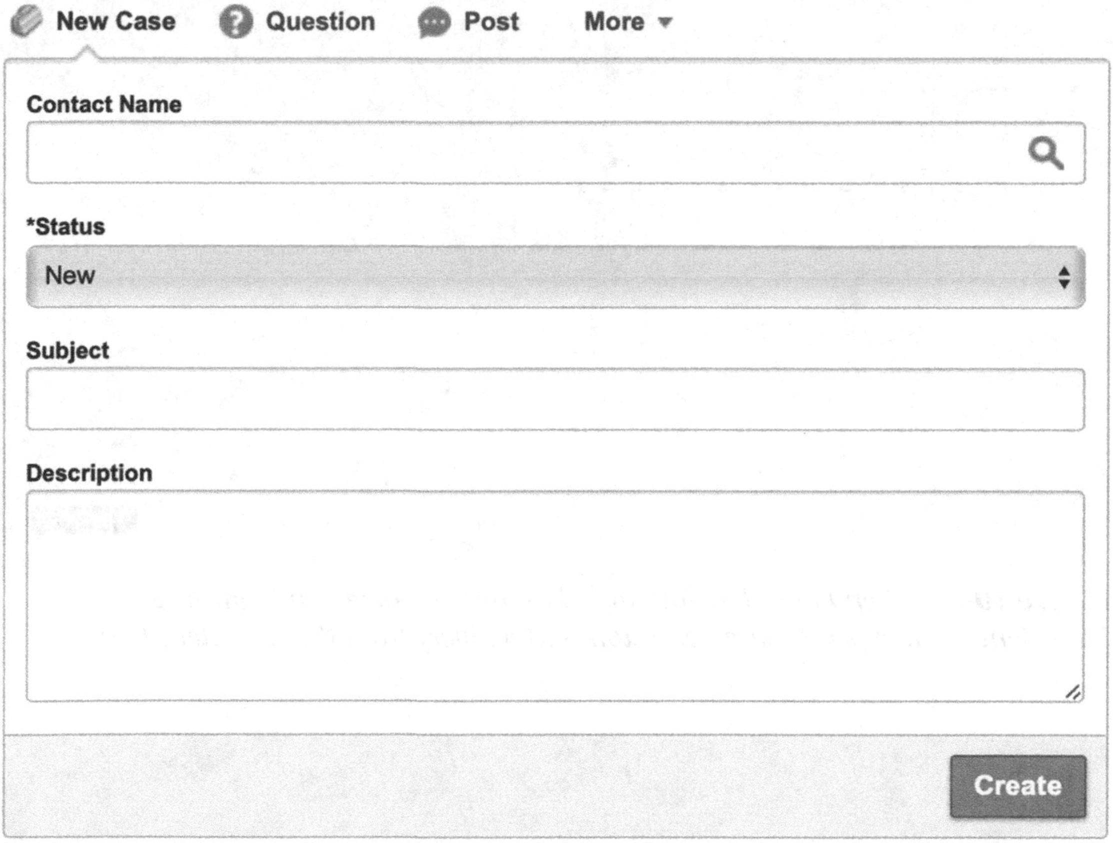

Figure 10-2. *This view (in classic) shows a layout that contains multiple actions, including New Case, a "create action"*

Send Email Actions

The Send Email action is fairly limited in scope, but is considered a standard action. Drop this action onto a Case detail page (or Case Feed) in Lightning to expedite the process of communicating with a contact via email. See Figure 10-3 for a view of a Send Email action from the Case object page and Figure 10-4 for a look at a Send Email action from a custom object page.

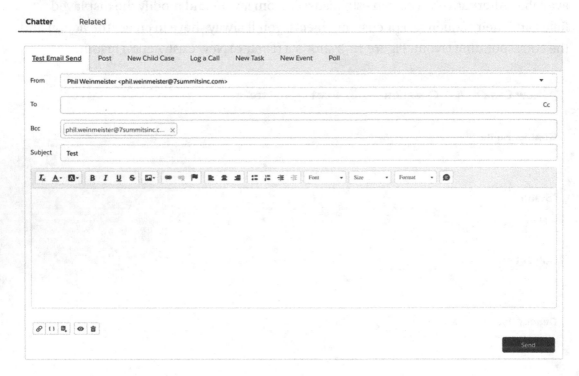

Figure 10-3. *A Send Email action added to the Case object in Lightning Experience can expedite email creation and delivery from the Case detail page*

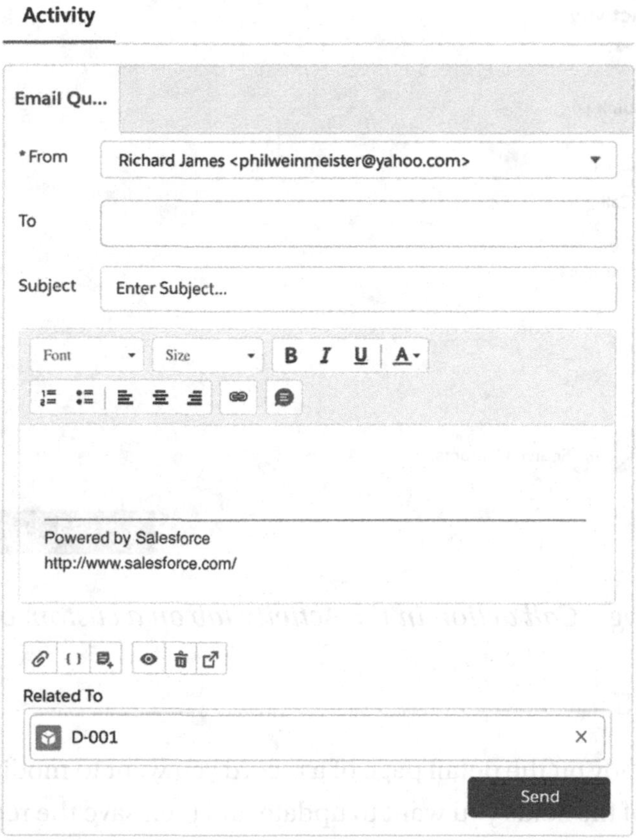

Activity

Email Qu...

* From   Richard James <philweinmeister@yahoo.com>   ▼

To

Subject   Enter Subject...

| Font ▾ | Size ▾ | **B** *I* <u>U</u> | <u>A</u>▾ |

¹₌ ⁝⁝ | ▤ ▤ ▤ | ∞ 💬

Powered by Salesforce
http://www.salesforce.com/

🖉 {} 🗟   👁 🗑 🗗

Related To

📦 D-001   ×

Send

Figure 10-4. A Send Email action added to the Activity tab of a custom object in Lightning Experience

Log a Call Actions

The Log a Call action offers a quick way for users to log a call, both with fewer clicks and less fields to fill out. This action allows you to do more than the name suggests. Although it is initially set up to record a Call activity, it can be configured to capture any type of Task (e.g., Meeting, Email, etc.). Of course, you can create any type of Task using the Create action, as well. This action automatically captures the corresponding record and populates the Related To field. Figure 10-5 shows a Log a Call action on a custom object page.

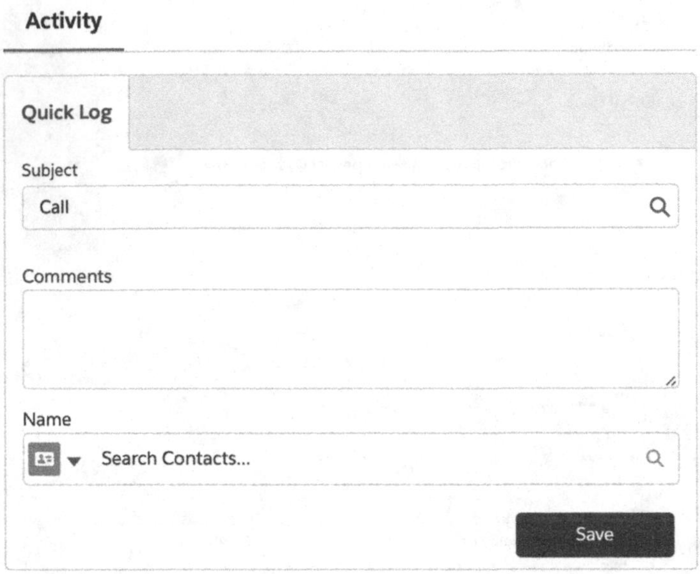

Figure 10-5. *A Log a Call action in the Activity tab on a custom object detail page*

Update Actions

Even if you are already on the detail page of a record you want to modify, it can be a bit tedious to find all of the fields you want to update and then save the record. With the update action, you can build what is essentially a "light" interface for common updates. Figure 10-6 shows an example Update Contact action.

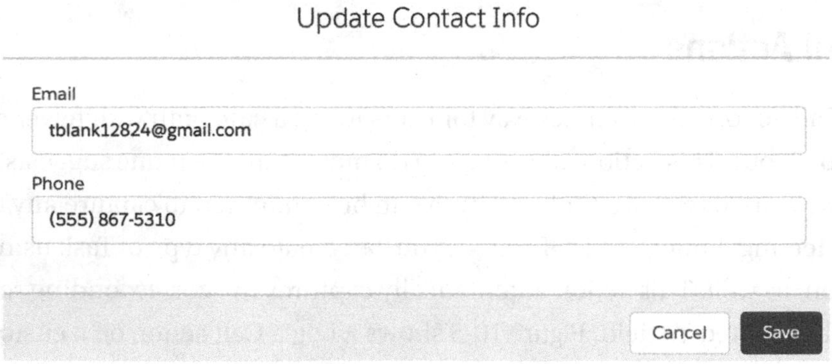

Figure 10-6. *The Update Contact action allows users to update a few specified fields on an existing Contact record*

Default Actions

Default actions are actions that are automatically set up by Salesforce. These actions are available for the following objects:

- Custom

- Account

- Case

- Contact

- Lead

- Opportunity

Figures 10-7 and 10-8 show the default quick actions and default mobile/Lightning actions, respectively, that are available for the Opportunity object, as shown from the Opportunity Layout editor.

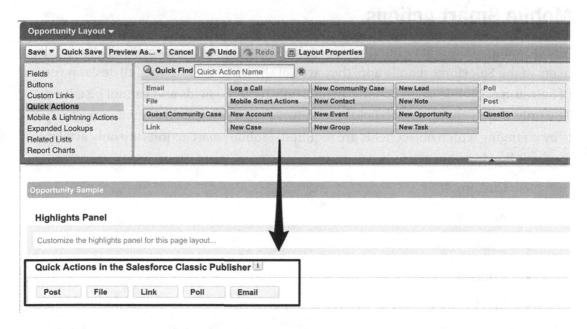

Figure 10-7. *A number of default quick actions are created for custom objects and a handful of standard objects; this image shows those associated with the Opportunity object*

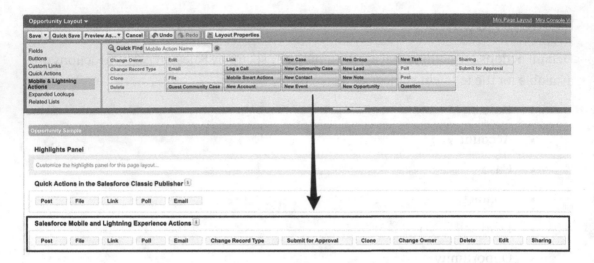

Figure 10-8. *A number of default mobile and Lightning Experience actions are created for custom objects and a handful of standard objects; this image shows those associated with the Opportunity object*

Mobile Smart Actions

Mobile smart actions are a bundle of predefined actions that are specifically for mobile users of the Salesforce mobile app; they are not shown to users of the full desktop version of Salesforce. Mobile smart actions include only required fields and cannot be edited. The only way to change which fields are shown as part of a specific mobile smart action is by changing which object fields are required. Mobile smart actions are only available for the following objects:

- Custom

- Account

- Case

- Contact

- Lead

- Opportunity

Custom Actions

The sky is the limit with custom actions. Custom actions can take advantage of Lightning components, Visualforce pages or Force.com Canvas apps, allowing you to define their behavior with precision. Anything that is not possible via the other action types is likely possible with custom actions. Since these actions require code, I won't be covering them in this chapter. However, I would encourage you to explore custom actions if the other action categories cannot facilitate your requirements being met.

Record Actions

A few additional object-specific actions are available within the Salesforce mobile app that cannot be modified. These actions may include

- Send Email
- Log a Call
- Map
- View Website
- Read News

Action Attributes

When you create an action, the type primarily defines the core behavior. However, some metadata will also contribute to the functionality. All actions require a Label and Name; the Label is what will appear in the Publisher to users. You can use a standard label type for quicker creation of an action; this allows you to use standard language to maintain consistency among your actions. Figure 10-9 shows some of the available standard label types.

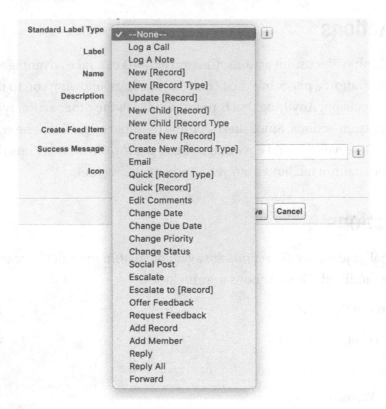

Figure 10-9. *You can use a standard label type or use your own custom label when creating an action*

Create actions have a few more attributes to be configured than other action types. One option is target object, which defines the object of the record to be created. This isn't present for update actions since those are only associated with the object for which they are created. It is important to understand that the relationships between objects can drive which objects are available for selection. For example, a create action for a custom object that is the master with another custom object in a master-detail relationship allows the detail object to be the target object in the parent's publisher layout. Another option with create actions is record type; this attribute only appears for create actions that have multiple record types.

Predefined Field Values

Salesforce did us all a favor when it decided to provide the ability to include predefined field values in an action. A predefined field value is a configuration record that identifies a default value for a particular field. What makes this particularly valuable is that it applies to all fields, including those that are not present in the page layout. You can use the predefined field value to

- Avoid forcing users to populate required fields

- Reduce the time required to fill out the record postcreation

- Prepopulate fields with likely/probable values for the particular action scenario

Figure 10-10 shows how an action layout and predefined field values can be combined in a hypothetical scenario.

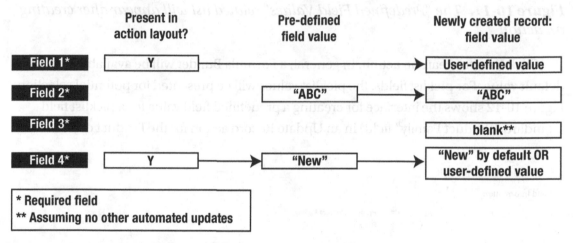

Figure 10-10. *You can place a field on the action layout and/or create a predefined field value to drive how a particular field is populated through an action*

To create a predefined field value, first create the action. Once the action has been built, you will be presented with action detail page. See Figure 10-11 for a view of this page.

Product Action
Quick Product Update

Help for this Page

Predefined Field Values [0]

Action Detail   Edit Delete Edit Layout

Label	Quick Product Update	Object Name Product
Standard Label Type		Action Type Update a Record
Name	Quick_Product_Update	Icon
Description		
Success Message		
Created By	Richard James, 11/11/2018 10:42 PM	Modified By Richard James, 11/11/2018 10:42 PM

Edit Delete Edit Layout

Predefined Field Values   New

No records to display

Figure 10-11. The "Predefined Field Values" related list will appear after creating an action

Click New to create an action. In general, a Formula Builder will be available to set the default value. For picklist fields, the picklist values will be presented for potential selection. Figure 10-12 shows the interface for creating a predefined field value for a picklist field (standard "Product Family" field) in an Update Record action for the Product object.

Predefined Field Value Edit   Save Cancel

Field Information

Field	Product: Product Family
Field Type	Picklist

Specify New Field Value

Specific Value	Pants
Formula Value	Show Formula Editor

Use formula syntax: Enclose text and picklist value API names in double quotes : ("the_text"), include numbers without quotes : (25), show percentages as decimals: (0.10), and express date calculations in the standard format: (Today() + 7)

Save Cancel

Figure 10-12. Setting the "Product Family" field on the Product object as a predefined field value for a Product-related action

Actions and Page Layouts

The Home Page, Chatter tab, and all of the record detail pages are associated with two types of layouts for pages: "Quick Actions in the Salesforce Classic Publisher" and "Salesforce Mobile and Lightning Experience Actions." By default, all record pages initially employ the default, global versions of each of these layouts, which can be found by searching for "Publisher Layouts" in the Quick Find menu. Like with other entities that have corresponding page layouts, you can customize the Global Layout or create additional layouts to be used for different profiles. Figure 10-13 shows your options for using the Global Layout or a custom layout based on the location of the feed.

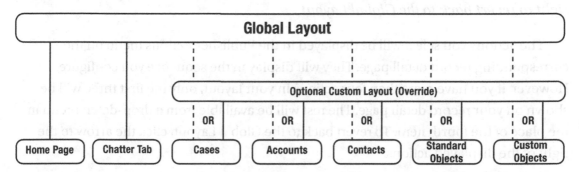

Figure 10-13. *The Home Page and Chatter Tab can only use the Global Layout, but you can create object-specific Publisher layouts for standard and custom objects*

The Home Page and Chatter Tab can only employ the Global Layout. However, you can override the Global Layout with an object-specific layout for standard and custom objects. Certain actions (e.g., Log a Call) are only available on object-specific layouts.

Publisher layouts are found within traditional record detail page layouts, just below the Highlights Panel section. You'll initially see a note confirming that the object is inheriting the parent Global Layout. To override the Global Layout, you simply click the wrench icon to the right of the text. Figure 10-14 shows the Quick Actions section of the "Page Layout" screen when the Global Layout default is enabled.

Figure 10-14. *The "Quick Actions" section on the Page Layout edit screen*

Clicking the wrench will allow you to configure the actions to be displayed on the corresponding record detail page. Figure 10-15 shows what the Publisher Actions layout section looks like after overriding the Global Layout default.

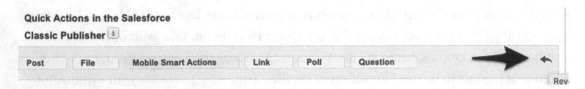

Figure 10-15. *Once an override has been applied, you can click the arrow on the right to revert back to the Global Layout*

The actions you select will be displayed in the Publisher Actions menu on the corresponding record detail page. They will display in the sequence you configure. However, if you have more than four actions in your layout, only the first three will be shown on your record detail page. The rest will be available from a drop-down menu in the place of the fourth item. To revert back to the Global Layout, click the arrow to the right of the displayed actions.

Action Layouts (How Actions Appear)

While the Publisher layout defines which actions appear within a given feed, the Action layout defines how a specific action appears to users. The Action layout editor is built on the same framework as record detail page layouts: you have the ability to add fields to and from the layout as well as reorganize them within the layout. Figure 10-16 provides a view of how an Opportunity-related action layout editor would appear.

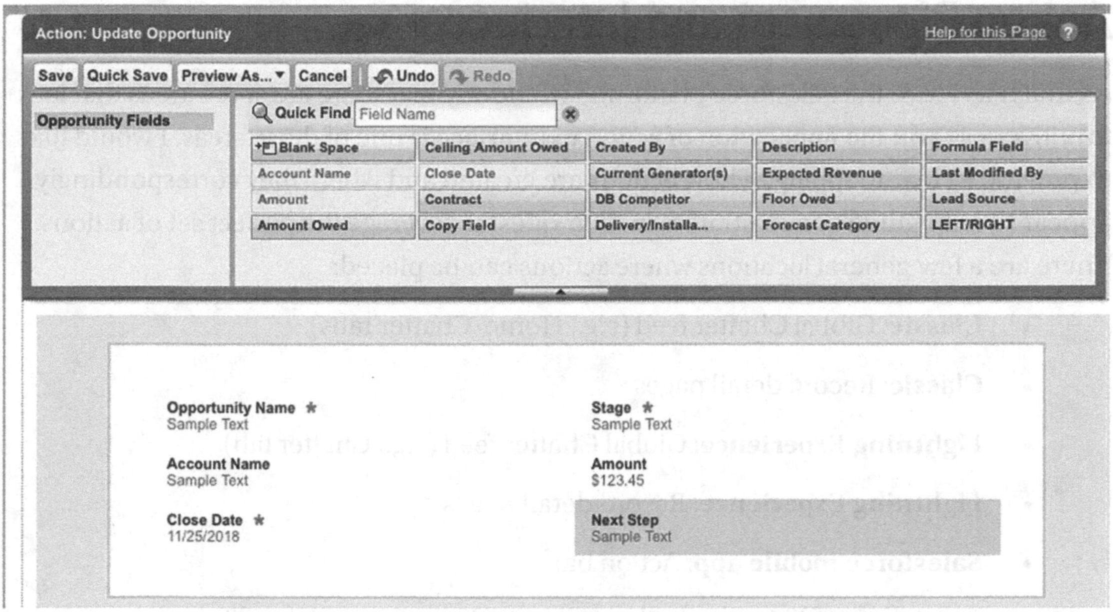

Figure 10-16. *The Action layout editor for updating an Opportunity*

Figure 10-17 shows you how the layout configured in Figure 10-16 would appear to a user.

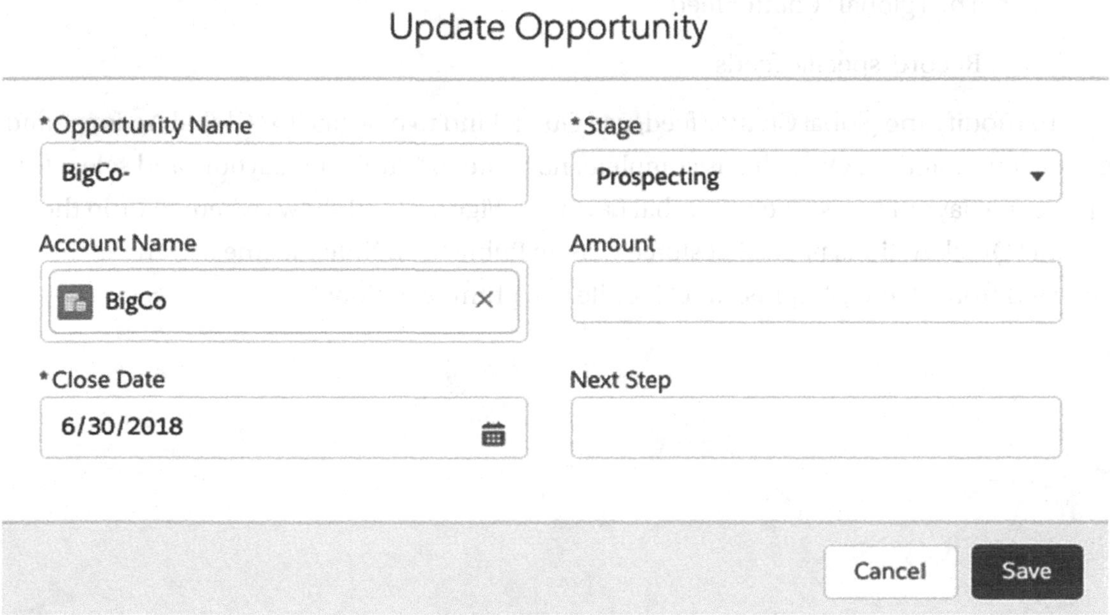

Update Opportunity

Figure 10-17. *The user's New Opportunity action, as configured in Figure 10-16 (LEX)*

Action Placement and Interfaces

As much as I love the Salesforce platform, I would say that there are some areas that lack intuitiveness and the application of action to interface is one of those areas. I would like to provide a clear mapping of how actions are created and where they correspondingly appear to help guide administrators in their quest to leverage the perfect set of actions. There are a few general locations where actions can be placed:

- **Classic**: Global Chatter feed (e.g., Home/Chatter tabs)

- **Classic**: Record detail pages

- **Lightning Experience**: Global Chatter feed (e.g., Chatter tab)

- **Lightning Experience**: Record detail pages

- **Salesforce mobile app**: Action bar

In this section, we will focus on Classic and Lightning Experience views.

Actions in Classic

Actions in Classic have two primary destinations:

- The (global) Chatter feed

- Record-specific feeds

To modify the global Chatter feed, use Quick Find to navigate to "Global Actions" and create a new action. Once that is complete, navigate to "Publisher Layout" and select the applicable layout (most likely, "Global Layout"). Figure 10-18 shows where to drop the action (Quick Actions in the Salesforce Classic Publisher). Note that the action must be selected from "Quick Actions," not "Mobile & Lightning Actions."

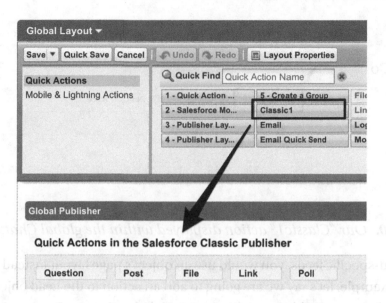

Figure 10-18. *Move an action to the "Quick Actions in the Salesforce Classic Publisher" section in the global publisher layout to display it within a global Chatter feed in Classic*

Figure 10-19 shows the action after placement in the layout editor.

Quick Actions in the Salesforce Classic Publisher

Figure 10-19. *Our "Classic1" action has been placed for display*

After saving the layout, the new action can be viewed from the Chatter tab in Classic (see Figure 10-20).

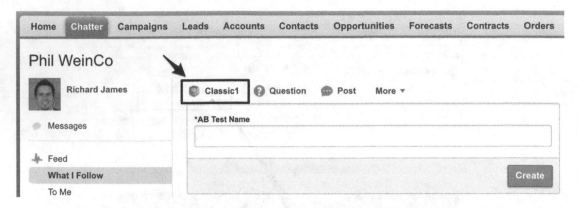

Figure 10-20. *Our "Classic1" action displayed within the global Chatter feed*

For record-specific feeds, you would use an object's page layout instead of the Global Layout. For example, let's say we are going to add an action to the Lead object. Note that the action can, as you would expect, be either a global action or a Lead-specific action. See Figure 10-21.

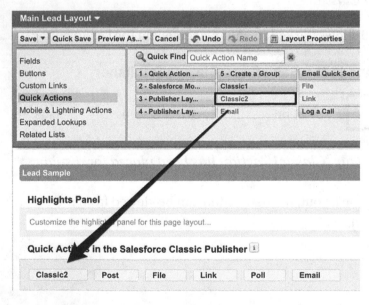

Figure 10-21. *Our "Classic2" action has been placed for display on the Lead object*

After placement, the action will appear in the Lead object feed, available on any Lead record. See Figure 10-22.

Figure 10-22. *Our "Classic2" action, as shown on a Lead record*

Note   For use of actions in Classic, make sure to select/drag from the "Quick Actions" group in the layout editor.

Actions in Lightning Experience

Actions in Lightning Experience (LEX) are not quite as straightforward as in Classic. That's not necessarily a bad thing, but does require some clarification. Salesforce has built LEX to be aware of action context. Instead of displaying all actions together (as done in Classic), actions, while placed together, are shown based on type, use, and so on. While this is great for end users, it can be a bit maddening as an administrator.

Unlike on the Classic Chatter page, only "standard" actions (e.g., Question, Post, Poll, etc.) will appear in the "Salesforce Mobile and Lightning Experience Actions" section to an end user. However, it will appear within the Global Action menu. Figures 10-23 and 10-24 show this behavior.

Figure 10-23. *Configuration of LEX actions on the Global Layout screen*

Figure 10-24. *The placement of actions in LEX based on configuration as shown in Figure 10-23 (Global Layout)*

Let's take a look at a record detail page in Lightning Experience. I created a custom object "Project" along with a few custom actions: "Record-specific Action" (a record update specific to the Project object) and "Global Action" (an Account record creation global action). I dropped those onto the Mobile/LEX actions section of the Project page layout as shown in Figure 10-25.

Figure 10-25. *Group types of LEX actions, including some custom actions*

In Figure 10-26, we can see how the actions configured in Figure 10-25 appear to end users.

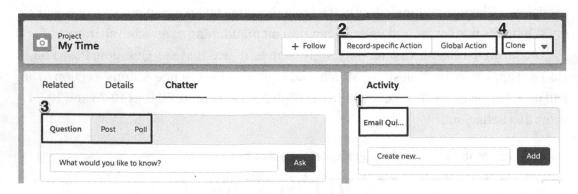

Figure 10-26. *This layout of the project custom object shows how the LEX actions, as configured in Figure 10-25, are displayed*

Creating an Action in Lightning Experience

This section offers a step-by-step guide for creating and configuring an action within Salesforce.

Business Scenario

In this hypothetical scenario, the sales team at your subscription-based software business is asking for additional efficiency in their sales process. The team feels burdened with the existing page layout, in that they have to scroll considerably to find and update important fields. Additionally, they have one very common Opportunity scenario that they would like to be able to create more quickly. After a detailed assessment of the process, you identify a few actions that would most dramatically aid the sales organization. The first phase of your action implementation is focused on the Account object. You plan on creating two actions: a quick update for the Account and a quick create for Child Opportunities related to software subscription renewals.

Example Action #1: Quick Account Update

This Quick Account Update will provide a "light" page with only minimal fields to quickly update an existing Account.

1. Navigate to the Account object (Search for "Object Manager" using Quick Find, then select "Account").

2. Click "Buttons, Links, and Actions."

3. Click "New Action."

4. Configure the new Account action shown in Figure 10-27 using the following settings:

    a. **Action Type**: "Update a Record"

    b. **Standard Label Type**: "--None--" (you will instead define your own label)

    c. **Label**: "Quick Update"

    d. **Name**: "Quick_Update"

    e. **Description**: A meaningful description for other administrators

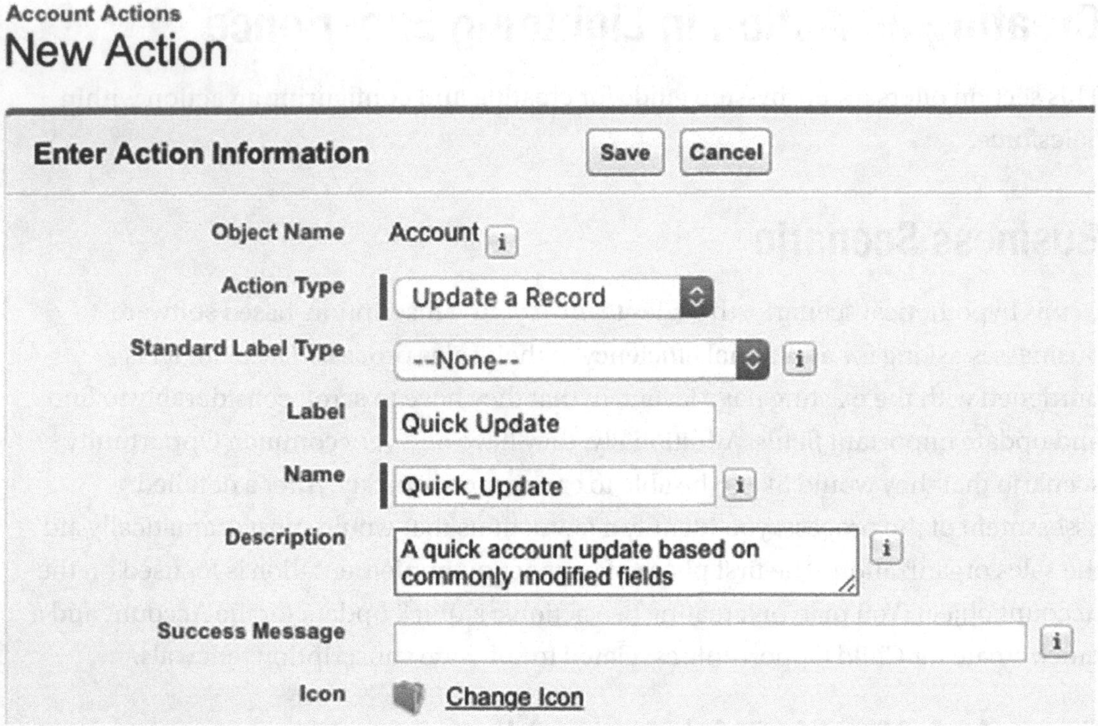

Account Actions
New Action

Enter Action Information	Save Cancel

Object Name	Account ⓘ
Action Type	Update a Record
Standard Label Type	--None-- ⓘ
Label	Quick Update
Name	Quick_Update ⓘ
Description	A quick account update based on commonly modified fields ⓘ
Success Message	ⓘ
Icon	📁 Change Icon

Figure 10-27. *Updating the action – main details*

5. Configure the Action layou for the new Account update as shown in Figure 10-28. These Account fields are those most commonly updated by the sales team.

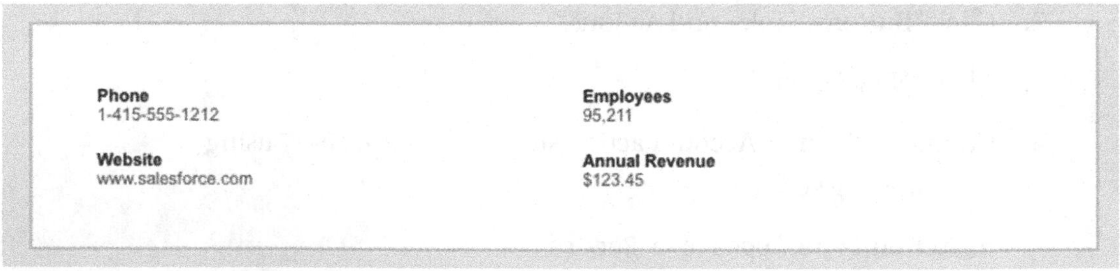

Phone	**Employees**
1-415-555-1212	95,211
Website	**Annual Revenue**
www.salesforce.com	$123.45

Figure 10-28. *Updating the Action layout*

6. Click "Yes" when asked if you want to continue saving, as shown in Figure 10-29. This is an existing record and will already have Account Name.

CHAPTER 10 CREATE EFFICIENT USER EXPERIENCES WITH ACTIONS

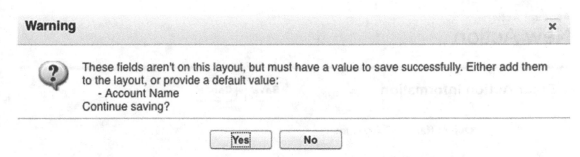

Figure 10-29. *You will be notified of any required fields that you do not have in the Action layout, as in this message*

7. No predefined fields will be needed since this is an update to the existing record.

Example Action #2: Creating a Child Opportunity from the Account

This Opportunity Creation action provides a quick way to create a common type of Opportunity from the parent Account page. To configure it:

1. Navigate to the Account object (Search for "Object Manager" using Quick Find, then select "Account").

2. Click "Buttons, Links, and Actions."

3. Click "New Action."

4. Configure the new Account action shown in Figure 10-30 using the following settings:

   a. **Action Type**: "Create a Record"

   b. **Target Object**: "Opportunity"

   c. **Standard Label Type**: "--None--" (you will instead define your own label)

   d. **Label**: "Quick Renew"

   e. **Name**: "Quick_Renew"

   f. **Description**: A meaningful description for other administrators

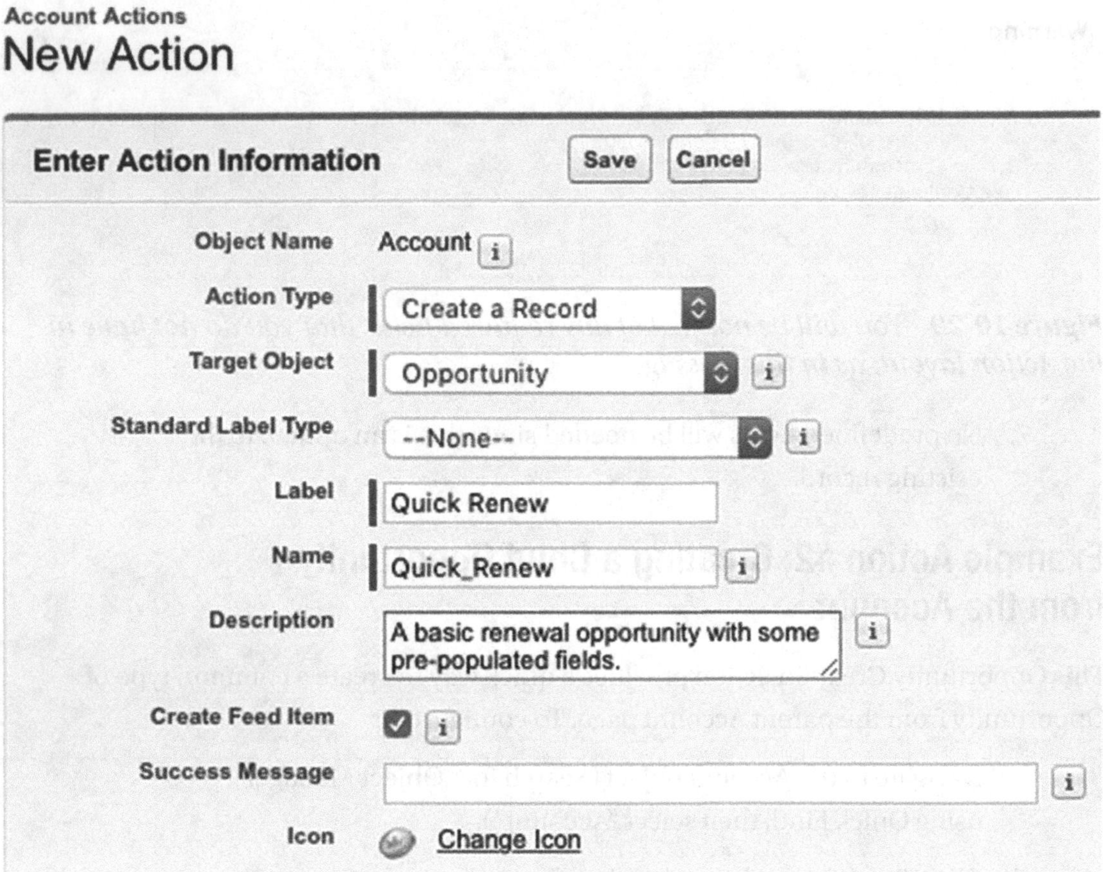

Account Actions

New Action

Enter Action Information   [Save]   [Cancel]

Object Name	Account [i]
Action Type	Create a Record
Target Object	Opportunity [i]
Standard Label Type	--None-- [i]
Label	Quick Renew
Name	Quick_Renew [i]
Description	A basic renewal opportunity with some pre-populated fields. [i]
Create Feed Item	☑ [i]
Success Message	[i]
Icon	Change Icon

Figure 10-30. *Creating the action – main information*

5. Configure the Create Action layout for the New Opportunity as shown in Figure 10-31. These fields are the minimum set of fields that need to be manually populated for a software subscription renewal.

Opportunity Name *
Sample Text

Close Date *
11/25/2018

Amount
$123.45

Figure 10-31. *Creating the action – layout*

6. Click "Yes" when asked if you want to continue saving. We will
    predefine Stage and a few other fields in the next step.

7. Click the "New" button in the "Predefined Field Values" section.
    Select "Stage" for the field and "Proposal/Price Quote" for the
    Value.

8. Click the "New" button in the "Predefined Field Values" section.
    Select "Type" for the field and "Quick Renewal" for the value in
    the "Specific Value" picklist. Note: You will need to add "Quick
    Renewal" to the list of picklist values before this.

Figure 10-32 provides a view of the predefined field values that have been configured
for the Child Opportunity example.

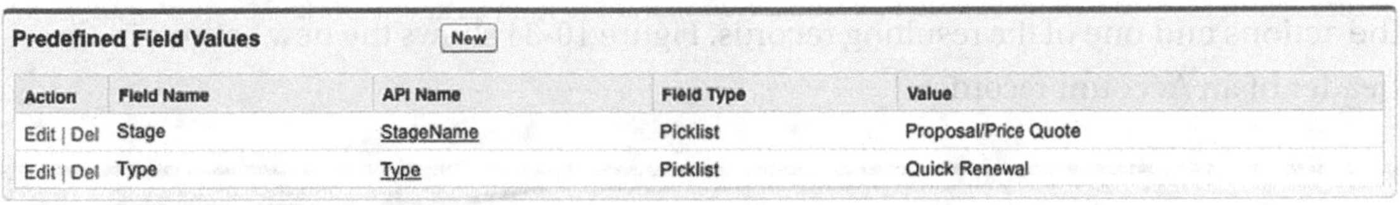

Predefined Field Values		New		
Action	Field Name	API Name	Field Type	Value
Edit | Del	Stage	StageName	Picklist	Proposal/Price Quote
Edit | Del	Type	Type	Picklist	Quick Renewal

Figure 10-32. *Creating the action – setting the predefined field values*

Establishing the Publisher Layout

The following steps will allow you to configure your Account object with a customized
Publisher layout:

1. Navigate to "Page Layouts" on Account setup screen.

2. After selecting the corresponding layout, scroll down to the
    "Salesforce Mobile and Lightning Experience Actions" section. If
    you are currently inheriting the Global Layout, click the wrench
    icon to override it and use a custom layout.

3. Remove all actions except for Post from the "Publisher Actions"
    section by dragging them up to the top layout section.

4. Click "Mobile & Lightning Actions" in the top section of the
    Account page layout editor.

5. Drag and drop "Quick Update" and "Quick Renew" down to the "Salesforce Mobile and Lightning Experience Actions" section, immediately after "Post." See Figure 10-33.

6. Click "Save."

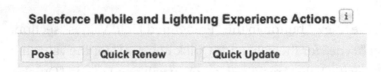

Figure 10-33. *The new LEX actions layout for the Account object*

View New Actions

Now that you've created a few new Publisher actions for accounts, let's take a look at the actions and one of the resulting records. Figure 10-34 shows the new actions in the header of an Account record.

Figure 10-34. *"Quick Update" action from the Account Chatter feed*

Figure 10-35 shows the Quick Update action (first example).

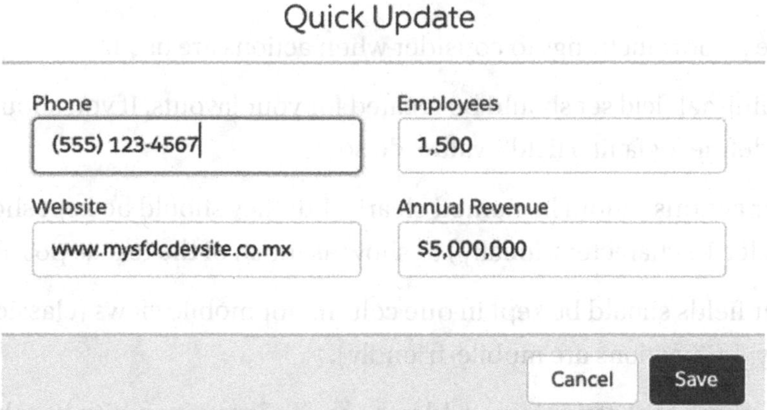

Quick Update

Phone	Employees
(555) 123-4567|	1,500
Website	**Annual Revenue**
www.mysfdcdevsite.co.mx	$5,000,000

Cancel   Save

Figure 10-35. *Quick Update (Account) action*

Figure 10-36 shows the Quick Renew action (second example).

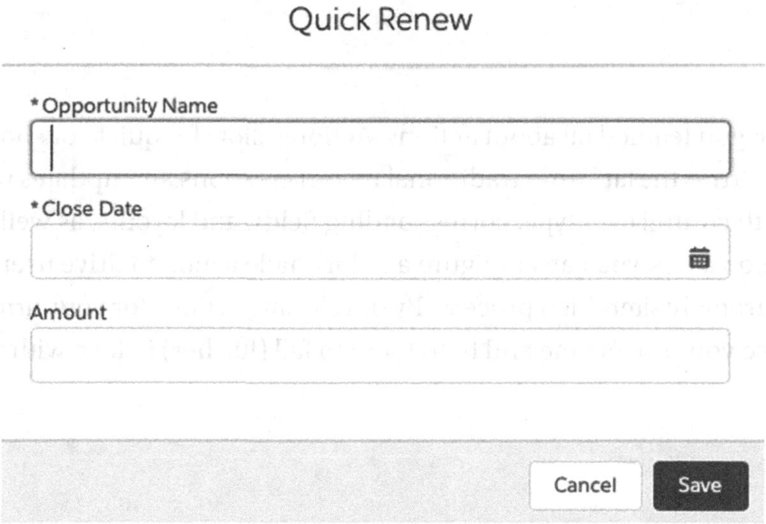

Quick Renew

*Opportunity Name

*Close Date

Amount

Cancel   Save

Figure 10-36. *Quick Renew (Opportunity) action from the Account Chatter feed*

Without a significant amount of work, you've just streamlined your sales team's process. With these actions, salespeople can make quicker updates to Accounts and create quick Opportunities for subscription renewals.

Considerations

Here are some important things to consider when actions are used:

- A minimal field set should be created for your layouts. If you should predefine/default a field's value, do so.

- Your actions should be named clearly, but they should be kept short (under 15 characters, ideally) to show as much of the text as possible.

- Your fields should be kept in one column for mobile views (classic only; LEX actions are mobile-friendly).

- The number of actions you add to a specific layout needs to be taken into account. More than four actions the full site will result in only the first three displaying without an additional click and only the first six appearing on the first page of the actions tray in the Salesforce app.

Recap

In this chapter, you learned all about actions. Actions allow for quick, or shortcut, behaviors that "trim the fat" from traditional record creations and updates within Salesforce. With control over type, corresponding fields, and layouts, as well as predefined field values, you can configure a tailor-made action to drive user behavior through an extremely simplified process. By developing actions for your firm, you can potentially save your user's time and help them to fall (further) in love with Salesforce.

CHAPTER 11

Using Web-to-Lead Effectively and Creatively

For years, Salesforce's Web-to-Lead tool has been a reliable means to capture sales inquiries from a web site outside an organization's Salesforce instance. While it may surprise some that it has persisted for so long, its simplicity and dependability has ensured its continued, official support from Salesforce. Web-to-Lead offers potentially significant value to those of us who would like to allow individuals without licenses (i.e., the public) to submit data into Salesforce without having to write any code to make that happen. The tool itself has not seen major modifications in years, but it is still a great feature to know. Additionally, there is depth to Web-to-Lead that is not immediately apparent to most users; in this chapter, I will explore its multiple levels to add another bow to your Salesforce no-code development quiver.

In this chapter, you will

- Understand the purpose of Web-to-Lead

- Learn the basics of the out-of-the-box tool

- Gain insight into modifying Web-to-Lead HTML to meet your needs

- Become familiar with certain considerations when using Web-to-Lead

- Explore how to combine Web-to-Lead with custom objects

Note Using Salesforce's Web-to-Lead tool does not require any previous knowledge of HTML. In this chapter, I will show you exactly what changes need to be implemented to effectively utilize Web-to-Lead. A basic understanding of HTML will provide you with some additional help when building out this functionality, however.

361

© Philip Weinmeister 2019
P. Weinmeister, *Practical Salesforce Development Without Code*,
https://doi.org/10.1007/978-1-4842-4871-3_11

Web-to-Lead 101

Before I go deeper, I'll start with the basics of Web-to-Lead. There are a few key components to understand:

- **Systems**: There are two systems involved – a client's web site and a Salesforce org. The only requirement of the web site itself is that it contains an HTML form that has Salesforce-generated Web-to-Lead HTML. The site can be public or private (e.g., Intranet). *Salesforce org* refers to your company's or client's instance of Salesforce of which you have administrative control.

- **Actors**: There is one actor involved – a web site user. This actor populates and submits the form on the web site previously mentioned.

- **Records**: A Lead record in Salesforce is created when the Web form is submitted.

- **Data**: The record's fields are populated based on how the Web form is filled out. The Web form fields can be visible to or hidden from the user.

Figure 11-1 provides an overview of how the Web-to-Lead process works.

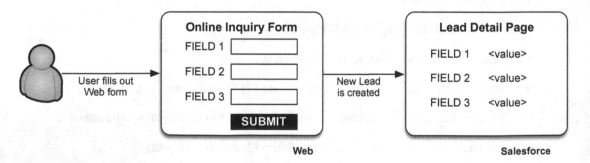

Figure 11-1. *The Web-to-Lead creation process*

Using the Web-to-Lead Tool

In order to get the most out of the Web-to-Lead tool, let's take a closer look at its various elements.

Web-to-Lead Settings

The first step in setting up Web-to-Lead is enabling the tool. To do this, find "Web-to-Lead" using Quick Find, click the "Edit" button, enable, and save (Figure 11-2).

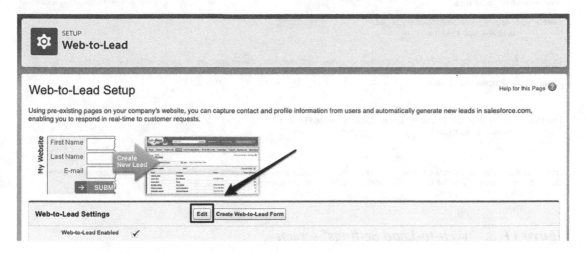

Figure 11-2. *Edit settings for Web-to-Lead*

Once you enable Web-to-Lead functionality, you have three settings to review:

- Require reCAPTCHA Verification

- Default Lead Creator

- Default Response Template

The first setting, "Require reCAPTCHA Verification," was an unexpected enhancement to the relativity constant tool that was delivered in 2017. Enabling this setting updates the Web-to-Lead HTML to display a reCAPTCHA form for the purpose of preventing unwanted submissions.

Setting a default lead creator is critical (and required). It refers to the individual who will be shown as creating a Lead generated via a Web-to-Lead form. The selection of your default lead creator may affect assignment rules, triggers, validation rules, and workflow rules that are based on the creator (and possibly owner) of Lead records, so select wisely.

As for the default response template, this is the e-mail template that will be sent if no template is determined based on the configured auto-response rules in the **Lead ➤ Auto-Response Rules** section. The default response template depends on how you have

363

configured your auto-response rules. The template is not required but is a good way to let users know that their submission was successful. Figure 11-3 shows the "Web-to-Lead Settings" screen.

Web-to-Lead Settings
= Required Information
Enable your organization to receive online leads.
Web-to-Lead Enabled
To reduce spam, require reCAPTCHA verification for customers' requests. When enabled, requests without verification don't generate leads. After enabling, confirm that your HTML includes the reCAPTCHA information.
Require reCAPTCHA Verification
The user who will be listed as Creator when a Lead is created online.
Default Lead Creator
Richard James
Use Lead Auto-Response Rules to select different email response templates based on attributes of the leads submitted online. Leads not matching any of the rules will be sent the default response template selected below.
Default Response Template
Web-to-Lead Email

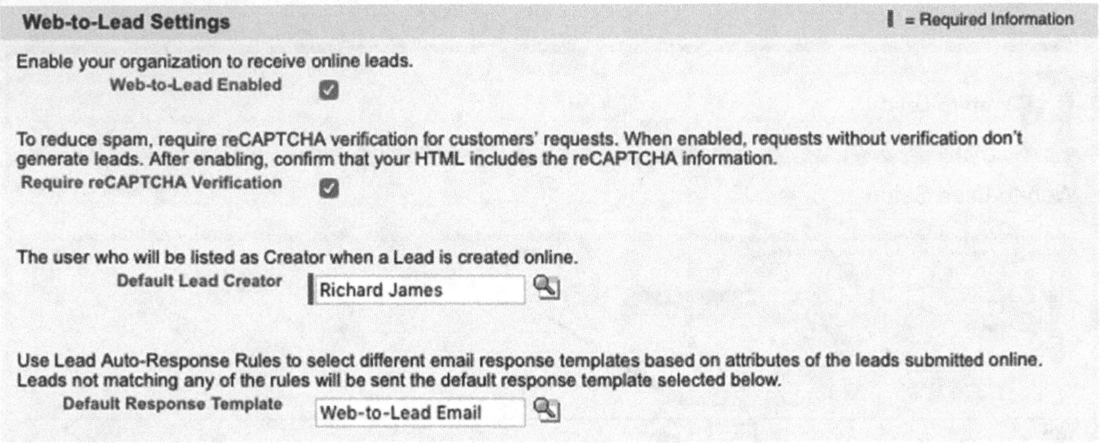

Figure 11-3. *"Web-to-Lead Settings" screen*

Selection of Fields/Configuration of Return URL

The fields you select will determine one key to the effectiveness of your Web-to-Lead form. Once you click the "Create Web-to-Lead Form" button (Figure 11-4), you will be able to determine the content of your Web form.

Web-to-Lead Settings
Edit
Create Web-to-Lead Form
Web-to-Lead Enabled
Require reCAPTCHA Verification
Default Lead Creator
Richard James
Default Response Template

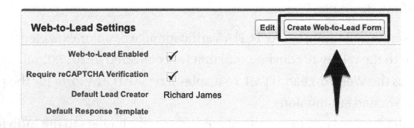

Figure 11-4. *Creating the Web-to-Lead form*

Include all fields you would like to be populated in the Web-to-Lead process regardless of how those fields are to be populated. Specifically, make sure all hidden and visible fields are selected for inclusion in the form. Figure 11-5 shows the available fields along with the selected fields that will appear in your Web-to-Lead form.

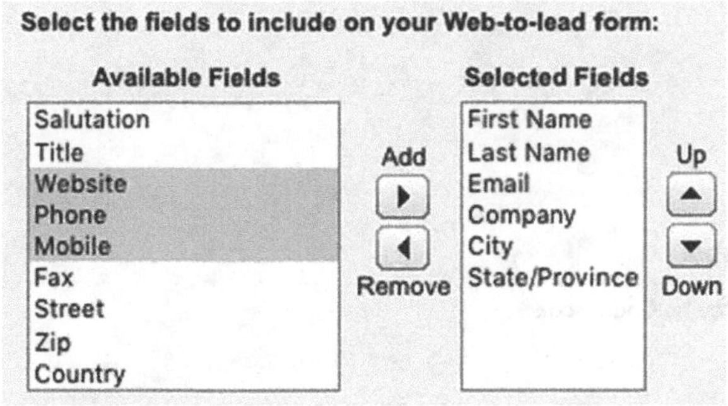

Select the fields to include on your Web-to-lead form:

Available Fields		Selected Fields	
Salutation		First Name	
Title	Add	Last Name	Up
Website	▶	Email	▲
Phone		Company	
Mobile	◀	City	▼
Fax	Remove	State/Province	Down
Street			
Zip			
Country			

Figure 11-5. *Selection of Lead fields for inclusion in your Web-to-Lead HTML form*

Additionally, Return URL (shown in Figure 11-6) is also available for configuration. This is the URL that your users will be directed to after submission of the form.

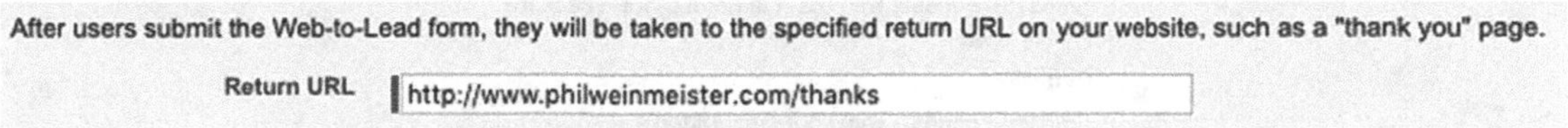

After users submit the Web-to-Lead form, they will be taken to the specified return URL on your website, such as a "thank you" page.

Return URL | http://www.philweinmeister.com/thanks

Figure 11-6. *Return URL configuration*

Next, we consider the reCAPTCHA settings, if they were originally enabled. First, you'll need to make sure that you have registered your site (the page on which you will be placing your Web-to-Lead form) with Google for reCAPTCHA. Search for "register Google reCAPTCHA" and you should find the site fairly easily. See Figure 11-7 for what the registration form looks like. I would recommend the "checkbox" option, although the other options are also viable.

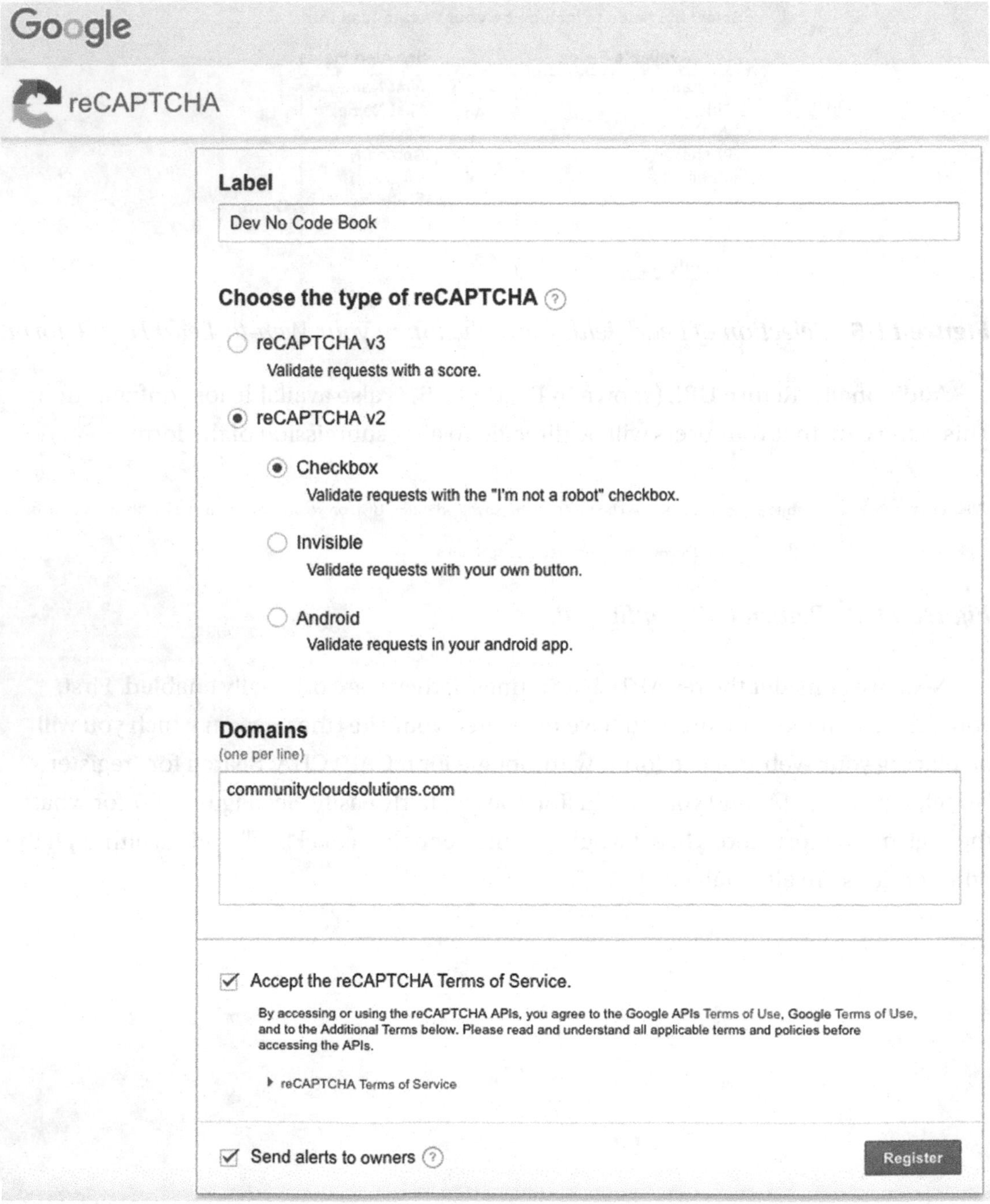

Figure 11-7. *reCAPTCHA registration form*

Once you have registered the site, go back to your Web-to-Lead form. Click the magnifying glass next to reCAPTCHA API Key Pair, then click the "New" button. See Figure 11-8.

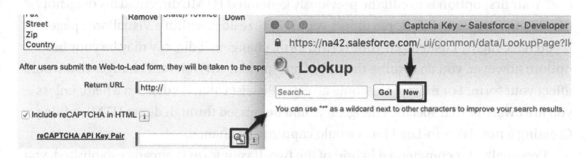

Figure 11-8. *reCAPTCHA API Key Pair management*

Enter the "Site Key" and "Secret" from Google's reCAPTCHA registration details and then save the record. See Figure 11-9.

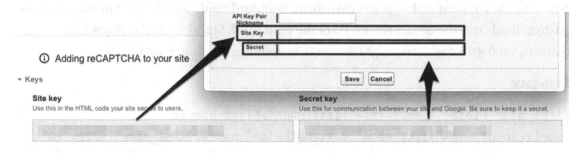

Figure 11-9. *Entering the Site Key and Secret*

Salesforce provides a "fallback" option in case the Google reCAPTCHA servers are down. If they are not available and "Enable Server fallback" will allow traffic (i.e., the form can be submitted). If the setting is not checked, traffic will not be allowed.

Generation of HTML

The selection of fields and configuration of the return URL field drive the specific HTML that is generated in the next step of the process. You will be presented with an HTML form that can then be used within a web page on any site you choose. One key aspect of Web-to-Lead to understand is that the generated HTML is not stored anywhere.

It is created once for you to copy and paste somewhere else; its content is unique to your settings at the time.

So, what should you do when changes occur to the Lead object within your internal org? Your first option is to edit the previously generated HTML directly. This does not require any access to Salesforce unless your HTML resides within a Visualforce page. If you have highly customized your HTML form, changing it directly may be your best option; however, you do assume the risk of not "picking up" relevant changes that would affect your form. For example, assume an extra Picklist value is added to a field; unless you are aware of that specific change, it would be missed through direct HTML editing. Creating a new Web-to-Lead form would capture that change.

Personally, I recommend a hybrid of the two. If your form is already established, you would typically not want to create it entirely from scratch. At the same time, you would not want to have any inaccuracies. Generate a new HTML form and compare it to your existing HTML form; copy the lines that are different and paste them in, as needed.

When reviewing your HTML, you may notice the difference in how standard and custom fields appear within the HTML form. Standard fields use the field name, whereas custom fields use the actual record ID of the field itself. Standard and custom fields within a Web-to-Lead form might generate output like the following HTML:

Standard

```
First Name Field: <label for="first_name">First Name</
label><input  id="first_name" maxlength="40" name="first_name" size="20"
type="text" /><br>
```

Custom

```
Twitter ID Field: <input  id="00N40000002Dj7E" maxlength="20"
name="00N40000002Dj7E" size="20" type="text" /><br>
```

The HTML that is generated includes all of the details specific to your org to allow a Lead coming through the resulting form to be able to properly route to your Salesforce org. Here is an example of generated HTML with commented rows removed:

```
<META HTTP-EQUIV="Content-type" CONTENT="text/html; charset=UTF-8">
<script src="https://www.google.com/recaptcha/api.js"></script>
<script>
```

```
function timestamp() { var response = document.getElementById("g-recaptcha-
response"); if (response == null || response.value.trim() == "") {var
elems = JSON.parse(document.getElementsByName("captcha_settings")[0].
value);elems["ts"] = JSON.stringify(new Date().getTime());document.
getElementsByName("captcha_settings")[0].value = JSON.stringify(elems); } }
setInterval(timestamp, 500);
</script>

<form action="https://webto.salesforce.com/servlet/servlet.WebToLead?
encoding=UTF-8" method="POST">

<input type=hidden name='captcha_settings' value='{"keyname":"API_Key_Pair",
"fallback":"true","orgId":"00DF000000061Hc","ts":""}'>
<input type=hidden name="oid" value="00DF000000061Hc">
<input type=hidden name="retURL" value="http://www.weinmeister.com/thanks">

<label for="first_name">First Name</label><input id="first_name"
maxlength="40" name="first_name" size="20" type="text" /><br>
<label for="last_name">Last Name</label><input id="last_name"
maxlength="80" name="last_name" size="20" type="text" /><br>
<label for="email">Email</label><input id="email" maxlength="80"
name="email" size="20" type="text" /><br>
<label for="company">Company</label><input id="company" maxlength="40"
name="company" size="20" type="text" /><br>
<label for="city">City</label><input id="city" maxlength="40" name="city"
size="20" type="text" /><br>
<label for="state">State/Province</label><input  id="state" maxlength="20"
name="state" size="20" type="text" /><br>

<div class="g-recaptcha" data-sitekey="6Lf2SHOUAAAAAEBvzATKwLa97R1Fc_LtuA8_
WQoa"></div><br>
<input type="submit" name="submit">
</form>
```

Modifying the HTML for Your Site

It's very likely that the HTML you've generated will require some modification. Unless you have an extremely basic site with no styling, this will be the case. Let's walk through some items that are candidates for tweaking.

Styling

Although I won't be delving into the world of web design here, suffice it to say that you will need to ensure that your HTML form renders properly within your site. This may mean employing CSS or identifying font properties within the HTML directly. Either way, you'll need to see how your form looks and update it accordingly. Using the HTML "as is" will not produce very aesthetic results within your site.

Hidden Fields

Just like with any HTML form, you can have hidden fields and input values in the Web-to-Lead form, which is a simple but powerful aspect. The fields are extremely valuable if you want to know the exact source of a Lead. For example, let's say you have ten Web-to-Lead forms spread across your web site. Without some specific identification within the form itself, it may be impossible to determine the original source of the Lead. To hide a form field, use the formatting shown in the following code for standard and custom fields:

Standard

```
<input type="hidden" name="fieldName" value="desiredValue">
```

Custom

```
<input type="hidden" name="fieldID" value="desiredValue">
```

The values in the name and value attributes can vary, but type must be equal to "hidden." Hiding fields provides two potential benefits:

- You can set a field to a specific value that cannot be modified by the user.

- You can hide the field from view on your web page.

Picklist Values

Picklist values are automatically generated for you during the process. However, you may want to omit some values or display them in a more user-friendly fashion on your site. Simply edit or remove them as needed. For example, HTML for a Picklist field can be changed from

```
<label for="industry">Industry</label>
<select  id="industry" name="industry">
<option value="">--None--</option>
<option value="Electronics">Electronics</option>
<option value="Government">Government</option>
<option value="Media">Media</option>
<option value="Other">Other</option>
</select><br>
```

to

```
<label for="industry">Industry</label>
<select  id="industry" name="industry">
<option value="">--None--</option>
<option value="Electronics">Electronics</option>
<option value="Media">Media</option>
<option value="Other">Other</option>
</select><br>
```

Here, the "Government" Picklist option was removed from the list.

Validations

Validations are a key and can easily be missed in the process. There are no validations that are automatically built into your generated form HTML. Users can enter whatever they would like in your form fields; it's up to you to restrict and control the information received, as desired. It is true that Salesforce will enforce system-level validations (e.g., a field of the number type cannot contain letters), but this will not be visible to the user; the form will "silently" fail. A key requirement that could be missed here would be ensuring that a field (e.g., Last Name) is populated when a form is submitted. Make sure to work with your web team to build in form validations accordingly.

Modifications for Sandbox Testing

A simple change that is often missed is the modification of a Web-to-Lead form to work with a sandbox org. If using Web-to-Lead in a sandbox, change the form's `action` attribute URL to `test.salesforce.com` as shown:

```
<form action="https://test.salesforce.com/servlet/servlet.WebToLead?
encoding=UTF-8" method="POST">
```

Lookup Fields/Campaigns

One valuable feature of Web-to-Lead is the ability to specify a Campaign. The formatting of a Campaign field is a bit different than that of other fields, since it is a lookup field. The values will be the ID of the Campaign records. You can specify the Campaign Member Status as follows:

```
<label for="Campaign_ID">Campaign</label><select id="Campaign_ID"
name="Campaign_ID">
<option value="">-None-</option>
<option value="CampaignID">Campaign1</option>
<option value="CampaignID">Campaign2</option>
<option value="CampaignID">Campaign3</option>
<option value="CampaignID">Campaign4</option>
</select><br>

<input type="hidden"  id="member_status" name="member_status" value="" />
<br>
```

Unfortunately, you cannot follow this same approach for other lookup fields. This is a feature that would be well received if ever offered by Salesforce.

Combining Web-to-Lead with Other Functionality

Although the only direct actions you can control with a Web-to-Lead form are creating Leads and Campaign Members, you can pair workflow rules with your generated records to greatly expand the capabilities. Like with standard workflow rules, you can create and assign a task, send an e-mail using a predetermined template, or update a different field on the Lead object. I believe that the most exciting synthesis will be with trigger-ready flows, however. These are the flows that can be kicked off from a workflow rule. It is absolutely conceivable that you could create a very creative solution associated with objects other than the Lead object using a combination of Web-to-Lead and a trigger-ready flow. I would definitely recommend exploring this option when this flow type is fully available to the public.

Other Web-to-Lead Considerations

What follows are some final items to consider when generating Web-to-Lead forms within Salesforce.

Debugging

Since failed Web-to-Lead requests do not show up anywhere by default, Salesforce has intelligently provided a debugging option for administrators. To do this, simply uncomment the two hidden input fields that follow (make sure to set them with your e-mail address) and you will receive details of failed Web-to-Lead submissions. You will receive a confirmation e-mail after submitting the form. See the following for the original and the revised HTML to activate debugging via e-mail. Bolded lines are those that require a modification.

```
<!--   ----------------------------------------------------------   -->
<!--   NOTE: These fields are optional debugging elements. Please    -->
<!--   uncomment these lines if you wish to test in debug mode.      -->
<!--   <input type="hidden" name="debug" value=1>                    -->
<!--   <input type="hidden" name="debugEmail"                        -->
<!--   value="pweinmeister@example.com">                             -->
<!--   ----------------------------------------------------------   -->
```

should become

```
<!--   ----------------------------------------------------------   -->
<!--   NOTE: These fields are optional debugging elements. Please    -->
<!--   uncomment these lines if you wish to test in debug mode.      -->
<input type="hidden" name="debug" value=1>
<input type="hidden" name="debugEmail" value="pweinmeister@example.com">
<!--   ----------------------------------------------------------   -->
```

Daily Limit

Another consideration you'll need to make when using Web-to-Lead is its daily limit. At the current time, the limit of Leads created using Web-to-Lead is 500 per day. However, that is subject to change in the future. This limit may not be a concern for your organization, but you should be aware of it when making related business decisions.

Recap

In this chapter, you examined a commonly used tool for capturing incoming Lead records in Salesforce from the Web, Web-to-Lead. You went over how to customize the HTML to meet your specific business needs and also reviewed considerations that should be made when using the tool. While this tool has been around for some time, a little extra time investigating its additional layers could potentially prove fruitful for you when working with Leads, especially if you are not using Pardot, Marketing Cloud, or another, similar application to handle this functionality.

CHAPTER 12

Optimizing Your UI Using Classic or Lightning

I have spent a considerable amount of time in this book discussing how to configure Salesforce to capture and store data as desired, provide users with critical functionality, build applications with clicks, and drive automated business processes to make your business efficient. However, this could all be for naught if you do not allocate the proper attention to the Salesforce user interface. While there are clear limits on what you can do with the interface via declarative methods, the extent to which you appropriately configure it for your organization or client can make a world of difference. Successfully designing and implementing your user interface will bring the following benefits to your organization:

- Increased user efficiency/reduction in process "waste"

- Appropriate and expected visibility of objects, fields, and data

- Reduced need for user training and assistance

- Enhanced user experience and increased user adoption

- Delivery of additional functionality

As with many other areas in Salesforce, you can significantly extend your control with code. You can employ Visualforce and/or Lightning components to deliver a customized experience, allowing you to potentially change colors, styles, and page elements (or to eliminate the Salesforce look and feel altogether). In this chapter, however, I will solely focus on the options available to you via "clicks, not code" and I'll cover some of the areas that will provide the highest return on your investment. A number of declarative options are available to you that can have a true material impact on your business.

375

© Philip Weinmeister 2019
P. Weinmeister, *Practical Salesforce Development Without Code*,
https://doi.org/10.1007/978-1-4842-4871-3_12

In this chapter, you will

- Become familiar with layout options for the record detail page

- Learn how to effectively configure page layouts

- Understand how to employ formula fields to present visual elements on a record's detail page

- Combine formula functions to increase your control of configurable page layout elements

- Review considerations to be made when configuring the Salesforce user interface

---

Note   In this chapter, I will address orgs using Classic, as well as those using Lightning Experience. When input only applies to one or the other, I will call that out. Also, "LEX" is an abbreviation for "Lightning Experience"; you will see that throughout the chapter.

The Record Detail Page

Since most of your users' time will be spent viewing or acting upon records within Salesforce, it makes sense that the biggest bang for your buck in terms of enhancing the user interface can be found in the standard page layout editor. This editor allows you to control the layout and the content in the "detail pages" that display the records from each of your objects. The following subsections review the key areas in the page layout that can bring value to your organization. Figure 12-1 shows a Lead record detail page in Lightning Experience.

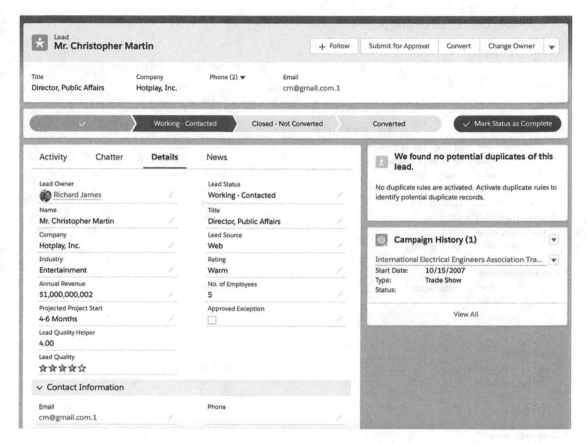

Figure 12-1. *The Lead record detail page in Lightning Experience*

Figure 12-2 shows the same Lead record detail page that is shown in 12-1, but with the Classic interface.

Mr. Christopher Martin

Customize Page | Edit Layout | Printable View | Help for this Page

Show Feed

Open Activities [0] | Activity History [0] | Campaign History [1] | HTML Email Status [0]

Lead Detail   Edit   Delete   Convert   Clone   Find Duplicates

Lead Owner	Richard James [Change]	Lead Status	Working - Contacted
Name	Mr. Christopher Martin	Title	Director, Public Affairs
Company	Hotplay, Inc.	Lead Source	Web
Industry	Entertainment	Rating	Warm
Annual Revenue	$1,000,000,002	No. of Employees	5
Projected Project Start	4-6 Months	Approved Exception	☐
Lead Quality Helper	4.00		
Lead Quality	★★★★☆		

▼ **Contact Information**

Email	cm@gmail.com.1	Phone	
Website		Mobile	
		Fax	
Description			

▼ **Custom Fields**

Migrated	☐	Date Field	
Text Area (Long)		Date Time	
Text Area (Rich)		Picklist (Multi-Select)	
Text Area (Encrypted)			

▼ **Custom Lookups**

Case		Property	
Solution			

Figure 12-2. The Lead record detail page in Classic

Displayed Fields

When thinking through the layout for your record detail pages, you'll want to make some decisions about the fields you intend to display. Arguably, the most important aspect of the page layout is the selection of the fields that you decide to present to users. If you fail to allow access to a key field, your users' ability to be productive will be avoidably inhibited. Less critically, but still important, is the inverse of that scenario. Littering the screen with extraneous fields will slow progress and potentially cause confusion while users perform standard business operations. If you can combine a thorough-yet-streamlined selection of key selection of fields with a strategic placement of those fields on the page layout, you can make a notable impact on the user experience. Here's a checklist of what to include to help you get started:

- **Required fields**: Add any required fields that are not present on the layout by default.

- **Fields critical for business processes**: Add fields that play a role in operational activities that are performed by your users.

- **Reference fields**: Add fields that may be referenced during operation or for reporting/analytics even if they are not always critical for viewing or editing.

Of course, there are a number of factors that will come into play when determining exactly which fields to place on your page layout. The main takeaway here is that you should not blindly dump all of the object's fields onto the page layout; you should have a reason for each field being present.

Record Detail Sections

Each field that you place on a record detail page is associated with a section. A section is a group of fields with a shared header and common navigation behavior. Figure 12-3 shows a Contact detail page layout with six sections.

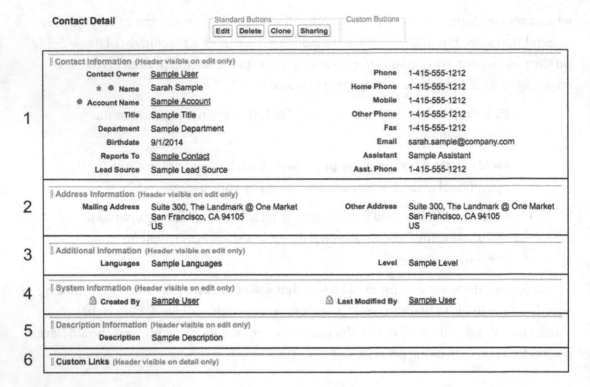

Figure 12-3. *A Contact detail page with various detail sections, as seen in the page layout editor. The numbered areas on the Contact detail page layout are field sections.*[1]

Here are some options and factors to consider when creating sections:

- **Balance of section count with field density**: You will want to find a happy medium between a layout that has a few sections that contain numerous fields and one that is loaded with small sections. You should consider breaking up some of your bigger sections for two reasons: First, a section with a moderate number of fields (five to ten) is easier to mentally digest than one that takes up half a page. Second, the opportunity to collapse a section is diminished as the volume of fields in a particular section increases. Don't forget that your users can collapse/hide sections. If you limit them to a few large sections, they will likely not be able to collapse these sections due to one or more key fields being included.

---

[1]All Salesforce screenshots in this chapter © copyright Salesforce, Inc. Used with permission.

- **Section names**: Section names, surprisingly, seem to be overlooked quite often. Adding them is simple and quick, and it provides important context for your users. Carefully consider the fields that will be placed within a section and assess how well they can be logically grouped. Would a user be surprised to see (or not see) a particular field in a certain section based on the section name? If so, handle the field accordingly, either by adding or omitting it to the section.

- **Use of screen space/number of columns**: Typically, page layout sections have two columns. This usually makes sense for minimizing white, or wasted, space. A one-column section is also twice as tall as a two-column section with the same field count. However, trying to force fields with large field values (e.g., because they have a long text area) into a section with two columns can sometimes present an odd look.

- **Header display**: While adding a section name can be very important, sections can be created specifically for layout purposes without needing to display a header. As previously mentioned, a long text field can sometimes look odd in the smaller columns. However, it may make sense to group one-column and two-column sections underneath the same header. To do this, you can create a new one-column section below the related two-column section and simply hide the header of the bottom (one-column) section. See Figure 12-4 for an example of how this looks to an administrator when the page is viewed in edit mode.

Figure 12-4. *A hidden header (on the bottom, the second section). Note that two sections exist in this view: a two-column section at the top and a one-column section at the bottom.*

Figure 12-5 depicts how the screen in Figure 12-4 would appear to a user.

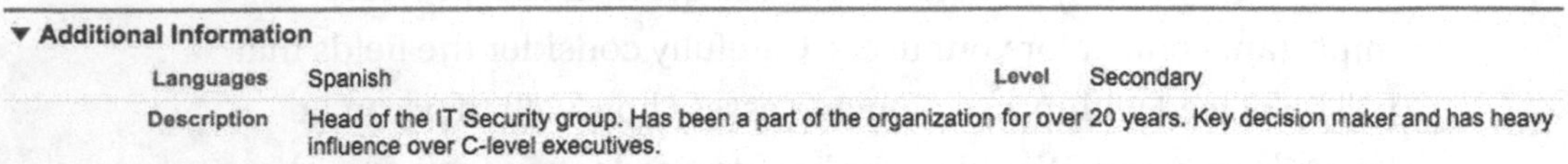

▼ Additional Information			
Languages	Spanish	Level	Secondary
Description	Head of the IT Security group. Has been a part of the organization for over 20 years. Key decision maker and has heavy influence over C-level executives.		

Figure 12-5. *A user's view of the page layout created in Figure 12-4*

Figure 12-6 shows the full page view of the section displayed in Figure 12-5.

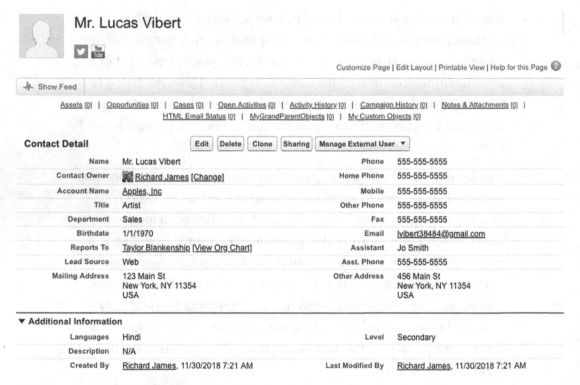

Figure 12-6. *Classic view of the detail sections on a record page*

While record pages in Classic view always show the detail sections at the top of the page, LEX record pages give the option of where to "drop" the detail component. Figure 12-7 shows a standard application of the detail component on a record page in LEX.

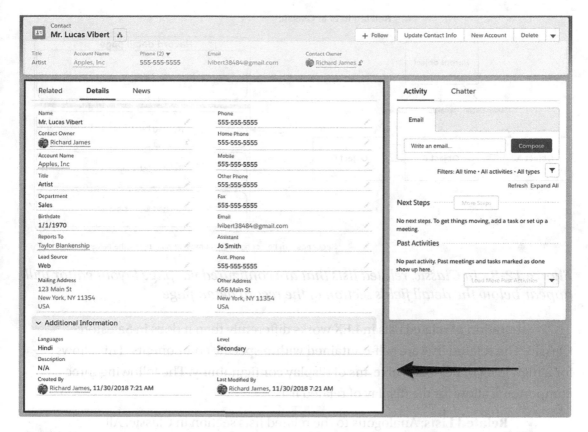

Figure 12-7. *LEX view of the detail section(s) on a record page*

Related Lists

Your setup of related lists, along with field configurations, will likely have the largest impact on the user experience in the page layout editor. Related lists contain sets of corresponding records from Child objects or, in some cases, certain related records (e.g., "Notes & Attachments"). Figure 12-8 shows how different child objects could be represented as related lists.

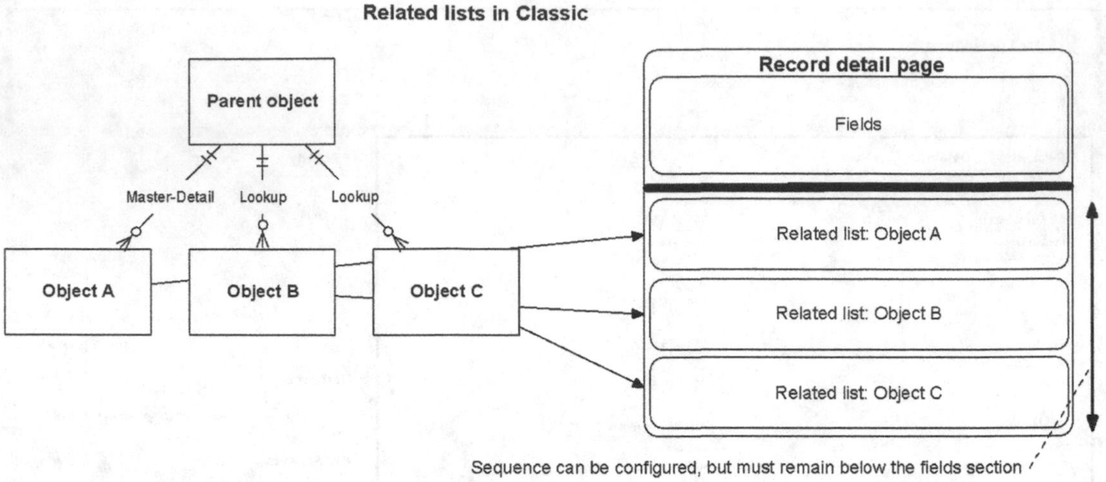

Related lists in Classic

Figure 12-8. *In Classic, related lists that are configured via page layout editor will appear below the detail fields section of the record detail page*

Presentation of related lists in LEX works differently than it does in Salesforce Classic. The related lists are self-contained within specific components. This allows for a high level of flexibility in terms of display configurability. The following three components allow for the display of related lists:

- **Related Lists**: Analogous to the related lists section in Classic. All related lists that are configured on the page layout are shown.

- **Related List Quick Links**: Similar to "Related Lists," but only displays links to the related list data (i.e., the records and fields are not displayed).

- **Related List – Single**: A single related list can be configured. This is extremely useful if you want to show different related lists in various places on a page without presenting the entire list.

Figure 12-9 shows how this works in LEX.

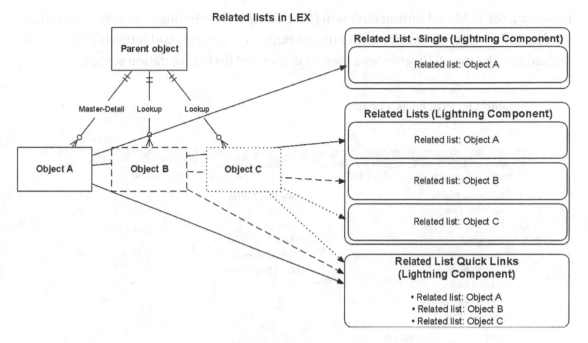

Figure 12-9. *Salesforce provides flexibility through three options for presenting related lists*

Some of the related records that can be represented as related records include

- Activity History

- Open Activities

- Approval History

- Campaign Influence

- Object Field History

- Content Deliveries

- Notes & Attachments

- Related Content

Although some related lists cannot be modified, the majority of the lists possess a few key elements that can be configured. You can add up to ten fields and assign a sequence to those fields, although only four of them appear as of Spring '19. It's worth mentioning that the standard Name field must be present as the first field in the list of selected fields. Additionally, you may be able to configure the sorting attributes, including the field and sorting direction (ascending or descending). Finally, depending on the Child object and any custom buttons built for it, you can add buttons to the related list. Figure 12-10 provides a view of the related list configuration screen.

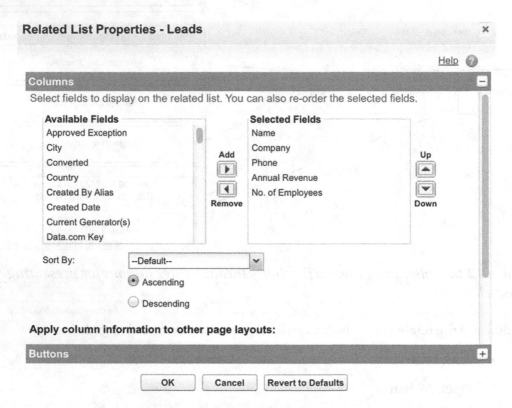

Figure 12-10. *The "Related List Properties" screen allows you to configure certain elements of some related lists, including fields, sorting method, and buttons*

Additionally, Lightning Experience offers a "Related Record" component that can be placed on a record detail page to show details of or actions associated with the related record. See Figure 12-11.

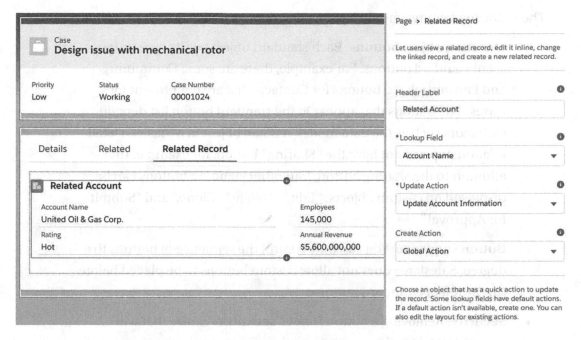

Figure 12-11. *The Related Record component in Lightning Experience*

Buttons

In Classic, you have the ability to determine which buttons are present on your page layout. You'll be given an initial default set of standard buttons when your org is set up, but it's highly recommended that you tailor these appropriately to your users' needs. Figure 12-12 shows a potential button layout for a Case object, with three standard buttons and one custom button.

Figure 12-12. *A possible Case button layout that includes a custom button*

Note   Technically, "buttons" are only available in Classic. However, button-like "actions" are available in Lightning Experience that equate to Classic buttons. See Chapter 10 for everything you need to know about actions.

The following features should be considered when building your set of buttons:

- **Standard object buttons**: Each standard object has its own unique set of standard buttons. For example, there are some Community- and Partner-related buttons for Contacts that are not present for Cases. The buttons that appear in the standard button list depend on factors such as the data model. A detail object in a Master-Detail relationship will not have the "Sharing" button, for example. In addition to the Sharing button, four other standard buttons can be displayed on custom objects: "Edit," "Delete," "Clone," and "Submit for Approval."

- **Button sequence**: You can only control the sequence of buttons to a degree. Salesforce does not allow custom buttons to be placed before (to the left of) standard buttons.

- **Security**: Removing a button is not a security measure that will prevent certain actions from occurring. For example, the removal of the Delete button does not prevent a user from deleting a record; it just prevents that user from deleting it via the standard button on the record detail page. If you are concerned about a user performing an inappropriate action, you need to restrict the user's permissions via their profile or a permission set. If a user is not able to delete a record, he or she will not see the Delete button even if it is present on the page layout.

Highlights Panel

Salesforce provides a "highlights panel" for consoles in Classic. The panel provides a quick reference to specified fields for use when working with a customer, client, prospect, or related contact. You can add up to eight fields within the highlights panel. Figure 12-13 provides a view of the highlights panel layout.

Case Sample

Highlights Panel

Case Number	Contact Name	Date/Time Opened	Status
GEN-2004-001234	**Sample Contact**	9/1/2014 8:52 PM	**Sample Status**
Case Owner	Contact Email	Date/Time Closed	Priority
Sample User	sarah.sample@company	9/1/2014 8:52 PM	**Sample Priority**

Figure 12-13. *Edit view of a Highlights Panel for a Case to be displayed within the Service Cloud Console*

Compact Layouts

Salesforce provides a few alternative layouts to support field configuration in different interfaces, including compact layouts. Compact layouts allow for configuration of key information related to a record. To modify the compact layout, navigate to the Compact Layouts section for an applicable object. Figure 12-14 shows a view of the layout page.

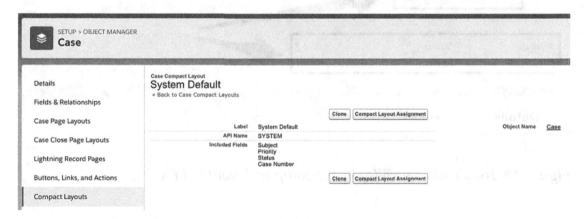

Figure 12-14. *Compact layout admin page*

To create a new compact layout, click "Clone" and set the desired fields. Once the new layout is present, you'll have to assign it via compact layout assignment. See Figure 12-15 for these buttons.

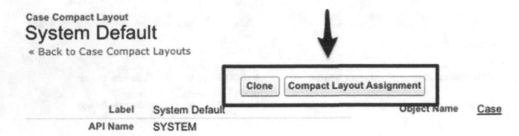

Figure 12-15. *Compact layout page layout editor*

A compact layout will manifest in two places. First, it will be displayed at the top of record detail pages in LEX (Figure 12-16). Additionally, it will be available for hover lookups in LEX (see FIgure 12-17). This is a critical item to keep in mind when creating a new object or modifying a standard object.

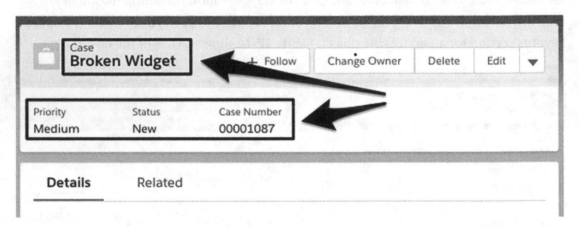

Figure 12-16. *Fields controlled by the compact layout in LEX*

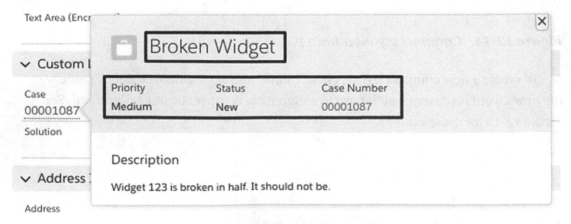

Figure 12-17. *Fields controlled by the compact layout via a lookup*

Mini Page Layout

A seldom-discussed but useful Classic interface tool for the within the page layout editor is the mini page layout editor. This layout editor determines which fields appear when hovering over a relationship field. When configuring a mini page layout, you will want to keep a minimal number of fields while making sure that you display relevant fields to users. Figure 12-18 shows a possible mini page layout for the Case object.

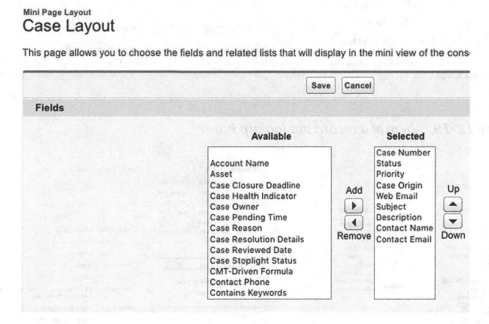

Figure 12-18. *Configuration of fields of the mini page layout for the Case object*

Figure 12-19 shows how the configuration in Figure 12-18 appears to end users. Note that the Web Email field is not displayed on the page layout; Salesforce is honoring field-level security by preventing the visibility of that field. Providing the appropriate field-level permission to the applicable user(s) will allow them to have this field displayed. Figure 12-20 shows the configuration and display together.

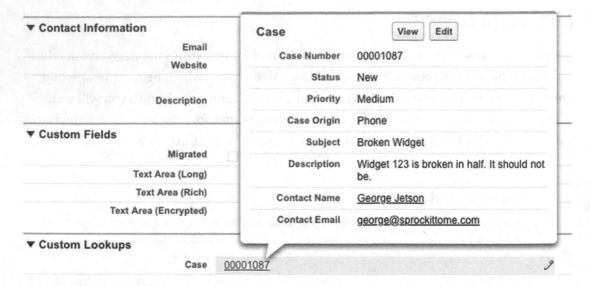

Figure 12-19. *View of a record via lookup hover*

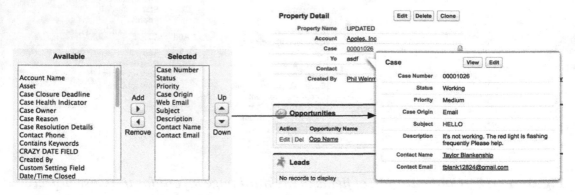

Figure 12-20. *A view of configuration and layout together; again, note that Web Email doesn't display. This is due to field-level security settings*

Actions

The layout of your actions has a significant impact on the value of record detail pages (and some nondetail pages). Chapter 10 gives the full scoop on configuring actions for your organization.

Properties

Certain standard objects have properties that can be configured in the page layout editor. These properties control key behavior related to your object, so make sure that you review each of them carefully. Here's a breakdown of the properties available for each object:

- **Task** (note that "Enable User Control over Task Assignment Notifications" – via **Activity Settings** in Quick Find – must be disabled to edit these properties)

  - Email Notification Checkbox: Show on edit page

  - Email Notification Checkbox: Select by default

- **Lead**

  - Lead Assignment Checkbox: Show on edit page

  - Lead Assignment Checkbox: Select by default

- **Case**

  - Case Assignment Checkbox: Show

  - Case Assignment Checkbox: Select by Default (note that the Select by Default checkbox is ignored if the Show checkbox is not enabled.)

  - Email Notification Checkbox: Show

  - Email Notification Checkbox: Select by default

  - Show Submit & Add Attachment Button

  - Show Knowledge Sidebar in the Console

- **Most Standard Objects** (including those mentioned earlier)

  - Show Highlights Panel in the Console

  - Show Interaction Log in the Console

Note   Although I do not cover it in this configuration-based book, Visualforce pages can be inserted into your page layouts. By adding Visualforce to a standard page in Classic, you can significantly enhance the look and feel of your page and add custom functionality, as well.

Profiles

When you are looking to craft a streamlined, relevant presentation of record data in Salesforce, you will need to inject an additional layer into your approach. Everything in this chapter so far has been outlined with one audience in mind. However, the overwhelming majority of Salesforce orgs include multiple audiences that need to be considered. This comes into play because each audience will likely care about different fields and functionality on your record detail pages. To help us incorporate this second layer of thinking, we need to consider profiles and permission sets.

Let's take a simple scenario with three audiences and look at how they come into play with an Account object that boasts a few custom fields. Here are the audiences and the custom fields that each audience needs to see:

- **Sales**: Account Tier (Picklist)

- **Service**: 12-Month Case Count (Number)

- **Marketing**: Prospect Referrals (Number)

If we ignore audiences, we end up with a page layout that displays two unnecessary fields to each audience (see Figure 12-21).

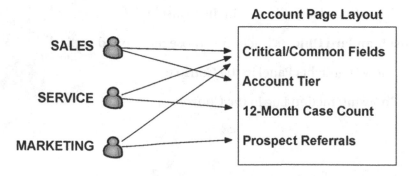

Figure 12-21. *Multiple profiles being presented the aggregate set of fields needed for all profiles*

By creating three page layouts, we can streamline and show only what is necessary to each audience (see Figure 12-22).

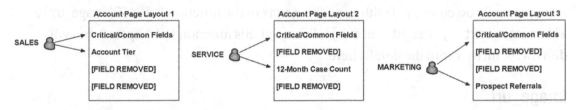

Figure 12-22. *By creating a page layout for each profile, extraneous fields can be removed for applicable profiles*

Permission sets can be useful here, as well. If, within an audience, slight variations are needed, permission sets can potentially provide streamlined views without generating an unmanageable number of profiles. Create your "base profile" without access to the field in question and then create and assign a permission set to grant access to it – but only to those who need to see it. End result? One page layout and one profile, but the field in question that warrants different visibility appears only to those with the permission set.

Bonus: IMAGE() in Formula Fields

I have covered formula fields in detail, but I've only touched on the visual impact they can have. Buried in the large list of functions that Salesforce provides is the IMAGE function. This function, which can be used in text formula fields, is extremely useful for making simple visual changes to the standard Record Detail page. Figure 12-23 shows an example of a visual icon that can be created with the IMAGE function.

Health Status Indicator

Figure 12-23. *An example of an image in a formula field created with the IMAGE function*

IMAGE Syntax

IMAGE allows an image to be inserted into a standard detail page. The inserted image can optionally be combined with text. The syntax of the function is IMAGE(image_url, alternate_text [, height, width]). I covered this function in Chapter 2, but will delve a bit further into the details here.

Image_url

Image_url contains the URL of the image to be displayed; it can be a relative reference to a file within Salesforce or an absolute reference to an image on the Web. If you are using a file in Salesforce, you have three options for how to upload and store your image: Documents, Static Resources, and Files.

To reference a Document in your IMAGE function:

1. Navigate to the "Documents" tab and upload your image.

2. Once the image is uploaded, get the URL of the image by right-clicking the image and either opening it in a new tab/window or viewing the file properties ("View File" or "Open Image in New Tab"). You'll see something like this for the URL: https://c.na42.content.force.com/servlet/servlet.ImageServer?id=0152A00 000AGO3m&oid=00DF000000061Hc&lastMod=1544446908000.

3. Go ahead and remove the https:// and everything before the next forward slash. This will allow you to provide a relative reference. Of course, if the document doesn't reside in your org, you'll need the full, absolute URL.

4. Optionally, you can remove "&lastMod" and everything after if you always want to show the latest version of the document. Do not do this if you want to show a specific version.

5. You'll end up with something like this: /servlet/servlet.Ima geServer?id=0152A00000AGO3m&oid=00DF000000061Hc&lastM od=1544446908000

Documents are handy when some degree of user modification may be needed. However, the URLs do not translate between orgs. Notice oid in the URL; this is the org ID. If you deploy something that references a Document record to another org, even if you include the Document, manual updates will be needed after deployment to update the reference.

Most likely, a better option for you when using images within your formula fields would be to take advantage of a Static Resource. A Static Resource can be deployed with its corresponding reference and no further updates will be needed. To upload a Static Resource, navigate to Static Resource (via Quick Find), click New, and upload your image. Click the "View File" link on the "Static Resource" page. You will see a URL similar to this: https://c.na42.visual.force.com/resource/1544447364000/YellowMan.

One great thing about using a Static Resource is that you can reference either the most recent version or a specific version (even if a new version is uploaded). To reference a specific version, you will follow a route similar to the one we followed for referencing a Document. Simply include everything after the base domain: /resource/1409553319000/ MyPhoto. To make sure that the most recent version is used, remove the unique value between "resource" and your Static Resource's name: /resource/YellowMan.

A third option is to use Salesforce Files. With Files, you can generate a publicly accessible URL that can be referenced. However, you will want to follow the same pattern as documents and static resources for referencing your File-based image in a formula. The URL of the image will look something like this: https://c.na42.content.force. com/sfc/servlet.shepherd/version/renditionDownload?rendition=ORIGIN AL_Gif&versionId=0682A000006BeVl&operationContext=CHATTER&contentId=05 T2A00000JTdRo. You can, once again, remove the https:// and everything before the next slash for a relative reference. The field might end up looking like what we see in Figure 12-24 in Lightning Experience.

Figure 12-24. *A File-based image in a formula field on a Case record*

Note   Make sure to include quotes around your URL within the IMAGE function.

Alternate_text

`Alternate_text` contains the text value that will be displayed if the image hasn't loaded yet or is prevented from loading. A description of the image is usually what you'll want to include here, but think through your scenario. If the image is critical for understanding the record, you may want to provide some additional detail in your `alternate_text` string.

Height, Width

Another option is to provide a height and width. Unless your image has been customized specifically for Salesforce, you may want to consider setting these dimensions.

Note   Height and width must be set together. Salesfore.com will not resize an image proportionately if you only define one attribute.

Here's an example of what one of the examples I used might look like:

```
IMAGE("/resource/MyPhoto", "My Photo", 50, 200)
```

Combining IMAGE with Other Functions

The real power of using a formula field to display images comes when you combine the IMAGE function with other functions. By doing so, you can further facilitate business processes by injecting additional functionality and conditions into the field. The following subsections cover some examples of potentially valuable combinations.

IMAGE and IF

Combining the IMAGE and IF functions allows you to display different images conditionally. This can be extremely useful if you want to catch a user's eye and communicate key data quickly. The Case Status and Opportunity Stage fields lend themselves to visual representation well. An image can ensure that users clearly understand the state of a particular record. Figures 12-23 and 12-24 provide two examples, both related to the Case record. For each example, I have uploaded the necessary images as Static Resources.

In the first example, shown in Figure 12-25, I represent different Case statuses with a stoplight theme. For Cases with a Status of "On Hold," I would show a yellow stoplight. For all other open Cases, I show a green stoplight. For closed Cases, I would just show the text "Case Closed." The resulting formula is

```
IF(ISPICKVAL(Status, "On Hold"), IMAGE("/resource/YellowLight", "On Hold",
32, 32), IF(NOT(IsClosed), IMAGE("/resource/GreenLight", "On Track", 32,
32), "Case Closed"))
```

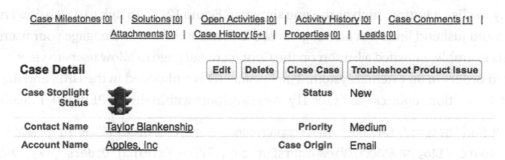

Figure 12-25. *Based on the formula, this Case displays a green stoplight for an open Case that is not on hold*

In the second example, shown in Figure 12-26, the scenario is similar. However, I map the Case statuses differently. Additionally, I employ a banner instead of a graphic and use a one-column section to show my visual field at the top of the Case page. The resulting formula is

```
IF(ISPICKVAL(Status, "New"), IMAGE("/resource/YellowNew", "New", 71, 800),
IF(NOT(IsClosed), IMAGE("/resource/GreenInProgress", "In Progress", 71,
800), IMAGE("/resource/RedClosed", "Closed", 71,800)) )
```

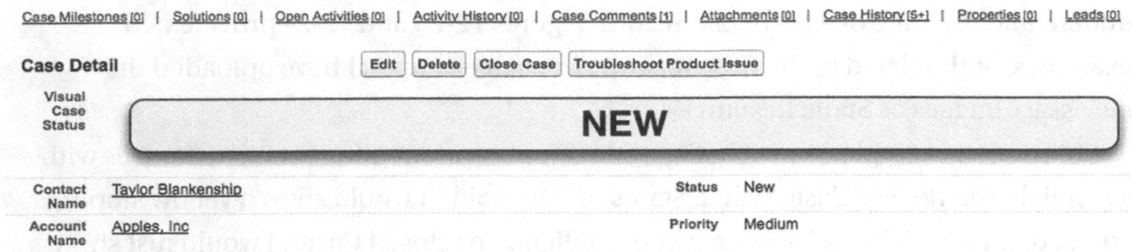

Case Milestones [0] | Solutions [0] | Open Activities [0] | Activity History [0] | Case Comments [1] | Attachments [0] | Case History [5+] | Properties [0] | Leads [0]

Case Detail   Edit   Delete   Close Case   Troubleshoot Product Issue

Visual
Case   **NEW**
Status

Contact   Taylor Blankenship   Status   New
Name
Account   Apples, Inc   Priority Medium
Name

Figure 12-26. In this example, a banner image showing the status has been created with a formula field

IMAGE and HYPERLINK

The IMAGE function can be combined with the HYPERLINK function to give users the ability to click a button, such as the one shown in Figure 12-27, to link to a website. True, you could just add links. But an image-based link will stand out and engage your users. In this example, I created a button on the Contact detail page to allow users to view related orders in an external system. The Contact ID is embedded in the URL, and the IMAGE function replaces the `friendly_name` attribute within the HYPERLINK function.

```
HYPERLINK("https://intranet.yourcompanydomainhere.com/orders/" & Id , IMAGE
("/resource/1409799656000/ViewOrdersButton", "View External Orders", 25, 250))
```

View Related Orders   **VIEW RELATED ORDERS (External System)**

Figure 12-27. A button created using a combination of the IMAGE and HYPERLINK functions within a formula field that is displayed on the page layout

IMAGE, IF, and HYPERLINK

If you want to get really creative, you can combine IMAGE, IF, and HYPERLINK to show conditional linked images to your users. In this example, I show an image if the Case is closed and an image hyperlink if the Case is open.

```
IF(
IsClosed,
IMAGE("/resource/CaseClosed", "Case is Closed", 50, 200),
HYPERLINK("https://intranet.yourcompanydomainhere.com/detailednextsteps/" &
Id, IMAGE("resource/DetailedNextSteps", "Next Steps", 50, 200))
)
```

400

Other UI Considerations

There are a number of other configurations that impact the user interface. While these topics would be more appropriate in a beginner/administrator book, they are still important aspects to consider when building an experience for your users. In particular, make sure to review the following elements:

- **Search layouts**: These layouts control the fields (and corresponding sequence) that are displayed in different search scenarios. Some of the layouts you can modify include standard search results, a lookup dialog (when populating a record in a lookup relationship field), and tab home pages.

- **Compact layouts**: You can configure compact layouts to drive the display of key fields for your objects within the Salesforce App. Compact layouts also affect which fields are displayed in the Chatter feed after creating a record via Publisher Actions.

- **Mobile cards**: Mobile cards are mobile-specific layouts that can be accessed from records of configured objects. They can be established for Parent records (via Lookup or Master-Detail relationships). Look into this if you are using the Salesforce app.

- **Tabs**: If you plan on navigating directly to or viewing the list views of records of a custom object you've created, you'll want to make sure to create an associated tab for the object. Your interface options will be significantly limited without a corresponding tab.

- **Apps**: You can create apps to present a logical grouping of tabs for a particular set of users. This setup is very straightforward and will notably enhance your users' experience.

- **Record types**: With record types, you can display different page layouts for one object to the same user depending on the underlying record data. This can be valuable if different types of records require different fields to be shown or edited.

- **User interface settings**: The user interface settings (available via Quick Find by searching for "**User Interface**") include a number of configurable options for controlling the look and feel of Salesforce for your users. Setting categories include **User Interface**, **Sidebar**, **Calendar**, and **Setup**.

- **Home page (Classic)**: The home page is a two-column page on which you can place certain components to determine their sequence. The home page can significantly impact your users' experience, as it will often be the first page they see when they log in to your Salesforce org. You can use some predefined components or you can create your own custom components such as the following: links, image/logo, HTML area, and Visualforce area. You'll want to carefully think through how you approach your layout. The HTML and Visualforce areas are great, as you can create a completely custom look and feel for this page

- **Themes and Branding (LEX)**: In 2018, Salesforce released themes in Lightning Experience. Until then, "Lightning Blue" (previously without a name) was the only theme option. This is an easy way to quickly enhance the look and feel of your LEX org. Search for "Themes and Branding" in Quick Find.

Recap

In this chapter, I took a slight detour from building solutions to focus on Salesforce's user interface. If you take some time to familiarize yourself with the plethora of options, you may be surprised how much you can control in the user interface without writing code. In particular, you'll want to methodically review the page layout for each of your objects and set up a streamlined look for each that has everything your users will need. Additionally, you can use a formula field or two to give your page a bit of flair and engage your users even more effectively.

CHAPTER 13

Using Lightning App Builder to Develop Declarative Apps

If it hasn't been clear in my writing up to this point, let me clearly acknowledge that there is immense value in traditional "customization" (i.e., code) on the Salesforce platform. While many of us reference the "clicks, not code" saying, that phrase doesn't actually capture the greatest value of the platform. It's not just the replacement of code with clicks that we should pay attention to; it's the application of declarative, clicks-based development *on top of* customization where the sky is truly the limit.

Overview

Lightning App Builder is a tool that completely and fully realizes this concept. It is a drag 'n' drop, WYSIWYG (what-you-see-is-what-you-get) editor that provides the ability to drag and drop the main building blocks of a Lightning app – Lightning components – to achieve the desired end state within the Lightning Experience UX. Figure 13-1 provides a view of this powerful tool.

© Philip Weinmeister 2019
P. Weinmeister, *Practical Salesforce Development Without Code*,
https://doi.org/10.1007/978-1-4842-4871-3_13

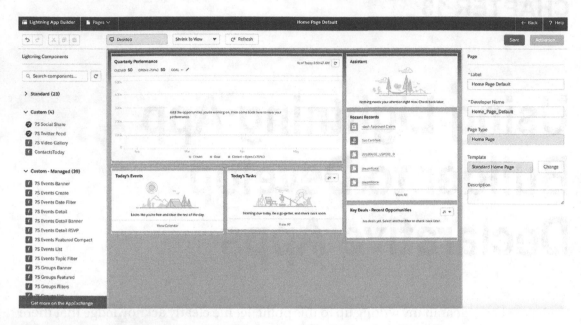

Figure 13-1. *Lightning App Builder, a tool for Lightning Experience*

Within Lightning App Builder, administrators can perform the following functions, among many others:

- Add, remove, position, and configure standard and custom Lightning components

- Configure page attributes

- Control visibility of individual components for specific audiences

- Active and assign pages, or "apps," to certain users

In this chapter, I will walk through each of the sections of Lightning App Builder and describe how to use them.

Getting to Know Lightning App Builder

Lightning App Builder is a broad, multifaceted application. To intimately understand how to use Lightning App Builder, a systematic, comprehensive walkthrough of each area is needed. I will divide it into four main sections, as shown in Figure 13-2:

1. Lightning Components Sidebar

2. Top Menu Bar

3.   Page Sections

4.   Property Editor/Page Editor

Figure 13-2. *Basic structure of Lightning App Builder*

Lightning Components Sidebar

The left sidebar in Lightning App Builder houses all of the components that are available for use when constructing Lightning apps. Components are segmented into three sections:

- Standard

- Custom

- Custom – Managed

As you can guess by the presence of a "managed" custom section, "Custom" implies unmanaged. While this actually does not always ring accurate, I would speculate that Salesforce is presenting these sections roughly equivalent as home-grown ("Custom") and third-party ("Custom – Managed"). However, some SIs (system integrators) do build apps that are delivered as unmanaged. See Figure 13-3 for a closer look at the left sidebar.

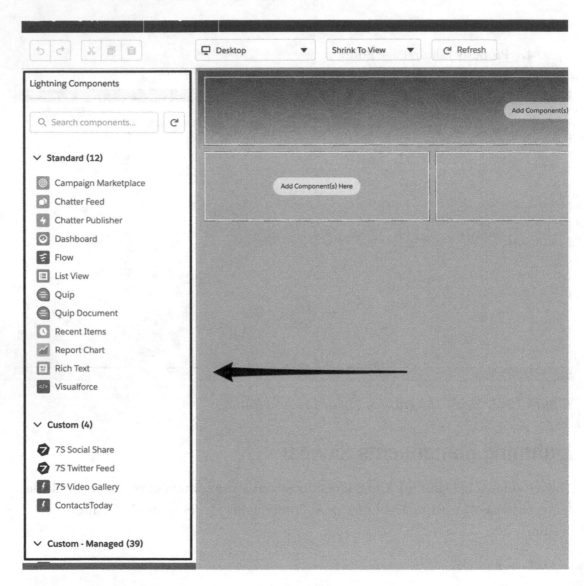

Figure 13-3. The left side contains all available Lightning components

Components Tab

If I go with the analogy that a Lightning component is to a Lightning app as an individual Lego piece is to a finished Lego project, then the left sidebar serves as a bag of various Lego pieces. This section is essentially a list of available Lightning components. Each component is represented by three items: a text label, an icon, and a description that is shown upon hovering over a component. See Figure 13-4 for an example.

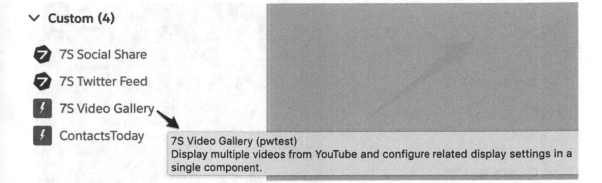

∨ Custom (4)

7S Social Share

7S Twitter Feed

7S Video Gallery

ContactsToday

7S Video Gallery (pwtest)
Display multiple videos from YouTube and configure related display settings in a single component.

Figure 13-4. *Each component listed in the left sidebar has a label, icon, and description*

In addition to finding by scrolling, you can search by a text string to filter for any component that contains that string. The section headers persist in the search results, which is very useful. See Figure 13-5 for an example of a possible search.

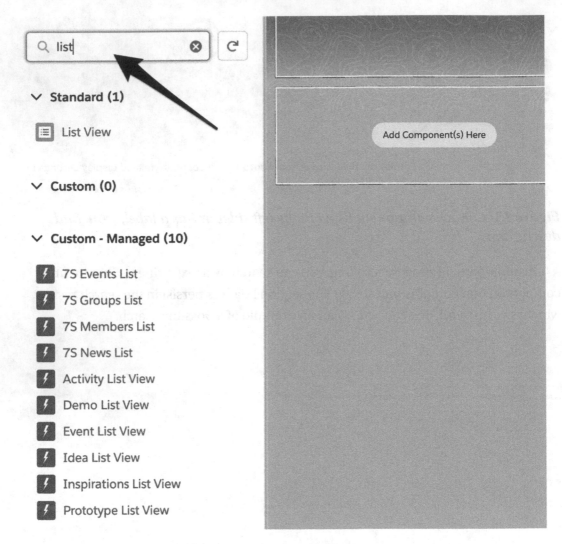

Figure 13-5. *Search results for "list" in the left sidebar*

To add a component from the sidebar to your app, simply perform the following (see Figure 13-6 for an example):

- Click the desired component.

- Drag the component to the appropriate section and position on the page.

- Drop the component by "dropping" (releasing from the click).

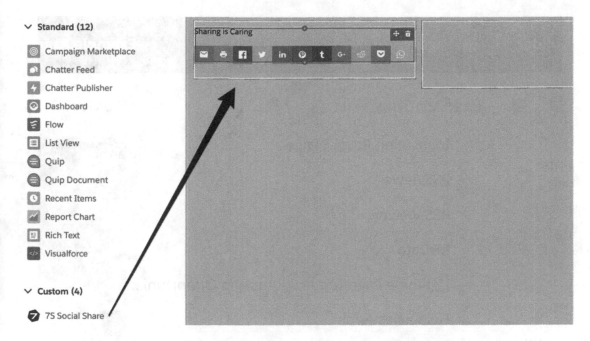

Figure 13-6. *Dropping a custom component onto a Lightning page*

Don't worry; if a component is placed in the wrong section on the page, it can be easily moved later.

Top Menu Bar

The top of Lightning App Builder has some key controls that admins need to be aware of. Let's have a look.

Page Manager

The page manager in Lightning App Builder enables two main functions:

- Navigation to an existing page

- Creation of a new, Lightning page

Figure 13-7 shows a screenshot of the panel with each section clearly delineated.

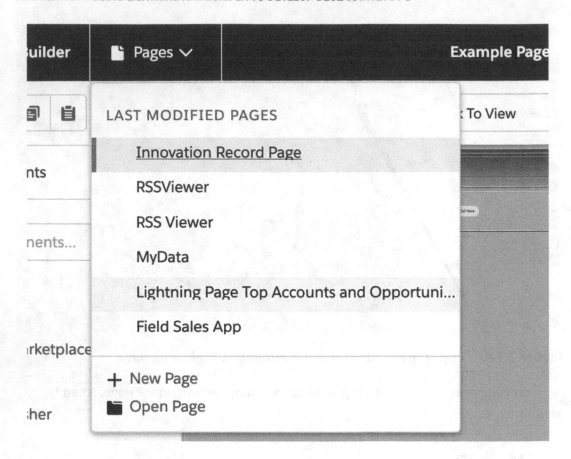

Figure 13-7. *The page manager menu in the top nav bar*

I will dive into page creation later in this chapter.

Editing Controls

The next section provides common editing controls for the following purposes (see Figure 13-8):

- Navigation (back and forward)
- Cut, Copy, Paste

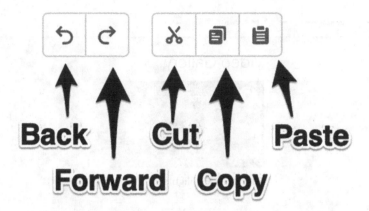

Figure 13-8. *A look at the editing controls in Lightning App Builder*

View Mode

The "View Mode" that is built into Lightning App Builder is extremely useful for admins to determine what the page will look like on a variety of device types. Specifically, four options are provided:

- Desktop

- Tablet – Portrait

- Tablet – Landscape

- Mobile

By using View Mode, the view can be adjusted to validate the responsiveness and positioning of components on the page. Figure 13-9 shows an example of the mobile view.

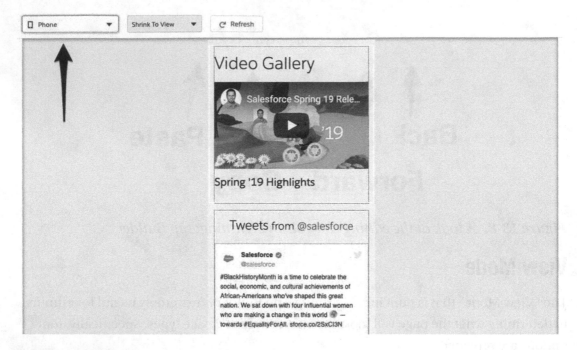

Figure 13-9. *Mobile view in Lightning App Builder*

View Options

While there is no "zoom" function currently available, Lightning App Builder does allow admins to toggle between the default "Shrink to View" and "100%" for view options. 100% will show the page as it will appear in actual size, although it's possible not all of the page will be visible. Figure 13-10 shows a view at 100%.

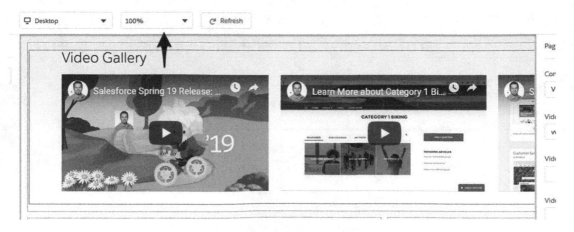

Figure 13-10. *Zoom to 100% option*

Actions and Controls

Certain basic actions are available in Lightning App Builder, including

- **Refresh**: Updates the content on the Lightning page

- **Save**: Saves the page

- **Activation**: Enables the page for actual usage

- **Back**: Exits the app

- **Help**: Provides help options, including

  - Take a tour

  - App Builder help

  - Keyboard help

  - Trailblazer Community

  - Reset Alert Preferences

The one action that requires additional information is Activation. Activation essentially applies, or publishes, the page vs. simply keeping it as a saved page that no one sees. For a page that is saved for the first time, "Save" will give the option to walk through the Activation process. Otherwise, you can manually click Activation to make it visible.

Activation includes three parts:

- Page Settings

  - App Name

  - Tab Visibility (All or System Administrator only)

  - Icon

- Lightning Experience

  - Add to Lightning Apps

- Mobile

  - Add to Mobile App

Figure 13-11 shows the Activation screen in Lightning App Builder.

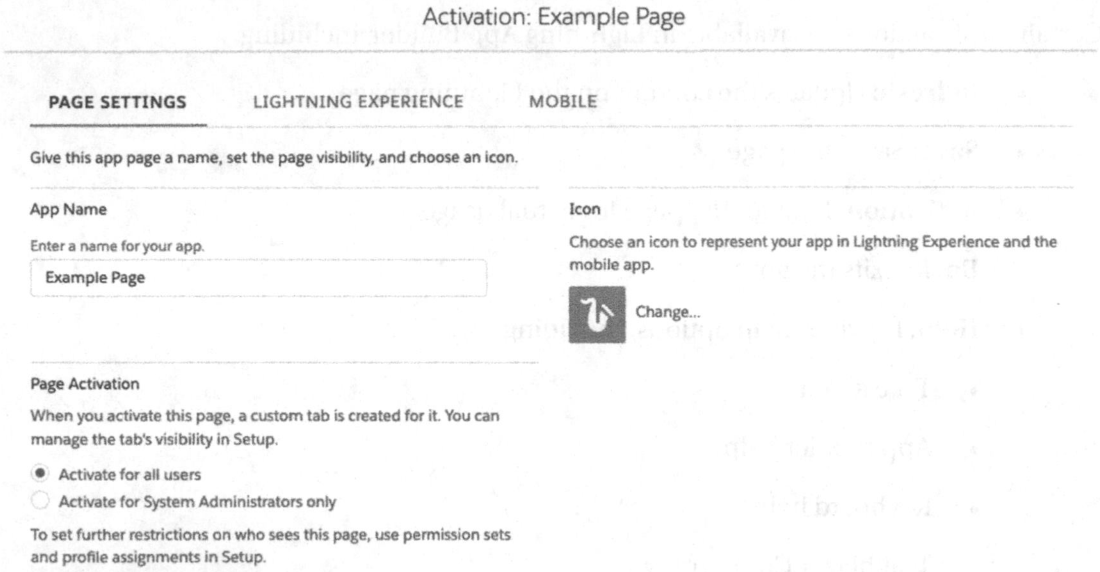

Figure 13-11. Activation screen

Page Sections

The main "canvas" in Lightning App Builder boasts the page sections into which components are to be positioned via drag 'n' drop. Figure 13-12 shows empty page sections before components are positioned.

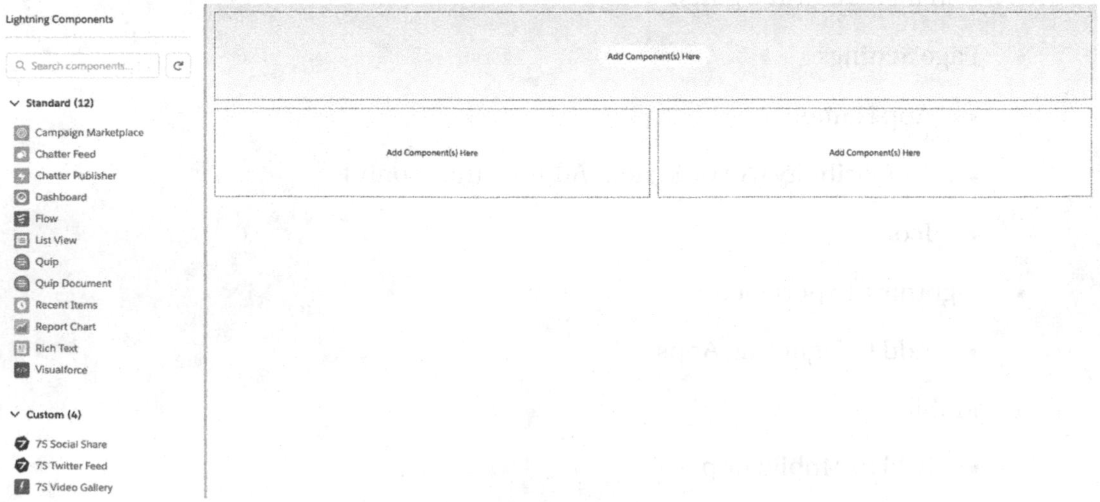

Figure 13-12. Empty page sections

Figure 13-13 shows page sections after components are positioned.

Figure 13-13. *Populated page sections*

With the page sections, there are three main functions. The first two are move and delete. Click and drag a component to another section or click the trash icon to remove the component completely. See Figure 13-14.

Figure 13-14. *Move or delete your component*

The final action is clicking a component, which brings up property editor. This leads us to our final section of Lightning App Builder.

Property Editor and Page Editor

The final section of Lightning App Builder is where the magic really happens. Let's take a look at the two types of editors that are available to admins in this area.

Page Editor

When a component is not selected (via clicking it), the page itself can be edited to the right of the page sections. See Figure 13-15.

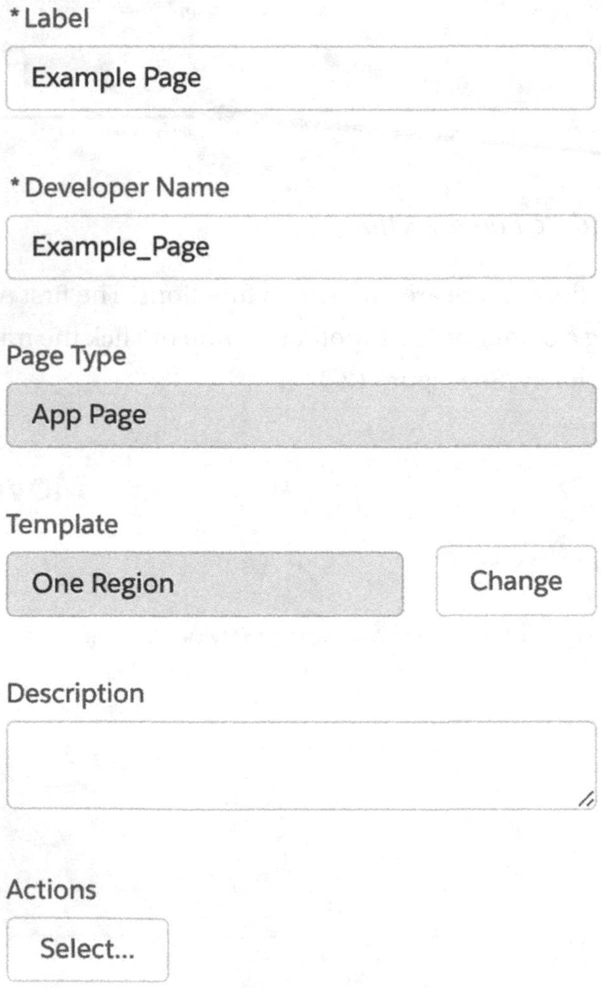

*Label

Example Page

*Developer Name

Example_Page

Page Type

App Page

Template

One Region   Change

Description

Actions

Select...

Figure 13-15. *Page editor in Lightning App Builder*

The following sections allow for page information and/or modification in page editor:

- Label: Visible name to users

- Developer Name: For reference in code

- Page Type (cannot be changed)

- Object (on Record Pages only; cannot be changed)

- Template

- Description

- Actions: An admin can add actions to the page (see Figure 13-16)

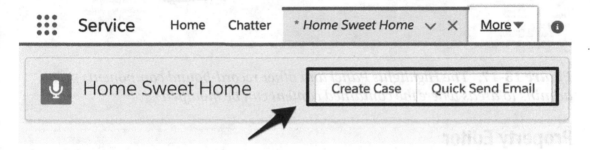

Figure 13-16. *Actions on a page of type "Home Page"*

Record pages boast a significant amount of additional functionality. When you click a component that is bound to a record (e.g., Highlights Panel, Record Detail, Related Lists, etc.), the right section points you to any areas that impact the *content* in the component. This is very different from regular Lightning component configuration. For example, this may facilitate the presence of an additional field via a specific layout (e.g., page, compact, etc.). This is a major time saver once you get familiar with how this works. See Figure 13-17.

Figure 13-17. *The Highlights Panel and other record-bound components point admins to areas where the contained content can be modified*

Property Editor

Once components are present on a Lightning page, clicking a component brings up the property editor for that particular component. This is where an admin can configure the settings for a particular component. You'll see a blue box around a selected component and the available settings will appear to the right of the page sections. See Figure 13-18 for an example of a component that has been selected.

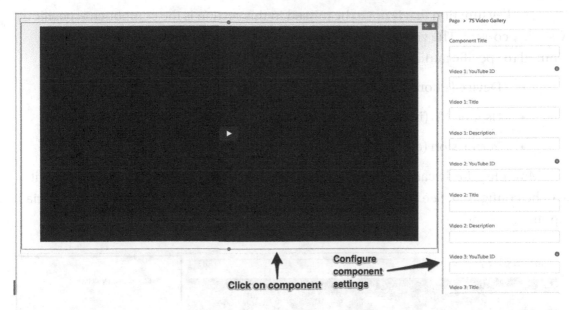

Figure 13-18. *Clicking a component brings up the component settings on the right*

Once a component is clicked, you can update settings on the right. Settings are determined at the component level, via customization. Figure 13-19 shows the same component, once configured.

Figure 13-19. *A display of how the settings directly impact the component from Figure 13-18*

419

One key function that is not to be missed in this section is the component-specific visibility control. The visibility of each component in Lightning App Builder can be limited to specific audiences or devices. The three types of criteria include

- Device (Phone, Tablet, Desktop)

- User Fields (includes parent objects)

- Permission (e.g., Moderate Chatter, Modify All Data, etc.)

Multiple criteria can be applied. Additionally, the logic is not strictly AND or OR; it can be configured. See Figure 13-20 for a look at a component that has visibility criteria applied.

Figure 13-20.   *Visibility controls can be applied to limit the audience of a component*

Thinking About Lightning Pages

Before diving in to build an app, let's take a step back. When thinking of the main elements involved in a Lightning app – namely, Lightning pages and Lightning components – we must first focus on the pages. A component's utility is minimal (nonexistent in a purely declarative framework) without a Lightning page to actually house the component. To break down the details of a Lightning page, we will start at the beginning with page creation.

Within Lightning App Builder, an admin can access the page manager, shown in Figure 13-21. In particular, note the "New Page" button at the bottom of the menu.

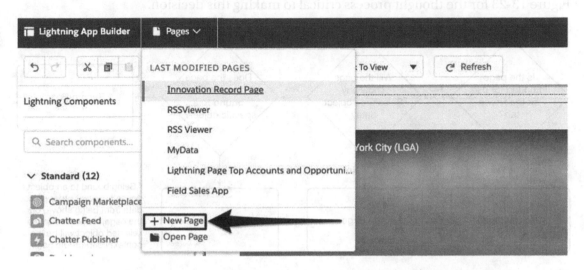

Figure 13-21. *Selecting "+ New Page" at the bottom starts the page creation process*

To create a new page, an administrator clicks the "+ New Page" button. The first step is a critical one: deciding whether the page will be an "App Page," a "Home Page," or a "Record Page." Figure 13-22 shows the choices available when creating a new page.

Figure 13-22. *The "Create a New Lightning Page" dialog provides three choices: App, Home, or Record Page*

One must ask him/herself whether the page will need to be bound to a specific object or not. If not, a standard page will suffice. If so, an object page will be needed. See Figure 13-23 for the thought process critical to making this decision.

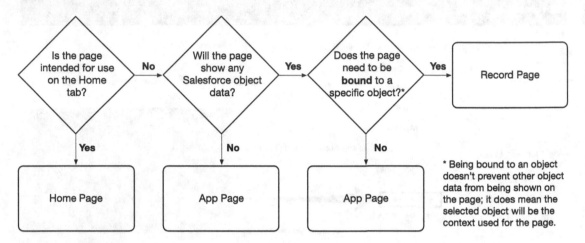

Figure 13-23. *Decision tree for creating a standard page or an object page*

After labeling the page, the next step is to select a page layout (actually called a "content layout"). The layouts that are available will include a number of out-of-the-box layouts but may also include some that are custom. See Figure 13-24.

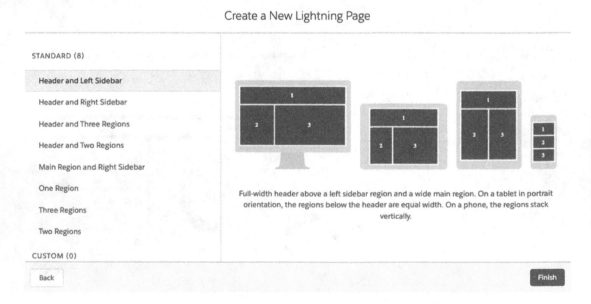

Figure 13-24. *Choosing a template for your new Lightning page*

An additional option is present if one has selected Home or Record Page. For these page types, an admin can choose whether to start from a preconfigured page ("clone a default page") or build from scratch (see Figure 13-25).

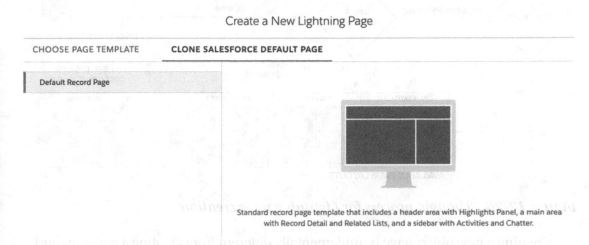

Create a New Lightning Page

CHOOSE PAGE TEMPLATE   **CLONE SALESFORCE DEFAULT PAGE**

Default Record Page

Standard record page template that includes a header area with Highlights Panel, a main area with Record Detail and Related Lists, and a sidebar with Activities and Chatter.

Figure 13-25. *Clone a default page to expedite the page creation process*

It is critical to understand what it means to clone a page from a Salesforce default page instead of creating a new, blank page. With a new, blank page, an administrator can select the page layout, but no content will exist on the page. When a default page is cloned, however, any components that are present on the selected page will be on the page at inception. Not only will the components be present, they will be positioned and configured exactly as they are on the selected page. Think of this as a page-level template. In Figure 13-26, I've tried to visualize the process of page creation process and the various selection points and activities.

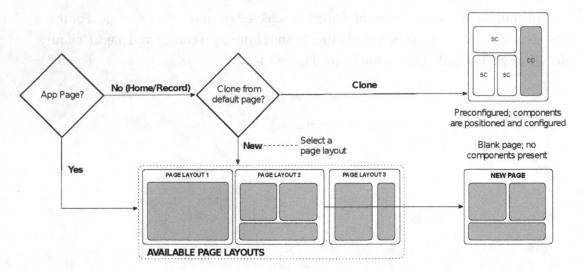

Figure 13-26. *Thought process for Lightning page creation*

Creating a new object page is fundamentally different from creating a new standard page, as it is bound to records of that object type. Unlike in Community Builder, Lightning App Builder only creates a record detail page. In Communities, the record list page and record related list page are also created. As an example, I'll create an object detail page for the product object (Figure 13-27).

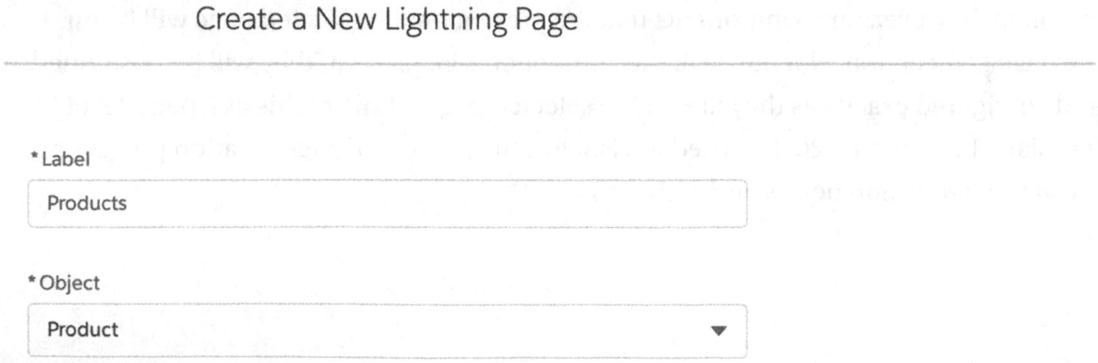

Create a New Lightning Page

---

* Label

Products

* Object

Product   ▼

Figure 13-27. *Creating new object pages for the Product object*

Figure 13-28 shows what the newly created product record page looks like in Lightning App Builder without any additional configuration.

Figure 13-28. *New, unmodified Product List page following creation*

Thinking About Lightning Components

I find it helpful to use metaphors in the context of Lightning apps (hence my previous example of referencing Legos). I'd like to use a slightly different one here. This time, let's use a neighborhood as the example for a Lightning app that involves multiple pages. Lightning pages serve as the "slabs" and Lightning components equate to elements of the homes themselves that sit on the slabs. While both slabs *and* the houses are absolutely essential, owners of houses really don't care about the slabs too much; the slabs exist to support and provide a layout for the house, but they don't provide much functional value to the owners.

It's the same with Lightning components and pages; most users don't think too much about the page itself, but instead, they care about the content (components) on the page. See Figure 13-29 for a visualization of this concept.

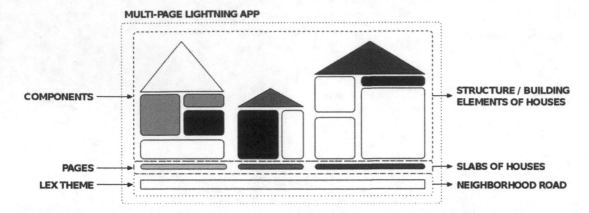

Figure 13-29. *Conceptualizing aspects of a Lightning app as neighborhood housing elements*

When we talk about Lightning apps, the components are at the core of the functional experience. Earlier in this chapter, I covered the components section of Lightning App Builder and discussed the presentation of the components (with components being grouped by whether they are standard or custom). Here, I will go a little deeper to help administrators go from concept to application in their journey to create the perfect app, specifically at the point of determining what to do with the plethora of Lightning components that are available.

Understanding Components Within Lightning Apps

Assuming a Lightning component is built properly for its intended purpose, I would make the statement that the value of a component within a Lightning app is predicated on three factors:

- Placement (Lightning pages on which the component is placed)

- Positioning (page section(s) in which the component is dropped)

- Configuration (configured settings of the component)

If any of these factors are not appropriately considered, the value of the component will decrease for users of the app. I'll briefly walk through each to ensure the concept is clear.

Component Placement

Before one can start configuring a component for its particular use, the decision as to which page(s) it should be associated with must be made. The absence of a high-value component on a particular page can be extremely impactful; similarly, the extraneous presence of a component on a page can be distracting and create a convoluted experience for a user. While many components can be placed anywhere within an app, it is critical to understand context and the fact that some components have a limited number of potential page homes. See Figure 13-30 for some examples of where and how components might apply to pages.

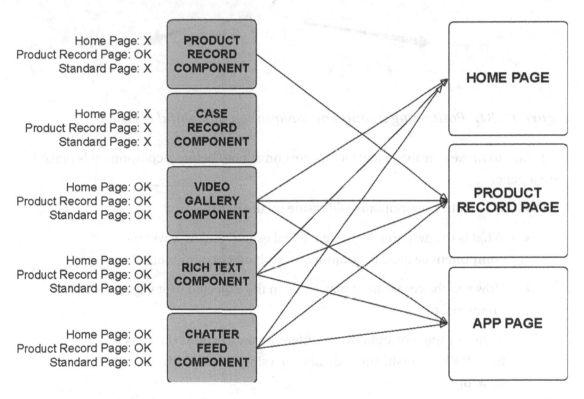

Figure 13-30. *Components have context and will not necessarily function on all Lightning pages*

Component Positioning

I discussed page sections in Chapter 5 and will let readers revisit that section for corresponding details. Here, I want to help answer the question: where on a page should a component be placed? There is typically no shortage of options; see Figure 13-31 for an example of what an admin might be faced with when choosing a component's positioning within a Lightning page.

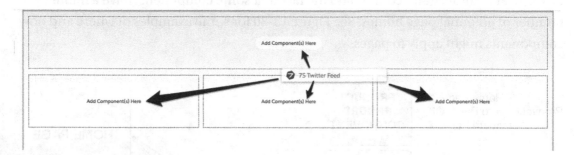

Figure 13-31. *Positioning a component requires a thoughtful decision*

I want to make sure that a few factors are considered before a component is placed onto a page:

- What other components will reside on the page?

- What is the available "experience real estate" and how will the component be used in conjunction with other components?

- How will the component play a role in the expected user experience on the page?

- Is the component suitable for different page sections (i.e., has it been built to satisfactorily display in a single, full-width column on a desktop)?

It is quite easy to fall into the trap of going drag 'n' drop crazy and letting user experience and context slip to the back of one's mind during an app build; administrators must fight against that potential slip and ensure that components are placed purposefully and intentionally within a specific page. If one asks these questions, successful positioning of the components will be much more likely.

Component Configuration

Even with the perfect placement and positioning of a Lightning component in your app, the component could render zero value if configured improperly. While this may seem obvious, an administrator needs to know his or her Lightning components very well. By that, I mean that it's important to learn most, if not all, of the available configurations for a particular component. First of all, knowing the configurations means knowing the underlying functionality and not missing out on some potential value for your app. Second, it's all about the context. Many components are contextual, providing different functions or capabilities depending on where they are placed.

Recap

In this chapter, I reviewed each aspect of the Lightning App Builder user interface, including the Lightning component sidebar, the top menu bar, the page sections, and the page/property editor on the right. Additionally, I transitioned from the Lightning App Builder tool in the previous chapter to the Lightning pages and Lightning Components that it supports. I provided an overview of how page creation and management works, along with the various options. I then dove into an example that featured a number of popular components, along with specific page placement and configuration, to provide a functional custom page within an app.

CHAPTER 14

Multifaceted Solutions Across the Platform with Lightning Bolt Solutions

While it's easy for us to focus on a particular tool as we establish a solid foundation to build Salesforce solutions without using code, it is critical to always remember that we are working with an immense and robust *platform*. Based on my years of experience with Salesforce, it is my fairly strong opinion that the most powerful and innovative solutions leverage multiple tools on the platform...not just one. Fortunately for us, Salesforce is proactively working to equip and enable us to produce multifaceted solutions. Lightning Bolt Solutions, introduced in 2018, are an example of this, supporting the delivery of solutions that include one or more of the following (see Figure 14-1):

- Lightning Bolt
- Custom App
- Flow Category

| Custom App | Flow Category | Community Template |

Figure 14-1. *The three parts of a Lightning Bolt Solution*

© Philip Weinmeister 2019
P. Weinmeister, *Practical Salesforce Development Without Code*,
https://doi.org/10.1007/978-1-4842-4871-3_14

Let's cut right to it. If you are not clear on what a "Lightning Bolt" is, you are not alone. For various reasons, a Salesforce Lightning Bolt has been a point of confusion for many. Don't worry, we'll work through that. By the end of this chapter, you should be able to explain not only what a Lightning Bolt is, but also what a Lightning Bolt Solution is.

Lightning Bolt Solutions: The Concept

The idea behind Lighting Bolt Solutions is that powerful, industry-specific solutions built on Salesforce typically leverage a broad slice of the platform. Years ago, implementation conversations usually focused solely on Service Cloud, Sales Cloud, Marketing Cloud, Community Cloud, or another specific Salesforce product. That's no longer the case. Today, solutions span these products as clients look to take advantage of as many use cases as possible on the platform. To help facilitate a clean, marketing-friendly delivery of these cross-cloud solutions, Salesforce created the Lightning Bolt Solution framework.

To be completely transparent, Lightning Bolt Solution technology does not really bring new functionality or capabilities to the platform. Wait, what? That's right; this isn't another "builder" tool. It is a delivery mechanism to better present multifaceted solutions.

A final note is regarding the what, why, and who regarding Lightning Bolt Solutions. At the most basic level, partners (Sis or ISVs) would build solutions using this technology and ship them to customers, who would deploy, configure, and use them. So, depending on your specific role and type of organization, you might look at this chapter differently. See Figure 14-2.

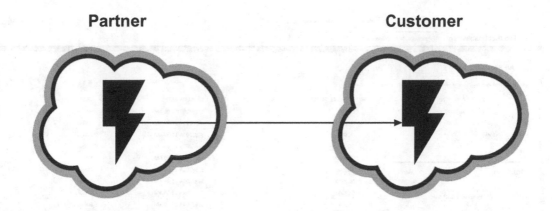

Partner   **Customer**

Organization Type: Partner   Organization Type: Customer
Roles: Consultant, Product Engineer   Role: Admin, BA, Developer
Actions: Build, Ship   Actions: Deploy, Configure, Use

Figure 14-2. *The organizations, roles, and actions associated with Lightning Bolt Solutions*

Lightning Bolt Solutions: The Parts

Before we discuss how to assemble a Lightning Bolt Solution, let's first break down its three parts.

Part I: Custom App

At their core, custom apps surface the appropriate data and apps to address one or more related use cases. These can be "traditional" apps in classic (i.e., a set of tabs), service or sales consoles, or robust Lightning apps that can leverage a suite of lightning components. Figure 14-3 shows an example app (a custom Lightning app). In a Lightning Bolt Solution, you will typically have one app, although you may have multiple if you are addressing multiple personas/audiences and they map to different use cases.

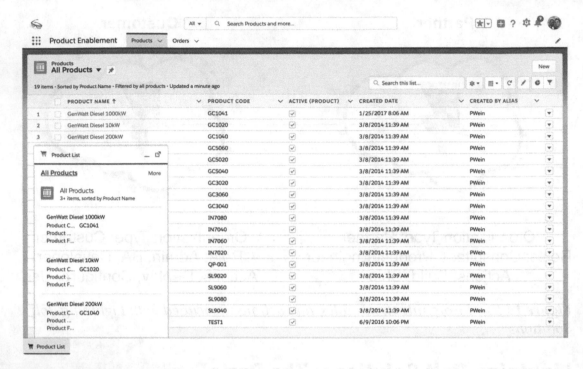

Figure 14-3. A custom "Product Enablement" app

Part II: Flow Category

We've talked about Flows, but haven't mentioned Flow Categories before. That's because their primary value, at least for now, is in Lightning Bolt Solutions. A Flow Category allows for the grouping of Flows that address one or more specific use cases. Assembling a Flow Category is pretty straightforward:

- Search for and click "Flow Category" in setup using Quick Find.

- Click "New Flow Category" (Figure 14-4).

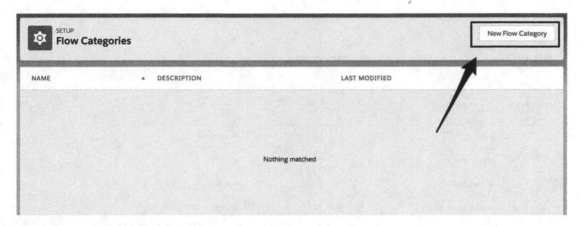

Figure 14-4. *Click "New Flow Category"*

- Click "+" next to each Flow to add (Figure 14-5).

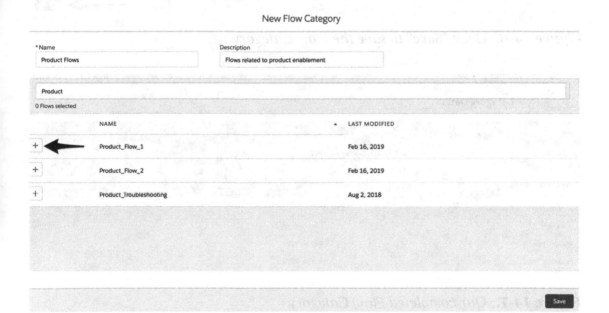

Figure 14-5. *Click "+" to add a Flow to the Flow Category*

- Click "Save" (Figure 14-6).
- View your completed flow (Figure 14-7).

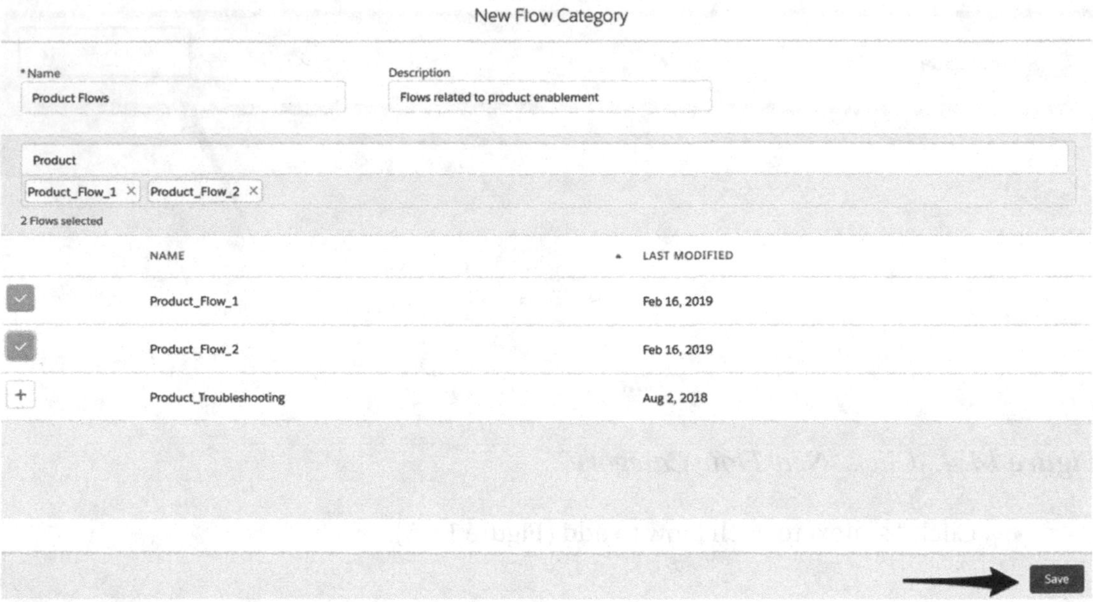

Figure 14-6. *Click "Save" to save the Flow Category*

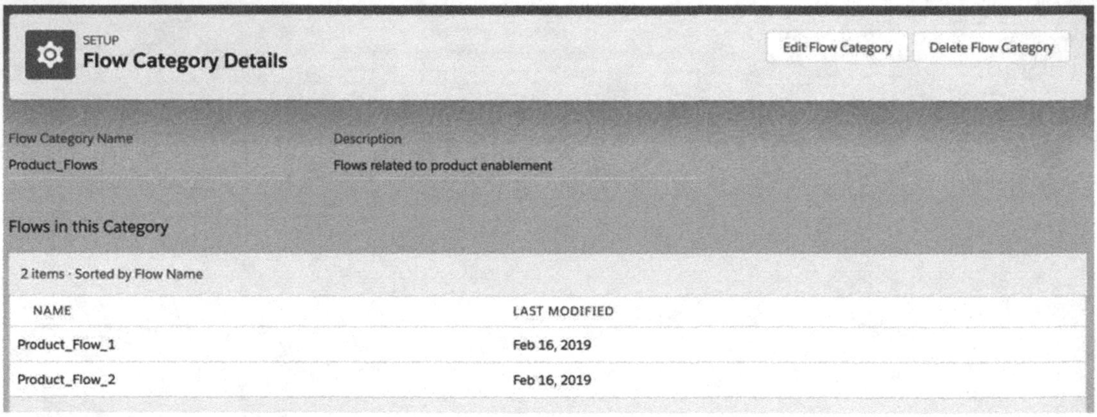

Figure 14-7. *Our completed Flow Category*

Part III: Lightning Bolt

The Lightning Bolt is the key to and central piece within a Lightning Bolt Solution. A Lightning Bolt solution provides the community template for partners, customers, and employees. This element facilitates robust external capabilities to complement the Flows and custom apps that extend to other user audiences. I won't go into a lot of detail on this topic in this book, but check out my book *Practical Guide to Salesforce Communities* to dive deeper. Figure 14-8 shows what a Lightning Bolt looks like on the Community creation page.

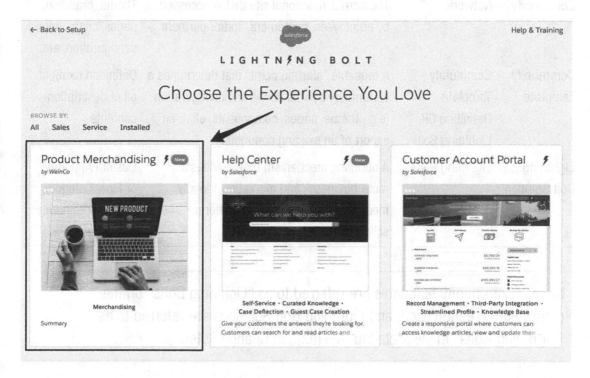

Figure 14-8. *A custom Lightning Bolt*

Let's establish something in this section: "Lightning Bolt Solution" is not a synonym for "Lightning Bolt." A Lightning Bolt is the term for a template that can be used to create Lightning Community. The process looks like this:

- A Lightning Bolt (community template) is created, either by Salesforce or by a Salesforce partner.

- The process to create a community is initiated and a Lightning Bolt is selected as part of that process.

- As a result of the Lightning Bolt "outline," certain pages, components, and configuration are applied to the new community.

I've created Table 14-1 to clarify some of the confusion around similar terms.

Table 14-1. *Breakdown of Lightning Bolt and Community Terminology*

Term	Also Known As	Description	Includes
Community	Network	The actual, functional site that is accessed by employees, customers, and/or partners	Theme, branding, pages, components, configuration, etc.
Community Template	Community Template Definition OR Lightning Bolt*	A reusable "starting point" that determines a community's initial scope and configuration (e.g., theme, pages, components, etc.); an export of an existing community	Definition (.xml) of all of description contents
Lightning Bolt Solution	Lightning Bolt*	A bundling mechanism that provides a more business- and marketing-friendly mechanism for distributing platform solutions	Custom App and/ or Flow Category and/or Community Template

Note   Community templates are referred to as "Lightning Bolts" on the community creation page, and Lightning Bolt Solutions are referred to as "Lightning Bolts" in the Metadata API (e.g., in Change Sets).

Lightning Bolt Solutions: The Creation Process

Let's walk through the process to create a product merchandising Lightning Bolt Solution. Our first step is navigating to the Lightning Bolt Solutions page, found via Quick Find in Setup (Figure 14-9). Then, click "Create the first one."

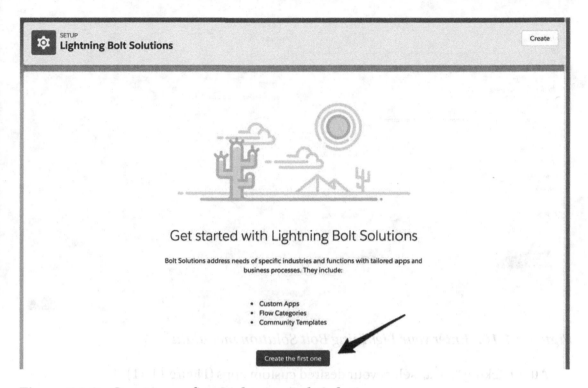

Figure 14-9. *Create your first Lightning Bolt Solution*

Next, enter Lightning Bolt Solution metadata, including name, description, and more (Figure 14-10).

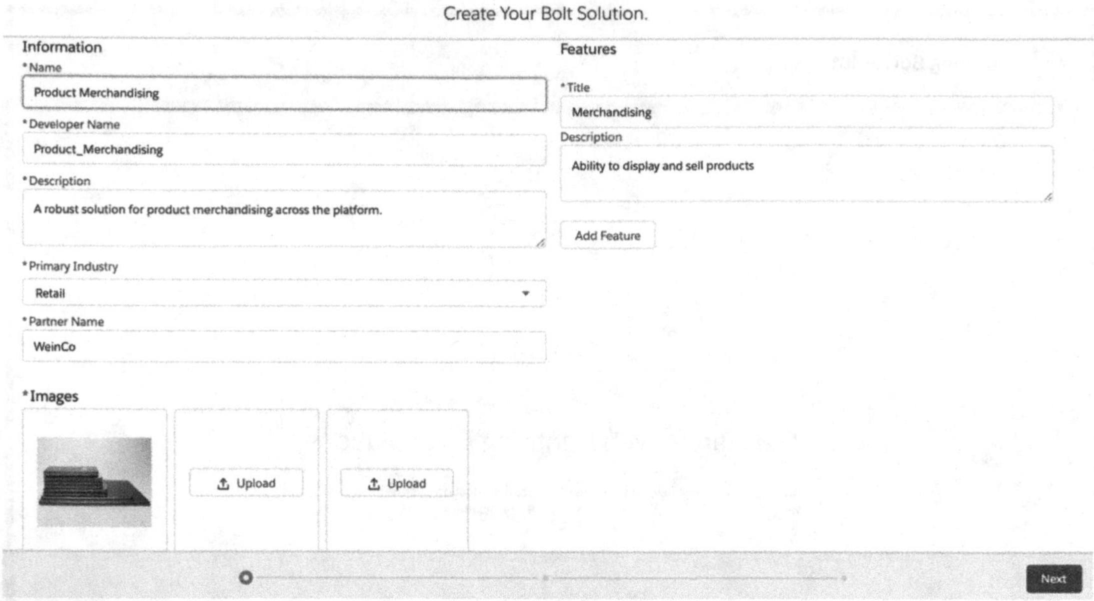

Create Your Bolt Solution.

Information

*Name

Product Merchandising

*Developer Name

Product_Merchandising

*Description

A robust solution for product merchandising across the platform.

*Primary Industry

Retail

*Partner Name

WeinCo

*Images

⬆ Upload   ⬆ Upload

Features

*Title

Merchandising

Description

Ability to display and sell products

Add Feature

Next

Figure 14-10. *Enter your Lightning Bolt Solution metadata*

After clicking "Next," select your desired custom apps (Figure 14-11).

CUSTOM APPS   FLOW CATEGORIES   COMMUNITY TEMPLATES

Search for Custom Apps...

Product_Enablement ✕

1 App Selected

	NAME	▲ LAST MODIFIED
+	Force_com	Mar 8, 2014
+	Module_Tracker	Jan 23, 2019
✓	Product_Enablement	Feb 16, 2019
+	Test	Sep 1, 2014

Back   Next

Figure 14-11. *Add one or more custom apps*

Click "Flow Categories" and select your desired flow categories (Figure 14-12).

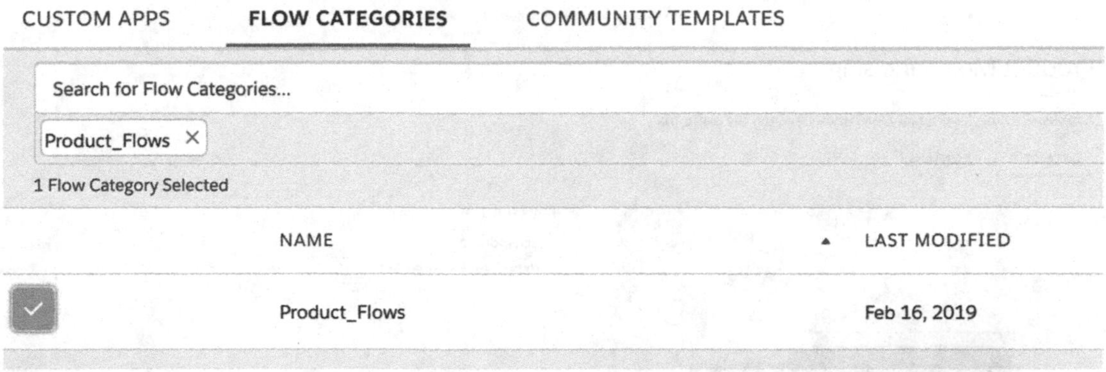

CUSTOM APPS	**FLOW CATEGORIES**	COMMUNITY TEMPLATES

Search for Flow Categories...

Product_Flows ✕

1 Flow Category Selected

	NAME	▲ LAST MODIFIED
✓	Product_Flows	Feb 16, 2019

Figure 14-12. *Add one or more flow categories*

Click "Community Templates" and select your desired community templates (Figure 14-13).

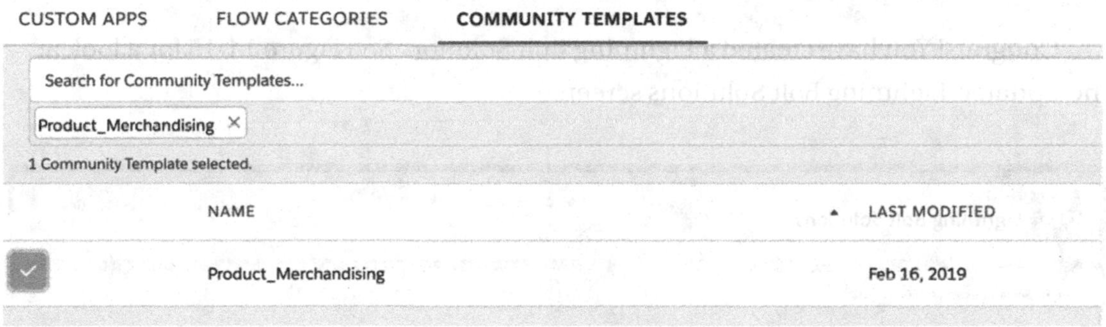

CUSTOM APPS	FLOW CATEGORIES	**COMMUNITY TEMPLATES**

Search for Community Templates...

Product_Merchandising ✕

1 Community Template selected.

	NAME	▲ LAST MODIFIED
✓	Product_Merchandising	Feb 16, 2019

Figure 14-13. *Add one or more community templates*

Review the details of your new Lightning Bolt Solution and click "Finish" (Figure 14-14).

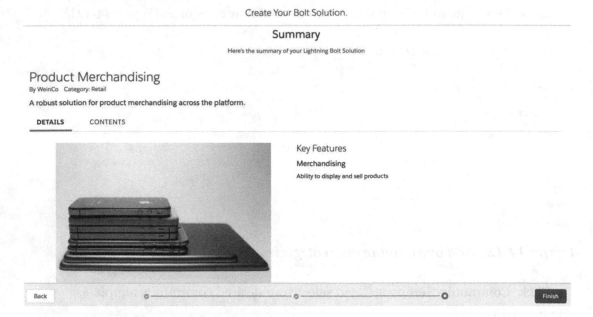

Figure 14-14. *Review and finish the process*

Congrats! You have created a Lightning Bolt Solution. See Figure 14-15 for a look at the updated Lightning Bolt Solutions screen.

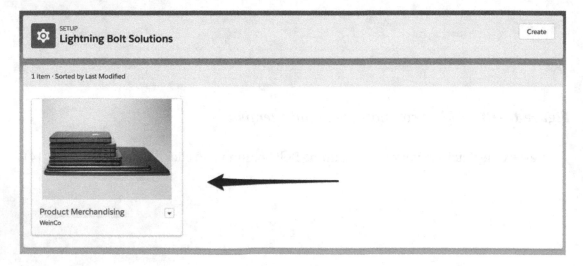

Figure 14-15. *Main Lightning Bolt Solutions screen, postcreation*

Finally, you can (optionally) add your new solution to a package. As previously mentioned in the chapter, you'll look for "Lightning Bolt" in the list of item types to add to your package. See Figure 14-16.

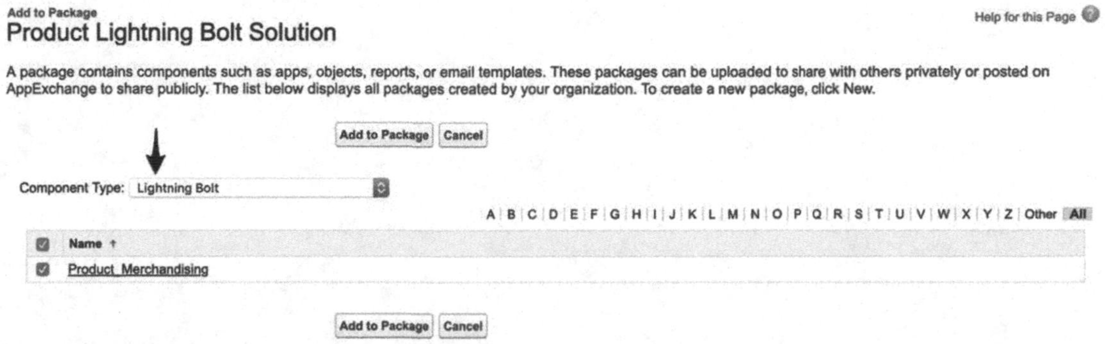

Figure 14-16. *Adding a Lightning Bolt Solution to a package*

Recap

In this chapter, we took a look at Lightning Bolt Solutions, a cross-platform framework for delivering multifaceted Salesforce solutions. First, we considered the concept and intent of the framework. From there, we looked at the three parts: custom apps, flow categories, and community templates. Finally, we constructed a Lightning Bolt Solution and prepared it for packaging.

CHAPTER 15

Solutioning with Security: Permissions and Sharing Considerations

Although one chapter is not nearly enough to cover all of its facets, I would be remiss to completely omit security considerations in this book. The world of Salesforce security is vast and involves a number of features and intricacies. However, I believe that I can break down the key security elements, as they relate to Salesforce development without code, in a meaningful, understandable way to help you as you build declarative solutions on the platform.

It's hard, if not impossible, to find two organizations with identical security models. Each organization has its own needs, considerations, and concerns, resulting in a unique sharing configuration. It hardly needs to be mentioned that security should be a cornerstone of any implementation. Even without specific security requirements from your client or organization, you will need to ensure that your solution has not put the company at an inappropriate, avoidable level of risk. I am purposefully using the word "inappropriate," as all solutions inevitably carry some security risks (even if the risk is that the system is too restrictive).

In this chapter, I'll walk you through specific security elements that should be assessed and updated, as needed, when developing declarative solutions within Salesforce and explain how they can be addressed together to build an effective, reliable

© Philip Weinmeister 2019
P. Weinmeister, *Practical Salesforce Development Without Code*,
https://doi.org/10.1007/978-1-4842-4871-3_15

security model. In particular, I will focus on those security elements that directly impact your users' ability to access data within an org. This chapter will cover the following topics:

- Object and field permissions

- Profiles

- Permission sets

- Organization-wide sharing defaults

- Sharing rules

This chapter's primary focus will be on how your users will interact with objects, fields, and records within Salesforce. I will not be covering any security topics related to login restrictions, such as IP ranges or login time. Additionally, since this book focuses on configuration-based solutions, I will not be addressing any items specifically related to code (e.g., access to Apex classes or Visualforce pages, Apex sharing rules). Of course, these aspects need to be examined and considered as well.

Establishing a Sensible Strategy

There is no one-size-fits-all solution that can be assumed to work perfectly across all organizations, even pertaining to those with similar security requirements. To that end, I will not provide a specific approach that you must always follow. However, there are some key considerations that you should review to ensure that you create a successful security component as part of your implemented solutions. The following are some questions that should be asked:

- *Q: What permissions will be needed to perform critical or required operational activities?*

    - *A*: Each user will need at least the permissions necessary to carry out her responsibilities within Salesforce. This may seem obvious, but it is overlooked quite often. This mistake will result in either inability to carry out critical tasks or frequent manual activities to provide the necessary access.

- *Q: Do requirements exist that call for the explicit prevention/restriction of access for specific individuals or groups of individuals?*

  - *A:* If so, you must be careful not to establish an oversimplified security model that grants too much access to certain individuals. In this scenario, you should only provide higher levels of access to those required to have it.

- *Q: Does an open-sharing model present notable risk?*

  - *A:* Just because a requirement to provide specific field or object permissions does not exist, it does not mean that restricting access to the field or objects for the related user(s) is your only option. You may decide that you are willing to allow individuals to have more access than is required per documented business needs. This comes down to an analysis of the potential value in providing the additional access vs. the associated risk in doing so.

- *Q: If you are rebuilding a solution from another system in Salesforce: were there any security configurations lacking in your previous app that you would have wanted? What about configurations that were present but did not prove helpful or effective?*

  - *A:* You may be able to glean significant value from looking at your own past experience to determine specific configurations that should or should not be included in your current solution.

No matter the size or complexity of the solution you are building, you will need to ask these questions and others to have a strong grasp of your organization or client's security requirements. Tread carefully and pay attention to detail. Repeated audits and deep testing of your security configurations are a wise investment.

Understanding the Salesforce Security Model

Before I dive into each element that impacts your users' ability to see and/or interact with data within your Salesforce org, I want to provide some context around how the security model works overall. There are two high-level groupings that are critical to understand:

- **Permissions**: Object and field access/permissions

- **Sharing**: Record access/visibility via sharing

Object and Field Permissions

A user's permission to modify a specific object or field can be broken down to four parts encompassed by CRUD ("Create," "Read," "Update," "Delete"). For standard and custom objects in Salesforce, *edit* is the term used in place of *update*. That explains why I previously referred to these permissions as "CRED." Logical rules exist in the program to ensure a sensible configuration of the CRED settings. For example, "Create," "Edit," and "Delete" cannot be granted if "Read" has not been granted, since "Read" is required for any of the dependent actions. Additionally, "Edit" is required in order for the "Delete" permission to be provisioned. Figure 15-1 shows full access being granted for the Account object.

	Read	Create	Edit	Delete
Accounts	✓	✓	✓	✓

Figure 15-1. *Full CRED permissions to Account records enabled for a specific profile in Salesforce*

Additionally, special permissions called "View All" and "Edit All" can be granted to ensure the highest-possible levels of "Read" and "Edit" access, respectively. If these permissions are enabled for a particular user, that user can view or edit all records for that object regardless of the organization-wide default sharing setting or any other sharing rules. To be clear, "View All" and "Edit All" are associated with record sharing for a specific object, not with object permissions.

Overlaying object permissions are field permissions, known as "Field-Level Security" within Salesforce. Two settings are presented at the field level. With the "enhanced" profile user interface, "read access" and "edit access" are available; with the "standard" interface, "Visible" and "Read-Only" are the options. To toggle your setting, search for "User Management Settings" in Quick Find and then look for "Enhanced Profile User Interface." Table 15-1 shows the equivalent object-level permissions for "Field-Level Security" settings.

Table 15-1. *"Field-Level Security" Permissions Translated to the Equivalent Permissions at the Object Level*

Enhanced Profile User Interface	Standard Profile User Interface	
	Visible	Read-Only
No Access		
"Read Access"	✓	✓
"Read Access," "Edit Access"	✓	

Figures 15-2 and 15-3 show possible configurations for the Created By field, as presented via the two profile user interfaces that are available within Salesforce.

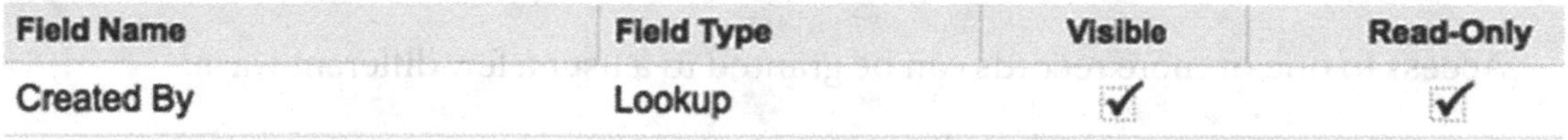

Field Name	Field Type	Visible	Read-Only
Created By	Lookup	✓	✓

Figure 15-2. *In this configuration, the profile has read-only permission for accessing the Created By field. This image shows the original view, in which the "Enhanced Profile User Interface" is disabled.*[1]

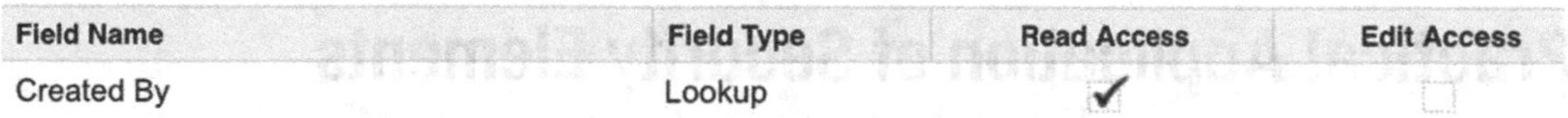

Field Name	Field Type	Read Access	Edit Access
Created By	Lookup	✓	☐

Figure 15-3. *This image shows how these permissions are displayed when "Enhanced Profile User Interface" is enabled. The profile has read permission for accessing the Created By field.*

Record Access via Sharing

Object permissions are not the only determinant of whether you can view or edit a record. If your org does not have an open-sharing model, the object permissions alone will not necessarily allow you to view or modify any records. In that case, you must also be granted the ability to view or manipulate the desired record via sharing. For example, although you may have the ability to read/view Account records, you will not be able

---

[1]All Salesforce screenshots in this chapter © copyright Salesforce, Inc. Used with permission.

to view those that have not been shared with you through your org settings. Table 15-2 breaks down how the CRED permissions work for record access in terms of allowing a user to view a specific record.

Table 15-2. *Combinations of Object Permissions and Sharing Access and How They Impact the Ability to View Records*

Account Read Permission	Access to Account Record "A"	Able to View Account Record "A"?
No	No	No
No	Yes	No
Yes	No	No
Yes	Yes	Yes

Access to one or more records can be granted to a user a few different ways:

- Organization-wide defaults
- Sharing rules
- "View All"/"Edit All" permissions

Practical Application of Security Elements

So far in this chapter, we've been looking at a high-level conceptual security framework for field-level and object-level security. Now it's time to dive into these areas in more detail and see how to apply these elements within your own org.

Field-Level Security

When you create a new field in Salesforce, you have an opportunity to properly configure the related security settings. Although it might be tempting to rush through the "Field-Level Security for Profile" screen to set up your new field, I highly recommend that you take the time to closely review the access that is granted to each profile and adjust the settings as needed. You might not need to create any new user profiles in conjunction with an implementation of functionality; however, you will need to at least ensure that related permissions have been properly set for your existing profiles. Figure 15-4 shows the screen you are presented with when creating a new custom field.

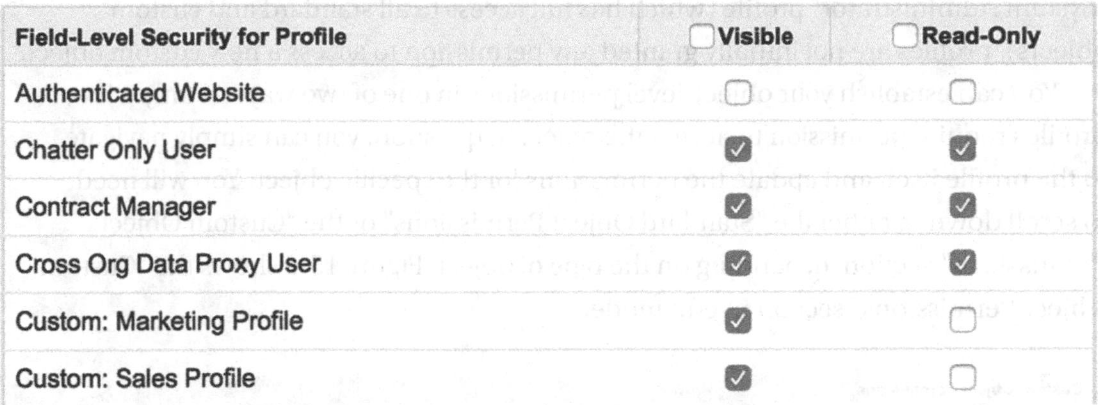

Field-Level Security for Profile	☐ Visible	☐ Read-Only
Authenticated Website	☐	☐
Chatter Only User	☑	☑
Contract Manager	☑	☑
Cross Org Data Proxy User	☑	☑
Custom: Marketing Profile	☑	☐
Custom: Sales Profile	☑	☐

Figure 15-4. *When you create a new field, you will need to review the security settings associated with existing profiles on the "Field-Level Security for Profile" screen*

Once you have configured the initial settings, you can update them by following these navigation paths:

- **Lightning Experience**: Navigate to "Object Manager" using Quick Find in Setup, select the object, then "Fields & Relationships."

- **Classic**:

  - *Standard objects*: Setup ➤ Customize ➤ [object name] ➤ Fields ➤ Field Label

  - *Custom objects*: Setup ➤ Create ➤ [object name] ➤ Field Label

Alternatively, you can also find specific fields via setup search (by using the search bar at the top of the page in Lightning or by clicking the "Enter" button after entering text into the Setup search field in classic). Once you are on the custom field detail page, click the "Set Field-Level Security" button. The screen format is identical to the screen shown in Figure 15-4.

Object-Level Security

Salesforce handles object-level security settings differently from how it handles field-level security. As you saw in Figure 15-4, you are prompted to set the permission level for each profile during field creation. However, no such screen exists to set profile permissions for the creation of custom objects. With the exception of the standard

"System Administrator" profile (which has full access to all standard and custom objects), profiles are not initially granted any permission to access a new custom object.

You can establish your object-level permissions in one of two ways: If only a few profiles require permission to access the object in question, you can simply navigate to the profile itself and update the permissions for the specific object. You will need to scroll down to either the "Standard Object Permissions" or the "Custom Object Permissions" section, depending on the type of object. Figure 15-5 shows the "Custom Object Permissions" section in edit mode.

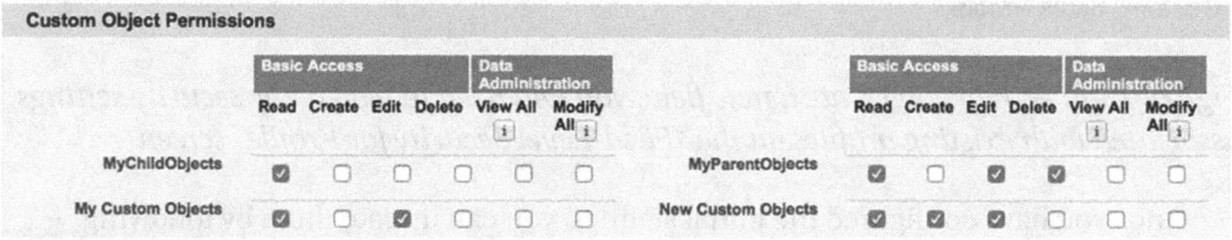

Custom Object Permissions

	Basic Access				Data Administration			Basic Access				Data Administration	
	Read	Create	Edit	Delete	View All	Modify All		Read	Create	Edit	Delete	View All	Modify All
MyChildObjects	☑	☐	☐	☐	☐	☐	MyParentObjects	☑	☐	☑	☑	☐	☐
My Custom Objects	☑	☐	☑	☐	☐	☐	New Custom Objects	☑	☑	☑	☐	☐	☐

Figure 15-5. *The "Custom Object Permissions" section of the "Profile Edit" screen, which allows you to modify object permission for a particular profile*

A valuable option for quickly applying object permissions across multiple profiles is enabling the "Enhanced Profile List View" permission and managing your profiles from the profile list view screen. To enable the appropriate view, search for "User Interface" using Quick Find and select "Enable Enhanced Profile List Views." This interface will allow you to update profiles with object permissions en masse. Once that is enabled, navigate to "Profiles" using Quick Find. There, you can create a list view that displays Profile Name and the related permissions. Figure 15-6 shows the desired settings that should be selected to apply permissions for an object called "New Custom Object."

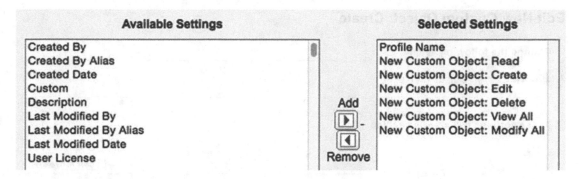

Figure 15-6. *When creating a list view for the enhanced profile list view screen,
you can select all permissions related to your new object(s) in order to quickly
apply a mass edit*

Once you've created your list view, select the profiles you want to update by checking
them and then double-click the permission to be added or removed. See Figure 15-7 for
a view of the screen just before double-clicking the permission.

☑	Action	Profile Name ↑	New Custom Object: Create
☑	Del | Clone	Custom: Marketing Profile	☐
☑	Del | Clone	Custom: Sales Profile	
☑	Del | Clone	Custom: Support Profile	
☑	Clone	Customer Community Login User	
☑	Clone	Customer Community User	

Figure 15-7. *To add or remove a permission to multiple profiles at once, select the
applicable profiles and double-click the applicable permission setting*

After double-clicking on the permission, the window shown in Figure 15-8 will
appear, allowing you to add or remove individual settings and apply the change to all of
the selected profiles.

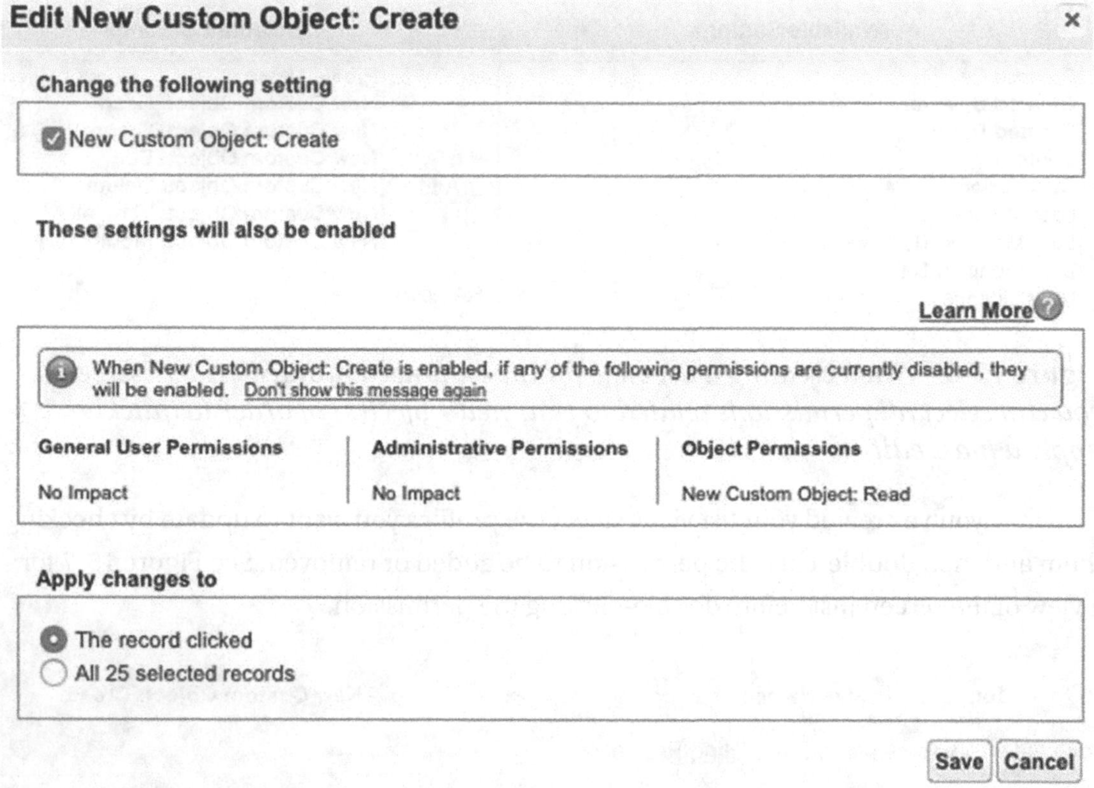

Edit New Custom Object: Create   ✕

Change the following setting

☑ New Custom Object: Create

These settings will also be enabled

Learn More ❓

ℹ When New Custom Object: Create is enabled, if any of the following permissions are currently disabled, they will be enabled. Don't show this message again

General User Permissions	Administrative Permissions	Object Permissions
No Impact	No Impact	New Custom Object: Read

Apply changes to

⦿ The record clicked
◯ All 25 selected records

Save   Cancel

Figure 15-8. *After selecting multiple rows (profiles) from an enhanced profile list view, double-clicking a field to edit it will bring up the "Edit New Custom Object" window. Here, you can apply the change to the record that was clicked or to all selected records*

Using Permission Sets and Validation Rules

As you've seen thus far, managing your field-level and object-level security requirements centers around the configuration of your user profiles. A few other features can be utilized to extend your security configuration further to meet certain requirements. While it is commonly the case that all users in an existing profile would need the same permissions to access a new field or object, there can be variance within that group of users. That variance might lead you to consider using permission sets or validation rules in your security model.

Take a user profile called "Tier 1 Support," with 50 users, as an example. Assume that 10 of those 50 support individuals need the ability to edit records for a new custom object called Asset Warranty; these users need to be able to update a few fields on that record based on customer input. The remaining 40 users within that profile, however, need only to view Product Warranty records. You have three primary options for providing the first group (the 10 users) with the required "Product Warranty Edit" permission. Figure 15-9 presents a visual representation of these options.

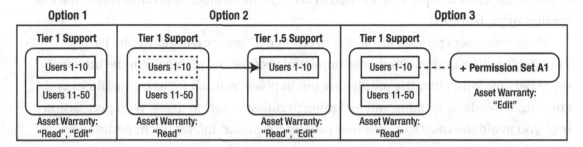

Figure 15-9. *Three possible options for providing additional permissions to a subset of Users in one profile*

So, which option is the best? As always, it depends on your situation.

- **Option 1**: In this scenario, you grant all of the Users within the group profile the "Account Read" and "Account Edit" permissions. This is the simplest approach and it may be a completely legitimate solution for your organization. However, you are potentially introducing risk by providing 40 individuals the extraneous ability to edit Asset Warranty records.

- **Option 2**: Here, you separate out the ten higher-access Users and provide only them with "Read" and "Edit" permissions to access the Asset Warranty object. This will definitely meet your needs, although you now have an extra profile to manage. If you frequently were to go down this route for similar situations, you would potentially find yourself with an inordinate number of profiles. Most likely, you would not want to create a completely new profile for minor permission differences.

- **Option 3**: Here, you use a permission set to grant "Edit" access only to specified individuals. This allows you to avoid Option 1, in which users have extraneous permission, and Option 2, in which a second profile must be maintained.

The permission set is an extremely effective feature within Salesforce; I highly encourage you to consider using it when it is applicable. Before the days of the permission set, all you had to work with for object and field permissions was the user profile. This required provisioning users a profile for each unique set of permissions; in some cases, those unique sets resulted in an extreme number of profiles (even in some smaller organizations).

Permission sets provide the ability to enforce a "least privilege" model by establishing the minimal number of impactful profiles and giving them the broadest set of permissions. Once the profiles are put in place, you can focus on variances and additional needs by creating and assigning permission sets to users. With permission sets, you avoid the need to create new profiles for minor differences in permissions. Instead, you can create one primary profile for the similar permission groupings and then layer a permission set on top of the profile for each unique group of permissions. Figure 15-10 shows the difference between a profile-only approach and one that uses permission sets.

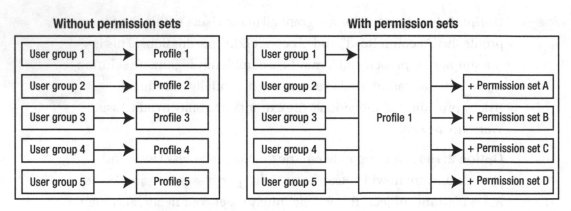

Figure 15-10. *Without permission sets, each unique grouping of permissions must be assigned its own profile. With permission sets, on the other hand, you can consolidate similar groupings and assign permission sets to handle the variances*

Another type of exception to the profile-only approach may emerge, as well. Say you have a hypothetical profile of 100 users. If you want 99 of them to have the ability to edit the NewObj object but 1 of them explicitly not to have editing permission, your options differ slightly from the "Tier 1 Support" example I used earlier in which you only wanted to grant 10 of 50 users access to edit records. Here, again, you could move one of the two groups to a different profile or you could add a permission set to grant the additional permission. You could also take a restrictive approach that would basically grant editing permission to the set of 100 users but block that access for that 1 user. Creating a validation rule would prohibit a specific user from editing the field in question. Figure 15-11 shows these two options.

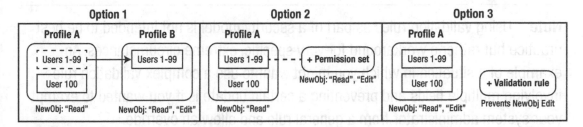

Figure 15-11. *If you have a very small subset of users that require reduced access, you can add a profile or restrict the access by creating a validation rule*

Option 1 or 2 may best meet your requirements. Although it should only be seen as a way to handle outlier scenarios and exceptions, Option 3 is available for consideration. By taking that approach, you minimize the setup and maintenance required for your profiles and permission sets. Of course, there's a cost (isn't there always?). In the case of Option 3, you have to manage the validation rule itself.

The validation rule can be formulated a few different ways for this example. One way is to construct it to restrict changes to the Name field for *new and existing records* for the user ID "005F0000004gHbf." You would build the following formula for the validation rule:

ISCHANGED(Name) && $User.Id = "005F0000004gHbf"

To restrict changes to the Name field for *existing records only* for this user ID, the formula would be

NOT(ISNEW()) && ISCHANGED(Name) && $User.Id = "005F0000004gHbf"

To apply this to an entire object, you would replace "Name" with "Last Modified Date." For example, to restrict changes to all records for a given object made by the same user, you would use

ISCHANGED(LastModifiedDate) && $User.Id = "005F0000004gHbf"

However, going with a validation rule for security elements also has trade-offs. The previous option requires additional administration responsibilities to maintain the security model. You can minimize those responsibilities by creating a custom setting or a custom metadata type and managing the affected users that way (as opposed to hardcoding the User ID), but you'll still need to make sure that your administrators are aware of these exceptions. See Chapter 9 for more on these options.

Note   Using validation rules as part of a security model is not intended to be best practice but rather a workaround for very specific, extreme circumstances. An example of a situation in which you might want to use a complex validation rule involving multiple fields and preventing a certain update is if you wanted to exempt your system administrator from a general rule and allow an override.

Record Access Through Sharing

As I mentioned earlier in the chapter, your profile-based permission to access a certain object does not necessarily mean that you can view or edit that particular record. The sharing model must be considered, as well. The following are a few key areas you should review related to record sharing when you are building solutions within Salesforce.

Organization-Wide Defaults

When you create a new custom object, an organization-wide default is set to control the sharing behavior for that particular object. These defaults allow you to "shut down" record access for an entire org before you open it back up for specific use cases via other sharing mechanisms. To manage these settings, navigate to **"Sharing Settings" within the Setup menu**. For each object, you have three main options in terms of settings:

- **"Public Read/Write" (default setting)**: Allows all users *with "Read" and "Edit" permissions for an object* to view and edit all records related to the object. This is known as an "open sharing" model.

- **"Public Read Only"**: Only allows all users *with "Read" permission for an object* to view all records related to it.

- **"Private"**: Restricts all users from viewing or editing an object. This is known as a "closed sharing" model.

Note   The "Public Read/Write/Transfer" setting is an additional option for Leads and Cases. This is similar to "Public Read/Write" but allows an additional sharing of the ability to transfer record ownership.

It is critical to understand that a user always needs to have the proper object permissions to view or edit a new custom object. Even if you set the organization-wide default to "Public Read/Write," a user without "Read" access for the object will not be able to view it. Figure 15-12 shows how this works.

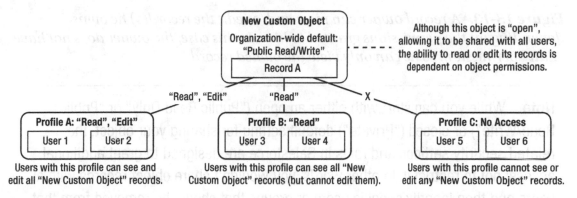

Figure 15-12.   *Even if your organization-wide default is set to "Public Read/Write," individual users will still need to have the proper permissions to read or edit records of that object type*

The obvious exception to the organization-wide default sharing rules is for the owner of a record since the purpose of a sharing rule is to share a record beyond its owner. The owner of a record interacts with it as though the organization-wide default is set to "Public Read/Write." For example, if the user Bunker Jones owns a record that is set to private, he can *potentially* see or edit the record. I say "potentially" because the object permissions still trump everything else. Bunker can only do what his permissions allow, even if he is the record owner. Figure 15-13 shows an object's access to a record when it has a "Private" sharing model.

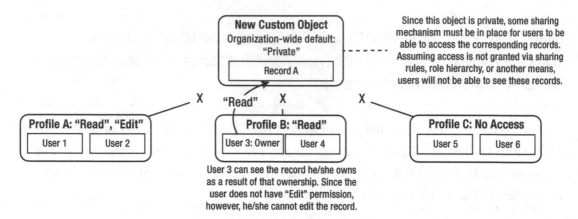

Figure 15-13. *A record owner can view and/or edit the record(s) he owns depending on the permissions granted to him. In this case, the owner does not have "Edit" permission, so he can only view the owned record*

Note   While you can start with either an open ("Public Read Only" or "Public Read/Write") or closed ("Private") default setting for sharing your object, the related security settings and rules in Salesforce are designed to grant additional access, not to restrict it. In other words, you wouldn't share object records with all users and then identify specific users or groups that should be removed from that group. Rather, you would start with a closed sharing model and then grant access to the appropriate users. This is sometimes referred to as the "principle of least privilege."

There are also two additional items related to organization-wide default settings that should be assessed and configured properly: The first is the "**Grant Access Using Hierarchies**" option, which is presented to you when you create a new custom object. When selected, it shares the record with all users who are higher in the hierarchy than the owner. This applies to users in public groups, as well. If a user is granted access to a record via a public group and that group is configured to grant access using hierarchies, that record will only be shared with users who are above the owner in the hierarchy. As with the previously discussed scenarios, for this to apply the impacted users must have the proper object permissions in place; if they do not have "Read" permission for a record that is shared with them, they will be prevented from viewing the record.

Figure 15-14 shows how this feature works. In this example, assume that the record owner has a Role 3c status and that "Grant Access Using Hierarchies" is enabled. Note that although Role 2a is higher than Role 3c, because they are not directly related in the hierarchy. Users in Role 2a are not granted access to the records owned by users in Role 3c when using this setting.

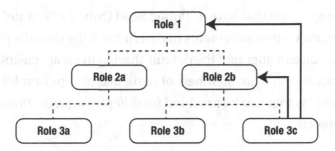

Figure 15-14. *When the "Grant Access Using Hierarchies" setting is enabled for an object, a record owned by a user in Role 3c would be automatically shared with users in Role 2b and Role 1*

The other configuration to take note of when establishing the default settings is the ability to set the **"Default Internal Access"** and **"Default External Access"** separately. This is extremely useful if you have a Community associated with your org. You could, for example, set the organization-wide default for your custom object to "Public Read/ Write" for internal users and "Private" for external users. Although I am not specifically covering Communities in this book, I encourage you to assess your internal and external sharing defaults separately and carefully if you are using either external feature. My book, *Practical Guide to Salesforce Communities*, covers community-specific sharing and access in more detail.

Note   For custom objects that look up to another object via a Master-Detail relationship, you have the option of inheriting the organization-wide default setting from the Master object or setting it up independently on the Detail object. The selection name is "Controlled by Parent."

Sharing Rules

If your organization-wide default setting for your new object(s) is set to "Public Read/Write," your sharing model is complete. All records for the applicable objects have been shared to the full extent with all users. There is no value in any additional sharing, as it would be redundant.

However, for any objects that have a "Public Read Only" or "Private" sharing default, you will need to review your requirements to determine if the defaults are sufficient. With sharing rules, you can augment the default sharing to create customized access for specific users or users that are members of particular groups or roles. Figure 15-15 shows the type of access that can be provided for different organization-wide defaults via sharing rules for objects.

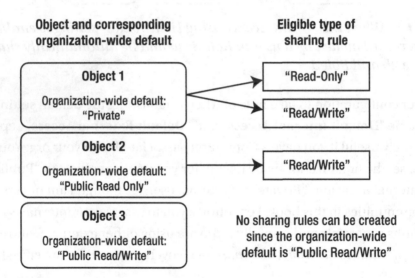

Figure 15-15. *The organization-wide defaults for a given object grant more access than already provided via sharing rules*

There are three primary types of sharing rules that you can configure yourself:

- Criteria-based sharing rules

- Owner-based sharing rules

- Manual sharing rules

All three rule types allow you to share records with users who are members of specified public groups or roles. Additionally, there are record-based sharing rules, which allow for more granular sharing made directly to users.

Criteria-based rules can satisfy fairly complex sharing needs. You can use Salesforce's criteria builder in the way that was discussed in Chapter 4. Figure 15-16 shows an example of a criteria-based sharing rule for a custom object.

New Custom Object Sharing Rules	New	Recalculate			New Custom Object Sharing Rules Help	⑦
Action	**Criteria**				**Shared With**	**Access Level**
Edit | Del	(New Custom Object: Number Field LESS THAN 5000) OR (New Custom Object: Percent Field GREATER THAN 50.0)				Role: Marketing Team	Read Only

Figure 15-16. *A criteria-based sharing rule for a custom object*

Note   If you want to venture outside of the "development without code" world, Apex sharing rules can go even further than criteria-based sharing rules in handling complexity.

Owner-based rules have only one criterion, and that is the role or group of the record owner. Records that are owned by a User with an applicable role or public group will be shared with users in one or more roles or groups. Figure 15-17 shows an owner-based rule that shares records with an owner in Role 1 with Users in Role 3a.

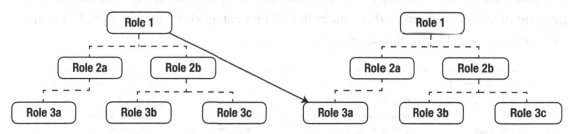

Figure 15-17. *This diagram represents an owner-based sharing rule that shares records owned by users in Role 1 with users in Role 3a*

In addition to identifying a particular role or group to share records with when using owner-based rules, you can include all Users in lower levels of that group by selecting them, either in the criteria or in the "Shared With" assignment. Figure 15-18 shows how records owned by Users in Role 2b or lower-level roles can be shared with Users in Role 2a.

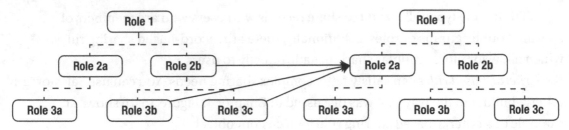

Figure 15-18. *An owner-based sharing rule that shares records owned by users in Role 2b or lower-level roles with users in Role 2a*

Figure 15-19 displays two owner-based sharing rules, each with unique criteria and access levels.

Sharing Rules

Action	Criteria	Shared With	Access Level
Edit | Del	Owner in Role: CEO	Role: CEO	Read Only
Edit | Del	Owner in Role, Internal and Portal Subordinates: CEO	Role: Marketing Team	Read/Write

New Custom Object Sharing Rules [New] [Recalculate]   New Custom Object Sharing Rules Help ⑦

Figure 15-19. *The "Sharing Rules" screen with two owner-based sharing rules*

Manual sharing rules are rules that allow records to be shared on an individual record basis. They are managed on the record itself, not on the "Sharing Settings" screen. The key difference between manual sharing rules and the other two types is that manual sharing rules allow records to be shared with specific users in addition to users in groups and roles. Figure 15-20 shows the screen that results from creating a record-based rule to provide Read-Only access to three users in different categories: users in a public group, users in a role, and individual users.

User and Group Sharing   [Add] [Expand List]   User and Group Sharing Help ⑦

Action	Type	Name ↑	Access Level	Reason
Edit | Del	Role	Eastern Sales Team	Read Only	Manual Sharing
Edit | Del	Public Group	After Hours Support	Read Only	Manual Sharing
Edit | Del	User	Jerome Walton	Read Only	Manual Sharing

Figure 15-20. *Three manual sharing rules. Record-based rules can be shared with individual Users in addition to groups and roles.*

Let's take a look at a scenario in which all three types of sharing rules are applied to records from the same object. Figure 15-21 shows the different sharing rules and the users that would be given access to the applicable record(s) as a result.

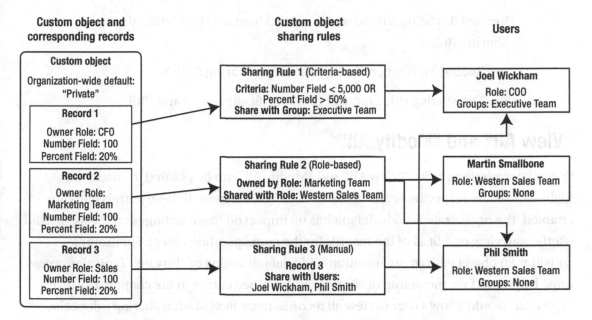

Figure 15-21. *In this example, multiple records for the same object are shared via different types of sharing rules. The users with whom the records are shared are shown on the right.*

It is important to understand the reasons why the sharing rules are being applied as shown in Figure 15-21:

- **Record 1** is being shared with Joel Wickham through Sharing Rule 1:

  - Record 1 meets the sharing rule criteria.

  - Jason is a member of the public group that Record 1 is shared with.

- **Record 2** is being shared with Martin Smallbone and Phil Smith through Sharing Rule 2:

  - The role of Record 2's owner matches the "owned by" role specified in the sharing rule.

  - Mike and Karl are members of the role that Record 2 is shared with.

- **Record 3** is being shared with Joel Wickham and Phil Smith through Sharing Rule 3:

  - Record 2 is being manually shared in Sharing Rule 3.

  - The sharing rule grants access specifically to Joel and Phil.

"View All" and "Modify All"

Special permissions called "View All" and "Modify All" can be granted to ensure the highest-possible respective levels of "Read" and "Edit" access. If these permissions are enabled, the organization-wide default has no impact on these settings and the associated user(s) can view or edit all of the records for the corresponding object. For example, consider an object with an organization-wide default setting of "Private." Typically, access must be granted via ownership or sharing, as described earlier in the chapter. However, "View All" would allow a user to view all records, regardless of what sharing rules exist.

Object Permission and Record-Sharing Overlap

Let's take a look at a few examples to make sure the basic framework is clear before we more closely review the specific functionality that will help you to accurately and reliably satisfy your security-related requirements.

Figure 15-22 shows three different objects and four corresponding records for each of them. A user's "View All/Read" access to each record is indicated by the shading. A white record represents a record that is accessible to the user in question and a shaded record represents a record that is inaccessible to the user. The record access granted via sharing is denoted by a line around the particular record and the object read permission is specified below each object. Each circled number is followed by a corresponding explanation for why the record is or is not accessible to the user.

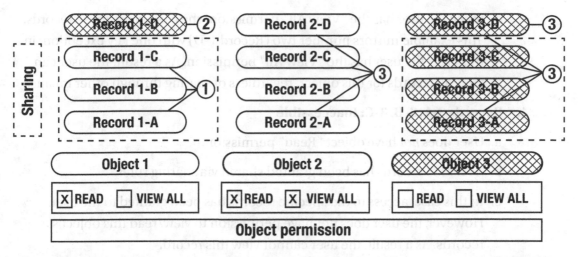

Figure 15-22. *This diagram shows how sharing and object permission granted for record access impact a user's ability to access (view) a particular set of records*

The records are or are not accessible for the following reasons:

1. **Records 1-A, 1-B, 1-C: Accessible**

   a. User has object "Read" permission.

   b. Access to records has been granted shared via sharing rules.

   c. The user has the ability to view records for this object and these particular records have been shared with her.

2. **Record 1-D: Inaccessible**

   a. User has object "Read" permission.

   b. Access to records has *not* been granted shared via sharing rules.

   c. Although the user has the ability to view records for this object, this particular record has not been shared with him. Therefore, the user cannot view it.

3. **Records 2-A, 2-B, 2-C, 2-D: Accessible**

   a. User has object "Read" permission.

   b. Access to records has *not* been granted shared via sharing rules.

   c. User has object "View All" permission.

    d. Since the user has the "View All" permission, she can access these records. This example mirrors number two (Record 1-D) with one key exception: in this case, the user has the "View All" permission. As a result, the user can view all records for this object, regardless of sharing through other means.

4. **Records 3-A, 3-B, 3-C: Inaccessible**

    a. User does *not* have object "Read" permission.

    b. Access to records has been granted shared via sharing rules.

    c. In this case, access to the specific records has been granted to the user. However, the user does not have permission to view/read this object's records. As a result, the user cannot view this record.

5. **Record 3-D: Inaccessible**

    a. User does *not* have object "Read" permission.

    b. Access to records has *not* been granted shared via sharing rules.

    c. In this case, access to the specific records has not been granted to the user and she does not have "Read" permission to access this object's records, so she cannot view the records.

Recap

The most critical takeaway from this chapter is that security requirements and needs must be analyzed as a part of all implementations, even if your security model is well established. Of course, that does not mean that you need to rehash every security-related element across your entire org every time an enhancement or fix is deployed. However, it does mean that any aspects related to permission, sharing, or visibility that pertain to your solution must be updated as needed. In this chapter, the security model was reviewed, specifically in regard to object and field permissions and sharing settings. With the right balance of permissions and access granted via sharing, you can ensure that your users will be able to perform the actions that are needed in their positions while minimizing risk for your client or organization.

CHAPTER 16

Managing Your Salesforce Data with Data Loader

Once you've built the perfect system using Salesforce, you can be assured that you'll have no lack of data to manage. If there's one guarantee with your implementation, it's that you will need to give that data some TLC and dedicated attention. While you should definitely employ validation rules, page layouts, and workflow rules to the fullest in your efforts to achieve and maintain data integrity, you'll also need to extract, transform, and load records to keep Salesforce in tip-top shape. Fortunately, Salesforce provides some useful tools to help you with this endeavor (and many third-party providers boast similar apps on AppExchange). In this chapter, I will focus on one indispensable tool, Data Loader, and how you can use it to manage your data.

Data Loader Overview

Data Loader is a client application that can be downloaded from within your Salesforce org (see Figure 16-1). To find it, **search for "Data Loader" using Quick Find in setup**. It provides the ability to extract, transform, load, and delete large amounts of data by following a simple step-by-step process. Anyone in a developer, consultant, or administrator role should be familiar with this tool or an equivalent.

Figure 16-1. *Main screen from Data Loader for Mac*

469

© Philip Weinmeister 2019
P. Weinmeister, *Practical Salesforce Development Without Code*,
https://doi.org/10.1007/978-1-4842-4871-3_16

Seven specific functions are available within Data Loader:

- **Insert**: Create new records.

- **Update**: Update existing records.

- **Upsert**: Create new records and/or update existing records, depending on whether existing records match those included in the input file.

- **Delete**: Move existing records to your organization's recycle bin.

- **Hard Delete**: Permanently delete existing records.

- **Export**: Export records that are not deleted (i.e., all records not in the recycle bin).

- **Export All**: Export records, including those that were previously deleted and are currently in the recycle bin (permanently/hard deleted records will not be included).

Each function possesses its own unique considerations; I'll walk through each in detail to provide a solid understanding of how you can use the specific function to successfully manage your organization's data. Figure 16-2 shows how each of the available functions is used within Data Loader.

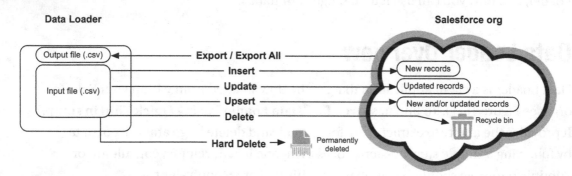

Figure 16-2. *Data Loader allows users to apply seven different functions to a specific set of data*

Setup

Once you download and install Data Loader, you'll need to perform some verification before proceeding. First, you'll need to make sure the proper access is set up. You must have been granted **"API Enabled"** permission, either through your profile or a permission set. Additionally, you'll need the corresponding permissions ("Create," "Read," "Edit," "Delete") for each applicable object. For example, you would need to have "Read" access for Cases to be able to export Case object data. Similarly, you'd need "Create" access on Opportunities to insert Opportunities. If you have the standard System Administrator profile, you won't need to worry about obtaining additional permissions.

The second step is selecting a login method. Salesforce now provides two ways to authenticate: OAuth and password authentication (see Figure 16-3).

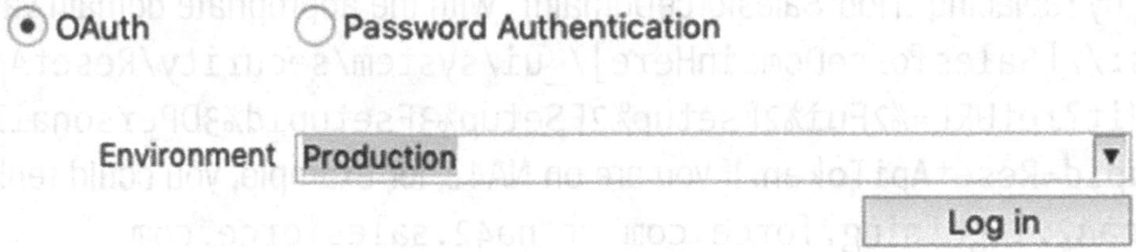

Figure 16-3. *Data Loader supports both OAuth and password-based authentication*

If using OAuth, you'll be provided with a standard Salesforce login via a pop-up window. Log in as you normally do via a browser and you'll be ready to use Data Loader. Note that you may need to provide a verification code.

The password authentication option is the original means to authenticate. For this path, you'll need to provide username, password, login URL, and possibly the security token. If you are working in production (i.e., your "live" instance), you'll need to keep the default URL (https://login.salesforce.com). This applies if you're using Data Loader for a trial or development org, as well. However, if you are managing data in a sandbox, you'll need to modify the URL to https://test.salesforce.com.

Note   One of the most common causes of login issues is using the wrong URL. Double-check the URL and adjust it based on org type. Development/trial/ production orgs use https://login.salesforce.com and sandbox orgs use https://test.salesforce.com.

Depending on your org's security settings, you may need to include the security token associated with your user when entering your password. The token is emailed to you when your User record is first activated. If you can't find the token in your email inbox, you can reset your token and have it emailed to you by navigating to "Settings" (click your avatar or name at the top right), then selecting "Reset My Security Token." If you had a password of "a1b2c34R" and a token of "79xyz22," you would enter the following for your password within Data Loader if a token was required: "a1b2c34R79xyz22."

Note   Depending on your org settings, you may not be able to see the "Reset My Security Token" menu item. In that case, a shortcut to directly access the following URL is by replacing "[YourSalesforceDomain]" with the appropriate domain value: `https://[SalesforceDomainHere]/_ui/system/security/ResetApiTokenEdit?retURL=%2Fui%2Fsetup%2FSetup%3Fsetupid%3DPersonalInfo&setupid=ResetApiToken`. If you are on NA42, for example, you could replace it with "`na42.lightning.force.com`" or "`na42.salesforce.com`".

Exporting Data

Exporting data via Data Loader is relatively simple and straightforward. The application can quickly become a trusted friend for those who need to manipulate a large number of Salesforce records quickly. First, however, I want to clarify the difference between the "**Export**" and the "**Export All**" options. "Export All" includes records that are in the Recycle Bin; "Export" does not. Typically, you'll want to use the "Export" feature, not "Export All." Of course, if you do need deleted records, you'll be very happy that the "Export All" feature exists.

To start the export, you'll need to select one object; you cannot export data from multiple objects simultaneously. By default, you'll see a list of the available standard and custom objects. It's key to pay attention to the "**Show all Salesforce objects**" checkbox at the top of the dialog window. If it is checked off, a number of additional objects will be exposed to you. These include, but are not limited to, objects related to

- Chatter
- Record history
- Sharing
- Search

- The Apex debug log

- Approval requests

- Communities

Once you select your object, you'll need to identify your directory and select a file name. If the .csv file you identify does not already exist, a new file will be created. In Figure 16-4, I have selected the Case object to be exported.

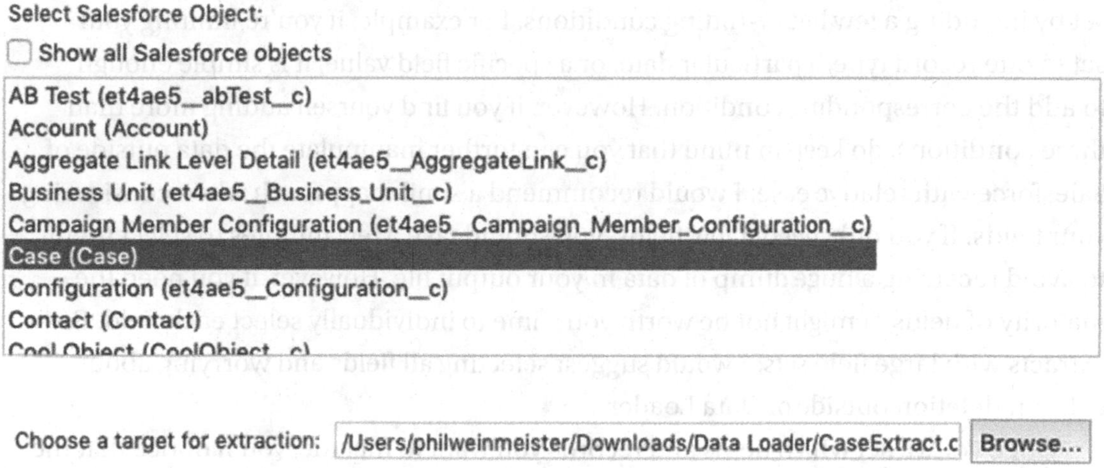

Select Salesforce Object:

☐ Show all Salesforce objects

```
AB Test (et4ae5__abTest__c)
Account (Account)
Aggregate Link Level Detail (et4ae5__AggregateLink__c)
Business Unit (et4ae5__Business_Unit__c)
Campaign Member Configuration (et4ae5__Campaign_Member_Configuration__c)
Case (Case)
Configuration (et4ae5__Configuration__c)
Contact (Contact)
Cool Object (CoolObject__c)
```

Choose a target for extraction: /Users/philweinmeister/Downloads/Data Loader/CaseExtract.c   Browse...

Figure 16-4. *Selecting an object is the first step for all functions within Data Loader*[1]

When you click the "Next" button (see Figure 16-5), you will be presented with an interface that allows you to configure two critical elements:

- The subset of records to be extracted

- The fields to be included in the output file

You can declaratively build a SOQL query to identify which records you want to include. You may not realize that every time you configure a workflow rule using criteria or build a list view, you are actually writing a SOQL query. SOQL is Salesforce's own language that can be used to manipulate data. You are not provided a lookup dialog,

---

[1]All Salesforce screenshots in this chapter © copyright Salesforce, Inc. Used with permission.

so you'll have to provide the record ID if you're using a relationship field in your query. Here's an example of a SOQL query that displays five fields and contains two conditions:

```
Select Id, CaseNumber, ContactId, AccountId, Status FROM Case WHERE
CreatedDate> 2015-01-01T01:01:01Z AND Status != 'Escalated'
```

You can get as precise as you want with your query to potentially limit your records to the exact set you desire. However, I'd encourage you to balance precision with invested time at this stage. I would definitely encourage you to reduce your record set by including a few heavy-hitting conditions. For example, if you're limiting your set to one record type, a particular date, or a specific field value, it is simple enough to add the corresponding condition. However, if you find yourself adding more than three conditions, do keep in mind that you can further manipulate the data outside of Salesforce with relative ease. I would recommend a similar approach when considering your fields. If you only need a few fields, you should take a few minutes to select them to avoid receiving a huge dump of data in your output file. However, if you need the majority of fields, it might not be worth your time to individually select each field. For extracts with large field sets, I would suggest selecting all fields and worrying about column deletion outside of Data Loader.

Once you've set which fields and records you want to include, you'll notice that the corresponding SOQL query is visible. If you feel comfortable, you can directly edit the query to make further modifications. After you confirm that you do want to proceed with the export, you'll get a confirmation of the number of successful and unsuccessful records. With exported data, you shouldn't see a positive number in the error column. Records are either exported or not and those that are exported are considered successful.

Figure 16-5 shows these key elements of this screen:

1. Select which fields will be included in the exported file

2. Where clause field (e.g., **CaseNumber** > 10,000)

3. Where clause operation (e.g., CaseNumber > 10,000)

4. Where clause value (e.g., CaseNumber > **10,000**)

5. Button to add the built condition to the where clause

6. View of the generated query (SOQL)

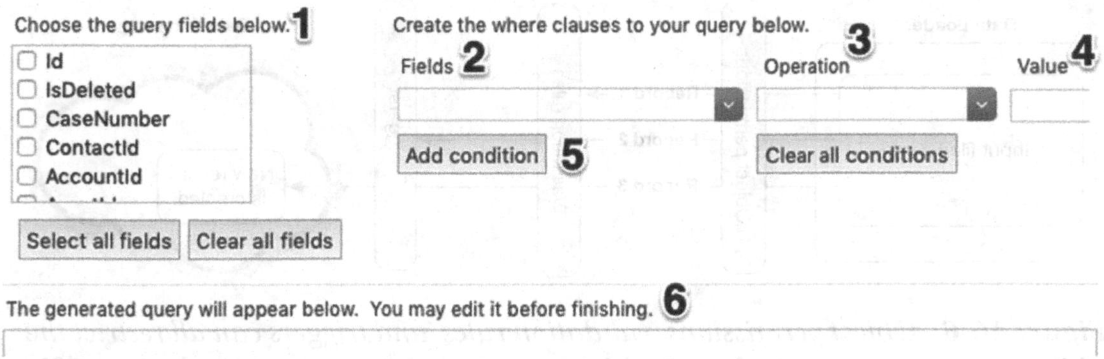

Choose the query fields below.**1**
- ☐ Id
- ☐ IsDeleted
- ☐ CaseNumber
- ☐ ContactId
- ☐ AccountId

Select all fields   Clear all fields

Create the where clauses to your query below.   **3**

Fields **2**

Operation

Value **4**

Add condition **5**

Clear all conditions

The generated query will appear below. You may edit it before finishing. **6**

Figure 16-5. *On this screen, you will build a query to determine which data to export*

Inserting Data

With Data Loader, you can insert large volumes of data to create new records in Salesforce. Like with exporting (and all other functions), you'll need to identify the target object. Additionally, you'll need to have a properly formatted .csv file containing the records to be created within your org. When preparing your file, keep in mind the following factors:

- Relevant **validation rules, workflow rules**, and **triggers** will apply. If you do not want them to be considered, you will have to update the rules, triggers, and/or data being loaded accordingly. For example, you could update rule criteria to exclude records with certain data present and then update your data to match that exclusion scenario.

- **Object permissions** and **field-level security settings** will apply. For example, if you do not have write access to a particular field, you will not be able to include that column in the insertion.

- **Page layout requirements** and restrictions will not apply. So, if a field is required on the one active page layout for an object, it has no bearing on the data being imported via Data Loader.

Figure 16-6 shows how permissions, rules, and triggers might impact a data insert when using Data Loader.

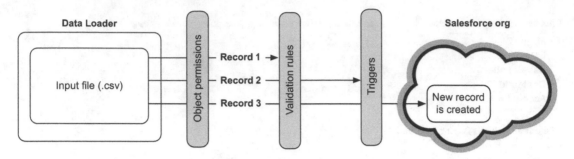

Figure 16-6. *Object permissions, validation rules, and triggers can all restrict the ability to manage specific data. In this example, three records are in the Insert file but only one ends up getting created.*

Once you have selected the file to be inserted and proceed, Salesforce will validate your file. You will be alerted of any empty columns and issues with the file that would guarantee a failure. However, it's critical to understand that a successful validation does not mean that your records will be inserted. The validation does not take any internal org rules into consideration.

Note   To avoid spending unnecessary time verifying the format of your file, consider exporting at least one record from the same object first. You can then use that export file as your template for importing. This will not only ensure that your columns are named properly but also that the field values are formatted correctly. Note that date fields in an export will need to be reformatted; more on that later in this chapter.

Once your validation has completed, you will map the column names within your .csv file to the object's "writable" fields. Read-only and system fields, for example, will not be available for mapping selection. If no existing maps exist, you will need to click "Create or Edit a Map" to define the field-mapping rules. As shown in Figure 16-7 (for the User object), the field-mapping interface includes two sections: the Salesforce fields and the file column headers. You can manually drag a Salesforce field down to match a file column header or you can "auto-match" Salesforce fields to columns. I use this feature frequently, but I would provide a word of caution here – only use the auto-match feature under the following conditions:

- You have appropriately named the file column headers (as previously mentioned, you may want to export a file via Data Loader and use that as your import template).

- You are familiar with the fields on the target object.

- You are attentive to detail.

Match the Salesforce fields to your columns.

| Clear Mapping | Auto-Match Fields to Columns |

Name	Label	Type
AboutMe	About Me	textarea
Alias	Alias	string
CallCenterId	Call Center ID	reference
City	City	string
CommunityNickname	Nickname	string
CompanyName	Company Name	string
ContactId	Contact ID	reference
Country	Country	string

Drag the Salesforce fields down to the column mapping. To remove a mapping, select a row and click Delete.

File Column Header	Name
Active	
Alias	
Company Name	
Department	
Division	
Email	
EmailEncodingKey	
Employee Number	
First Name	
Language	
LanguageLocaleKey	

| OK | Save Mapping | Cancel |

Figure 16-7. *Field-mapping interface with object fields at the top and file column headers at the bottom. You can auto-match the fields or manually drag the object fields down to map them to file column headers.*

Once you've mapped your fields, you will want to carefully review them before proceeding. In Figure 16-8, you can see how your file's headers (on the left) match up with applicable fields (on the right).

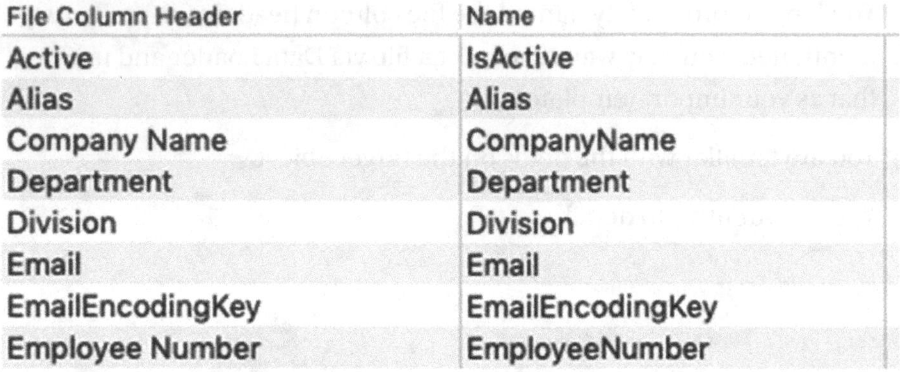

File Column Header	Name
Active	IsActive
Alias	Alias
Company Name	CompanyName
Department	Department
Division	Division
Email	Email
EmailEncodingKey	EmailEncodingKey
Employee Number	EmployeeNumber

Figure 16-8. *A view of file column headers postmapping*

Once you've gone over the information, you have the option of saving that mapping for future use. This is especially helpful for deployments. Since you may have to hand off data creation responsibilities, it's much more reliable to provide a mapping file that can simply be loaded than to assume someone else will set the proper mappings.

After optionally identifying a directory for the success and error files, you'll proceed to insert the records from your file by clicking the "Finish" button. As with the export process, you will receive a confirmation of successes and errors. Make sure to carefully review your errors to determine if they were expected or not based on your org's configuration.

Updating Data

Updating data via Data Loader overlaps significantly with the process of inserting data, with a few key differences. The main difference with updating is that you must include the record ID of the record you are updating. To do this, you export the data you need and make sure to include the ID in the selected fields list. With that exported file, you can simply update your field values in other columns and submit the modified file for update. The key is to make sure that you do not modify the ID column, as it is the only place to identify existing records using Update. Figure 16-9 shows a scenario in which data is exported using Data Loader, edited, and then updated (once again, using Data Loader).

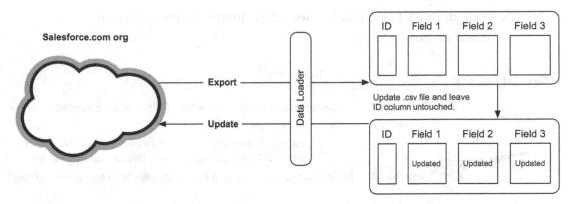

Figure 16-9. *In this example, a three-step process includes extraction ("Export"), transformation (manual editing via a spreadsheet application), and load ("Update"). The ID field will need to be left untouched for a successful update.*

Note   Make sure that your spreadsheet application does not automatically change your file format from `.csv` to something else. Only `.csv` files will work with Data Loader.

Upserting Data

If you've ever used an ETL (Extract, Transform, and Load) tool in the past, you won't find too many surprises with the "Insert" or "Update" functions within Data Loader. The "Upsert" function, however, is a different beast altogether. "Upsert" allows to you submit a data set that includes existing and/or new records; Salesforce will make the proper determination and either insert a new record or update an existing one. This activity centers around the External ID field shown in Figure 16-10. Unless you include a column containing the Salesforce record ID, you must have a field designated as an External ID on your target object to perform an upsert. You should be aware of the following factors when considering external IDs:

- The Email, Geolocation, Number, Phone, Picklist, Text (not Text Area), and URL fields can be set as external IDs.

- You may identify more than one field per object as an external ID (up to seven).

- The External ID field that is selected to identify the records via an upsert cannot be blank.

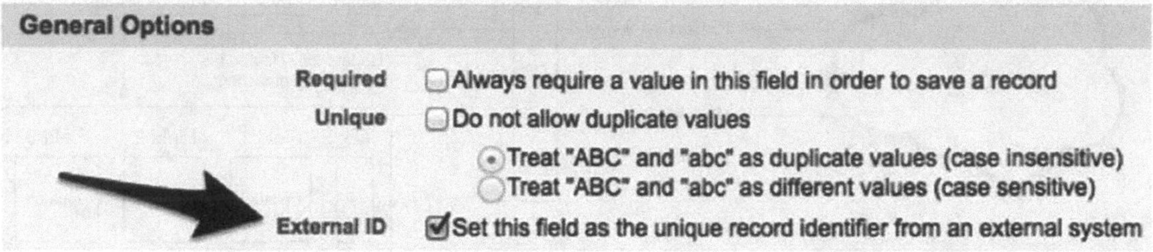

Figure 16-10. *Checking off the "External ID" checkbox when editing a field to identify it as an external ID*

When you are upserting within Data Loader, you will be given the option to select either the Standard ID field or a different field that has been designated as an External ID. Figure 16-11 shows a custom Case field, External Ticket ID, that can be selected during the Data Loader upsert process as an External ID field.

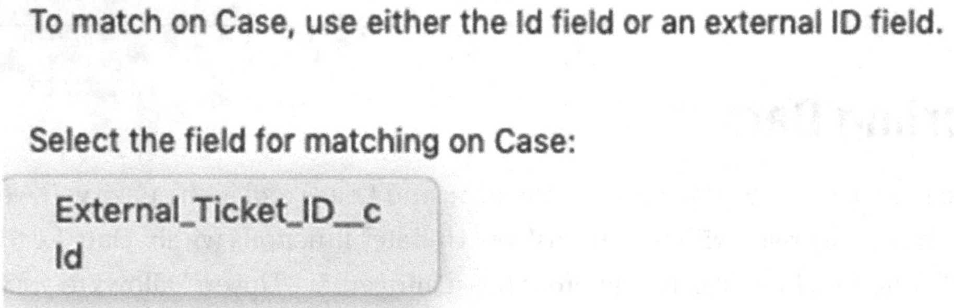

Figure 16-11. *You can select the Salesforce record ID or an external ID to be used as the primary identifier in an upsert. Here, the record ID and the field External_ Ticket_ID__c (an external ID) are both available for selection.*

Next, you will identify the field to use for related objects. This field would be used if the records you're upserting have a relationship to another object via a Relationship field and you are referencing an External ID field value instead of a Salesforce record ID.

Once the upsert is complete, you will receive notification of the result. You'll notice that the results column will show one of two different values for successfully submitted records: "Item Updated" or "Item Created." If no existing record matches an external ID in the submitted file, a new record will be created. Figure 16-12 gives an overview of a hypothetical scenario involving an upsert.

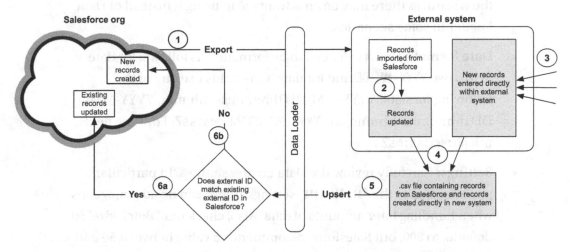

Figure 16-12. A potential step-by-step process for an "Upsert" use case

Deleting Data

In addition to exporting, inserting, and updating data, you can delete records as well. You have two options for doing so: "Delete" or "Delete All." The only difference between the two is that "Delete" performs a "soft" deletion, placing the records in the organization's recycle bin, and "Delete All" performs a "hard" deletion, from which records cannot be recovered. To delete data, you only need the record IDs. Upload your file containing the IDs of the records to be deleted, and that's all there is to it. Obviously, be careful to double-check your data before you perform a deletion.

Other Considerations

There are, of course, numerous options and alternatives for the approaches discussed in this chapter. You should consider the following:

- **Exporting via reports**: If you want to quickly export data outside of Salesforce to be used in a future update, consider using the available report builders and make sure to include the record ID in your selected fields. You can export the data directly as a .csv file.

- **Data Import Wizard**: Salesforce offers a standard "Data Import Wizard" tool to guide you through importing data. Get familiar with the wizard, as there may be an advantage to using it instead of Data Loader in some scenarios.

- **Date formats**: Dates will need to be formatted as follows: for date fields, use YYYY-MM-DD and for date/time fields use one of the following formats: YYYY-MM-DDThh:mm:ss+hh:mm, YYYY-MM-DDThh:mm:ss-hh:mm, or YYYY-MM-DDThh:mm:ssZ. For time fields, use hh:mm:ss:msZ.

- **Settings**: Carefully review the Data Loader settings. In particular, pay attention to the "**Bulk API**" settings. These can be advantageous when handling later amounts of data. Also, check out "Batch size"; it defaults to 200, but Salesforce recommends a value between 50 and 100 when Bulk API is not checked. For Bulk loads, you can set batch size up to 10,000.

- **History/Backup**: Make sure to back up your Salesforce data often. Take a look at the "**Data Export**" option and consider scheduling an export of your org's data.

- **Command line**: Data Loader can be programmed at the command line (in Windows) to schedule activities to manage your data.

Recap

In this chapter, I discussed the need to manage your data, specifically focusing on how to use the Data Loader tool for your approach. Any solution you build will affect data and, if you're the one responsible for managing that data, you'll be thankful to have a powerful solution such as Data Loader to facilitate that activity. You learned about seven Data Loader functions, paying special attention to "Export," "Insert," "Update," and "Upsert." If you get familiar with Data Loader, you'll have no problem quickly managing large amounts of data within your org.

CHAPTER 17

Managing Your Environments and Deploying Your Solutions

In the scramble to produce valuable and impactful functionality for your organization or clients, it can become all too easy to overlook the need to have a solid plan in place to manage the development/testing instances associated with your production environment (called "sandboxes" within Salesforce) and deploy your work. However, I would implore you to prioritize this highly in your overall Salesforce development life cycle process. A thoughtfully configured sandbox model combined with a well-planned deployment approach will significantly increase your chances for long-term success as you build and deliver solutions. In this chapter, I will delve into the world of sandboxes and deployment within Salesforce and provide guidance on the way to approach them and key considerations that should be made.

Note   The world of Salesforce deployment extends beyond sandboxes, specifically with separate development orgs, Salesforce DX, Metadata API, and more. As this book focuses on development without code, I won't dive into those areas area. However, make sure to research those if you are looking for a more advanced way to deploy solutions.

483

© Philip Weinmeister 2019
P. Weinmeister, *Practical Salesforce Development Without Code*,
https://doi.org/10.1007/978-1-4842-4871-3_17

The Salesforce Sandbox

The term *sandbox* refers to a development or testing environment (org) on the Salesforce platform that is associated with a production org. At creation, a sandbox is typically initiated as a copy of the current production org and is provisioned with all of the configuration, code, and setup data (i.e., metadata) from that org. Record data may be included, depending on the type of sandbox and its configuration. While the sandbox is initially a replica of production, it is not automatically synced with production in any way. It is important to understand that changes in production will not automatically be reflected in a sandbox. See Figure 17-1 for a view of the initial sandbox screen.

Sandboxes   Help for this Page ❓

Sandboxes are special organizations that are used to test changes or new apps without risking damage to your production data or configuration. Sandbox Templates are used to create new Sandboxes containing specific data sets.

Available Sandbox Licenses

Developer	Developer Pro	Partial Copy	Full
89 Available (11 in use)	3 Available (2 in use)	0 Available (1 in use)	0 Available (1 in use)

Sandboxes   Sandbox Templates   Sandbox History

New Sandbox

Action	Name	Type	Status	Location	Current Org Id	Completed On	Description	Copied From
Clone | Del | Refresh | Log In	BoltDev1	Developer	Completed	CS19	00D290000008rNz	3/28/2018 12:05 PM		
Clone | Del | Refresh | Log In	BoltDev2	Developer	Completed	CS19	00D290000008rNL	3/28/2018 12:06 PM		
Clone | Del | Refresh | Log In	BoltDev3	Developer	Completed	CS20	00Dm0000000DVGu	3/30/2018 9:57 AM		
Clone | Del | Refresh | Log In	BoltDev4	Developer	Completed	CS21	00Dq000000010SQ	4/3/2018 2:35 PM		
Clone | Del | Refresh | Log In	BoltDev5	Developer	Completed	CS21	00Dq000000011eQ	4/6/2018 11:41 AM		
Clone | Del | Refresh | Log In	BoltDev6	Developer	Completed	CS19	00D290000008tQd	4/6/2018 12:03 PM		
Clone | Del | Refresh | Log In	BoltDev7	Developer	Completed	CS91	00D2F0000000aQP	4/18/2018 6:47 PM		
Clone | Del | Refresh | Log In	BoltDev8	Developer	Completed	CS91	00D2F0000000alZ	4/18/2018 7:01 PM		

Figure 17-1. *A view of the Sandbox main menu/dashboard*

Note   It is now possible to clone a sandbox from another sandbox. While this action is much less common than creating a sandbox from Production, it is important to know that it is available for situations that could warrant a sandbox-to-sandbox clone. Keep in mind that both sandbox types must match.

Sandbox Copy Engine

To assist with the generation of new or "refreshed" sandboxes, Salesforce leverages what is referred to as the "sandbox copy engine." This engine determines a few key factors intelligently to optimize the overall process:

- The destination instance of the sandbox (e.g., CS58 vs. CS90)

- Data copy (including the data selected and the copy protocol)

- Postcreation reconciliation to address changes to production during the sandbox copy

- Progress monitoring

Sandbox Templates

To assist with the relevant selection of data during the copy of Full and Partial Data sandboxes, templates can be created. Sandbox templates allow objects to be specified for inclusion. Note that some objects must always be included and certain related objects may be included, depending on the object selection. See Figure 17-2.

New Sandbox Template

Sandbox Template Information		
Name		
Description		

Select Objects to copy into the new sandbox.

Objects   Show All | Show Selected   **Object Details:** Click an object to see its details

Name	Required Objects	Selected
Account	1	☐
Account Brand	2	☐
Activity	4	☐

Figure 17-2. *The New Sandbox Template screen*

Figure 17-3 shows an overview of the process.

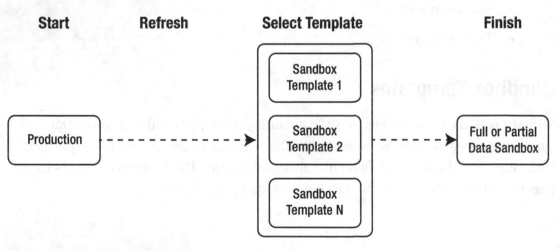

Figure 17-3. *Using a sandbox template*

Types of Sandboxes

Salesforce offers a few different types of sandboxes that can be created. It is useful to be familiar with each to understand the pros and cons of provisioning a new sandbox of a particular type. Figure 17-4 provides an overview of sandbox types.

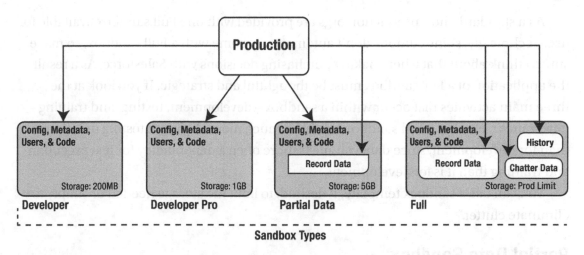

Figure 17-4. *You can create four different types of sandboxes. All of them include a mirror of production metadata; Partial Data and Full sandboxes include data in addition.*

Full Sandbox

A Full sandbox includes all of the configuration, metadata, code, users, *and* data from your production org. All object records, custom setting records, and the like will be available in your Full sandbox. This would, for example, include all of the Case records created in your production environment as part of your customer support department. Likewise, all Opportunities created by your Sales team would be copied to the sandbox. A few additional options are also made available:

- **Field history**: You have the option of copying a configurable amount of field history data from production.

- **Chatter data**: You can include the Chatter posts and activity from production if desired.

There are two primary considerations you'll want to make when setting up these options: First, do you have concerns about file storage limits in your sandbox? If so, consider avoiding inclusion of Chatter data. On the other hand, field history data does not count against your data storage limits. Second, are you looking to provision the sandbox as quickly as possible? If so, avoid copying any field history or Chatter data. Overlooking these items will expedite the provisioning time of a Full sandbox.

As a standard, most production orgs are provided with one Full sandbox available for use. Technically, some editions don't automatically come with a Full sandbox, so make sure to think about that when making purchasing decisions with Salesforce. As a result, the application of a Full sandbox must be thoughtful and strategic. If you look at the three main activities that occur within a sandbox – development, testing, and training – it becomes clear that a Full sandbox would be much more useful for testing or training than for development, since data volume is more often a dependency for test execution and training than it is for development.

You can use a sandbox template, if desired, to limit the storage needed or simply to eliminate clutter.

Partial Data Sandbox

Partial Data sandboxes are very similar to Full sandboxes except that they only allow a subset of data to be copied to the sandbox from production. Additionally, the options to capture field history and/or Chatter data are not available in Partial Data sandboxes. Salesforce's sandbox copy engine intelligently selects data to be copied from applicable objects. Based on the data storage required during the copy, up to 10,000 records of each selected object will be included in the copy. Additionally, file and data storage limits of 5 gigabytes apply (although this could increase at a later date).

Using a sandbox template is a key piece of the partial data sandbox process. Create a sensible template that contains the critical objects for your needs, but avoids bloat by omitting those objects that are not required.

Note   Each sandbox type has a different limit for file and data storage. Object records count against data storage; content, files, and Chatter feeds count against file storage.

Developer and Developer Pro Sandboxes

Developer and Developer Pro sandboxes include no data from production; they only consist of metadata. This is often sufficient for testing needs. If additional data is needed, you can manually create it via the UI (as a production user would) or load in a set of data via Data Loader. If you needed a smaller set of data, there's really no need to provision a Full or Partial Data sandbox. For example, let's say you need a sample of Accounts, Contacts, Opportunities, Cases, and Leads; you can create files of 10–100 records for each quickly with relative ease.

The only differences between Developer and Developer Pro sandboxes are the limits for file and data storage. A Developer sandbox can hold up to 200 megabytes of each, while a Developer Pro sandbox can hold up to 1 gigabyte of each.

Refreshing a Sandbox

When you create a sandbox, you can be confident that its metadata precisely aligns with the metadata in production. However, the two environments will inevitably diverge, and your sandbox will, to some degree, fall out of sync with your production org. In order to make them consistent again, Salesforce provides the ability to refresh a sandbox after a specific period of time has passed since the last refresh or the creation date if it hasn't yet been refreshed. The process is illustrated in Figure 17-5. In reality, a refresh is essentially the same as replacing your existing sandbox with a new sandbox of the same name. All of the metadata from production is copied to your sandbox, overriding the existing configuration, code, and setup data. Additionally, the existing data in the sandbox is wiped out.

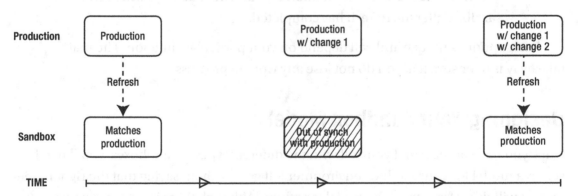

Figure 17-5. *Over time, your sandbox will diverge further and further from the production org. However, you can refresh your sandbox to sync it up with production again. Depending on the sandbox type, the current data in production will be copied to your sandbox during a refresh.*

It is a good idea to refresh your sandbox at the following intervals:

- **Full**: Every 29 days

- **Partial Data**: Every 5 days

- **Developer Pro**: Every day

- **Developer**: Every day

The refresh feature can be extremely beneficial when developing solutions. New functionality may be based on metadata or records that exist only in production. A refresh can mirror records in production in your sandbox for you. You may find that your sandbox is in need of a refresh while you are working on something. However, before you do a refresh, be extremely careful that there is nothing in progress that is stored only in your sandbox, as there is the possibility of it getting overwritten. To avoid this happening, you have three primary options:

- Complete your work and deploy it to the parent environment.

- Save your work outside Salesforce in a way that will allow a quick recreation of the solution if need be.

- Deploy your work to a "sibling" environment (another sandbox connected to the same production org) and then deploy back to your sandbox after the refresh has completed.

Each option is unique and will depend on your particular situation. The main takeaway is to ensure that you do not lose any work in progress.

Designing Your Sandbox Model

Once you have familiarized yourself with the different types of sandboxes, you'll need to set up a model for your sandbox environment. It goes without saying that the right model for you will differ from the right model for others. Although there is no one-size-fits-all setup that will meet the needs of all organizations, what follows are some common considerations that will set you up for potential success.

Determining Your Needs

Before you start creating sandboxes on a whim, think about how you'll use them. Here are some possible activities that may be required:

- Development

- Unit testing

- System/integration testing

- Performance/load testing

- User acceptance testing (UAT)

- Training

- Demos

By thinking through how your environments will be utilized, you'll have a better idea of how many sandboxes you'll need and which types. For example, if you have only one or a few developers building solutions to be implemented in production, you likely won't need a large number of development sandboxes (Developer or Developer Pro). On the other hand, if you have large organizational departments that require detailed training and demonstrations, you'll benefit from a Staging/UAT sandbox (ideally, a Full sandbox).

Assessing Availability and Cost

When your production org is initially set up, you'll have a certain number of each type of sandbox available for use. The number can differ significantly based on your agreement with Salesforce. Typically, you'll have one Full sandbox and multiple Developer sandboxes, although this depends on various factors. Extra sandboxes are usually not cheap, so have a solid justification prepared if you feel that you need to purchase one. Figure 17-6 shows the sandbox availability and use within an example production org. To get to this screen, search for "Sandbox" in the setup menu using Quick Find.

Sandboxes

Help for this Page ❓

Sandboxes are special organizations that are used to test changes or new apps without risking damage to your production data or configuration. Sandbox Templates are used to create new Sandboxes containing specific data sets.

Available Sandbox Licenses			
Developer	**Developer Pro**	**Partial Data**	**Full**
18 Available (3 in use)	0 Available (1 in use)	0 Available (0 in use)	0 Available (1 in use)

Figure 17-6. *By viewing your sandboxes from your production org, you can confirm how many of each sandbox are available or in use. This screenshot is just an example; each org is different.*[1]

Designing and Building the Sandbox Environments

After determining your sandbox needs and availability, you can create a logical model for your sandbox environment. As I previously mentioned, there is not a cookie-cutter approach that will work for everyone; however, I will propose one possible model that could be used as a baseline. Your exact situation may warrant additional sandboxes or a smaller footprint.

Development

The lowest tier of your sandbox model will represent those environments that see the greatest frequency of change, which would be your development environments. Additionally, there may be multiple developers or development teams working simultaneously; it is recommended that each development group have a separate sandbox to prevent conflicts. These would likely be Developer or Developer Pro sandboxes.

System/Integration Testing

When you have multiple development environments, you should consolidate the disparate development activities into one environment. To achieve this goal, you will need to create a system/integration testing environment that all of the development environments feed into. Broader testing can be performed in this type of environment

---

[1]All Salesforce screenshots in this chapter © copyright Salesforce, Inc. Used with permission.

since it includes all development activity. It would likely be a Developer or Developer Pro sandbox. Figure 17-7 shows a possible configuration of development and system/integration sandboxes.

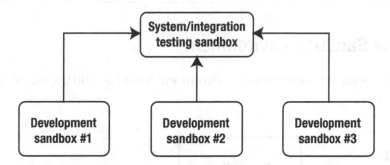

Figure 17-7. *Multiple development sandboxes and a parent integration sandbox will allow you to consolidate all development work in one org. All of these would likely be Developer or Full sandboxes in Developer.*

User Acceptance Testing/Staging

Although your system/integration testing sandbox should contain all of your changes, you may want to have an additional sandbox for the purpose of user acceptance testing and/or staging. This environment will be a mirror of production the majority of the time; the exception would be when new functionality is pushed to the environment to be user acceptance tested or staged for a short period of time. This serves two purposes: it allows a stable, controlled environment to be used for UAT or staging, and it provides an org that can be used for a production deployment "dry run." You can run through your full deployment and it should be completely successful. If not, you have another opportunity to correct your deployment process and steps before anything reaches production. This environment would typically be a Full sandbox.

Performance/Load Testing

Depending on your needs, you may choose to have a separate environment for performance/load testing. If you'll be performing a significant number of automated activities in an org or measuring the speed of particular actions, you may want to consider obtaining a second Full sandbox. The content in this sandbox would not go directly to production but would instead be an endpoint for deployment. In other words, the latest changes would be deployed both to this sandbox as well as to the UAT/staging sandbox; in the final release you would move the UAT/staging sandbox to production.

Note   Contact Salesforce directly if you need additional sandboxes. Keep in mind that they must be purchased.

An Example Sandbox Environment

Figure 17-8 shows an overall sandbox environment based on the hypothetical sandboxes mentioned earlier.

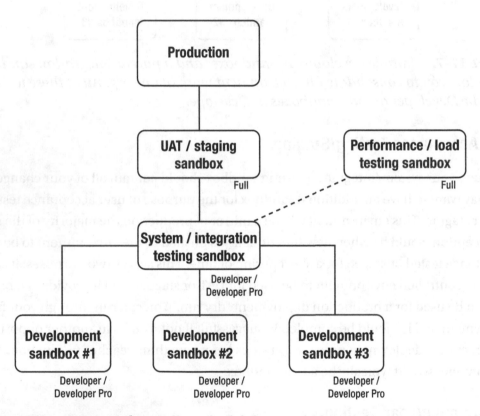

Figure 17-8. *An example sandbox model that could be used to manage organization changes and enhancements*

Deployment

Once you have designed and created your sandbox model, you will need to establish a plan to deploy your changes from your original environment to the next sandbox "tier." Outside a few exceptional situations, it is highly recommended that you create a clear deployment plan and adhere to it. Although a "quick fix" in production may seem to be a harmless time-saver in the moment, the true cost may end up being many hours of lost time as a result of miscommunication and/or a conflict at some point in the future.

To deploy your Salesforce functionality, you'll need to use an appropriate tool to move the corresponding changes. A number of tools and environments are available to you, including

- Change sets

- Salesforce DX

- Ant Migration Tool

- Force.com IDE

- Metadata IDE

To follow the path of development without code, I will only focus on the primary declarative option, change sets, in this chapter. Personally, I use Illuminated Cloud in addition to change sets and would recommend reviewing it and some of the other tools available, especially if you are familiar with code migration tools outside of Salesforce.

Change Sets

Change sets are groupings of components (in the general sense, not necessarily Lightning components) that can be deployed from one org, the source, to another org, the target or destination. Both the destination and the target org can be either a sandbox or a production org. The factor that makes change sets truly unique is their declarative nature – the entire process can be done within the Salesforce user interface with only clicks (in addition to naming some text and describing the set).

Deployment Settings

The first step in using change sets is to configure your deployment connections, or authorization directions. Deployment connections define which orgs (sandboxes or production) are allowed to serve as a destination org for a specific target org. To set up your deployment connections, you will need to log in to the destination org and check off which orgs may push change sets to it. To do this, search for "Deployment Settings" via Quick Find. Figure 17-9 shows the edit screen for this setting.

Figure 17-9. In the "Upload Authorization Direction" section, you can enable deployment connections by checking off "Allow Inbound Changes" and "Allow Outbound Changes" so that the changes will be received from the target org

Figure 17-10 depicts the sandbox model, now with direction to show the allowable path of change set deployment.

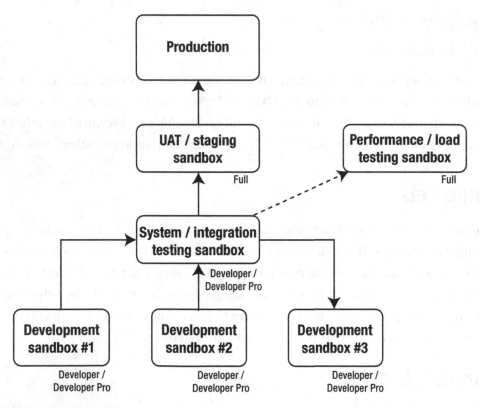

Figure 17-10. This diagram adds direction to the sandbox model represented in Figure 17-8

Change Set Content

To add content to your change set, search for "Outbound Change Sets" with Quick Find in the setup menu. Once your set has been created, you can add a large variety of Salesforce development components to it. Among many other components, you can include the following types:

- Custom objects

- Custom fields

- Page layouts

- Workflow rules, field updates, and e-mail alerts

- Validation rules

- Custom report types

- Record types

- Sharing rules

- Code-related items (Lightning components, Apex classes, etc.)

To add a component, select the component type, click the specific component you want to add, and click the "Add to Change Set" button, as shown in Figure 17-11.

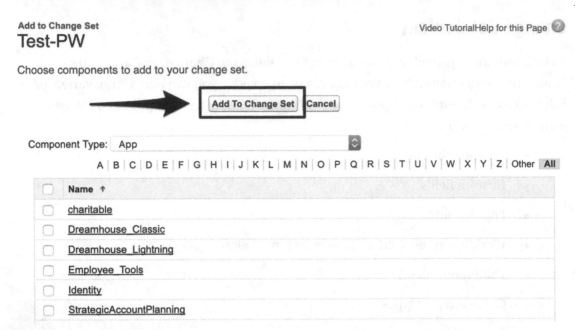

Figure 17-11. *You can select a component and click "Add to Change Set" to include it in your change set*

Additionally, you can include profiles to be a part of your change set. This will carry over certain profile-specific attributes in the deployment. For example, let's say you have a new custom field with field-level security configured differently for various profiles. If you do not include profiles in the deployment, no profiles will have access to your new field; however, by including the applicable profiles, your field-level security settings will carry over. Do note that field-level security settings will only be carried over to the destination org via the change set for items that are included. This may seem obvious, but it can easily be missed. For example, since the Case object is not available in change sets (because it is a standard object), you will not be able to pass profile-specific field-level security updates via a change set.

You should also take advantage of the "View/Add Dependencies" button that is available within your change set before proceeding. This button will identify any potentially dependent components that should also be considered for deployment. After clicking the button, carefully review the components to determine whether they should be included. Page layouts can be used to illustrate an example. Assume that your set includes an updated page layout that exposes a brand-new custom field; the "View/Add Dependencies" functionality will reveal the new custom field to you and allow you to add it to the set.

Deployment Process

Once you have finalized your change set, you are ready to deploy it to the desired target org. To do so, click the "Upload" button from within your change set and select an available org as your target org, as shown in Figure 17-12. Click the "Upload" button to submit your set.

	Name	Description	Type	Platform Version
	dev1	Developer sandbox Ask Meighan for access	Developer	45.0
	dev2		Developer	45.0
	LDVUAT	Large data volume UAT	Developer Pro	45.0
	Partial	Partial copy for testing sales process new features and implementing new business processes.	Partial Copy	45.0
	FullSbox		Full	44.0

Figure 17-12. *To deploy your change set, select the appropriate org and click* *"Upload"*

You'll need some patience here; it can take a while (10–15 minutes) before your set is available within the target org. You will be notified by e-mail of a successfully submitted change set, but it may take another 5 minutes before the set can be accessed.

At this point, you'll have two options: you can simply validate the deployment of the change set or go ahead and deploy it. A validation of the deployment will simulate a deployment and inform you of whether the process will be successful if actually deployed; no components in the set will actually be introduced to the target org. This can be a huge time-saver in the deployment process. Let's say you have a deployment planned for Friday at 10 p.m. If you attempt your deployment for the first time on Friday at 10 p.m., you may be disappointed to find out that an error was encountered. This means creating a new change set and redeploying it, which can take up your valuable time. By validating the deployment earlier in the day on Friday, you can identify potential errors and get your set ready for a punctual deployment free of any errors.

When you are ready to make changes to the target org, click "Deploy." Like with the validation process, this will validate your deployment and, if applicable, run all Apex tests. If successful, everything in your change set will now exist in the target org.

Deployment Approach

In an ideal situation, you would package up everything related to a specific release and deploy it via one change set. This should be attempted whenever possible. If successful, you'll be done with deployment relatively quickly. The reality, however, is that an all-at-once approach can be extremely time consuming if deployment issues are encountered. If you have more than a few errors, peeling back the layers can require numerous iterations and analysis and potentially waste your time. As an alternative, consider grouping related components and deploying them separately. For example, you might place all new objects and fields in one change set, and follow that with another set containing workflow rules and validation rules. There is no perfect solution for all users. Consider your situation and choose an approach that makes the most sense for you.

Other Considerations

Keep in mind the following considerations when deploying change sets:

- **Deploying "down"**: You can deploy down (e.g., from production to a sandbox) in addition to deploying up. There may be times when a change is made in a higher-level environment and you need to sync it up without making all changes manually or performing a complete refresh. In these cases, consider a deployment connection that is bidirectional.

- **Manual changes**: Some changes must be done manually. For example, "Case" and "Email-to-Case" settings cannot be deployed from one sandbox to another. Make sure you plan your deployment accordingly.

Recap

No matter how amazing your work is, it won't provide much value if it never sees the light of day (i.e., if it fails to get deployed to production). To successfully manage your solutions within Salesforce, you will need to create the appropriate sandboxes to meet your needs and establish a thorough, sensible plan for deployment. Your deployment can be done via change sets or a variety of other tools. Make sure to assess your options carefully. With an effective sandbox model and an effective deployment strategy, you'll be able to deliver functionality where you want and when you want with relative ease.

CHAPTER 18

Next Steps in Your Path to Declarative Development Excellence

So, what's next? Besides taking the obvious step of applying what you've learned in your everyday job and building up your experience in the different areas, there are additional opportunities for continuing your path of learning within the world of declarative development on the Salesforce platform. This book is only one of many resources available on the path to becoming an expert at building solutions on the Salesforce platform. In this final chapter, I'll suggest some supplementary options for forging ahead.

Success and Developer Communities

Salesforce has done an amazing job of building collaborative sites where you can get involved and interact with peers in the ecosystem. The following two communities are particularly valuable:

- **Trailblazer Community**: (https://trailblazer.salesforce.com) This community is designed for administrators, power users, consultants, and basic-to-intermediate developers.

- **Salesforce Developer Community**: (https://developer.salesforce.com) This community provides an outlet for developers, including those at advanced skill and experience levels.

In both communities, you can find useful articles, ask questions, get answers, submit ideas, and more. They are both valuable resources for anyone who likes to learn more or help others to do the same. Set up a profile and start collaborating!

© Philip Weinmeister 2019
P. Weinmeister, *Practical Salesforce Development Without Code*,
https://doi.org/10.1007/978-1-4842-4871-3_18

Official Salesforce Help

Salesforce has spent many thousands of hours compiling extremely useful help documentation. Some very intelligent, eloquent employees have devoted detailed attention to providing information on each piece of the platform, allowing you to take full advantage of the entire system. You can find the main help page at `https://help.salesforce.com`. As part of the overall help documentation, Salesforce produces a number of guides to using specific features in PDF format.

Local Trailblazer Groups and Volunteering

You may be surprised to know how many other solution builders are in your local area who would love to share thoughts on Salesforce solutioning with you and others. A number of different types of groups regularly meet and share the experiences, tips, and tricks they've gained through their own development. You can find Salesforce's list of Trailblazer Community groups at `https://trailblazercommunitygroups.com`.

One creative and helpful way to grow your skill set and benefit others at the same time is to volunteer your time at a nonprofit. Take a look at `www.salesforce.com/volunteers/probono` for more information on how to find organizations looking for help.

Trailhead

How could any breadth of educational Salesforce material be considered complete without Trailhead? Trailhead (`http://trailhead.com`) is an online learning management application that is self-paced and free that has helped thousands of individuals improve their understanding of and capabilities on the Salesforce platform.

Release Notes

While the volume of information can be overwhelming, getting to know the release notes three times a year is critical for those who want to stay ahead of the curve. The official release notes URL is `https://releasenotes.docs.salesforce.com` and is typically updated a few months before each release. Make sure to look for official "release readiness webinars" from Salesforce that provide useful summaries and recaps of major releases.

Twitter

Admittedly, there is a lot of noise in the world of social media and Twitter is not an exception. However, by following the right accounts, one can get a steady flow of useful information. Here are some recommended accounts to follow:

- **@PhilWeinmeister**: Hear from me with useful updates! I share my blog posts and other insights here.

- **@SalesforceAdmns**: This is the main Twitter account for the Salesforce Admin team. It allows you to stay up to date on news and announcements for declarative developers.

- **@SalesforceDevs**: This account sends out tweets about a variety of development topics. It is a great resource for staying on top of the latest within the world of Salesforce development. A good portion of the content involves coding, but it's also valuable for declarative solutions.

- **@Trailhead**: Here, you can get the latest news, updates, tips, and tricks to help you get the most out of Salesforce training and certification.

- **@AppExchange**: The Salesforce1 AppExchange (`https://appexchange.Salesforce`) sends out tweets about thousands of different apps.

- **@salesforce_labs**: Salesforce Labs publishes apps written by Salesforce employees and sends out its updates here.

- **Salesforce and Force.com MVPs**: This group includes some of the best and brightest, who bring insight and new content to the Salesforce ecosystem, sharing a ton of helpful tips and feedback for the larger community (`https://twitter.com/salesforce/lists/salesforce-mvps`).

Dreamforce, TrailheaDX, and World Tours

Dreamforce (`www.dreamforce.com`) is Salesforce's bigger-than-life annual megaconference held in San Francisco each fall. If you pay attention to advertised offers and start looking early, you can snag a discounted pass that will give you full access to the event. This conference offers a plethora of resources. I would specifically recommend the following two areas of the conference:

- **Sessions**: Salesforce offers hundreds of sessions in which you can hear from employees, customers, and partners about best practices, real-world lessons learned, and helpful tips. These sessions can serve as minitraining for you to level up your skills.

- **Developer/Admin/Trailhead Campgrounds**: At Dreamforce, you'll find extensive resources for coding or declarative developers of all skill levels. Visit the zone and get involved. You may even score some swag while you're learning the latest-and-greatest development features.

In addition to Dreamforce itself, a number of city-specific events are held around the world. Salesforce hosts smaller, Dreamforce-like events as part of the Salesforce World Tour. Look for an event coming to your town in the near future.

Finally, there's TrailheaDX. This one is highly recommended for developers and declarative solution builders fall into that bucket. You'll find less fluff and more learning here.

Salesforce Training and Certification

If you're not already familiar with Salesforce's certification program, you should be! Salesforce provides a thorough, well-organized offering of meaningful certifications that allow you to convey your knowledge in a particular area. As of 2019, at least 25 different certifications exist, with more likely to come. This book's content relates most directly to the following certifications:

- Platform App Builder
- Platform Developer I
- Advanced Administrator

To learn more about these exams or to obtain a free study guide, navigate to http://certification.salesforce.com. Good luck getting certified!

A Final Word

The world of Salesforce is vast and dynamic, with opportunities to build solutions on the platform growing each year. A unique facet that sets it apart is the fact that you can develop powerful, meaningful applications without producing a line of code, and Salesforce places a strong emphasis on this ability to build solutions declaratively. An array of new features and functions are released triannually, allowing you to take what you produce with "clicks" to the next level. I am honored to be a part of this ecosystem and I hope this chapter (and entire book) provides valuable information and guidance on your personal career journey. It's an exciting time to be a part of the Salesforce network, and I wish you the best in all of your future Salesforce development endeavors!

Index

© Philip Weinmeister 2019
P. Weinmeister, *Practical Salesforce Development Without Code*,
https://doi.org/10.1007/978-1-4842-4871-3

Printed in the United States
By Bookmasters